State Atrophy in Syria

State Atrophy in Syria

War, Society and Institutional Change

Harout Akdedian

EDINBURGH
University Press

Edinburgh University Press is one of the leading university presses in the UK. We publish academic books and journals in our selected subject areas across the humanities and social sciences, combining cutting-edge scholarship with high editorial and production values to produce academic works of lasting importance. For more information visit our website: edinburghuniversitypress.com

© Harout Akdedian, 2023, 2024

Edinburgh University Press Ltd
13 Infirmary Street
Edinburgh, EH1 1LT

First published in hardback by Edinburgh University Press 2023

Typeset in 11/15pt EB Garamond by
Cheshire Typesetting Ltd, Cuddington, Cheshire

A CIP record for this book is available from the British Library

ISBN 978 1 3995 1026 4 (hardback)
ISBN 978 1 3995 1027 1 (paperback)
ISBN 978 1 3995 1029 5 (webready PDF)
ISBN 978 1 3995 1028 8 (epub)

The right of Harout Akdedian to be identified as author of this work has been asserted in accordance with the Copyright, Designs and Patents Act 1988 and the Copyright and Related Rights Regulations 2003 (SI No. 2498).

Contents

Acknowledgements	vi
Introduction: On Abolition, State Capture and Atrophy	1
1 State Capture and Devolution in Syria: A Paradoxical Landscape	30
2 Institutions of Violence and Proliferation	69
3 Ethno-religious Subjectivities: Dynamics of Communitarianism and Sectarianisation	106
4 Institutional Ecologies during State Atrophy: The Religious Field as Case Study	134
5 Civilian Agency and its Limits: Community Protection in Deir Hafer and Kasab	172
Conclusion: The Future of State–Society Relations	228
Bibliography	241
Index	265

Acknowledgements

In the summer of 2011, I could not believe words I was hearing over dinner tables, family reunions, social gatherings and at workplaces in Aleppo City. I had been to Aleppo almost every summer of my life until then. In 2011, the Aleppo that I so intimately knew felt different, and so did its people. I had questions. Literature on Syria had answers. But narratives about embedded sectarianism in society driving a conflict that was in the making for so long seemed contrary to lived experience – or at least contradicted the reality of so many. My hope in writing this book is to have contributed to answers and conceptual frameworks that are underutilised when applied to notions such as sectarianism, Islamism, culture, politics and society in the Levantine Middle East.

Each chapter is written to stand alone for those with little patience for theoretical discussions. As dry as they are to read, it remains the responsibility of scholars to bring out the theoretical and conceptual premises that inform knowledge production. I took this imperative seriously while also trying to keep chapters accessible for those only skimming through parts they deem of interest.

Before delving into the subject further, first and foremost, I am forever indebted to my wife, Emily, and my two kids, Demi and Marx, for their support and sacrifices that are far too many to recount. To mention one, I finished writing my PhD dissertation in 2017 sitting behind the wheels of a 1994 Toyora Rav-4 parked in the shade of eucalyptus trees by the sports fields at the University of New England while my oldest slept in the back seat. I would not have been able to finish my dissertation had it not been for Demi's preference for prolonged naps in the car. On a more serious note, I am grateful to my PhD supervisors, Anthony Lynch, Bertram Jenkins and Howard Brasted, for their support throughout my doctoral studies and beyond. I am also indebted to Juan Carlos Sainz-Borgo for his support in initiating my academic journey at the postgraduate level. I am equally indebted to Aziz Al-Alzmeh and Nadia al-Bagdadi for their mentorship and support throughout my postdoctoral fellowships. I was able to resist the pressures of rapid and voluminous publishing, competing for grants or teaching, and instead spent time conducting fieldwork and engaging with broader scholarship. I am specifically indebted to Syrian friends, acquaintances and strangers who participated in this research and were keen to generously engage and contribute. Of specific mention is Ali AlJassem, for his assistance with data collection on Deir Hafer, and many others who assisted in various capacities but opted to remain anonymous at the time of the book's publishing.

A multitude of scholarships and grants made this project possible. The Australian Postgraduate Award and the International Postgraduate Research Award at the University of New England funded the content on ethno-religious subjectivities and Jihadi groups as a part of my doctoral studies. A brief consultancy for UN-ESCWA allowed me to expand on civilian community protection efforts. The core sections of the book on the religious field as well as the overall framework of the book on state atrophy were funded through postdoctoral fellowships within the 'Striking from the Margins' research project housed at the Central European University in Budapest and Vienna through a grant by the Carnegie Corporation of New York.

At the time of writing this acknowledgment, I can hardly muster the appetite to speak about the book's content. The Syria that I have spent so long studying and experiencing is hardly recognisable to me and to many others. It is painful to look at this in its most gruesome details. Gratitude to everyone who continues to do so, despite the trauma and estrangement.

Introduction
On Abolition, State Capture and Atrophy

Between 2010 and 2011, public squares from Morocco to Bahrain witnessed millions of people huddled together chanting in unison: 'The people. Want. To topple the system' [*Al-sha'b. yourid. Isqat al-nizam*]. Despite the specificities of each country that witnessed protest movements during the Arab Spring, the famous slogan came to be the sonar symbol of the historic protests across the MENA region. By proclaiming the *nizam* (system or regime) as public enemy, the masses of the Arab Spring expressed their perceived, felt and experienced challenge of maintaining a functional distinction between government policy and state institutions, or state officials and state institutions. The term 'regime', as the go-to word choice as translation for *nizam*, garnered popularity and common usage in literature and public vernacular to denote both government and state precisely for expressing the difficulty of contesting governments without having to challenge the state, or contesting public officials without having to challenge the public institutions they occupy. For protestors, meaningful political change seemed to require more than a mere change of government personnel.

More recently in the United States and in response to the killings of George Floyd, Breonna Taylor and a long line of innocent African-American individuals murdered at the hands of law enforcement officers, the Black Lives Matter protests similarly expressed that meaningful change requires more than mere change of law enforcement officers. Demands such as 'defund the police' redefined social justice in the United States in abolitionist terms to address systemic flaws rather than merely demand holding specific law enforcement officers guilty of police brutality accountable for abuse of power.¹ Protestors across the Middle East, North Africa and North America over the past decade voiced that so long as oppression is systemic, change in personnel will not yield a meaningful outcome. It is in this context that abolitionist platforms received a growing public appeal and rallying capacity internationally.²

The idea of abolition, within its nineteenth-century classical as well as derivate contemporary repertoires of abolitionist slogans voiced over the past fifteen years, fundamentally rejects the notion of the state as an unquestioned field of power to be taken as a given. From an abolitionist perspective, the modern state is the product of hierarchical and unavoidably oppressive relations of power, and not the end point of human collective progress or the product of an evolutionary political process.³ Unlike conservative and right-wing political platforms, abolitionist platforms (contemporary or historic) trust in the idea of dismantling the state as a step towards communal liberation rather than advocate for limited government or minimal state regulations.⁴ Such propositions are not mere intellectual exercises in imagining an alternative political reality. In the Syrian context, for instance, the autonomous region of Rojava in the northeast, under the control of Kurdish-led Syrian Democratic Forces since late 2013, is administered

---

[1] Dayvon Love, 'Police Accountability', *Human Rights Magazine* 46, 2 (2021), available online: https://www.americanbar.org/groups/crsj/publications/human_rights_magazine_home/civil-rights-reimagining-policing/police-accountability/; Sean Illing, 'The "abolish the police" movement', *Vox* 12 June 2020, accessed 12 July 2022: https://www.vox.com/policy-and-politics/2020/6/12/21283813/george-floyd-blm-abolish-the-police-8cantwait-minneapolis.

[2] Despite repeated claims about the lack of questioning of the state, specifically in the Middle East, abolitionist frames and slogans have in fact been a fundamental component of popular mobilisation across protest movements in the MENA region. For slogans and framing of protest movements, see Malu Halasa, Zahra Omareen and Nawara Mahfoud, *Syria Speaks: Art and Culture From the Frontline*, (London: Saqi Books, 2014). For a counterpoint, see Moris Ayiq, 'الانتفاضات العربية وسؤال الدولة', *aljumhuriyya*, 7 January 2022, accessed 6 July 2022: https://aljumhuriya.net/ar/2022/01/07/%d8%a7%d9%84%d8%a7%d9%86%d8%aa%d9%81%d8 %a7%d8%b6%d8%a7%d8%aa-%d8%a7%d9%84%d8%b9%d8%b1%d8%a8%d9%8a%d8%a9-%d9 %88%d8%b3%d8%a4%d8%a7%d9%84-%d8%a7%d9%84%d8%af%d9%88%d9%84%d8%a9/.

[3] See Peter Kropotkin, *Mutual Aid: A Factor of Evolution* (New Haven: self-published, 2022); Mikhail Bakunin, *Statism and Anarchy* (Cambridge: Cambridge University Press, 1990). For more recent formulations, see for instance the *New York Times* bestselling book, Mariame Kabe, *We Do This Until We Free Us: Abolitionist Organizing and Transformative Justice*, (Chicago: Haymarket Books, 2021); on the Arab Spring and statism, see Ayiq, 'الانتفاضات العربية وسؤال الدولة'.

[4] Bakunin, *Statism and Anarchy*, pp. 136–8; Kabe, *We Do This Until We Free Us*, pp. 4–5.

according to similar political imaginaries. Inspired directly by the founder of Kurdistan Worker's Party, Abdullah Ocalan's Democratic Confederalism, Rojava is an existing system that represents itself as an alternative to state-based systems of social and political organising.[5]

Ocalan's propositions on Democratic Confederalism are directly based on readings from American social theorist and self-prescribed eco-anarchist Murray Bookchin, who in turn grounded his work in Peter Kropotkin's notion of 'mutual aid' written originally for the pre-Soviet Russian peasantry more than a century ago.[6] Kropotkin's ideas on mutual aid are still echoed today in many contemporary abolitionist treatises such as the 2021 *New York Times* bestseller *We Do this Until We Free Us: Abolitionist Organizing and Transformative Justice* by Mariame Kabe.[7] Pre-Soviet popularity of anarcho-communism aside, the recent public appeal and rallying capacity of abolitionist slogans represent a significant shift in public opinion towards questioning the state and towards refusing to assume its inevitability as an organising structure.

Questions of the Book

This book raises two fundamental questions about the growing abolitionist appeal and answers them within the Syrian context. The first question relates to the factors leading to increased public questioning of the state altogether. The book addresses this question by looking at the role of state institutions. What kind of institutional arrangements and exercises of state power make it seemingly impossible to mount a challenge to prevailing systems of hierarchy while separating government and state, or officials and institutions? The answer of the book is that state capture by power constituents neither responsive nor accountable to the public pits the state against the public in diametrical opposition.

---

[5] Michael Knapp, Anja Flach and Ercan Ayboga, *Revolution in Rojava: Democratic Autonomy and Women's Liberation in Syrian Kurdistan* (London: Pluto Press, 2016).
[6] Abdullah Ocalan, *The Political Thought of Abdullah Ocalan: Kurdistan, Women's Revolution and Democratic Confederalism* (London: Pluto Press, 2017), 39; Murray Bookchin, *The Ecology of Freedom: The Emergence and Dissolution of Hierarchy* (Oakland: AK Press, 2005).
[7] Kabe, *We Do This Until We Free Us*, p. 4. See also Derecka Purnell, *Becoming Abolitionists: Police, Protests, and the Pursuit of Freedom* (New York: Astra House, 2021).

Despite the foundational nature of the first question about state capture for this book, it is the second question that occupies the bulk of the content: what are the consequences of undermining the state as a strategy for political change? This is due to the specific value of the Syrian case in relation to consequences of abolition not as a set of ideas but as actuality. The Syrian case reveals consequences, intended and unintended, that came about during the Syrian conflict when state institutions were directly undermined, contested or stopped functioning on their own.

Ironically, outcomes of state atrophy in Syria seem to contain statist elements. For instance, even anarchist social theorist David Graeber noted after visiting Rojava that the democratic self-administration

> looks very much like a government, replete with ministries, parliament and higher courts. If you simply read the formal constitution of the Rojava cantons you would have very little sign this was anything other than an enlightened social democratic, or perhaps at most democratic socialist, state.[8]

Groups such as Daesh (known as ISIS) and Hay'at Tahrir al-Sham (previously known as the al-Qaeda-affiliated Nusra Front) also contested state control and established parastate structures.[9] Therefore, in addition to Rojava, large swathes of territory across Syria came under the control of a variety of armed groups vying to establish alternative political orders. Emergent political orders shifted in form throughout the conflict, and some, as in the case of Daesh's Islamic State, came to an end. Regardless of the fluidity of outcomes, the book's attention is on processes of transformation unintentionally unleashed as a consequence of dismantling or undermining the state as an organising structure. State atrophy is empirically consequential,

---

[8] David Graeber, 'Foreword', in Michael Knapp, Anja Flach and Ercan Ayboga (eds), *Revolution in Rojava: Democratic Autonomy and Women's Liberation in Syrian Kirdistan* (London: Pluto Press, 2016), xvii.

[9] As Russia and the Islamic Republic of Iran came to the rescue of the Assad rule, the attention of armed opposition groups turned towards maintaining territorial control and establishing parallel states even when lacking official recognition. It is in this context that the militarisation of the uprising against the Assad rule quickly transitioned the conflict against the state rather than the Assad government.

regardless of the uncertainty of its outcomes or the normative standing of the state experiencing atrophy.

Synopsis

The Assad rule lost considerable military capacity since the 2011 uprisings and the militarisation of the Syrian conflict. However, the devolution of state capacity in the military field proved neither a terminal stage nor an unsurmountable challenge for the Assad rule. Similar to other countries such as Colombia, Sri Lanka and Mozambique, the armed conflict in Syria targeted and compromised state capacity without imploding the state or central government.[10] State atrophy and reduced military capacity acted as a generative force that unleashed myriad dynamics of transformational change in Syria, including simultaneous processes of devolution and reconstitution of power – state power as well as the power of the Assad rule.

Echoing the premise of functionalist theorists of the state such as William Reno and David Keen, this book argues that based on the Syrian experience, state atrophy is not simply the collapse of a particular system, but rather a process of reconfiguring power structures (institutions and elites) that presents threats as well as opportunities for profit and power consolidation.[11] This reconfiguration of power structures takes place within state institutions and beyond. In this book, the functions and consequences of state atrophy are examined in five areas: (1) state capture, (2) proliferation and devolution of violence, (3) sectarianisation, (4) the expansion of the religious field and (5) civilian efforts of community protection.

Where state authority is reinstated in Syria, it is done through novel actors (elite re-accommodation) and reconfigured power relations (new co-dependencies and hierarchies), even when pursued through recognisable and familiar strategies of the Assad rule (combination of coercion and

---

[10] Jonathan Di John, 'Conceptualizing the Causes and Consequences of Failed States: A Critical Review of the Literature', *LSE: Crisis States Working Papers* 2, no. 25 (2008): 27.

[11] William Reno, *Warlord Politics and African States* (Boulder: Lynn Rienner, 1998), 4; David Keen, *Useful Enemies: When Waging Wars Is More Important Than Winning Them* (New Haven: Yale University Press, 2012).

favouritism/clientelism).[12] While the emergent institutional arrangements and regulatory mechanisms of the state are wired to buttress the Assad rule, they do so at further expense of the state's public functions. As a result, the blurring of private and public domains, a constitutive feature of state capture by the Assad rule since 1970, took unprecedented predatory intensity towards both the private and public since 2011.

As the Assad rule and its allies continue to solidify their military exploits, the state has emerged as a reward in and of itself due to its capacity to institutionalise the extraction of wealth and power for a set of private interests represented by 'concordant or discordant' warlords and patrons of war-economies that spawned throughout the conflict.[13] In this sense, activities generally described as corrupt in public vernacular emerge in Syria, similar to other war-impacted contexts, to constitute the very system of appropriation of state structures and state functions, rather than an institutional or alleged cultural (organisational or societal) derangement.[14]

The Assad rule nurtures a new process of accommodating elites and clients by extending privileges for fealty and services, while its own economic, military, political and diplomatic reliance on Russia and Iran in turn require it to serve as a client of foreign sponsors. This comes at the further expense of the Syrian state's autonomy with ominous consequences for state–society relations going forward. As Tilly points out, the consequences for the reliance of states or armed groups on resources and support from other states, as is the case with the Assad rule, is the further loss of incentives to be internally responsive, which further undermines any vestiges of deterrence against predatory practices targeting the state or its citizens.[15]

---

[12] Reno, *Warlord Politics*, 15–18; Jean-François Bayart, *L'État en Afrique* (Paris: Fayard, 1989); Stathis N. Kalyvas, *The Logic of Violence in Civil War* (Cambridge: Cambridge University Press, 2012), 52–86; Max Bergholz, *Violence as a Generative Force* (Cornell: Cornell University Press, 2021).

[13] Balint Magyar, 'Towards a terminology for Post-Communist Regimes', in Balint Magyar (ed.), *Stubborn Structures: Reconceptualizing post-Communist Regimes* (Budapest: Central European University, 2018), 139–40.

[14] Aziz al-Azmeh and Nadia al-Bagdadi, 'Introduction', in Aziz al-Azmeh, Nadia al-Bagdadi, Harout Akdedian and Harith Hasan (eds), *Striking from the Margins: State, Religion and Devolution of Authority in the Middle East* (London: Saqi Books, 2021), 1–24.

[15] Charles Tilly, 'War Making and State Making as Organized Crime', in Peter Evans, Dietrich Rueschemeyer and Theda Skocpol (eds), *Bringing the State Back* (Cambridge: Cambridge University Press, 2010), 185.

Scope of Study

The book's primary time frame is focused on the period of social strife extending from 2011 onwards. Circumstances before 2011 only feature when significant for processes of state atrophy after 2011. Namely, two areas of inquiry consider pre-2011 dynamics: (1) institutional arrangements for seizing the state instilled at the onset of Hafez Assad's rule and (2) devolution of state functions through neoliberal policies after Bashar Assad replaced his father in the year 2000. The institutional architecture at the intersection of strategies of state capture by Hafez Assad and the restructuring of state–society relations through the reconfiguration of socio-economic functions of state institutions under Bashar Assad set the stage for post-2011 institutional dynamics.

The geographic coverage of the book provides an overview of developments Syria-wide as well as granular case studies through in-depth analyses from Aleppo City (Aleppo Province), Kasab (Latakia Province) and Deir Hafer (Aleppo countryside). While the book considers relevant transnational dynamics, it does not focus on Middle East geopolitics and international dynamics, which are widely analysed in other works. Chapters prioritise internal developments rather than international ones because the aim is to identify trends and trajectories of emergent developments in state–society relations primarily through empirical data and fieldwork at the local level within Syria's relatively bounded territorial space, despite the porosity of its borders. Transnational aspects are discussed only when the data indicates their relevance and in the context of highlighting linkages between macro-institutional transformations and micro-level realities. Answers therefore stem from in-depth studies with reference to localities.[16]

---

[16] The book maintains a fluid understanding of internal and external factors as these categories often mark distinctions based on ideal type models rather than an existing or actual variance. Examples include Syrian actors who were forced or chose to operate outside the country but were portrayed as external actors as an effort to delegitimise them. This strategy was pursued by the Assad government as well as armed factions who strove to alienate diplomatic and political opposition groups active abroad.

Conceptually, the book stands as a counter-argument against culturalist or exclusively geopolitical interpretations of the Syrian conflict – narratives that often reduce Syria's socio-political developments to either essential and static local features (such as alleged inherent popular Islamism and sectarianism) or exclusively to foreign imposition and meddling.

Knowledge Production about Syria: War, Locality and Paradigm Shifts

Public protests since 2011 and patterns of militarisation thereafter took different forms in Syria's different towns and cities. Syrians underwent highly contrasting shifts before 2011 too, and the trajectories of change have been different in different areas. Through distinct features of class structure, rates of poverty, unemployment, education, demographics of (un)employment, scale of destruction and patterns of displacement and migration, each locality functioned in different conditions.[17] These contrasting shifts led to disparate responses and reactions to public unrest. In line with this, oppositional-armed activism after 2011 had explicit local roots and operational frameworks too. Syrian armed groups generally formed at the neighbourhood level before coalescing or becoming a part of larger armed factions.[18]

As state institutions were contested, shrank in reach and diminished in capacity, localities found themselves, to varying degrees, left to their own devices to organise and govern themselves. Locality thus emerges as a field of power where a multitude of actors, groups and new power relations are forged. This applies to rebel held and government held areas alike. In other words, locality in the context of the Syrian conflict is both a relatively bounded territorial area or 'place' where socio-political transformations unfold as well as a unit of analysis in relation to fluctuating topographies of

---

[17] Isam al-Khafaji, 'De-Urbanizing the Syrian Revolt', *The Arab Reform Initiative*, 6 March 2016, https://www.arab-reform.net/publication/de-urbanising-the-syrian-revolt/. (accessed 4 January 2018).

[18] Prior to the rise of the Nusra Front or ISIS, local military formations and defections from the Syrian army were the primary constituents of early armed actors. For a detailed portrayal, see Chapter Two.

power. Locality thus became a significant lens for post-2011 studies about developments in Syria.

The aggregate knowledge produced through the lens of locality, however, faces methodological challenges, specifically in its representational capacity and generalisability.[19] Since 2011, while there is a growing need for scholarly documentation and analysis due to rapidly changing circumstances, field access remains limited even for researchers and scholars from the region. Emergent knowledge about the Syrian conflict displays a sharp local emphasis as scholars and researchers continue to focus on the limited areas they have access to. The aggregate outcome of this is multifaceted. In the Syrian context, where knowledge, journalistic and academic alike, is securitised and suppressed by the security apparatus of the Assad rule or armed groups in place after 2011, local visibility and documentation remain highly sought after for purposes of knowledge production. Analytically, however, as Shami and Miller-Idriss point out, snapshots, reportages and caricature images of events, incidents and local developments became equivalent to generalised analysis in contexts where in fact localities underwent divergent experiences.[20] In other words, studying the locale while disregarding broader processes at work (such as dynamics of state atrophy in the form of war economies, trans-local power dynamics, trajectories of displacement and shifting modalities of violence and order) may lead to 'fetishising' locality.[21] Localities, no matter how isolated, cannot be considered separate categories or levels of analysis as their isolation could have an impact on, or be the outcome of, broader and trans-local processes. Rather than account for trans-local and multi-causal

---

[19] According to the 2015 report of the Arab Social Science Monitor, out of 732 articles in eight leading Arab peer-reviewed periodicals between 2010 and 2014, 'field studies, including both pure field studies, and those framed theoretically, do not exceed 22% of the total articles', with *Majallat al-Ulum al-Ijtima'yyah* and *Al-Majallah al-Ijtima'iyyah* featuring the majority of those works with as many as 50% of their publications grounded in field work. See Mohammad Bamyeh, *Social Sciences in the Arab World: Forms of Presence* (Beirut: Arab Social Science Monitor, 2015), 68–9. In addition, of all the research methods mentioned in these publications, direct observations (7.3%) and direct interviews (6.6%) only comprise 13.9% of the total mentioned methods. See Bamyeh, *Social Sciences in the Arab World*, 74.

[20] Seteney Shami and Cynthia Miller-Idriss, *Middle East Studies for the New Millennium: Infrastructures of Knowledge* (New York: New York University Press, 2017), 1.

[21] David Harvey, *The Condition of Postmodernity: An Enquiry into the Origins of Cultural Change* (Oxford: Wiley-Blackwell, 2000), 117.

dynamics, the focus on locality in knowledge production about Syria constrains researchers and scholars to answering broad questions about the Syrian conflict through the lens of the 'here and now'. This is problematic for many reasons.

Localism came to serve a triadic function, as a methodology (method of deriving findings), a unit of analysis (subject of analysis) and findings (as a depiction of prevailing patterns of fragmentation) all at once. Considering the body of work that projects normative attributes of 'tradition' and 'authenticity' to that which is geographically, socially, culturally or politically 'local' in the sub-national sense, localism gained prognostic and prescriptive values as well.[22] This is evident in peace-building frameworks, represented by an ensemble of distinct yet interconnected interventions, measures, policies, structures and conceptual frameworks that are typically deployed under the premise of conflict resolution or termination at later stages or aftermath of intra-state armed conflict. Much of those prescriptions are bundled within what came to be known since the early 1990s as the 'Liberal Peace Paradigm' and its critical counterpoints known as 'post-liberal peace'.[23]

---

[22] This often expressed itself in the literature under 'governance', 'decentralisation' and 'civil society'. See Aziz al-Azmeh, *Secularism in the Arab World: Contexts, Ideas and Consequences* (Edinburgh: Edinburgh University Press, 2019), xxv–xxx. For more on the local turn of post-liberal peace paradigm as a mechanism of conflict resolution see, Harout Akdedian and Aziz al-Azmeh, 'Introduction', in Aziz al-Azmeh, Harout Akdedian and Haian Dukhan (eds), *Spoils of War In the Arab East: Reconditioning Society and Polity in the Arab East* (London: Bloomsbury, 2023).

[23] Thania Paffenholz, 'Perpetual Peacebuilding: A New Paradigm to Move Beyond the Linearity of Liberal Peacebuilding', *Journal of Intervention and Peacebuilding* 15, no. 3 (2021): 367–85; Oliver Richmond, 'Resistance and the Post-liberal Peace', *Journal of International Studies* 38, no. 3 (2010): 665–92; Roger Mac Ginty and Oliver Richmond, 'The Local Turn in Peace Building: a critical agenda for peace', *Third World Quarterly* 34, no. 5 (2013): 763–83. Some of the most recognisable components of the peace-building register are 'post-conflict reconstruction, transitional justice and reconciliation, economic reintegration, disarmament, demobilisation, and reintegration (DDR) schemes, democratisation including most especially elections, constitutional- and security sector reform (SSR), and various transformatory approaches to help deal with the past (DWP), re-establish social cohesion, and promote cultural change'. See Balazs Kovacs, 'Peace-Building: From Liberal State Building Imperative to the Post-conflict Register? Perspectives from Comparison' in Aziz al-Azmeh, Harout Akdedian and Haian Dukhan (eds), *Spoils of War In the Arab East: Reconditioning Society and Polity in the Arab East* (London: Bloomsbury, 2023).

The fundamental criticism levelled against the Liberal Peace Paradigm, which came to prominence in the post-Soviet historical context, was that post-conflict frameworks were too often dismissive of locality, and embedded in or reliant on political actors that contributed to social strife in the first place. Institutional arrangements proposed as antidotes to open conflict under the liberal peace framework were deemed counterproductive because they were superimposed in a statist top-down format without consideration for local specificities.[24]

The critical counterpoint to the Liberal Peace Paradigm that came to dominate the post-conflict register in the global humanitarian field, United Nations agencies and the peace-building literature more broadly, emphasised the importance of local peace-building, instead of national state-building, as a more effective mode of conflict resolution and prevention. This transition is framed as 'a critical agenda of peace' in Peace and Conflict Studies.[25] As a result, the peace-building scholarship witnessed growing and well merited emphasis on psycho-social needs, victim-centred approaches and trauma-informed programmes of social and economic rehabilitation of localities impacted by political violence. The local turn, however, did not eliminate pre-existing pitfalls (neoliberal tendencies) and continued to be the subject of much scholarly debate, raising questions about the role of locality in processes of power consolidation that take place during armed conflict but also perpetuate under conditions of conflict abatement.[26] Localised peace-building schemes were applied to war-impacted countries such as Lebanon and post-invasion Iraq under the banner of consociationalism, again as a conflict resolution strategy, which led not only to the consolidation of warlord politics, but also entrenched sectarian actors at the local level in both

---

[24] Balazs Kovacs and Paddy Tobias, 'Questioning Peace Infrastructure and Peace Formation', *Peace and Conflict Review* 9, no. 1 (2016): 1.

[25] Mac Ginty and Richmond, 'The Local Turn in Peace Building'.

[26] For specific explorations on Syria and Iraq in relation to the Liberal Peace Paradigm and its counterpoints, see Paffenholz, 'Perpetual Peacebuilding' and Tobby Dodge, 'The Failure of Peacebuilding in Iraq: The Role of Consociationalism and Political Settlements', *Journal of Intervention and Statebuilding 15*, no. 4 (2021): 459–75, respectively. For a broader overview, see special issue 'Questioning Peace Infrastructure and Peace Formation', *Peace and Conflict Review* 9, no. 1 (2016): 1–105.

countries.²⁷ The outcome is the unequivocal empowerment of factional and sectarian contenders for state capture at the expense of 'the coherence of the state' as well as its 'autonomy'.²⁸

This logic of localism deems separatism and decentralisation as desirable and natural.²⁹ By default, 'artificiality' and 'inauthenticity' are extended not only to the unravelling order but also to any notion of unity or cohesion, institutional or otherwise. Within this logical structure, the frame of locality comes to reinforce broader analyses that project Syrian politics and society, similar to depictions of Iraqi politics and society according to the Bush and Obama administrations, as defined by an underlying centrifugal ethos, innately wired to pull apart and segregate unless prevented from doing so by force. As a result, common and formulaic thematic categories, such as Kurdish separatism, tribal primordialism, intertribal hostilities, religious intolerance and sectarian unease continue to essentialise the Syrian context despite the rise of nuanced scholarship paying attention to the variety of forces and processes behind sub-national dynamics.³⁰

Two specific clusters of literature echo this underlying debate regarding locality and its meanings in the Middle East and Syria: one prevalent in Islamic Studies, and the other in the ever-growing field of Syria Studies. The first is concerned with meta-narratives sceptical of modernity. Rooted in post-colonial and post-structural narratives, the likes of Wael Hallaq, Talal Asad and Saba Mahmoud received ample responses from a long line of scholars such as Hadi Enayat, Aziz al-Azmeh and Aijaz Ahmad for their 'obscurantism', 'logical inconsistencies', 'abstraction'

---

[27] Samir Makdisi and Marcus Marktanner, 'Trapped by Consociationalism: The Case of Lebanon', *Topics in Middle Eastern and African Economies* 11 (2009): available online https://meea.sites.luc.edu/volume11/PDFS/Paper-by-MakdisiMarktanner.pdf; Dodge, 'The Failure of Peacebuilding in Iraq', 459–60.

[28] The institutional fragmentation of the state is a result of partitioning state power amongst factions with ties to foreign support. This leads to undermining state coherence and autonomy. See, Dodge, 'The Failure of Peacebuilding in Iraq', 459.

[29] Similar statements made were by the Bush, Obama and Trump administrations justifying US foreign policy in the Middle East.

[30] Yassin-Kassab and Leila al-Shami, *Burning Country: Syrians in Revolution and War* (London: Pluto Press, 2016).

and 'state-phobia'.³¹ The scepticism regarding the state stems from interpretations of the state based on its artificiality and critical assessments of modernity in its institutional and ideological permutations. While providing a convincing negation of the modern state as an end point of an evolutionary and progressive political process, post-structural frames of analysis, as in the works of Saba Mahmoud and Talal Asad, also extend an alternative teleological justification of that which is local as being 'traditional' or 'authentic' without taking into account the predation, repression and violence that takes place within those categories.³² Fundamentally, the categorical anti-statism leaves no room for exploring differences between distinct systems of government, their historicities and the institutional arrangements that produce outcomes and structure state–society relations.

In Syria Studies, and specifically in the context of the emergent scholarship on the Syrian conflict, a comparable dismissal of the state as a category of analysis is noticeable through the common use of the term 'regime' to refer to the Assad rule and the Syrian state alike. As mentioned, the use of the term 'regime' as a translation of '*nizam*' pays homage to the public frustration voiced throughout the Arab Spring regarding state capture. In academic jargon, the term 'regime', specifically in the field of political science, refers to rogue states, as in governments that have seized the state and rendered state policy less responsive (even hostile) to public needs, democratic processes or other regional actors.³³ Despite its adequacy for purposes of classifying and categorising political systems, the use of the term beyond comparative politics has the tendency to obfuscate consequential distinctions between institutions and policies, or systems of power and people in positions of power. Those distinctions are consequential because they directly answer questions about how to change specific outcomes of political processes in place. Without the distinction between state and government in analytical

---

³¹ Hadi Enayat, *Islam and Secularism in Post-Colonial Thought: A Cartography of Asadian Genealogies* (London: Palgrave Pivot, 2017); al-Azmeh, *Secularism in the Arab World*; Aijaz Ahmad, *In Theory: Classes, Nations, Literatures* (New York: Verso, 2008), 164–66; On the notion of 'state-phobia' see M. Dean and K. Villasden, *State Phobia and Civil Society: The Political Legacy of Michael Foucault* (Stanford: Stanford University Press, 2016), 1.
³² See, Enayat, *Islam and Secularism*; al-Azmeh, *Secularism*.
³³ Andrew Heywood, *Politics* (London: Bloomsbury, 2019).

efforts, answers about the role of actors, strategies, conditions and processes remain vulnerable to mystifying that which is a social construct by concealing its material conditions.[34]

Shifts in knowledge production about the Syrian conflict came to address previous gaps in knowledge while also generating new questions specifically in the context of state–society relations. State atrophy speaks directly to the question about institutional changes needed, in addition to change of government, for meaningful political change in Syria. The conceptual framework that this book proposes addresses the need for a renewed focus on state–society relations through a vocabulary of state atrophy that links micro and macro dynamics of change within the state and without. The next section explains the vocabulary the book uses to gauge the extent to which the Syrian tragedy is an expression of modern state institutions revealing their violent tendencies under conditions of state atrophy when compared to the role of Assad rule's strategies and direct actions in shaping the characteristics of the Syrian state.

Keywords and Conceptual Framework

Having spent much of their intellectual efforts on discerning the notion of society, classical sociologists such as Max Weber and Émile Durkheim well established the challenges of capturing its material form. Geographically or socially bounded societies that form a single or uniform entity are impossible to locate.[35] Thus, the notion of society requires identifiable boundaries to serve as a unit of analysis.[36]

---

[34] Specifically, the conflation of state structures with the Assad dictatorship and its practices through the widespread use of the term 'regime' in literature to denote both the Syrian state and government practice. This not only dismisses the consolidation of state capture by the Assad rule under drastically changing circumstances, but also restrains discussions about transformations in state structures and their outcome for society. Thomas Pierret's *Religion and State in Syria: The Sunni Ulama from Coup to Revolution* is a case in point. Although the book is a foundational contribution to the field of Syria Studies, it fails to acknowledge or account for distinctions between state and government, which is crucial for accurate assessment of the religious field. Pierret, *Religion and State in Syria* (Cambridge: Cambridge University Press, 2013). For a counter-point see, Line Khatib, *Islamic Revivalism in Syria: The Rise and Fall of Ba'thist Secularism*. (New York: Routledge, 2011).
[35] Michael Mann, *The Sources of Social Power* (Cambridge: Cambridge University Press, 2012), 1.
[36] Anthony Giddens, *A Contemporary Critique of Historical Materialism. Vol. 1. Power, Property and the State.* (London: Macmillan, 1981), 45–6.

The Latin *societas*, the plural form of *socius*, historically meant an ally or a group of companions.[37] Similarly in Arabic, as in some Indo-European languages, the word for society (*mujtama'* in Arabic or *engerutyün* in Armenian) literally translates to 'that which is combined together' as an alliance, partnership or companionship. The contingent and 'acted upon' nature of associations comprising society is central in the original etymology of the word. Michael Mann argues that the binding force that forms society, giving it specific boundaries, is 'the organisation of power'.[38] Sources of power, such as economic, political, military or ideological, provide the organisational means for collective social action and thus allow social groups to be structured as socio-political actors, hence becoming bounded units of analysis within specific spaciotemporal coordinates.[39]

Merit could be given to unitary conceptions of society, provided that the density and patterns of interactions and exchanges within a given collectivity are discernible from patterns of interactions and exchanges outside of that collectivity.[40] Otherwise, regardless of imaginaries in place, given the plurality and fluidity of overlapping social networks that constitute any given population, the concept of society remains hyperbolic.[41] Society, regardless of its nature or attributes, is too messy to be systematised or spatially delimited. Social networks are often informal and fluid. And societal boundaries are permanently in the process of (trans)formation, including those that seem stubborn.[42] What exists instead is a multitude of continuously shifting and intersecting networks that form a variety of overlapping social spaces.[43]

The institutional approach that this book proposes focuses primarily on the spatiotemporal constellation of multiple overlapping social institutions and networks that form society.[44] Processes of structuration of human

---

[37] Mann, *The Sources of Social Power*, 14.
[38] Mann, *The Sources of Social Power*, 2.
[39] Joel Migdal, *State in Society: Studying How States and Societies Transform and Constitute One Another* (Cambridge: Cambridge University Press, 2001).
[40] Giddens, 1981, 45–6; Mark Granovetter, 'The Strength of Weak Ties', *American Journal of Sociology* 78. No. 6 (1973): 1360–80.
[41] Mann, *The Sources of Social Power*, 13–14.
[42] Ibid.
[43] Mann, *The Sources of Social Power*, 20.
[44] Dennis Wrong, *The Problem of Order: What Unites and Divides Society* (Cambridge, MA: Harvard University Press, 1995), 8–11.

behaviour, social relations and political mobilisation through institutional arrangements do not eliminate deviancy nor operate with predetermined functions. In other words, 'order is never so fully present in concrete social reality as to exclude all deviations, unpredictabilities, mistaken perceptions and accidents. Nor is it ever so utterly absent that complete random behaviour . . . prevails' and social interactions become 'confined to the minimum required biological necessities'.[45] As Barbara Fields notes, social formations never cease from being historical phenomena by transforming into 'an external motor of history; according to the fatuous but widely repeated formula, "it takes on a life of its own"'.[46] The institutional approach of this book explores social ordering – the relational arrangements between institutional domains and networks that shape social formations. This approach analyses the impact of state atrophy as in transformations in institutional domains on social groups rather than attribute the presence or behaviour of social groups to essential cultural traits or exclusively attribute them to prevalent imaginaries.

Institutional domains and networks

Institutional domains are macro-level societal structures that enclose specialised and differentiated organisational bodies. Examples of institutional domains include economy, religion, law, politics, arts, sport, and education amongst others.[47] They are specialised fields comprised of (1) networks of organisational bodies, (2) internal rules and regulations (formal and informal) and (3) circulating resources (material or symbolic) that provide networks, organisations and institutional domains a level of autonomy and influence. Each domain is specialised in unique codes. For instance, the religious field, regardless of the diversity of actors and organisations within, is dedicated to notions of religiosity and piety. Politics is dedicated to notions of power and influence. Law is dedicated to legal doctrine and jurisprudence. Those specific codes define each institutional domain but may also inform and influence other domains depending on the institutional

---

[45] Wrong, *The Problem of Order*, 9–10.
[46] Barbara Fields, 'Slavery, Race and Ideology in the United States of America', *New Left Review* 181, no. 1 (1990): 103.
[47] Abrutyn and Turner, 'The Old Institutionalism', 287.

ecology and inter-institutional power dynamics in place. In other words, institutional ecology stands for the nature of relational arrangements and overall power relations between institutional domains.[48] The primacy of specialised codes or influence of specific institutional domains over others is determined through the prevailing power relations and actual systems of hierarchy between institutional domains. The relative primacy of one or a multitude of domains over others might be reflected through the salience of its specialised codes and rules, in explicit or implicit terms.[49] 'Depending upon the relative dominance of one or more institutional domains, the environment can be disproportionately influenced by the ideologies of these dominant domains'.[50]

Institutional theory has its foundations in early functionalist sociology focusing on processes of institutional differentiation in the evolution and growth of societies.[51] As populations grew, societal structures and social institutions grew more complex and specialised to regulate distinct aspects of the collective experience. The functionalist thrust of early sociology resides in the attribution of predetermined functions and purpose to social institutions. Institutional theory has been mostly preoccupied with causes of social differentiation, but until relatively recently little attention was given to inter-institutional dynamics – specifically in relation to questions of institutional ecologies, autonomy and primacy.[52] In other words, the early focus was on institutions as macro-level social actors and how they evolve, adapt and influence changing circumstances. Popularised today through Bourdieu's notion of 'field', institutional domains have become subjects of analysis not only as actors but also as contested fields where institutional

---

[48] Abrutyn, 'Toward a Theory of Institutional Ecology', 168.
[49] Implicit primacy here is referred with reference to designate the Gramscian notion of hegemony where the dominant culture has reached a stage where its dominance is naturalised to the extent that it is a natural feature of socio-political existence and therefore almost invisible. See Gilbert Achcar, 'Hegemony, Domination, Corruption, and Fraud in the Arab Region', *Middle East Critique* 30 no. 1 (2021): 57–66.
[50] Abrutyn and Turner, 'The Old Institutionalism Meets the New Institutionalism', 287.
[51] Émile Durkheim, *The Division of Labor in Society* (New York: The Free Press, 1893); Herbert Spencer, *The Principles of Sociology* (New York: Appleton and Company, 1896).
[52] Seth Abrutyn, 'Toward a General Theory of Institutional Autonomy', *Sociological Theory* 27. no. 4 (2009): 449.

functions are not predetermined but contingent upon power relations within and without institutional domains.[53]

Power struggles within and between institutional domains are shaped by social networks and relational mechanisms that allow the flow of human transactions and define intra-institutional and inter-institutional power dynamics.[54] Social networks are able to operate in multiple social fields and penetrate a multitude of institutional domains.[55] Hence, relationships that constitute a network are flexible enough to interact, compete, cooperate and even become a part of other networks (formally or informally).[56] Processes of inclusion and exclusion through favouritism, nepotism, promotions, credibility, trust and the allocation of resources and benefits are key processes and mechanisms of power structuration.[57] The nature of exchanges and transactions within and between networks is key for uncovering emergent institutional arrangements and power relations.[58]

Any institutional domain, be it religion or state, can only be assessed and its power relations highlighted from a relational standpoint.[59] For instance, to look at the religious domain to understand its broader place and functions, institutional arrangements, relations and interactions with other domains need to be explored. The predominance of the religious field might not necessarily be attributed to the increased and expanded intensity of exchanges and interactions between religious actors and a given population. Rather, the prominence of the religious or any other domain may also be related to the relative relegation of other domains, such as the economy

---

[53] Pierre Bourdieu, 'Social Space and Symbolic Power', *Sociological Theory* 7, no. 1 (1989): 14–25.
[54] Seth Abrutyn and Jonathan Turner, 'The Old Institutionalism Meets the New Institutionalism', *Sociological Perspectives* 54, no. 3 (2009): 287; Barry Wellman, 'Network Analysis: Some basic Principles', *Sociological Theory* (1983): 155–200; for Syria specific application see Kevin Mazur, 'State Networks and Intra-Ethnic Group Variation in the 2011 Syrian Uprising', *Comparative Political Studies* 52, no. 7 (2019): 995–1027.
[55] Barry Wellman, 'Network Analysis: Some basic Principles', *Sociological Theory* (1983): 155–200.
[56] Peter Blau, *Exchange and Power in Social Life* (New York: John Wiley and Sons, 1964).
[57] Joel Podolny and James Baron, 'Resources and Relationships: Social Networks and Mobility in the Workplace', *American Sociological Review* (1997): 673–93; Margaret Greico, *Workers' Dilemmas: Recruitment, Reliability, and Repeated Exchanges – An Analysis of Urban Social Networks and Labour Circulation* (London: Routledge, 1996).
[58] David Jones, Anne Lane and Paul Schulte, *Terrorism, Security and the Power of Informal Networks* (Northampton, MA: Edward Elgar Publishing, 2010).
[59] Abrutyn and Turner, 'The Old Institutionalism Meets the New Institutionalism', 287.

or the state. Given the primacy of the institutions of coercion in Syria, the gradual prominence of the religious field, for instance, over the past two decades cannot be analysed without accounting for state-religion relations. However, the role of the religious domain is not limited to its relations with the state. Religious entities, activities and even subjectivities have a broader spatial attendance. The endowment of structuring and regulating functions to religion and even religiosity can also materialise if the field of religion permeates other domains, including the economy as an institutional domain.[60]

State and state atrophy

The state, as a distinct institutional domain, distinguishes itself from other domains, including the broader field of politics in general, through its authority over other domains as the ultimate regulator of institutional ecologies.[61] The state in this sense is an institutional superstructure that has the self-ascribed authority to regulate other domains with varying capacities to do so.[62] The notion that modern state structures represent a global condition of institutional supremacy over other domains has come under adequate scrutiny.[63] However, even where state power is limited and greatly relinquished, the modern state hardly ever loses all relevance or influence over other domains.[64] In instances where the state loses territorial control,

---

[60] Seth Abrutyn, 'Toward a Theory of Institutional Ecology: The Dynamics of Macro Structural Space', *Review of European Studies* 4, no. 5 (2012): 168.

[61] Jonathan Turner, *Human Institutions: A Theory of Societal Evolution* (Lanham, MD: Bowman & Littlefield Publishers, 2003); Karl Marx, 'The German Ideology', in Robert C. Tucker (ed.), *The Marx-Engels Reader* (New York: W. W. Norton & Co., 1972), 146–202; Spencer, *The Principles of Sociology*; Christopher Chase-Dunn and Thomas D. Hall, *Rise and Demise: Comparing World-Systems* (Boulder, CO: Westview Press, 1997).

[62] For an overview of debates regarding the subject, see Seth Abrutyn and Kirk Lawrence, 'From Chiefdom to State: Toward an Integrative Theory of the Evolution of Polity', *Sociological Perspectives* 53, no. 3 (2010): 419–42.

[63] Regarding Foucaultian takes on power beyond the state, see Ole Sending and Iver Neumann, 'Governance to Governmentality: Analyzing NGOs, States, and Power', *International Studies Quarterly* 50, no. 4 (2006): 889–910; on performativity and modalities of power beyond the state or institutions in general, see Judith Butler, *Bodies That Matter* (New York: Routledge, 1993), 184.

[64] On the question of post-colonial state see Klaus Schlichte, 'A Historical-Sociological Perspective on Statehood', in Thomas Risse et al (eds), *The Oxford Handbook of Governance and Limited Statehood* (Oxford: Oxford University Press, 2018,) 53–60. On the Islamic Republic of Iran see Sami Zubaida, *Islam, The People and The State: Political Ideas and Movements in the Middle East* (London: I. B. Tauris, 2009), 38–63. On Saudi Arabia, see Aziz al-Azmeh, *Islams and Modernities*

or where the state no longer operates in its capacity as a regulator of other domains, as in Somalia, Democratic Republic of Congo, Liberia and Sierra Leone, the state is transformed into a belligerent entity contending with a multitude of other domains.[65] Regulatory capacity of the state is therefore never absolute or stationary. Nevertheless, losing its relative supremacy does not imply the absence of the state altogether. Regulatory capacity is dependent upon fluid power dynamics within each domain as well as the broader institutional ecology in place. It is in moments when the state's capacity to regulate other domains is abruptly compromised that a meaningful break and transition from one social order to another may come about, making way to a new institutional ecology.

Scholars such as Joel Migdal and James C. Scott look at instances where the state has only limited influence over many social institutions and domains, or where the prevalence of the state over one domain, such as the military, does not necessarily translate to regulatory capacity over other domains.[66] Rather than presenting a static representation of the state as present or absent, Migdal looks into contests and bargaining processes between state institutions and other domains and actors. This line of questioning is pertinent for the post-2011 Syrian moment of transformational change where state institutions and social institutions are reconfigured. This book offers what Seth Abrutyn labels a 'meso-level' analysis of institutional developments.[67] This meso-institutional perspective focuses on organisational units and actors equally embedded in macro-level institutional domains and ecologies as they are in micro-level dynamics of intra-organisational networks and organisational cultures.[68]

(London: Verso, 2009), 157–73.

[65] Amongst the often cited exceptions are Somalia, Sierra Leone and Democratic Republic of Congo. See Robert Rotberg, 'The Failure and Collapse of Nation-States: Breakdown, Prevention and Repair', in Robert Rotberg (ed.), *When States Fail: Causes and Consequences* (Princeton: Princeton University Press, 2005), 5. For distinctions between the state as a regulator of other domains as opposed to its presence or absence based on performance in service provision or public administration, see Eric Stollenwerk, 'Measuring Governance and Limited Statehood', in Thomas Risse et al (eds), *The Oxford Handbook of Governance and Limited Statehood* (Oxford: Oxford University Press, 2018), 109–18.

[66] James C. Scott, *Seeing Like a State: How Certain Schemes to Improve the Human Condition Have Failed* (New Haven: Yale University Press, 1999); Migdal, *State in Society*.

[67] Abrutyn and Turner, 'The Old Institutionalism Meets the New Institutionalism', 284, 289.

[68] Ibid., 284.

Despite the centrality of the notion of the state as a distinct institutional category, the book neither presupposes the state as a unitary actor with coherent decision making processes nor does it negate the ephemeral nature of its powers.[69] Rather, in line with premises found in historical sociology, the book identifies 'core components of a political and social order, the state, ideology and society and focuses specifically on how institutions, be they political or social/religious power, are established, and maintained', or contested.[70]

The state, as an institutional superstructure with relative capacity and predisposition to regulate other institutional domains, combines symbolic as well as material forms of influence. Given the variety of these forms and the tentative and fluid nature of power, institutional forms of state power are constantly 'in motion' and should be re-examined and studied as such.[71] Not only are governing strategies, regulations and institutional arrangements subject to change, but even territorial control, as post-colonial approaches point out, is so often assumed as a given when in fact it is rather contingent upon relational arrangements and institutional forms of presence.[72] The state may be present in some institutional capacity but absent in others at the same time. This fluidity notwithstanding, territorial control (passive or coercive) is key in introducing an element of fixity through what Paasi labels as 'bounded spaces'.[73] Paasi elaborates that despite cross-border or transboundary flows of people, goods and information, territorial identities and systems of regulation and jurisdiction somewhat overlap and intertwine to form the territorial extent of sovereign authority.[74] As mentioned, levels of success in establishing such territoriality vary, and the specific forms they

---

[69] For a brief review of these perspectives, see Fred Halliday, *The Middle East in International Relations: Power, Politics and Ideology* (Cambridge: Cambridge University Press, 2005), 34.

[70] Halliday, *The Middle East in International Relations*, 34 ; Andrew Brandel and Shalini Randeria, 'Anthropological Perspectives on the Limits of the State', in Thomas Risse et al (eds), The Oxford Handbook of Governance and Limited Statehood (Oxford: Oxford University Press, 2018), 79–81.

[71] Victor Konrad, 'Toward a theory of borders in motion', *Journal of Borderlands Studies* 30, no. 1 (2015): 1–17.

[72] Brandel and Randeria, 'Anthropological Perspectives', 68–75.

[73] Anssi Paasi, 'Bounded spaces in a "borderless world": Border Studies, power and the anatomy of territory', *Journal of Power* 2, no. 2 (2009): 216–17.

[74] Ibid.; see also Vladimir Kolossov, 'Border Studies: Changing perspectives and theoretical approaches', *Geopolitics* 10, no 4 (2005): 611.

take are context dependent, but the state as an institutional domain plays a structuring role to shape socio-political communities based on notions of national belonging or citizenship. As Newman affirms, state atrophy does not imply the loss of all forms of state territoriality or boundedness.[75] Inversely, loss of territory (losing territorial control to belligerent armed factions), loss of territoriality (relinquishing territorial control by withdrawing from certain areas) or diminished forms of territorial presence (such as the collapse of state capacity as a service provider) do not imply the loss of the state altogether. This is due to the varying capacities of enforcement and influence that can persist or resume despite the contested and elusive nature of territorial control.

Throughout processes of de-territorialisation and reterritorialisation of the state as an institutional domain in the Syrian conflict, novel bargaining processes and contests between the state and other domains shape trajectories of social ordering and emergent state–society relations.[76] State atrophy therefore implies the relatively abrupt and uneven unravelling of institutional arrangements from a state regulated ecology to another where political power, social boundaries and military frontiers disarticulate and are distinctly contested.[77]

The Syrian State: A Background

The pre-2000 Syrian state (prior to Bashar Assad) exhibits three post-Soviet (or post-socialist) features: (1) developmentalism, (2) military authoritarianism and (3) (neo)patrimonialism.[78] The developmentalist aspect of

---

[75] David Newman, 'On borders and power: A theoretical framework', *Journal of Borderlands Studies* 18, no. 1 (2003): 16.

[76] Thomas Blom Hansen and Finn Stepputat, 'Sovereignty revisited', *Annual Review of Anthropology* 35, no. 1 (2006): 305.

[77] Harout Akdedian and Harith Hassan, 'State atrophy and the reconfiguration of borderlands in Syria and Iraq: Post-2011 dynamics', *Political Geography* 80, no. 1 (2020).

[78] The different terms used in the literature on Syria (such as the Pretorian state, Bonapartist state, the Mafia state) conceptually fall under the three categories above. See Klaus Schlichte (ed.), *Dynamics of States: The Formation and Crisis of State Outside the OECD* (Aldershot: Ashgate, 2005); Klaus Schlichte, 'A Historical-Sociological Perspective on Statehood', 53–7; Balazs Trencsenyu, 'What Should I Call You? The Crisis of Hungarian Democracy in a Regional Interpretative Framework', in Balint Magyar and Julia Vasarhelyi (eds), *Twenty-Five Sides of a Post-Communist Mafia State* (Budapest: Central European University Press, 2017), 3–19; for Syria specific analysis, see Raymond Hinnebusch, *Syria: Revolution from Above* (New York: Routledge, 2002); Khaled

the Syrian state resided in the central role of the state in economic planning and implementation, welfare provisions and distributive functions.[79] Developmentalist institutional arrangements of the Syrian state were established in the 1970s and were intertwined with processes of the personalisation of state power by Hafez Assad.[80] In other words, the expansion of state bureaucracy and administrative institutions into provinces beyond urban centres was intertwined with the structures of the ruling Ba'th Party in rural areas.[81] Agrarian reforms and land redistribution under state guidance took place alongside the capture of state institutions and the redistribution of privileges and resources, such as access to state power. Between 2000 and 2011, Bashar Assad radically reconfigured the distributive functions and roles of the state but only to reinforce neo-patrimonial institutional arrangements, which stand for the effective blurring of personal and bureaucratic authority. State atrophy in its institutional forms after the year 2011 implied the reconfiguration of the presiding institutional arrangements in place at the onset of peaceful protests in March 2011, specifically the reconfiguration of institutions of violence, which have been the bedrock of the Assad rule.

Social ordering in areas under rebel control is also integral to emergent institutional arrangements. Distinct areas of territory controlled by competing factions did not always bring about rigid institutional ruptures.[82] In some instances, the Assad government took care to preserve the state, to the point of paying official salaries in opposition areas. Residents in opposition held areas remained somewhat dependent on the state for certain services.

Abou El Fadel, 'The Pretorian State in the Arab Spring', keynote lecture at the University of Pennsylvania Law School Symposium *Democracy in the Middle East*, 11 November, 2011, https://scholarship .law.upenn.edu/cgi/viewcontent.cgi?article=1041&context=jil (accessed 6 November 2021). The post-Soviet designation indicates not only the collapse of the Soviet Union as an international actor and sponsor but also as an exporter of state systems known as presidential republics that differentiate functions of power in government without separation of powers. See Robert Freedman, *Moscow and the Middle East: Soviet Policy Since the Invasion of Afghanistan* (Cambridge: Cambridge University Press, 1991).

[79] Hinnebusch, *Revolution from Above*.
[80] See Chapter Two on State Capture.
[81] Hinnebusch, *Revolution from Above*; Samer Abboud, *Syria* (Malden, MA: Polity Press, 2016).
[82] Kalyvas, *Logic of Violence*, 111–15. Megan Stewart, *Governing for Revolution*, 6.

Consequences of state atrophy include security dilemmas, social cleavages and economic degradation that create institutional arrangements of their own: institutional ecologies of war that fluctuate between high-intensity and low-intensity cycles of violent contestation and continue to undermine the state's capacity to regulate other domains.[83] This is not solely driven by oppositional activism competing over territorial control. Survival strategies used by the Assad rule continue to cannibalize state resources and privatize state functions.

Book Structure, Methods of Research and Findings

In Chapter One, the state's coercive apparatus and the bureaucracy of violence receive specific attention as they played a foundational role in defining broader institutional transformations after 2011. Alongside efforts to consolidate state capture, the state under Hafez Assad increased its regulatory role and authority over other institutional domains such as the economy and the religious field. The neoliberal turn of the Syrian state under Bashar Assad, however, created paradoxical institutional trajectories with regards to the regulatory capacity of the state.

These contradictions are expressions of strategies of power consolidation by Bashar Assad. They allowed the Assad rule to reproduce its power over state institutions as well as over specific segments of society while further undermining the state's civic capacities (regulatory capacity of civilian institutions over the military and religious domains) and developmental capacities (vis-à-vis the economic domain). The seemingly contradictory strategies of power consolidation produced, intentionally or otherwise, asymmetric power relations within and between institutional fields such as religion, the economy, the military and the state. Asymmetric power relations also affected the socio-political role and influence of each institutional

---

[83] The book does not attempt to theoretically model processes of state atrophy or causes that lead to it. The broader literature on subjects such as state failure, state collapse and state weakness is primarily preoccupied with predictive indicators and interventionist policies with regards to civil wars rather than local dynamics. Indicators include gender-based literacy rates, mortality rates based on age demographics, life expectancy at birth and gross national income per capita. See, for instance, Robert Rotberg, 'The Failure and Collapse of Nation-States', 20–51. Robert Rotberg (ed.), *When States Fail: Causes and Consequences* (Princeton: Princeton University Press, 2005).

domain in question. The cumulative impact of institutional rearrangements between the years 2000 and 2011 not only shaped public dissent in 2011 but also defined the instruments of control that the Assad rule held in the midst of mounting civil unrest, militarisation and economic incapacitation since 2011.

In addition to the formal coercive capacity of the state, the dictatorship also relied on informal networks and relationships that have been the bedrock of its rule. These networks and relationships developed primarily through the transformation of the state from a regulator of resources and national wealth to a resource in and of itself. In Chapter Two the book explores informal aspects of institutional arrangements specifically in the military field. The chapter looks at the organisational and operational devolution of state violence, in formal and informal capacities before and after the uprising in government-controlled areas and beyond. The devolution of violence and institutional changes in this field after 2011 created far-reaching socio-political repercussions. Prominent groups within the military domain functioned as sect-based reservoirs of military recruitment. Sect-based strategies of mobilisation and power consolidation unleashed a process of sectarianisation that overwhelmed the Syrian context.

The spatial component of the devolution of violence after 2011 is also integral to unpacking the socio-political and economic consequences of state atrophy, which rendered many Syrian regions unrecognisable. While urban–rural divides largely shaped military frontlines early in the conflict, borderlands too emerged as geostrategic zones with distinct military dynamics and projects of socio-political engineering. After the solidification of internal frontlines by 2014, the coercive capacity of the state proved insufficient for the Assad rule to suppress dissent and maintain or regain control through its own devices. This led to the retraction and concentration of the state to limited areas, the spiralling of pro-government paramilitary formations and the effective end of the monopoly of violence.

In some localities, emergent military formations unsettled the state security apparatus. In other places, military vacuum created space for new militias and armed groups to form and operate. The devolution of state violence in an organisational sense did not reduce the deployment of state violence by the Assad rule because blanket targeting of entire areas, populated by civilians and militants alike, remained commonplace. Paramilitary groups, pro- and anti-government alike, also emerged as unhinged armed formations within localities. Violence was deployed for novel purposes of contesting or establishing territorial control as well as to redefine the body politic. Political violence during the Syrian conflict operated within ethno-religious ideological frames, and mass violence intensified the social appeal of such frames both intentionally and unintentionally, effectively redefining social and political subjectivities alike.

To explore the social repercussion of the devolution of violence and its impact on subjectivities, Chapter Three takes the reader on a tour of the social landscape in Syria through the perspectives of a diverse and contradictory sample of Syrian voices and narratives about their experiences and interpretations of socio-political transformations. Social reactions to violence and strategies of mobilisation by armed groups (government forces and beyond) rendered sectarianism a strong feature of social subjectivities at the onset of the militarisation of the uprising between 2012 and 2014. Supported by sixty-three semi-structured interviews collected between 2011 and 2014 from Syria and Lebanon, the chapter reveals two distinct narratives about sectarianism simultaneously at work: narratives of pre-existing ethno-religious belonging, and a more recent dehumanising sectarianism that emerged during the conflict. While the two reinforced each other, they are the outcome of different processes and conditions. The emergent sectarianisation cannot be attributed to a pre-existing ethno-religious condition liberated from authoritarian suppression. Rather, this is the ideological output and outcome of emergent institutional arrangements. Sectarian modes of mobilisation and the disproportionate impact and level of violence in different areas reinforced notions of relative harm and victimisation.

In addition to the institutions of violence, developments in the religious field also intensified sect-based structures as well as sectarian outlooks. As the state's territorial control and monopoly of violence was contested, state structures did not collapse altogether. Rather, the bureaucratic apparatus of the state maintained varying levels of presence and was used as a method of projecting power, establishing control and maintaining order. Despite its bureaucratic presence, the state's primary function as a regulating superstructure of other institutional domains as well as its capacity to act as such were effectively compromised. This brought forward significant changes to institutional hierarchies and public functions of different institutional fields: namely, with regard to the socio-economic roles of the religious domain and that of the state. To depict the reconfiguration of institutional arrangements while state capacity to regulate institutional domains is undermined, Chapter Four looks into state-religion relations as an illustration of institutional developments and transformations in broader state–society relations since 2011. The chapter looks into a variety of roles and functions that the religious field played in everyday life, before the conflict and throughout. The chapter also looks into the efforts of the Assad rule to strengthen the state's regulatory capacity over the religious field as a strategy of power consolidation.

Based on fieldwork in Geneva, Beirut and Amsterdam, the data in Chapter Four is derived from detailed case studies from Aleppo City and Kasab through interviews with key actors from the religious field in Syria between 2011 and 2018, as well as from a broad review of the existing scholarship about religion as an institutional domain in Syria. The chapter reveals that religious networks emerged as local socio-economic actors with significant socio-economic capacity, and were functionally weaponised in the course of the conflict through their targeted efforts to maintain basic conditions of liveability in specific areas and populations along political fault lines. Thus, the consolidation of local-level sect-based constituencies produced novel power structures that often dominated specific areas, reconfigured norms of religiosity or tradition, and replaced the state through distributive (socio-economic) functions. This did not translate into the weakening of the Assad rule. Clientilist arrangements reinforced the Assad rule and neo-patrimonial power structures, while continuously undermining state functions. The outcome is a more limited presence of the state in the areas of socio-economic responsibility in favour of an expanded presence for sect-based and religious actors.

Despite processes of sectarianisation and consolidation of local sect-based societal structures, civilian agency did not express itself in sectarian terms alone during state atrophy. Often dismissed as inconsequential, civilians and civilian organisations were actively involved in efforts of community protection during conflict. Community-protection efforts by civilians at the local level are expressions of civilian agency. Chapter Five documents such efforts in Deir Hafer and Kasab, and focuses on three main variables influencing the outcome of those efforts: (1) local autonomy, (2) organisational capacity and (3) social trust. Based on two divergent case studies of communities that faced different modalities and scales of violence, Kasab and Deir Hafer, and informed by forty-two in-depth interviews with local community organisers and civilian stakeholders during outbreaks of violence, surveys with 191 participants (10% margin of error), and focus group discussions, the chapter depicts variations in local circumstances, patterns of community mobilisation throughout the conflict and variables impacting the outcome of efforts to resist, cope and adapt to dynamics of state atrophy. Sectarianism was not the organising principle behind patterns of social trust, civilian cooperation or decision-making. Instead, specific modalities of violence and threats within local communities (Deir Hafer and Kasab) and local organisational capacities of civilian actors determined the efforts in place and their limits. The rarity of such efforts and the limits of their successes reflect the impact of state atrophy for civilian populations and the limits it entails for civilian agency.

The book concludes by juxtaposing the outcome of civilian efforts in Deir Hafer and Kasab with the outcome of institutional transformations in state–society relations. Overall, neither the sectarian nor the religious facets witnessed in Syria over the past ten years are due to essential characteristics of state or society. They are the product of multi-causal momentous transformations in institutional ecologies and elite politics that unleashed various transformational vectors. Emergent pathways in state–society relations, the alignment of sect-based factionalism (societal and institutional), along with the devolution of state functions and resources, yield socially destabilising institutional contradictions. As the state is incapacitated, external patronage and dependency will continue to be more intimately intertwined with local developments. From a state–society perspective, the state will be further alienated from public functions. This alienation of the state results in the further alienation of the public as well, as it surrenders the body politic, the instruments of political power and platforms of public service to private interests, both endogenous and exogenous. This reinforces path dependencies and conditions that further entrench institutions of war and predatory practices against the state and its citizens even when military contests settle.

I

State Capture and Devolution in Syria: A Paradoxical Landscape*

This chapter tracks processes of continuity and change with regards to the institutional architecture of state capture from the rule of Hafez Assad in 1970 until the militarisation of the Syrian uprising in 2012. The informality of the Assad rule – arrangements that fall outside the scope of state institutions – play a crucial role in reproducing state capture. The chapter shows how the formality of state capture and its formative institutional arrangements in Syria gave prominence to actors and processes outside the formal realm of the state to reinforce the Assad rule.

The Institutional Architecture of State Capture

The transitional period of thirty-seven days between Hafez Assad's death on 10 June 2000 and Bashar Assad's inauguration as president on 17 July 2000 encapsulates, with great precision, the institutional features of state capture in Syria. Upon the death of his father, Bashar Assad came to power in July 2000 through a constitutional amendment that changed the age requirement for presidential candidates. Under the second title ('The Powers of The State') of the 1973 constitution presiding at the time, Article 83 stipulated that 'the candidate for the presidency must be an Arab Syrian, enjoying his civil and political rights and be aged forty years at least'.[1] The constitutional process

---

* An earlier draft of this chapter was presented at the Bruno Kreysky Forum for International Dialogue in Vienna in 2018.
[1] Karim Atassi, *Syria, The Strength of an Idea: The Constitutional Architectures of Its Political Regimes* (Cambridge: Cambridge University Press, 2018), 313.

for bringing about the amendment that lowered the age requirement was also laid out in the same 1973 constitution. Constitutional amendments required a proposal by one third and approval by two thirds of the People's Assembly (*majlis al-sha'b* or the Syrian parliament). The person overseeing the process of constitutional change after Hafez Assad's death was defence minister Mustafa Tlass who owed his position to Hafez Assad and had a vested interested in maintaining the status quo.[2] The very same evening of Hafez Assad's death on 10 June 2000, the People's Assembly introduced the amendment to change the age threshold to thirty-four, Bashar Assad's age. Vice President Abdel Halim Khaddam announced the decision the next day. Khaddam, who had served as vice president since 1984, was assigned Minister of Foreign Affairs in 1970 by Hafez Assad. Every aspect of the transition of power that took place between 10 June and 17 July of the year 2000, from previous president Hafez Assad, to vice president Khaddam, to the new president Bashar Assad, was predetermined by institutional arrangements introduced by Hafez Assad after he seized the state in 1970.

Article 84 on executive powers of the 1973 constitution allocated the prerogative to assign a president to the joint responsibility of the leading Ba'th Party's Regional Command in proposing candidates and the People's Assembly's simple majority vote to select the president. Article 84 of the constitution about designating the president was introduced in the 1971 provisional constitution prior to becoming endorsed in the official constitution of the country in 1973. Article 86 of the constitution stipulated that if the president was unable to carry out his function as executive authority, the vice president was to perform those functions.[3] Furthermore, Article 88 of the 1973 constitution stipulated that in the event of the president's death, a referendum should represent the will of the people and confirm the new president.[4] In the period between Hafez Assad's death and Bashar Assad's ascension, Abdel Halim Khaddam acted as interim president between 10 June 2000 and 17 July 2000 until a referendum was held on 10 July 2000 – the only

---

[2] Patrick Seale, *Assad: The Struggle for the Middle East* (Berkeley, CA: University of California Press, 1989), 144; Atassi, *Syria, the Strength of an Idea*, 316.

[3] The article was introduced in an amendment on 1 July 1991, just as Hafez Assad's health started to deteriorate.

[4] Atassi, *Syria, the Strength of an Idea*, 313.

candidate was Bashar Assad. On 17 July 2000 Bashar Assad delivered his 'Oath Speech' before the People's Assembly and officially became the new president of the Syrian Arab Republic.

Capturing the state: constitutional and para-constitutional processes

The formal constitutional process for assigning Bashar Assad president consisted of formal and informal arrangements that defined the functions of executive, judicial, legislative and coercive (enforcement) branches within the state apparatus. The 1973 constitution embodies the refined version of the Syrian state in its captured and personalised version under Hafez Assad. This constitution stayed in place until 2012. The institutional arrangements it lays out featured in the 1969 provisional constitution drafted by the Ba'th as well as the 1971 provisional constitution after Hafez Assad's takeover in 1970. The undermining of separation of judicial, legislative and executive powers initiated with the Ba'th and was inspired by Stalinist one party-systems, institutional templates that acknowledged distinctions in functions of state power without any distinction in the authority over each function.[5] The 1969 Ba'th constitution was, however, unprecedented in two major ways compared to the previous constitutions in Syria since the 1928 constitution of the first republic. First, it had the longest preamble of all constitutions, and second, it was the first to introduce officially (de jure and de facto) a one-party system under the Ba'th.[6] The long preamble represents a formalisation of the Ba'th's efforts to redefine the place and role of the Syrian state under its rule. The three titles comprising the 1969 constitution laid out the institutional arrangements within the state, as well as between the state and the Ba'th, officially formalising state capture by the Ba'th.[7]

---

[5] For more on the subject see Raymond Hinnebusch, *Syria: Revolution from Above* (London: Routledge, 2002), 44–60.

[6] Atassi, *Syria, the Strength of an Idea*, 290. The Ba'th were already in control of executive and legislative functions within the state through Decision 2 of the 1966 Ba'th Regional Congress (25 February 1966). This was not officially codified in constitutional frames until the 1969 provisional constitution; Atassi, *Syria, the Strength of an Idea*, 295.

[7] The three titles were: (1) 'Fundamental Principles of the State and Society', (2) 'On the Rights and Obligations of Citizens, Popular Organisations, and Cooperative Associations' and (3) 'On the Constitution and Organisation of State Administration'.

Of significant note is Article 10 of the 1969 constitution, which defined the functions of the armed forces and institutions of coercion within the state. Article 10 stated that in addition to the protection of the country from external threats and attacks, the armed forces were responsible for 'the protection of the objectives of the unitary socialist revolution' – placing the armed forces of the Syrian Arab Republic at the service of the Ba'th.[8] The ideology of the Ba'th Party was not only imposed on the armed forces but also on the state's primary educational and cultural functions featuring under Chapter III of the first title of the constitution, which defined spreading the purpose of the Ba'th as the ultimate goal of public education.[9] The Ba'th had effectively captured the key branches of the country's armed forces prior to the new constitution, but the formal ideological conditioning of the state's armed forces came about through the 1969 provisional constitution.

Hafez Assad's journey towards state capture was not a pre-planned and strategised pathway finding success at every turn. Rather, this trajectory was characterised by a series of events, actions and reactions, which saw Assad gradually and oftentimes unsuspiciously attain a position of unmatched power enabling state capture. After all, Assad had effectively lost much of the air force under his command during the 1967 confrontation with Israel. It is hard to imagine how events over just three years since then could deliver Hafez Assad to the position of dominance he attained in 1970. Initially, after the disastrous outcome of the 1967 war with Israel, Hafez Assad's removals and appointments of army officials was a defence mechanism as the party leadership under the guidance of Salah Jadid placed the blame of defeat on Hafez Assad personally. Hafez in turn framed discharged officers as responsible for the performance of the Syrian armed forces against Israel. The calamitous outcome of the war gave allegations against Hafez momentum and support within the Ba'th. The political and military days of Hafez seemed numbered. It was in the midst of such pressure that Hafez Assad built around himself a 'personal power base in the armed services [. . .]

---

[8] Atassi, *Syria, the Strength of an Idea*, 291.
[9] Under Chapter III on the 'Principles of Education and Culture' Article 17 states the purpose of the state: 'to create a socialist, national Arab generation attached to its history, proud of its heritage driven by a spirit of combat, to achieve the objectives of the nation in unity, freedom and socialism'. See, Atassi, *Syria, the Strength of an Idea*, 292.

forged loyalty to himself by distributing favours and rendering services, and assiduously furthered the careers of friends like the tank officer Moustafa Tlass'.[10]

If there was ever an overall strategy employed by Assad, it could be vaguely described as an attempt to control both the Baʻth Party and the Syrian state through the armed forces of party and state. His primary competitor heading the Baʻth Party, on the other hand, Salah Jadid, had gradually shifted his attention towards civil matters since the 1963 takeover of the Baʻth Party, becoming less involved in military affairs. Salah Jadid, in contrast to Hafez Assad, tried to control the armed forces through the political leadership of the party. Ironically, as pointed out by Munif al-Razzaz, the civilian party leader of the Baʻth who had himself been ousted by Jadid in 1966, had lost his power to Jadid due to the same dynamics. Jadid's shift of attention towards party politics and policy was due to his trust in the security apparatus he had created around himself. This led to a polarity in the Baʻth military structures between Hafez Assad and Salah Jadid, which ultimately gave Salah Jadid a sense of stable parity and a level of detachment from military matters.

The broader context of the struggle between Jadid and Assad was more than a mere power struggle. Ideologically, Jadid was closer to the Communist Party and Assad postured a more pragmatic and conservative disposition. Furthermore, Jadid received stronger support from the Soviet Union compared to Assad. There were also strong disagreements between the two regarding the role of Syria in the Palestinian question, especially in neighbouring countries such as Jordan and Lebanon.[11] Ultimately, however, it was the tactics employed by Assad within the army to overcome adversity in the aftermath of the war with Israel and to consolidate power that led to his prominence. Moustafa Tlass states that removals of key contenders were carried out 'one by one, as one might take the leaves off an artichoke'.[12] The heart of the artichoke was Salah Jadid, surrounded by layers upon layers of loyalists in the military

---

[10] Seale, *The Struggle for the Middle East*, 144.
[11] For a detailed discussion about the broader context and meaning of issues at stake in the struggle between Assad and Jadid see Freedman, *Moscow and the Middle East*.
[12] Seale, *The Struggle for the Middle East*, 149; Lucien Bitterlin, *Hafez al-Assad: Le Parcours d'un Combattant* (Paris: Editions du Jaguar, 1986), 80; Atassi, *Syria, the Strength of an Idea*, 296; Moustafa Tlass, مرآة حياتي, vol. III, 345.

and political ranks of the Ba'th. In his memoirs, Tlass admits to replacing officers of significant rank on a weekly basis.[13] Tlass himself replaced previous chief of staff, Ahmad al-Suwaydani, a Jadid loyalist, in February 1968.[14] The loyalty of Tlass towards Hafez was not only based on mutual interest, but was also profoundly personal as Assad senior and Tlass had met in 1951 at the Homs Military Academy and had climbed the ladder of power together.[15] Their efforts saw influential Jadid loyalists, such as Colonel Izzat Jadid and Abd al-Karim al-Jundi, removed from the command of the most well equipped and technologically endowed 70th Armoured Brigade of the army and internal security services respectively.[16] The most consequential post was that of 'Abd al-Karim al-Jundi, who provided the protection that Salah Jadid needed to be able to focus on party politics and pursue ideological goals. If Jadid was the heart of the artichoke, Jundi represented the stem holding the artichoke together.[17] Along with Tlass, Rif'at Assad, the brother of Hafez, pre-emptively and effectively stifled al-Jundi by swiftly detaining his entire personal security apparatus.[18] Prior to that, they also controlled primary media outlets in the country by overtaking government and party newspapers and radio stations in Damascus and Aleppo.[19]

Patrick Seale, the author of Hafez Assad's sole biography with direct access to him and to archives, wrote that al-Jundi eventually committed suicide as he was about to be detained and most likely tortured, tried and ultimately executed. The case of al-Jundi is not only decisive in its consequence for Assad's ascent to power, but also decisive in the tactics employed by the security and intelligence services once Hafez Assad came to control them. Patrick Seale describes al-Jundi as a ruthless and cunning military man who controlled the intelligence services by the age of thirty-six.[20] Seale credits him for expanding the reach and repression of the security apparatus towards the

---

[13] Tlass, مرآة حياتي.
[14] Seale, *The Struggle for the Middle East*, 148.
[15] Ibid.
[16] Ibid., 149, 150.
[17] For a more detailed account of the significance attributed to al-Jundi by Salah Jadid himself, see Seale, *The Struggle for the Middle East*, 148–51.
[18] Ibid., 151.
[19] Ibid., 150–1.
[20] Ibid., 150.

public at an unprecedented scale, laying the foundations of ruling by terror against the public rather than targeting political opponents per se. Hafez Assad found al-Jundi's methods convenient and effective as he continued expanding his army of petty informants, increasing arbitrary arrests, and normalising unrelenting and undiscriminating torture practices. The only practice that Seale credits Assad with reining in, in line with other efforts of projecting and expanding state power and order, was the unchecked looting of private property and residences (now known colloquially as de-furnituring or *ta'feesh*) by the security apparatus.[21] With the elimination of Jadid loyalists from significant security posts, the elimination of Salah Jadid was a matter of formality. Not everyone met the same fate as al-Jundi. Many were offered posts in embassies abroad.[22] Others, such as Salah Jadid, were imprisoned. Although many were eventually released decades later, Salah Jadid was held in the Mezze prison until his death in 2012. Simultaneously, other names such as General Fuad Kallas, commanding the Air Force College, Ali Dhadha, acting as Head of Military Intelligence, Colonel Naji Jamil as Chief of Air Operations and Muhammad al-Khuly as Chief of Air Force Intelligence, came to positions of prominence.[23]

The personalisation of state capture: Syria's presidential system and the institutionalisation of Assadism

Commenting on the 1971 provisional constitution, Karim Atassi, an expert on Syrian constitutions, states that as 'a rare enough feat in Syrian history that merits special mention, the 1970 Corrective Movement was the only coup that kept the existing constitution in place'.[24] In this sense, the constitutional framework remained unchanged except for a few key features, which transformed the Syrian state model towards a presidential republic tailored to Hafez Assad's rule. Under Article 78 of the constitution, the President of the Republic became the head of state, no longer to be elected by the People's

---

[21] Seale, *The Struggle for the Middle East*, 150. After 2012 the practice of de-furnituring came to be known as *ta'feesh* (de-furnituring a private place of residence) and linked to the practices of the modern Shabbiha. This will be covered in the next chapter on the devolution of violence.
[22] Seale, *The Struggle for the Middle East*, 164.
[23] Ibid., 149, 151; Nikolaos Van Dam, *The Struggle for Power In Syria: Politics and Society under Assad and the Ba'th Party* (London: I. B. Tauris, 2012), 86–7.
[24] Atassi, *Syria, the Strength of an Idea*, 300.

Assembly but through a public referendum after candidates are proposed by the Ba'th Regional Command and shortlisted by the People's Assembly. In practice, what was described as a referendum was in fact a plebiscite. While a referendum is a source of law and has a binding effect on government practice, a plebiscite is an advisory step to confirm an already established policy orientation or government decision. The choices that were provided to the public until the 2014 presidential elections were 'yes' or 'no' regarding the candidate of choice (Hafez Assad pre-2000 and Bashar Assad post-2000).[25]

Despite the fact that the 1971 provisional constitution formally maintained separate branches of government, the prerogatives given to the president ensured that the legislative, judiciary and executive powers were held by the position of the president. For instance, unlike the 1969 provisional constitution, the 1971 version rendered the council of ministers solely accountable to the president and no longer responsive to the People's Assembly (under Article 65 of the 1971 constitution).[26] Similarly, proposals for constitutional amendments as well as legislation in between parliamentary sessions were withdrawn from the Council of Ministers and passed to the president's authority (Article 54).[27] The constitutional powers of the Ba'th were also substantially transferred in favour of the presidency, rendering the president no longer responsive, in any meaningful way, to the Ba'th Regional Command.[28] For instance, the Ba'th's Regional Command no longer had the power to dismiss, accept the resignation or appoint a head of state, or declare war, as was stipulated under the 1969 constitution. Ahmad Khatib became interim head of state on 20 November 1970, only to resign from the post after the 12 March 1971 plebiscite, which saw Hafez Assad receive 99.2 per cent approval rate and be announced as president.[29] Hafez made sure to appear as the person in control only after consolidating his capture and after having instilled a constitutional framework that enabled him to mobilise state structures to protect and further consolidate his position of power.

---

[25] This changed after the endorsement of the 2012 constitution, which altered the presidential electoral system. From then on, presidential elections featured multiple candidates.
[26] Atassi, *Syria, the Strength of an Idea*, 301.
[27] Ibid., 301–2.
[28] Ibid., 302.
[29] Ibid., 303.

This did not necessarily come at the expense of state structures as such. In other words, as Patrick Seale and Raymond Hinnebusch argue, Hafez Assad was invested in bolstering state institutions and expanding the state's institutional reach through Ba'th structures as long as he effectively controlled the decision-making process within state and party.[30] This ensured the capacity to mobilise and expand state institutions without attributing autonomy or meaningful decision-making power to state institutions. Hafez Assad's efforts to create a centralised system of presidential government effectively transformed the Syrian Republic into a neo-patrimonial regime where all sources of bureaucratic power emanated from the position of the presidency through the person of Hafez Assad. For example, in the final 1973 constitution, Article 115 in Chapter II of Title II established the council of ministers, as 'the highest executive and administrative organ' within the state, while Article 117 established the council and the ministers as only accountable to the president. The president was effectively the source of all state authority. The council of ministers ultimately served as an expanded secretariat for the president.[31]

This personalisation of state power was not at the expense of the state's bureaucratic and institutional reach – rather it was at the expense of decision-making powers in government institutions specifically with respect to the prerogatives and autonomy of the different branches. For instance, by reinstating the High Constitutional Court, the 1973 constitution reversed previous constitutional provisions introduced by the Ba'th since 1964 to undermine the judiciary and its judicial powers.[32] Interestingly, the 1971 provisional constitution under Hafez Assad, mirroring the 1969 constitution, did not feature a High Constitutional Court. This institution was not consequential for Hafez Assad's state capture. In fact, the lack of such judicial authority made capturing the state easier. However, upon capturing the state and attaining a monopoly on state authority, the expansion of the state apparatus in every domain was crucial for Assad's power consolidation. Reinstating a High

---

[30] Hinnebusch, *Revolution from Above*, 62–4; Seale, *The Struggle for the Middle East*, 175–8.
[31] Article 127 of the 1973 constitution delimits the responsibilities of the council, specifically in participatory, coordinating, procedural and enforcement roles. See Atassi, *Syria, the Strength of an Idea*, 315.
[32] A similar structure featured in previous constitutions (1920, 1928, 1950 and 1962) but was removed from constitutions proposed by the Ba'th in 1964 and 1969.

Constitutional Court under the guidance, supervision and micromanagement of Hafez Assad allowed the creation of an additional layer of bureaucratic authority within the state, which checked the authority of other branches of government but was effectively subservient to the president. On paper, Articles 144, 145 and 147 of the 1973 constitution acknowledged the court's authority on establishing the legality and constitutional character of electoral processes, legislative decrees and even the trial of the president in the event of high treason.[33] Hafez Assad never lifted the emergency laws instated by the Ba'th in 1963, which rescinded most constitutional authorities of the High Court. The constitutional court ultimately served as a legal veneer to frame all predatory and oppressive practices, including arbitrary detentions and torture, within a framework of legality. The operational modes of the court, however, reflected the same arrangements of state capture inflicted upon the legislative and executive branches.

In light of the restrictions and limitations on the legislative process and the effective hollowing of the state as a decision-making authority, the number of presidential decrees issued by Hafez Assad between 1971 and 1999 matched the total number of all bills passed by the People's Assembly during the same period.[34] As Atassi observes, since 1971, the legislative branch, represented through the People's Assembly, never objected to a single presidential decree despite having the constitutional prerogative to do so.[35] The nature of decrees also reflects a clear distinction between the procedural nature of assembly statutes compared to the substantive nature of presidential decrees.[36] For instance, the electoral laws under Hafez Assad were passed through a presidential decree on 14 April 1973, which provided him greater influence in determining lists of candidates as well as defining the process for allocating government seats. This reinforces loyalty of the legislative branch to the executive.[37] Similarly, in

---

[33] Atassi, *Syria, the Strength of an Idea*, 316.
[34] 1,134 presidential decrees compared to 1,158 assembly statues. Originally sourced from the People's Assembly services in Damascus. See *Atassi, Syria, the Strength of an Idea*, 374.
[35] Atassi, *Syria, the Strength of an Idea*, 318.
[36] This distinction remains a characteristic feature of legislation under Bashar Assad. See Chapter Four for examples of decrees regarding the religious field.
[37] Innovations included the division of assembly members between two distinct categories: (1) workers and farmers on one hand and (2) the rest of the population on the other. This saw the allocation of seats in rural areas as rewards or prizes while also countering the influence and presence of well-established urbanites with significant financial or symbolic power and standing within cities

a clear expression of blurring distinctions between the executive and legislative branches, the 1973 presidential decree on electoral laws enabled members of the People's Assembly to be members of the Council of Ministers and hold ministerial offices and portfolios. In addition to undermining the separation of powers, this arrangement introduced a competitive process within the People's Assembly for more favours, privileges and authority within state structures directly distributed by the president through the appointment process of ministerial positions.[38] The president became the equivalent of state authority, effectively controlling all key decision-making powers within the three branches of government as well as the distribution of privileges and powers within administrative and political structures alike.

As the head of state and commander in chief, Hafez Assad reiterated at every opportunity that he was a 'man of institutions'.[39] Patrick Seale reported a concerted effort since the early 1970s by Assad to project state presence operating for the people even if not by the people. The institutional expansion of the state beyond the confines of urban centres represented a sharp contrast to Assad's predecessors who did not match his strategic appreciation of the state's public functions. The 1973 constitution maintained a strong developmental economic outlook for purposes of social alleviation. Free education, health services and robust government subsidies supporting the agricultural sector further engrained the state's institutional and public presence. Needless to say, Hafez Assad was not motivated by ideological predispositions per se. The developmental and public functions of the state were carried out hand in hand with the personalisation of the Syrian state in decision-making processes, as well as legitimisation projects that projected the image of Hafez Assad as the symbol of nation and state. Statues and posters of Hafez Assad in public spaces and government buildings with labels such as 'the honour of the nation' were impossible to avoid.[40]

---

such as Damascus and Aleppo. Aleppo, specifically, was targeted through an additional arrangement where representation within the Muhafaza was divided between two representatives: one for the city of Aleppo and one for Aleppo's countryside. For more see Atassi, *Syria, the Strength of an Idea*, 316–7.

[38] See Atassi, *Syria, the Strength of an Idea*, 317.

[39] Seale, *The Struggle for the Middle East*, 175–8.

[40] For more on the spectacle of domination and personalisation of political power see Lisa Wedeen, *Ambiguities of Domination: Politics, Rhetoric, and Symbols in Contemporary Syria* (Chicago: University of Chicago Press, 1999).

Constituents and informal inclusivity

Constitutional provisions and formal structural arrangements in Syria since Hafez Assad's takeover reveal the transformation of the Syrian state into an instrument for nurturing loyalty and patronage by limiting entry points to political power through exclusive institutional provisions. Analysis of state capture in Syria through vocabularies of political institutions and constitutional features, as laid out so far, emphasise the universality of contemporary Syrian political history. Strategies to undermine separation of powers or checks and balances are political developments that continue to take place around the world with varying degrees of success. The distinctiveness of Syria as a case study is in the success of the political administration to capture the state and preside politically and bureaucratically despite recurrent episodes of crises and violent contestation after state capture by Hafez Assad.

The resilience of the Assad rule is due to multiple factors.[41] In addition to exclusive measures through formalised institutional provisions, state capture equally rested on inclusive practices through informal arrangements. The Assad rule continuously generated and co-opted various constituents of power to serve it and fill up the state apparatus. By serving as clients, power constituents garnered bargaining capacity vis-à-vis the state as well as the Assad rule. This created constraints (institutional and otherwise) for the exercise of power by the Assad rule. Various power conglomerates and hierarchies emerged within different government branches including the security apparatus leading to contradictory vectors in government policy and practice.[42]

The interactions between Tlass's military networks and other emergent classes of affluent bureaucrats illustrate how formal and informal practices interlock and to shape system of hierarchy that they operate within. The competition between Prime Minister Alraouf Alkasm (1980–7) and the generals

---

[41] Raymond Hinnebusch and Tina Zintl (eds), *Syria From Reform To Revolt, Volume 1: Political Economy and International Relations* (New York: Syracuse University Press, 2015), 14–17.

[42] Examples include the networks of vice-president Abdel Halim Khaddam, and the networks of Defense Minister Moustafa Tlass. See Raymond Hinnebusch, 'President and Party in Post-Ba'thist Syria: From the Struggle of "Reform" to Regime Deconstruction', in Raymond Hinnebusch and Tina Zintl (eds), *Syria From Reform To Revolt, Volume 1: Political Economy and International Relations* (New York: Syracuse University Press, 2015), 37.

under the patronage of Moustafa Tlass included disputes over hiring processes of government employees, and government contracts regarding nuclear waste management, construction and development planning and agricultural reform projects.[43] Despite having the backing of Hafez Assad, the prime minister at the time and his associates were not able to reckon with the immunity of Tlass generals despite the efforts of the General Director of Customs Bashir Najjar to curb illicit smuggling activities.[44] Generals under the patronage of Tlass operating the smuggling routes from Lebanon fed into an informal market that comprised a staggering ten per cent of the GDP at the time.[45] When those confrontations escalated, the Assad rule did not take an active role in supporting the efforts of state bureaucrats against Tlass. Instead, when the conflict between Tlass associates and Prime Minister Alkasm reached an impasse, Hafez Assad removed Alkasm and replaced him with Muhammad Alzou'bi.[46] Those on the commanding heights of the security apparatus prevailed even if their opponents were assigned by Hafez Assad for crucial tasks such as confronting the economic crisis in the 1980s amidst diminishing economic support provided by the Soviet Union. Prime Minister Alkasm's efforts were not motivated by personal vendetta against Tlass. Instead, it was his efforts to curb nepotism and improve the administrative performance and efficiency of the Syrian state that saw the formal apparatus of the state in conflict with the informal practices and power constituents of the Assad rule that were a part of the state yet immune from the law.[47]

Despite those power dynamics, the state continued to play a crucial role in social reform that benefited many, specifically through agrarian reform in rural areas and the expanded bureaucracy of institutionalised clientelism.[48]

---

[43] See detailed findings from first-hand interviews by Muhammad Jamal Barout in العقد الأخير في تاريخ سورية: جدليّة الجمود والإصلاح (Doha: Arab Center for Research and Policy Studies, 2012), 36–7.
[44] Ibid.
[45] Ibid.
[46] Ibid., 37.
[47] Alkasm's efforts included forbidding the use of government vehicles (civil and military) outside of official work hours. Government vehicles belonging to Tlass were used by his associates for smuggling purposes. Alkasm also published a prolonged study in the *Al-Thawra* newspaper supporting his rejection of a development project in rural Damascus on agricultural land that would have compromised the sustainability of the agricultural practices in the region. Ibid., 36–7.
[48] Hinnebusch and Zintl (eds), *From Reform To Revolt*, 4–5.

The primary benefactors from the steady transformation of the state into a reward for loyalty and services were select ex-rural elite officers in the army, the Ba'th's rural constituency and select urbanite merchants in the major cities of Damascus and Aleppo.[49] Not all constituents were rewarded equally as privileges, such as exceptions and immunity from the law, the use of coercive force, formal and informal licences of capital accumulation and rent-seeking, were not distributed equally. Discrepancies in rewards aside, the reconfiguration of the state under Assad senior was sufficient to maintain the loyalty of a core constituency that remained loyal despite episodes of violent confrontation with the Muslim Brotherhood and austerity measures introduced in the 1980s.[50] With every crisis that the Assad rule faced in the 1980s, such as the Muslim Brotherhood's uprising in Hama, mass protests in Aleppo or austerity measures, constituents (old and new) found opportunities to benefit while the Assad rule found opportunities to consolidate power. The limited revival of a private sector, expanding government contracts and endorsement and expansion of state-backed religious actors brought new constituents of power into the Assad fold. While clientelism is a pervasive feature of political systems everywhere, it is the effective capture and partitioning of the state in its fullest administrative, coercive as well as decision-making aspects that rendered the Assad rule resilient.

The informal practices and constituents that prevailed over the state apparatus did so through entry points into the state and through the capacity to determine exceptions to laws. Ultimately, arrangements within the coercive apparatus of the state under Hafez Assad and later under Bashar Assad came to shape patterns of state violence and atrophy after 2011.

State Capture under Bashar Assad

The 1973 constitution and its amendments remained substantively intact under Bashar Assad until a new constitution was devised between October 2011 and February 2012, and later approved by referendum on 26 February 2012. In the words of Atassi, the 2012 constitution 'is more a logical continuation and modernisation of the 1973 constitution than a radical departure

---

[49] Hinnebusch, *Revolution from Above*.
[50] Hinnebusch, 'President and Party', 22.

from it'.⁵¹ Bashar Assad handpicked the committee members devising the new constitution, and a final draft was ready at breakneck speed, taking under four months. The new constitution contained a new title on 'Rights, Freedoms and the Rule of Law' as well as an entire title on 'the Supreme Constitutional Court'. In terms of differences between the two constitutions, the 2012 constitution is stripped of all references to socialism, effectively redefining the economic functions of state institutions in liberal terms.⁵² The 2012 constitution also makes specific mention of 'war and disasters' and allows the state to confiscate private property under those circumstances through legislation and 'against fair compensation'.⁵³

Another fundamental constitutional change came about with reference to the role of the Ba'th in leading the state.⁵⁴ Article 8 of the new constitution established the political system of the state based on the principle of 'political pluralism'.⁵⁵ Furthermore, the fifth clause of Article 8 stated that 'public office or public money may not be exploited for a political, electoral or party interest'.⁵⁶ Despite this verbiage, contradictory vectors dominate the new constitution as Article 11 continues to state that the role of the armed forces in the country is not only to protect Syrian territories, but also to safeguard the objectives of the Ba'th – 'union, freedom and socialism'. This dichotomy between inklings of political change while shielding armed forces and the security apparatus from any reform is a characteristic feature of Bashar Assad's rule and one that defined the foundations of his rule along the exact same lines as that of his father, Hafez Assad. It is for this reason that the constitutional verbiage regarding 'Rights, Freedoms and the Rule of Law' or omitting the role of the Ba'th as the party leading the state, remain little more than ink on paper without any change in recruitment patterns or oppressive practices of the security apparatus. State capture remains founded

---

51 Atassi, *Syria, the Strength of an Idea*, 387.
52 Government practice and policies in line with the language of the constitution had a decisive impact on the rule of Bashar Assad in a variety of ways, which will be covered in the forthcoming sections of this chapter.
53 Given than presidential decrees are still the norm, the definition of 'fair compensation' remains at the sole discretion of the president. The case of Rami Makhlouf and the seizure of his assets in 2020 is a case in point.
54 Radwan Ziyadeh, السلطة والاستخبارات في سوريا (Beirut: Riad El-Rayyes Books, 2013), 67.
55 Article 8 (1).
56 Article 8 (5).

on the control of armed forces, the Baʿth Party remains the producer of leading cadres within the armed forces, and the president remains in control of the Baʿth as well as both legislative and executive powers despite constraints from constituents.

The primary differences in government practice under Bashar Assad as well as with reference to the 2012 constitution stem from the divergence in the state's designated economic functions. All other elements of constitutional reform were shielded from meaningful change. For instance, despite the fact that the 2012 constitution sets a limit of seven-year presidential terms with the possibility of one successive re-election, it does not specify a total limit of two terms per president.[57] In addition, under Article 155, the new constitution allows the president holding office at the time of the new constitution's endorsement to be eligible for two more terms. This effectively maintains Bashar Assad's hold on the presidency for another successive twenty-eight years and potentially longer through non-successive terms thereafter. Despite the fact that the electoral process is open to direct competitive vote, candidates should first secure the support of at least thirty-five members of the assembly with members being able to support only one candidate at a time.[58] Given the distinction in the People's Assembly between workers/farmers in one camp and all others in the other, candidates are unlikely to garner support across the aisle. This means that candidates are most likely competing for 35 votes out of a potential 125. Although the new constitutional process provides greater meaning for popular votes in presidential elections, this does not diminish the ability of Bashar Assad to remain in control of the state. Karim Atassi provides an incisive depiction of the dynamics at play:

> The constitution has tied the legitimacy of the future president to that of the members of the assembly. Anyone doubting the legitimacy of assembly members, whose representative character is subject to caution, [due to] interference by the authorities in the election of assembly members, will ipso facto cast doubt on the legitimacy of the representative character of a president sponsored by members of a doubtfully representative assembly.[59]

---

[57] Articles 86 (2) and 88.
[58] Article 85.
[59] Atassi, *Syria, the Strength of an Idea*, 401–2.

In other words, electoral processes in Syria do not guarantee representation unless the security apparatus and the judiciary maintain the integrity of the electoral process. Unless the armed forces and the judiciary are detached from the presidency, no electoral process, regardless of constitutional framing, can bring about meaningful political change in institutional structures. The 2012 constitution's content under title IV stipulates that all seven judges of the Supreme Court are appointed by the President of the Republic.[60] Furthermore, appointed judges do not serve for life but rather serve renewable terms of four years.[61] In other words, there are no protections for maintaining the position except by appealing to the will and favour of the president. Article 148 also limits the powers of the Supreme Constitutional Court regarding laws submitted by the head of state (the president) and approved by referendum. Despite the fact that title IV provides improvements to judicial authority compared to previous constitutions in Syria, the fact remains that the neutrality, impartiality and objectiveness of the supreme judges are not protected, and the judiciary remains in the hands of the presidency. In this sense, lifting emergency laws in 2012 made no difference to the autonomy of the judiciary in relation to the executive.

Along with the control of armed forces and neutralisation of the judiciary, the third institutional bedrock of state capture under Bashar Assad has been the continuous hold over both executive and legislative powers by the presidency. The 2012 constitution perpetuated the framework of unchecked presidential decrees outside of parliamentary sessions. In practice, since Bashar Assad came to power the rate of presidential decrees increased even more, from the staggering rate of fifty per cent under Hafez Assad to approximately sixty per cent.[62] A quick survey and comparison of the nature of the decrees passed by the president and those passed by the People's Assembly reflects the way the state machinery is run by presidential decrees.[63] Although Article 113 (3)

---

[60] Article 140.
[61] Article 143.
[62] Between 2001 and 2010 there were 699 presidential decrees and 542 legislative decrees by the People's Assembly. Numbers are from the People's Assembly services in Damascus found in Atassi, *Syria, the Strength of an Idea*, 403. fn, 44.
[63] Decisions such as cancelling the position of the Grand Mufti of Syria, for instance, were carried out through presidential decrees.

allows the People's Assembly to amend or revoke presidential decrees, such powers are yet to be exercised.

Foundations of power under Bashar Assad and the reproduction of state capture

The elimination, reappointment and reassignment of key security figures were a major component of Hafez Assad's strategies of state capture. He also worked tirelessly to restructure the organisational structure of the army in general. For instance, the Syrian Air Force was transformed into a quasi-personal security organism comprised of tight-knit loyalists and dependents of the president.[64] This was the result of Hafez Assad's hold over the air force even before his ascent to a leadership position since the Ba'th takeover in 1963. Hafez not only expanded the Syrian Air Force but also redefined its assignments and prerogatives within the army and beyond. The infamous Air Force Intelligence (known colloquially as *al-Jawwiyeh*) is renowned for monitoring other intelligence branches as well as direct involvement in public security matters deemed most urgent and critical by the president. The Air Force Intelligence, however, is only one of four intelligence agencies operating in Syria. The Military Intelligence Directorate (colloquially known as *moukhabarat Jeish*), the Political Security Directorate (colloquially known as *amn Siyasi*) and the General Intelligence Directorate (known as *amn 'am*) are all situated within different branches of the armed forces. Each provides surveillance within their specific ranks, over other intelligence agencies as well as over the public. This creates a system of hyper-surveillance, institutionally structured through parallel agencies and overlapping bureaucracies that monitor themselves, each other and the public, while reporting separately to the same head of state. The Military Intelligence Directorate falls within the Ministry of Defence and was restructured in 1969.[65] The General Intelligence Directorate is a part of the Ministry of the Interior and is dedicated to civil intelligence. It was formed in the early 1970s when the Political Security

---

[64] Seale, *The Struggle for the Middle East*, 151; Van Dam, *The Struggle for Power In Syria*, 87–8.
[65] Shmuel Bar, 'Bashar's Syria: The Regime and its Strategic Worldview', *Comparative Politics* 25 (2006): 353–445.

Directorate, which also falls within the Ministry of the Interior but has both internal (within Syria) as well as external (outside Syria) bureaus, was also formed.[66]

Those agencies are situated in every province of Syria, with the sole exception of the Air Force Intelligence, which is stationed out of Damascus, Lattakia, Daraa and Homs but does mobilise nationwide.[67] The four intelligence services report directly to the National Security Bureau of the Ba'th's Regional Command (*Maktab al 'amn alkawmi lilkiada alkoutriya*), which also has its own offices all over Syria and adds yet another layer of surveillance over intelligence agencies as well as the public.[68] The National Security Bureau responds directly to the Regional Command of the Ba'th headed by Hafez Assad prior to Bashar Assad.[69] Regionally, each province in Syria is represented through a governor (*Muhafiz*) under the direct command of the president. The fourteen governors of Syria are the administrative heads of each province and of government institutions therein. In case of emergencies, the governor is also in charge of local police as well as armed forces within the Syrian army, positioned within the province.[70] The governor and his office overlap with the regional representative and provincial branch of the Ba'th, also reporting directly to the president. In addition, intelligence forces operate within all provinces. Unlike suggestions about a pyramid-like structure or chain of command between those entities, the only common chain of command between all agencies is that of Bashar Assad as head of state and party. This neo-patrimonial system of hierarchy and power structuration, in outcome, is closer to parallel circles of asymmetric and uncoordinated networks of power that exchange information, favours and services only through a central node represented by the president and his appointees heading those key institutions. These networks are asymmetric, as exchanges do not happen reciprocally, or

---

[66] Andrew Rathmell, 'Syria's Intelligence Services: Origins and Development: Origins and Development', *Journal of Conflict Studies* 16, no. 2 (1996): 75–96; Radwan Ziyadeh, السلطة والاستخبارات في سوريا (Beirut: Riad El-Rayyes Books, 2013), 67; Alan George, *Syria: Neither Bread Nor Freedom* (London: Zed Books, 2003), 2–3.

[67] Human Rights Watch, *Torture Archipelago: Arbitrary Arrests, Torture, and Enforced Disappearances in Syria's Underground Prisons since March 2011* (July 2012), 56–62.

[68] Ziyadeh, السلطة والاستخبارات في سوريا, 67.

[69] Ibid.; David Roberts, *The Ba'th and the Creation of Modern Syria* (London: Routledge, 1987).

[70] Ziyadeh, السلطة والاستخبارات في سوريا, 63.

with similar intensity and frequency. In fact, within the central node, appointees in positions of power rarely report to each other but report directly to the president. The aggregate outcome of this type of power structuration is a loyalty system based on what Bassam Haddad labels 'relations of mistrust' that generate checks and balances for one another but reinforce the rule of the central node.[71] This stands as a system of proofing against power constituents.

The Ba'th's role is crucial in all intelligence and key army positions. Since the personalisation of state capture by Hafez Assad, recruitment has been driven by the intersection of two primary loyalties: to the Ba'th Party and to the president. Those two loyalties are distinguishable. On one hand, loyalty to the Ba'th is institutional as it is measured by the years and nature of service within the Ba'th Party (armed forces as well as political activism within the party), as well as the network of support and loyalty one holds within the party. This kind of appointments are key as the co-optation of key figures of such stature generate loyalties within the Ba'th ranks while also countering the influence of other Ba'thists in the party or within the institutions of violence and coercion of the Syrian state. The second loyalty to the president is distinguishable by its personal, rather than institutional, characteristics, as it does not stem from a loyalty to the position of the presidency, loyalty to public service or constitutional commitment within the army to state institutions including the head of the state. Rather, loyalty to the president implies direct loyalty to the person of Bashar Assad or Hafez Assad before him. It is for this reason that personal connections and loyalties produced an overwhelming Alawi presence within the army. This was not the product of a primarily sectarian predisposition that defined Alawis as trustworthy and non-Alawis as untrustworthy by Bashar or Hafez Assad.[72] In fact, many Alawi officers were also excluded from promotions within the army in favour of others who were deemed better connected, more dependent and by extension more dependable due to their personal connections to the ruling family.[73]

---

[71] Bassam Haddad, *Business Networks in Syria: The Political Economy of Authoritarian Resilience* (Stanford: Stanford University Press, 2012), 12–13.
[72] Seale, *The Struggle for the Middle East*.
[73] Carsten Wieland, 'Alawis on the Syrian Opposition', in Michael Kerr and Craig Larkin (eds), *The Alawis of Syria: War, Faith and Politics in the Levant* (Oxford: Oxford University Press, 2015), 274–90.

This system of appointments continued under Bashar Assad but gradually yielded a new group of loyalists to the new president as opposed to those who were loyal to his father, Hafez Assad. In fact, Bashar Assad's primary efforts at power consolidation after coming to power were motivated by ridding of those who brought him to power upon his father's death. The shift in dependency structures and symmetries of power preoccupied Bashar in the first years of his reign, between 2000 and 2003. The invasion of Iraq by the US, and the direct challenge against the presence of Syrian armed forces in Lebanon in the aftermath of the brutal assassination of Lebanese Prime Minister Rafik Hariri in 2005, both complicated and exacerbated Bashar Assad's tactics thereafter. Although he owed the transition of power from his father to the 'old guard' who held the fort for him, Bashar Assad knew that to rule as the sole authority, individuals in charge of key institutions within the state and beyond needed to owe their positions to him rather than the other way around.[74] Bashar Assad regularly changed heads of intelligence services, fostered internal competition within agency ranks through increased possibilities for higher appointments and frequently demoted individuals when he deemed it appropriate.[75] By 2002 all four intelligence agencies had new directors. A significant break from Hafez Assad's pattern of appointments under Bashar Assad has been the more frequent changes in higher ranks and shorter periods that heads of intelligence agencies tended to hold office for.[76]

Despite the fact that intelligence branches were constantly involved in the day-to-day operations of government and surveillance, the Syrian Army was mobilised more selectively and strategically, specifically during moments of crisis under Hafez and Bashar Assad alike. Unlike the intelligence agencies,

[74] See for instance, Sam Dagher, *Assad or We Burn the Country: How One Family's Lust for Power Destroyed Syria* (Boston: Little, Brown & Co., 2019), 113, 115, where he reports through interviews with Manaf Tlass, the son of Moustafa Tlass, who grew up and worked with Bashar Assad throughout his transition from an obscure son of Hafez Assad to being the designated successor upon the death of Hafez Assad, as well as the early years of his presidency. Manaf Tlass defected and joined family members in Paris in July 2012. A similar depiction of Manaf Tlass was portrayed by Rif'at Assad, the once exiled brother of Hafez Assad, in 2007. See his statement in a phone interview on minute 42:02 to 42:40 of Al Jazeera's documentary about Ghazi Kan'an's mysterious death: https://youtu.be/BAlaBfK6BUQ?t=2521.

[75] Gary Gambill, 'The Military Intelligence Shake Up in Syria', *Middle East Intelligence Bulletin* 4, no. 2 (2002), https://www.meforum.org/meib/articles/0202_s1.htm (accessed 12 May 2021).

[76] For a summary of these placements see Hicham Bou Nassif, '"Second-Class": The Grievances of Sunni Officers in the Syrian Armed Forces', *Journal of Strategic Studies* 38, no 5 (2015) Appendix.

the structuring of the army was not for purposes of effective mobilisation. Rather, the purpose was to ensure the taming of army divisions and render any possible insurgency or rebellion within the army inconsequential. The outcome was a hierarchy within army divisions where the most well-equipped divisions were headed by close associates of Assad, including immediate family members such as Bashar's brother Maher Assad, who controlled the Republican Guard and the Elite Fourth Division, which were equipped with the heaviest weaponry available to the Syrian Army.[77] Other extended family members and close friends included Hafez Makhlouf (maternal cousin) as previous head of the Damascus branch of the General Intelligence Directorate (*amn 'am*), the defected Manaf Tlass, the son of Moustafa Tlass, the lifelong associate of Hafez Assad (heading the 104th Brigade in the Republican Guard before his defection) and Atef Najib, another maternal cousin heading Dar'a's branch of the Political Directorate (*amen siyasi*) before 2011.

As indicated, it was government policy by Bashar Assad to frequently change personnel in key positions. This did not imply an immediate marginalisation of those whose roles had changed. Rather, reassignments also took the form of horizontal movement or upward mobility within the state bureaucracy. Demotions and promotions reinforced internal competition while simultaneously never allowing a single individual to become irreplaceable within the constellation of power. As a result, the army's role throughout the militarisation of the power struggle in Syria from late 2011 onwards played out as designed. Defections were inconsequential and mainly limited to lower ranking officers within divisions and brigades. The assassination of Assef Shawkat in 2012, the defection of Manaf Tlass in 2011 and the reassignment of Atef Najib away from Dar'a in 2011, did not pose any insurmountable challenge to Bashar Assad's reign over the expansive security apparatus.

The downside for Bashar Assad was that despite the size of the armed forces in the country, mistrust within the institutions of violence prevented state institutions from achieving full mobilisation and deployment. In other words, armed forces were not successful in quelling the uprising in 2011

[77] Bou Nassif, 'The Grievances of Sunni Officers', 632–3.

nor in maintaining or regaining territorial control with the militarisation of oppositional activism. This was and remains the Achilles heel of the Assad rule and the specific methods of state capture it employed to reproduce and consolidate authoritarian power. Despite the size of the Syrian Army, its four sections (1) Infantry, (2) Air Force, (3) Air Defence Force and (4) Navy are not structured to operate in harmony, within each force or with one another.[78] The same applies to the parallel intelligence agencies operating primarily to repress dissent. The security apparatus operates under mistrust and in competition within itself. Within each section or agency hundreds of sub-divisions and brigades are endowed with disparate capacities and roles creating a vast terrain of uneven topographies in resources and capacity as well as gradations in autonomy and influence. Those at the commanding heights, either in the chain of command or in capacity of mobilisation, are always closest to the president.

The machinery of coercion: selective recruitment, arbitrary detentions and the bureaucracy of torture

Institutions do not operate without individuals playing a key role in allocating roles and responsibilities, mobilising and directing personnel. The first step in ensuring that institutional arrangements operate according to their designated functions is recruitment. Patrick Seale, Nikolaos Van Dam and Hanna Battatu employed first-hand data, including direct interviews with officers, internal army and Ba'th documents, as well as memoirs and autobiographies to prove that key and high-ranking officers of the most powerful army divisions and brigades were handpicked after rigorous background checks and often selected because of personal affiliations.[79] In this sense, three main categories emerge as decisive in determining personal allegiance in the recruitment process (besides affiliation to the Ba'th): (1) region, (2) kinship (including tribal

---

[78] A fifth malleable category was that of paramilitary groups primarily dedicated to Palestinian forces operating on Syrian territories that were absorbed within state structures.

[79] Often referred to as coup-proofing in the literature. See for instance, Hicham Bou Nassif, 'Generals and Autocrats: How Coup-Proofing Pre-Determined the Military Elite's Behavior in the Arab Spring', *Political Science Quarterly* 130, no. 2 (2015): 245–75. The purpose of clientelism within the army is not solely coup-proofing. The institutions of violence provide more wide-ranging functions and possibilities of mobilisation.

where relevant) and (3) ethno-religious affiliation.[80] In other words, selected officers are assigned to their positions due to their dependencies as well as their intersectional embeddedness (regional, familial, professional and other communitarian associations) within the same networks as the ruling group. This reinforces interdependency of the high-ranking officers in the political status quo as well as the personal well-being of their family members. Those elements reinforce the loyalty of key officers serving the Assad rule.

The selection process excludes members of the same communities that are overrepresented in the army, based on regional and kinship distinctions. However, the outcome of such recruitment practices over the course of fifty years yields both uneven patterns of marginalisation disproportionately impacting some communities more than others, and fosters notions of relative deprivation and communal grievances within the army and beyond. The research of Hicham Bou Nassif relying on first-hand data on the grievances of Sunni officers in the Syrian Armed Forces is an invaluable addition to the literature. Bou Nassif documents how overrepresentation of the Alawi denomination has intensified over the years since Bashar Assad came to power. Bou Nassif derived findings from interviews with eighty-one defected officers occupying senior military positions under Bashar Assad.[81] Between 1970 and 1997 more than 61.3 per cent of all new officers appointed by Hafez Assad came from the Alawi community.[82] Between 2000 and 2011 all newly assigned Directors of Airforce Intelligence (*jawwiyyeh*) and Military Security (*amn Jeish*) hailed from the Alawi community.[83] Similarly, between 2000 and 2011, the Republican Guard and the Fourth Armoured Division were entirely led by officers who were Alawi by affiliation.[84] By the year 2011 and prior to the uprising, of the twelve infantry divisions surveyed by Bou Nassif, eighty-five per cent of the top commanders were from the Alawi community.[85] Furthermore, the top commanders and sub-commanders

---

[80] Van Dam, *The Struggle for Power In Syria*; Hanna Battatu, *Syria's Peasantry, the Descendants of its Lesser Rural Notables and Their Politics* (Princeton, NJ: Princeton University Press, 1999), 215–26.
[81] Bou Nassif, 'The Grievances of Sunni Officers', 627.
[82] Batatu, *Syria's Peasantry*, 215–26.
[83] Bou Nassif, 'The Grievances of Sunni Officers', 647.
[84] Ibid., 648.
[85] Bou Nassif surveys divisions 1, 3, 4, 5, 7, 9, 10, 11, 14, 15, 17 and 18. Ibid., 647.

of all Special Forces across all sectors of the Syrian Army were Alawi, with the sole exception of the leadership of the Special Forces within the Air Force.[86]

It is important here to focus on sectors of leadership that do not follow the same pattern of Alawi overrepresentation and reflect greater diversity in affiliation. While the top commanders of the Air Force between 2000 and 2011 were split evenly between Sunni and Alawi, recruits and sub-commanders within the ranks of those units were predominantly handpicked over a period of fifty years by Hafez Assad and Bashar Assad. Similarly, despite the fact that within the Ministry of Defence (2000–11) Alawis rarely featured as ministers of defence or chiefs of staff, divisions within the army are almost entirely led by commanders with Alawi affiliation. Similarly, before 2011 only two out of ten minsters of defence and chiefs of staff were of Alawi affiliation (Ali Habib and Ali Ayyoub).[87] One could derive that where the position is symbolic and inconsequential for purposes of mobilisation, non-Alawis were preferred to counter the narrative of overrepresentation of Alawi officers. In other words, even when a top commander defects or hypothetically mobilises a segment of their division, others within the same division or other entire divisions remain unaffected by their actions and may possibly counter them. Simultaneously, discrepancies in capacity and equipment within army sectors and divisions further reinforced this mechanism, as segments that were not closely controlled and deemed reliable were under-equipped. According to Major Iyad Jabra, defected commander from Air Defence: 'Combat preparedness is good when eighty per cent of a company's heavy weaponry (tanks, artillery and military transport) is operational. Military inspectors on tours have often found that less than forty per cent of the equipment is properly maintained.'[88] The underequipped nature of the army is not accidental or due to lack of resources, particularly in light of the over-equipped reality of select divisions such as the Republican Guard and the Fourth Armoured Division under the command of Maher Assad.

---

[86] Bou Nassif, 'The Grievances of Sunni Officers', 647.
[87] Bou Nassif surveys divisions 1, 3, 4, 5, 7, 9, 10, 11, 14, 15, 17 and 18. Ibid., 647.
[88] Ibid., 637.

With regards to surveiling the public, each individual intelligence agency is represented through its branches all over Syria and each set of offices and facilities function as independent prisons and torture centres.[89] The journey of the detained is not limited to their experiences within those local detention centres and the torture that takes place therein. Upon the first round of forced confessions, specifically when the accusations are of a political nature, captives are transferred to the headquarters of the respective intelligence agencies where martial courts of special jurisdiction are often located, then moved to centralised military prisons where detainees from all branches are amassed.[90] Detention centres contain prison cells (communal and solitary), interrogation rooms and torture chambers.[91] Prior to the detention centres operated by the intelligence agencies, local law enforcement facilities are also used as initial sites of detention before prisoners are relocated to local intelligence branches. The time spent in each facility varies, with most political detainees waiting for years before being transferred to one of the central prisons such as Saydnaya, Idlib or Tadmur.[92]

After providing forced confessions under torture, detainees are returned to an assigned judge within the directorate for sentencing. The courts of special sentencing became commonplace under emergency laws in Syria and had become the foundations of the presiding legal system, specifically in relation to political conduct deemed contentious by the security authorities. In the absence of due process, arbitrary sentencing was routine even for those who had legal representation. For example, Malek Daghestani, a previous member of the Communist Labour Party, reports that after the prolonged torture he was subjected to, he found himself in front of a judge and was represented

---

[89] Human Rights Watch, *Torture Archipelago*.
[90] George Sabra, 'Ya hurriyyeh', interview by Suad Qatanani, *Syria TV*, 19 July 2018, https://www.youtube.com/watch?v=9N8Amxu4riQ.
[91] Human Rights Watch, *Torture Archipelago*.
[92] George Sabra recounts staying in the local facility of the General Intelligence Directorate in Damascus, known as Fir' al-Khatib, for almost two years prior to being transferred to the court of the General Intelligence Directorate in Damascus and then to the notorious Saydnaya Prison. For detailed descriptions of facilities, including locations, chamber structures and practices therein see Human Rights Watch, *Torture Archipelago*; the Tadmur prison was blown up by ISIS in 2015. It was the only other military prison in Syria that could compete with the scale of Saydnaya prison, which carried out what amounted to extermination policies. See Amnesty International, *Human Slaughterhouse: Mass Hangings and Extermination at Saydnaya Prison* (London: Amnesty International, 2016).

by independent, voluntary and pro bono lawyers who tried to defend him out of their commitment to the profession and rule of law.[93] Such advocates included Mounir al-Abdallah, Sami Dahi and Khalil Ma'touk – the latter being detained himself after the 2011 uprising.[94] Sam Dagher held interviews with Samer Darwish, a similar independent defence attorney and human rights activist who represented detained individuals in the wake of arrests targeting civil society members and intellectuals mobilising for political reform between late 2000 and early 2001. Samer Darwish reports that even when judges agreed with the legal arguments of the defence attorneys, they explicitly admitted to having instructions from intelligence officers as to the pre-determined length of sentences that they were obliged to hand down.[95]

The fact that intelligence officers were orchestrating courts of special jurisdiction is not surprising. The performative aspects of legal observances or procedures on the other hand are surprising and are analytically significant as well. In the absence of due process, performances of legality and the presence of judges or attorneys are effectively void of any legal meaning. Detainees are neither guilty until proven innocent nor innocent until proven guilty. Every detainee, specifically those suspected of political dissidence, is unavoidably found guilty. What then is the value of such performances and exhibitions of legality when the Assad rule is capable of killing and oppressing dissidents or suspects without accountability? Superficial forms of legality and judicial processes are remnants of state institutions and the rule of law in Syria. That these practices are performed within a shell of legal and institutional processes is an illustration of effective state capture where repression operates within the state bureaucracy and through the institutional structures of the state. This intentional blurring of government practice and state institutions is in line with the personalisation of the state where the Assad rule and the Syrian state become almost indistinguishable. State capture indicates the importance attributed to state institutions by the Assad rule and the crucial role of those institutions in expanding the reach, oppression and domination of the Assad rule.

---

[93] Malek Daghestani, 'Ya hurriyyeh', interview by Suad Qatanani, *Syria TV*, 29 March 2018 Time Stamp: 18:00–19:20, https://youtu.be/f3SiDRJj_Sk.
[94] Ibid.
[95] Dagher, *Assad or We Burn the Country*, 108.

Intelligence services operate every institutional junction in the bureaucracy of torture, such as the transfer of detainees and the administration of facilities.[96] This bureaucracy of torture on an industrial scale is not only punitive in its outlook but also pre-emptive in its own assessment of its efforts. Given that the existing structures of hierarchy are founded on relations of mistrust, the Assad rule expects the security apparatus to identify and pre-empt betrayals, rebellions and attempts at seeking vengeance against the ruling establishment and power structures in place. Parallel security agencies therefore compete with one another to present their achievements to the Assad rule as the evaluation of their success depends on it. It is primarily for this reason that suspicion alone is sufficient for the security apparatus to not only apprehend but also force confessions, which ultimately results in prolonged sentences in prison and death.[97] The personal testimonies of previous prisoners and officers who defected after the uprising in Syria reveal that there were direct instructions from interrogators and officers to tortured detainees to write self-incriminating reports that 'seem' credible and convincing even when they were aware that the person was innocent of the accusations levied against them.[98] It is only possible to rationalise the absurdity of such morbidity at the personal level when one takes into account the macro dynamics of inter-organisational competition within the security apparatus as well as the effect of such practices on the general population (beyond the personal dynamics between the prisoner and their captor). The cumulative sum of the bureaucracy of terror and the expansive reach of security services through petty informants in every corner of the country, combined with the unrelenting loyalty of privileged and 'clientelised subjects' cultivated over fifty years, resulted in multigenerational terror wherever the

---

[96] The Idlib Central Prison, for instance, consisted of five floors. The Political Security Directorate (*Amen Siyasi*) operated on the third floor whereas the military intelligence operated in the basement. See Human Rights Watch, *Torture Archipelago*, 76–7.

[97] Amnesty International, *It Breaks the Human: Torture, Disease and Death in Syria's Prisons* (London: Amnesty International, 2016).

[98] See the series of documentaries and interviews broadcast by *Syria TV* (*tlfzyon Sourya*) under the title 'Ya Hurriyyeh' with political dissidents from the Communist Labour Party, such as Malek Daghestani and George Sabra, or citizen journalists such as Riyad Avlar. Interviewer: Suad Qatanani, 29 March 2018. For a conclusive report documenting the perpetuation and post-2011 intensification of such practices, see Anne Barnard, 'Inside Syria's Secret Torture Prisons: How Bashar al-Assad Crushed Dissents', *The New York Times*, 11 May 2019.

intelligence agencies operate (in Syria and beyond).⁹⁹ Mere suspicion or an accidental personal grievance with an inconspicuous informant is enough for an arbitrary report to be created.¹⁰⁰ With little accountability or due process, security agencies have no repercussions or restraints against harming or killing detainees. In fact, with each murder of a detainee, security services can claim to have aborted and neutralised a serious threat against the establishment.¹⁰¹

Institutional Reconfiguration and Constituents of Power under Economic (Neo)Liberalisation

The hereditary nature of Bashar Assad's rule implied that the foundations of state capture and practices therein remained the same despite the fact that Bashar Assad reassigned and reshuffled individuals holding key positions. From an institutional standpoint, as mentioned, the primary break in relation to state structures came in the context of the state's socio-economic roles within society. Bashar Assad's presidency had other defining features in relation to its unique government practices and policies responding to internal and regional developments. These aspects pertain to government practice and did not alter the structural features of the Syrian state or the institutional arrangements of the political system in general.

Internationally, Bashar Assad came to power in a context of limited regional partners and even scarcer international allies. The isolation of the Assad rule worsened in the first six years of Bashar's rule. The US invasion of Iraq threatened the possibility of a similar invasion in Syria and the Assad rule needed reassurances against the Bush Administration's post-9/11 hawkish endeavours. This coincided with the post-invasion rise of trans-local Jihadi activism in Iraq, which required broader regional cooperation for effective

---

[99] Such practices were not unique to the operations of the Assad rule in Syria. Lebanon, until the withdrawal of Syrian forces in 2005, was under the direct command of Ghazi Kanaan and the Lebanese branch of Syrian security forces headquartered in the small town of Anjar on the Syrian–Lebanese border. For further reflections regarding the impact and function of extreme surveillance and rampant indiscriminate practices of violence, see Mamdouh Adwan, حيونة الانسان (Beirut: Dar Mamdouh Adwan Lil nashr wal-tawzi', 2016); see also Mustafa Khalifa, القوقعة (Beirut: Dar al-Adab, 2008); Bassam Yousef, حجر الذاكرة: بعض من جحيم السجون السورية (Paris: Maysaloun Press, 2018).
[100] Amnesty International, *It Breaks the Human*, 21.
[101] Salwa Ismail, *The Rule of Violence: Subjectivity, Memory, and Government in Syria* (Cambridge: Cambridge University Press, 2018), 32–8.

intelligence gathering and intervention. Syria's isolation came in the context of regional and international pressures against the Assad rule in the aftermath of Lebanese Prime Minister Rafik Hariri's detonated assassination that left a thirty-feet crater and 240 casualties (twenty killed) in broad daylight in downtown Beirut. Syrian forces withdrew from Lebanon amidst mass anti-Syrian protests in Lebanon, international condemnation and strong suspicion regarding the Assad rule's involvement in the brutal assassination. Simultaneously, the Damascus Spring saw local mobilisation of Syrian activists demanding political reforms within a state-sanctioned framework of civil society. This context encouraged the neoliberalisation of the Syrian state and economy. The international context aside, it is the internal economic threats facing the Assad rule and Bashar Assad's reformist dispositions that primarily led to neoliberalisation of the Syrian state and the full-fledged commitment of the Assad rule to crony capitalism.[102]

There is a clear and explicit logical thread and common denominator between the inaugural speech of Bashar Assad on 17 July 2000, the five-year plan endorsed at the Ba'th's Tenth Regional Congress in 2005 and the 'Economic Principles' of the 2012 constitution (Chapter II (13) of Title I).[103] While central economic planning was a primary function of the state and was aimed at abolishing 'all forms of exploitation' during the era of Hafez Assad, Bashar Assad's vision and commitment since the first day of his presidency was to transfer the burden of economic responsibility from state structures to private interest. It is in this context that the 2012 constitution's economic outlook omits all references to 'socialism'. Despite the fact that the language of social responsibility semantically features in the 2012 constitution (that is, references to social justice, free access to education and healthcare), the logic and ethos of the constitution endorses liberal modes of economic government.[104] The premise that economic responsibility and social responsibility can be divorced and therefore economic management and social justice are two distinct and separate fields of policy represents the primary foundation

---

[102] Mohammad Jamal Barout, العقد الأخير; Emile Hokayem, *Syria's Uprising and the Fracturing of the Levant* (London: Routledge, 2013).
[103] Jamal Barout and Shams alDin Kaylani (eds), سورية بين عهدين: قضايا المرحلة الانتقالية بيانات ووثائق، حوارات وسجالات، مقالات (Amman: Dar Sindbad Lilnashr el'am, 2003).
[104] Atassi, *Syria, the Strength of an Idea*, 391.

of neoliberal economic government.¹⁰⁵ This radical shift in economic government policy and outlook reconfigured state–society relations and had far reaching implications that can be summarised under the following headings: (1) new expertise and a technocratic cadre of neoliberal policy-drafters within state structures, (2) the generation and expansion of private capital, (3) relative deprivation at multiple levels of society and (4) the effective devolution of social responsibilities from the state to private interests.

In his inaugural speech, Bashar Assad explicitly indicated the need to modernise the Syrian economy and enhance the circulation of domestic and foreign investment in the form of private capital. Less than six months after his speech, select private banks were allowed to open and a new cadre of leadership had already been recruited and assigned to key positions. Ghassan Rifa'i, an economist working at the World Bank in Washington, DC, became minister of economy by 2001.¹⁰⁶ Issam al-Za'im and Nibras Fadel, expatriates living abroad, took on responsibilities as early as 2001 to reform public administration and economic management practices within state institutions.¹⁰⁷ By June 2005, Abdallah al-Dardari was in charge of overall economic affairs of the Syrian state as deputy prime minister.¹⁰⁸ These early appointments spanning the first five years of Bashar's rule were tasked with spearheading efforts of economic modernisation and the reconfiguration of the role of the state in economic government.¹⁰⁹

The paradoxical landscape

The emergence of a new class of technocrats and policy makers was directly orchestrated by the president, but lacked the broader support of the system

---

[105] David Harvey, 'Neoliberalism as Creative Destruction', *The Annals of the American Academy of Political and Social Science* 610 (2007): 22–44, http://www.jstor.org/stable/25097888.
[106] Caroline Donati, *L'exception Syrienne* (Paris: La Découverte, 2009), 219.
[107] Atassi, *Syria, the Strength of an Idea*, 367.
[108] Ibid.
[109] Haddad, *Business Networks in Syria*, 31. The economic pressures that pushed for changes in economic government were due to the imminent transition of Syria's economy from oil exporting to oil importing. This was not only due to diminishing resources but also due to an increase in local demand and a decline in foreign aid. For more on economic dynamics see also Shamel Azmeh, 'The Uprising of the Marginalized: A Socio-Economic Perspective of the Syrian Uprising', *LSE Middle East Centre Paper Series*, no. 6 (November 2014): 16.

in which they operated.¹¹⁰ Internally, a schism emerged between the new, educated and cosmopolitan technocratic elites and the old guard of party politicians and partisans who had climbed the political ladder through dogmatic and ritualised commitments to the Assad family, Baʿthist bureaucracy and ideology. These emergent schisms were not instigated by Bashar Assad, yet they were not unpredictable either. In a political establishment where status quo is sanctified, new faces breaking onto the political scene with direct and close access to the president were guaranteed to create friction in the broader political arena. Intellectually, the schism was between two groups: (1) those who prioritised concerns over economic projections in the country, and (2) those who advocated for maintaining the status quo on ideological grounds and/or out of personal concerns over the redistribution of wealth.¹¹¹ The new technocrats were aware of these tensions and tried to find a practical modus operandi.¹¹² However, economic liberalisation inevitably implied some undermining of rent-seeking politicians who had acquired economic privileges through their political posts and then used their economic privileges to further engineer clientelistic arrangements and networks of dependency.¹¹³ When those conflicts came to a tipping point, Bashar Assad did not intervene to protect reformists.¹¹⁴

---

[110] Despite the fact that new faces were in charge of economic modernisation under Bashar Assad the class of the 'bureaucratic bourgeoisie' was not a recent phenomenon. A far more limited and contained privatisation took place under Hafez Assad which allowed those in significant positions of power and their relatives, such as previous vice president Abd el-Halim Khaddam and his sons or generals such as Bashir Najjar, previous General Director of Customs, to capitalise on any government contract, such as nuclear waste management programmes. For more on Hafez Assad's policies and the dynamics of the bureaucratic bourgeoisie see Barout, 36–37, العقد الأخير.

[111] The bureaucrats imported by Bashar Assad were not of uniform academic, intellectual or ideological dispositions as the new cadre included those of Marxist views, such as Issam Izzat, some with socialist inclinations, such as Muhammad Jamal Barout, and those who leaned towards free market economies such as Abdallah al-Dardari. See Barout, العقد الأخير, 50; Atassi, *Syria, the Strength of an Idea*, 367. The plurality of views and visions regarding economic policies were also evident in deliberations about city planning projects, the creation of industrial zones and the management of informal settlements (*ʿishwaʾiyyat*) around urban centres such as Aleppo city. See The Aleppo Informal Settlement Task Force, 'Informal Settlements in Aleppo', *Aleppo Urban Development Project*, January 2009, http://madinatuna.com/downloads/IS-Book_en.pdf.

[112] This included the use of slogans such as 'change within continuity' or the broad label of 'social market economy' to straddle the emergent divides; Haddad, *Business Networks in Syria*, 177–8.

[113] Haddad, *Business Networks in Syria*, 70–1, 177–9.

[114] For instance, Issam al-Zaʿim, Ghassan Rifaʿi, Nibras Fadel and Abdallah al-Dardari all eventually lost their jobs.

The presidency, similar to the Syrian state in general, were reconfigured as neutral and separate from both politics and society. By doing this, neither the state nor the president were accountable for government practice and state policies. This devolution of responsibilities and state functions was intertwined with a further devolution of accountability. When economic policies backfired, the new technocrats were held responsible. Economic modernisation was designed to maintain the repressive features and coercive foundations of political power in Syria. The Assad rule aimed to adapt to local and international economic pressures while attempting to not only maintain but also reinforce its position of power.[115] When neoliberal government policies came under scrutiny, Bashar Assad did not hesitate to replace technocrats without much change in models of economic government, state policies or government practice.[116] Changes in personnel did not interrupt the granting of government contracts and partial privatisation deals (*'uqud tasharukiyya*), trade deregulations (specifically with neighbouring Turkey) and the formation of the Syrian Business Council (2007) or the Damascus Stock Exchange (2009).[117] Despite the fact that the scale of the planning phase for economic modernisation was unmatched in the history of modern Syria, the vast majority of recommendations and plans, specifically for institutional reforms, were ultimately disregarded.[118] Jamal Barout was in charge of the 'Syria 2025' project, which was tasked with setting the blueprint and developmental plans preceding the endorsement of the tenth five-year plan in 2005. He was present in the plenary sessions, which drew unprecedented national and international participation from experts and scholars who scrutinised Syria's institutional status in economic management and suggested recommendations. In his book, *Syria in the Last Decade: The Dialectic of Stagnation and Reform*, Barout states that the deadline for the planning phase was the tenth conference by the Regional Command of the Ba'th for endorsement.[119]

---

[115] Often labelled as authoritarian upgrading by scholars such as Raymond Hinnebusch, Steven Heydemann and Volker Perthes.
[116] Issam al-Za'im and Ghassan Rifa'i both lost their jobs in 2003, as early as two years after their appointment.
[117] Haddad, *Business Networks in Syria*, 177–9; Azmeh, 'The Uprising of the Marginalised', 16.
[118] Barout, العقد الأخير, 51.
[119] Ibid., 50.

What took place during the conference was a clear indication of the nature of economic modernisation that was to follow in Syria:

> When the project was presented to the 10th Regional conference of the Baʿth party, the economic office [of the Baʿth] omitted from it sections on institutional reform. The plan was still endorsed but eventually was placed on the shelf [. . .] Instead, what was implemented was a naïve politicised liberal agenda even compared to 'the Washington Consensus' [. . .] What followed was a policy of liberalisation that resembled the Mexicanisation of the Syrian economy which was comprised of trade deregulations with severe outcomes.[120]

The omission of institutional reforms during the tenth regional congress is yet another reminder of the nature of state capture in Syria. Institutional reforms submitted for consideration included both sector-by-sector government models and cross-sectoral reforms needed to create the institutional infrastructure required to modernise Syria's stagnant economy, which once relied primarily on oil income. The proposed institutional infrastructure was not mere bureaucratic and organisational landscaping with further compartmentalisation. At heart, those suggestions were ultimately about decision-making processes concerning economic government (licensing, government regulations, deregulations, fiscal policies and banking amongst others) and the capacity to mobilise and coordinate relevant state institutions. Suggestions for institutional reform contradicted the very ethos of state capture in Syria. What ensued, instead, was an intensification and expansion of privatisation and deregulation schemes that generated a new class of tycoons closely associated with Bashar Assad controlling every major privatised space of the Syrian market.[121] Meanwhile, domestic economic sectors, such as industrial and agricultural sectors, suffered tremendous losses due to a number of factors, including trade deregulations and the inability of these sectors to compete with neighbouring markets, such as Turkish exports, which operate on a global scale.[122]

---

[120] Barout, *The Past Decade of Syrian History*, 51.
[121] For a detailed account of these business partners or crony capitalists, see Barout, *The Past Decade of Syrian History*, 54–88. See also Haddad, *Business Networks in Syria*.
[122] For detailed studies of specific economic policies of deregulation, government contracts and

State-society relations

Despite the socio-economic repercussions of neoliberal policies, the state effectively abandoned its commitment to social welfare provisions.[123] Before 2000, the state was responsible for the provision of social services such as education, healthcare, subsidised food products (such as sugar and bread) and other subsidies targeting the agricultural sector.[124] Experimentations with the private sector remained limited before 2000. According to the International Labour Organisation, until early 2000, more than half of the workforce was employed in agriculture and industry, two sectors heavily supported and subsidised by the state.[125] Furthermore, the number of registered associations (charity, social, cultural) was stagnant, declining from 596 in 1962 to 512 in 2000.[126] The state continuously limited the role of associations, as it considered itself the primary authority responsible for socio-economic welfare.

Between 1990 and 2010 the population in Syria nearly doubled from approximately 12 to 21 million, which exacerbated the economic hardships that hit the country after the year 2000, such as drought in the agricultural areas of al-Jazira and Houran, which increased youth unemployment and caused mass internal migration from rural to urban areas.[127] Balancing the country's economic and social needs was largely dependent on revenue from the energy sector, and this was becoming gradually untenable as Syria began transitioning from an oil-exporting to an oil-importing country.[128] Between 1990 and 2000, Hafez Assad nurtured intimate linkages with wealthy individuals and families

---

social repercussions, see Joseph Daher, *Syria After The Uprisings: The Political Economy of State Resilience* (London: Pluto Press, 2019), 9–37; Azmeh, 'The Uprising of the Marginalized'; Samer Abboud, 'Locating the "Social" in the Social Market Economy', in Raymond Hinnebusch and Tina Zintl (eds), *Syria From Reform To Revolt, Volume 1: Political Economy and International Relations* (New York: Syracuse University Press, 2015), 45–65.

[123] Daher, *Syria After The Uprisings*, 22.
[124] Azmeh, 'The Uprising of the Marginalised', 10–11.
[125] 'World Development Indicators: Databank (Syrian Arab Republic: Preview)', *The World Bank*, 21 March 2020, https://databank.worldbank.org/reports.aspx?source=2&country=SYR.
[126] Laura Ruiz de Elvira and Tina Zintl, 'The End of the Ba'thist Social Contract in Bashar al-Asad's Syria: Reading Sociopolitical Transformations Through Charities and Broader Benevolent Activism', *International Journal of Middle East Studies* 46, no. 2 (2014): 333. State responsibilities included subsidies, tax cuts, the protection of domestic products against foreign imports and the provision of social services. See Azmeh, 'The Uprising of the Marginalized'.
[127] The World Bank, 'World Development Indicators'.
[128] Azmeh, 'The Uprising of the Marginalised', 16.

in urban centres.¹²⁹ These linkages and clientelist arrangements with private entities expanded between 2000 and 2011, forming the bedrock of the private sector in Syria.

Assad's answer to the socio-economic circumstances was to adopt neoliberal policies by fostering economic privatisation, increasing openness to importing and devolving social responsibility to private interest. It is in this context that the number of registered associations grew from 513 in 2000 to 1,485 in 2009.¹³⁰ Similar to business partners, social associations were also handpicked. Government contracts (*'uqud tasharukiyya*) became commonplace where public services including health services, refugee resettlement and humanitarian assistance devolved to private entities such as charities, religious organisations or government-sanctioned civil society organisations.¹³¹ Overall, privatised mechanisms of wealth extraction and circulation were prioritised while the state surrendered social responsibility to private actors. These policies are comparable with the neoliberal models of the 1980s, known as the Washington Consensus, enforced in Latin America. Syria refrained from substantial involvement with international financial institutions such as the IMF or the World Bank. Syria's new Social Market Economy also refrained from any meaningful form of political liberalisation. However the neoliberal substance was in the separation of economic responsibility from social responsibility, and the treatment of both fields, economic and social, as detached from the state.

The administrative functions of the state bureaucracy were reconfigured in two primary ways. Firstly, the ministerial portfolios in the executive transitioned from the role of central planning to an interventionist model of operation. This entailed reactive policy making as the new modus operandi of state institutions.¹³² Secondly, neoliberal policies further diminished the

---

[129] Haddad, *Business Networks in Syria*.
[130] Laura Ruiz de Elvira and Tina Zintl, *Civil Society and the State of Syria: The Outsourcing of Social Responsibility* (Boulder, CO: Lynne Rienner, 2012). It is important to note that Jamal Barout reports the number of registered associations in Syria as 1,049 in 2010. Barout, العقد الأخير, 150–1. This is consistent with the analysis provided by other authors including de Elvira, that after 2009 the Syrian state started its attempt to curb the expansion and influence of private associations.
[131] De Elvira and Zintl, *Civil Society and the State of Syria*.
[132] There were no substantive changes to ministerial portfolios except for the merge of the ministry of expatriates with the ministry of foreign affairs in 2011 (the same model exists in Lebanon and was introduced during circumstances of mass external displacement), and the elimination of

public functions of state institutions, which ultimately became dysfunctional bureaucratic shells that provided employment opportunities and other forms of privilege. Despite the fact that the public function of state institutions diminished, administrative structures specifically in areas of service provision and civil service maintained their bureaucratic apparatus.[133] Public salaries in Syria remained diminutive throughout Bashar Assad's rule even with currency devaluation during the Syrian war.[134] However, public employment within the bureaucracy provided other revenue streams and advantages such as bribes, favours and access to possible promotions. The organisational culture of public institutions in Syria in their corrupt, dysfunctional and incompetent forms are not incidental or a mere fault of character of the personnel operating them. Those functions are precisely the mechanisms through which public institutions are captured to serve wide reaching clientelistic networks of dependents that ultimately reinforce the status quo and uphold prevailing systems of hierarchy. In this sense, the dysfunctional nature of the administrative apparatus of state institutions is in line with the incapacitation of state autonomy and the discouragement of initiative within state institutions at all levels. In fact, when the Assad rule needed state institutions to be functional, even when located under opposition control, those institutions resumed a level of public function amidst the most prohibitive of circumstances imaginable.[135]

---

the ministry of irrigation in 2012, which was merged with the ministry of water resources. The number of ministries stands at twenty-four, which includes the following: foreign affairs and expatriates; finance; defence; higher education; local administration and environment; tourism; agriculture and agrarian reform; education; economy and trade; health; justice; *awqaf* (religious endowments); social affairs and labour; oil and mineral reserves; interior; information; culture; electricity; housing and construction; transport; industry; communication and technology; water resources; and administrative development. See their respective websites on Syria.gov.

[133] The twenty-four ministerial portfolios are headquartered in Damascus and regionally divided based on their areas of operation within regional subdivisions at the levels of the country's fourteen administrative governorates (also known as provinces). The fourteen governorates are subdivided into sixty-five districts (*manatiq*), which are also in turn subdivided into sub-districts (*nawahi*) and villages (*qura*). In fact, based on relative size of population and economic activities, many areas, such as the Aleppo countryside, were upgraded into separate sub-districts (*nahia*) with separate and expanded bureaucracies. For a detailed account of such dynamics, see Chapter Five on Deir Hafer. See also Abboud, 'Locating the "Social"', 53.

[134] Daher, *Syria After the Uprisings*.

[135] For detailed examples, see the case study of Deir Hafer in Chapter Five.

Corruption, incompetency and dysfunctionality in public administration emerge only through possibilities afforded by the state bureaucracy itself.[136] The bureaucratisation of the Assad rule stands for the appropriation of state bureaucracy, public assets and decision-making processes as a mechanism to consolidate power. In this sense, clientelism and informality, despite being features present in political systems beyond Syria, receive distinctive scale and role in Syria as a derivative phenomenon of successful state capture.

Conclusion

The contradictory strategies of power consolidation allowed the dictatorship to reproduce its position of power and perpetuate its control over the state, despite the weakening of the state's developmental outlook and curtailing its regulatory functions before 2011. The undermining of regulatory and public functions of state institutions after the year 2000 is unprecedented in intensity and scale but not in nature, as Hafez Assad also introduced limited measures of privatisation. The decline in regulatory and public functions is not equivalent to lack of all capacity to perform such tasks. Rather, before 2011 those were strategies and mechanisms of power consolidation by the Assad rule.

After the uprisings and the militarisation of the Syrian conflict, the state lost considerable regulatory capacity over the military field. The devolution of state capacity even in the military field was neither a terminal stage, nor an insurmountable challenge for the Assad rule. In fact, new opportunities presented themselves in the face of mounting military challenges while the state atrophied and devolved in unprecedented ways. It is in this context that the 2020 parliamentary elections in Syria saw the domination of three categories of candidates: (1) warlords, (2) patrons of war economies and (3) religious/tribal leaders.[137] Previously, those given access to state bureaucracy garnered access to economic privileges. Now, those with local power, economic or otherwise, are granted access to the state as a measure of political co-optation and integration.

---

[136] Gero Erdmann and Ulf Engel, 'Neopatrimonialism reconsidered: Critical review and elaboration of an elusive concept', in *Commonwealth and Comparative Politics*, vol. 45, no 1 (2007) 114.

[137] Ziad Awad and Agnes Favier, 'Elections in Wartime: The Syrian People's Council (2016–2020)', *Robert Schuman Centre for Advanced Studies*, 30 April 2020, https://medirections.com/images/dox/RPR_2020_07.pdf.

The outcome of devolution of state capacity in the military field is a reconfiguration of power relations between institutional domains such as the military, the state and the religious field. It is through state capture and the subsequent partitioning of state authority to clientelised associates, first under Hafez Assad and later under Bashar Assad, that informality ultimately circumvented state authority. Although emergent and contingent in its formation, as elaborated in the next chapter in relation to networks of violence, informal practices strive to reproduce themselves once granted the immunity, resources and freedoms to thrive. It is in this context that informal networks of violence, cross-border trafficking and arbitrary detentions are intimately connected with formal state security institutions. Eventually, informal arrangements and mechanisms defined the strategies of survival that the Assad dictatorship relied on in the military field in the midst of mounting civil unrest and militarisation after 2011.

2

Institutions of Violence and Proliferation*

The militarisation of the Syrian uprising began a few months after the March protests of Darʻa in the Syrian south. On 25 April 2011 government forces besieged Darʻa and attacked protestors in response to mounting non-violent mobilisation. Following that, government forces perpetrated numerous massacres against unarmed civilians.[1] For example, on 3 May 2013, the town of al-Bayda in the province of Tartus off the Mediterranean coast witnessed brutal massacres and summary executions of unarmed civilians by government forces, pro-government paramilitary groups and local mobs.[2] After brief clashes between government forces and armed opposition groups in the nearby coastal town of Baniyas in the morning, armed opposition groups withdrew, and the village of al-Bayda saw government forces making their way in by 1pm.[3] Until four o'clock in the afternoon, pro-government forces repeatedly entered specific complexes of homes of select families in

---

* Earlier versions of this chapter were presented in closed workshops on Political Violence in Syria at Utrecht University in 2018, and on Tribes and Jihadi groups in Syria and Iraq at the Isam Fares Institute (American University of Beirut) in 2017. Parts of this chapter feature under Harout Akdedian and Harith Hassan. 'State atrophy and the reconfiguration of borderlands in Syria and Iraq: Post-2011 dynamics', *Political Geography* 80, no. 1 (2020); and Harout Akdedian, 'On Violence and Radical Theology in the Syrian War: The Instrumentality of Spectacular Violence and Exclusionary Practices from Comparative and Local Standpoints', *Politics, Religion & Ideology*, 20, no. 3 (2019) 361-80.

[1] See for instance, Syrian British Consortium, *A Decade after Daraya: Documenting a Massacre* (London: Syrian British Consortium, 2022); Martin Chulov, 'Massacre in Tadamon: how two academics hunted down a Syrian war criminal', *The Guardian*, 26 April 2022, https://www.theguardian.com/world/2022/apr/27/massacre-in-tadamon-how-two-academics-hunted-down-a-syrian-war-criminal.

[2] 'No One's Left: Summary Executions by Syrian Forces in al-Bayda and Baniyas', Human Rights Watch, 13 September 2013, https://www.hrw.org/report/2013/09/13/no-ones-left/summary-executions-syrian-forces-al-bayda-and-baniyas.

[3] Human Rights Watch, 'No One's Left', 1.

the area, 'separated men from women, rounded-up the men in one spot, and executed them by shooting them at close range'.[4] As a Human Rights Watch investigation reveals, the violence of the day was targeted, and the indiscriminate killings of the day were not random.[5] Although the men and women were separated, the report documents at least twenty-three women and fourteen children, including infants, killed on the day.[6] In addition to killing 167 individuals, pro-government forces burned the bodies of the deceased and some perpetrators recorded the violence as it unfolded and uploaded the footage to YouTube.[7] Mass looting and burning of properties ensued, before armed forces withdrew from the area on Saturday at 5pm.

Mass violence, such as the massacre in al-Bayda, has broad spatial attendance beyond the targeted unarmed civilians, as it encourages retribution from opponents and hastens polarisation more broadly. As Salwa Ismail notes, in August 2013, when opposition groups, including Suqur al-'Iz and al-Farouq Battalion, launched an attack on Latakia countryside, their massacres reflect a mimetic reproduction of the violence witnessed in al-Bayda.[8] Ismail argues that this 'modus operandi of the actors produces the regime and the armed opposition as fetishes of each other'.[9] What is significant here is the capacity of mass violence to bring civilians (loyalists, oppositionists and the silent majority – *ramadiyyin*) alike, into a spiralling polarisation.[10] Ismail also notes that such dynamics render narratives of victimisation interchangeable and contested even where the identity of perpetrators is evident – pro-government

---

[4] Human Rights Watch, 'No One's Left', 1.
[5] Ibid.
[6] Ibid.
[7] http://www.youtube.com/watch?v=_tYK8AAW1sY.
[8] Salwa Ismail, *The Rule of Violence: Subjectivity, Memory, and Government in Syria* (Cambridge: Cambridge University Press, 2018), 183; see also '"You can still see their blood": Executions, Indiscriminate Shootings, and Hostage Taking by Opposition Forces in Latakia Countryside', Human Rights Watch, 10 October 2013, https://www.hrw.org/report/2013/10/10/you-can-still-see-their-blood/executions-indiscriminate-shootings-and-hostage.
[9] Ismail, *The Rule of Violence*, 183.
[10] Emile Hokayem, *Syria's Uprising and the Fracturing of the Levant* (London: Routledge, 2013), 53. These attacks included suicide bombs and car bombs in urban areas such as Damascus and Aleppo City. Other massacres recurred in different parts of Syria. See for instance the massacres of Houla in Homs that saw forty-nine children and thirty-four women killed in May 2012. See UN General Assembly's Human Rights Council's report A/HRC/21/50, https://undocs.org/pdf?symbol=en/A/HRC/21/50.

or anti-government alike.[11] This interchangeability of victimhood became a generative force that drove social polarization in Syria.

Social polarisation, however, does not explain transformations in the military field in Syria during state atrophy. Rather, military developments in Syria exhibited simultaneous dynamics of increased anti-government militarisation as well decentralisation of state violence. For example, the forces that carried out the violence in the village of al-Bayda included uniformed members of government forces, uniformed members of pro-government paramilitary groups and others participating in the violence in civilian clothing. Each of these groups represents a different military formation that emerged during the conflict, and the nature of their relations evolved throughout. The devolution of the state's monopoly of violence, organisationally and in deployment, did not solely stem from the emergence of oppositional armed activism. The specific forms of the devolution of violence were also shaped by novel institutional arrangements within state structures and their unintended consequences. The first section of this chapter looks into the devolution of violence within state structures.

Violence as Generated Force: Government Policy and State Violence

Many factors played a role in the unravelling of the state as regulator of the military field. These factors include defections, restricted command structures, restrained capacity for full military mobilisation and emergent geographies of war, such as military concentration in areas prioritised by the Assad rule or military withdrawal (strategic or forced) from areas with relatively limited government capacity for territorial control. The state, having already been divested of any effective autonomy over the military domain in the forty years prior to the uprising, devolved into an active participant in the military mobilisation by the Assad rule as a contestant with other armed groups – opposition groups and pro-government paramilitary forces alike. In other words, the pro-Assad stance of armed groups is not equivalent to a pro-state disposition or recognition of state authority. In fact, many pro-government armed factions active in Syria, including local Syrian militias, Lebanese Hezbollah forces or affiliates of the Revolutionary Guards of the Islamic Republic of Iran (IRGC), actively

[11] Ismail, *The Rule of Violence*, 178–82.

prop up the Assad rule but to the determinant of the state's regulatory capacity. The state must directly contest those groups, through bargaining processes or coercive force, to gain any regulatory capacity over them.[12] The institutional reconfiguration of the state's monopoly over the military field throughout the conflict followed two trajectories. On one hand, pro-government armed groups outside the directives of the state proliferated, but on the other, the state simultaneously consolidated its regulatory capacity over some of these groups, albeit in a limited capacity.

As evident from the first instances of deployed state violence in April 2011 in Darʿa, the Assad rule relied on the privileged armed groups closest to it. Throughout 2011 the factions that led attacks against protestors were the intelligence agencies, the Republican (Presidential) Guard and Special Forces.[13] Within the army, the third, fourth, fifth, ninth and eighteenth divisions were amongst the most utilised segments.[14] These divisions were not mobilised in their entirety, as only select sub-units were favoured over others.[15] It is notable that the segments mobilised within the army were comprised of divisions (*firqa*), brigades (*liwaʾ*) and regiments (*foj*) ranging in size from 3,000 to 15,000 conscripts, and were accompanied by intelligence forces and paramilitary formations.[16]

When the conflict expanded geographically, the core security apparatus (intelligence agencies and Special Forces), geared primarily towards internal repression, was insufficient for effective crackdown countrywide. The conventional army, on the other hand, underequipped and primarily trained to combat external threats, was called upon in desperation without having capacity to quell protests or insurgencies and maintain or regain territorial control

---

[12] Sarah Dadoush, 'Iran is putting down roots in eastern Syria, outcompeting Assad's regime in signing up fighters', *The Washington Post*, 28 January 2022, https://www.washingtonpost.com/world/2022/01/28/iran-syria-militias-deir-al-zour/.

[13] Specific units within the Republican Guard include 101st and 102nd Regiments and 104th, 105th and 106th Brigades. See Human Rights Watch, 'By All Means Necessary', 82–7.

[14] Ibid.; see also Joseph Holliday, *The Assad Regime: From Counterinsurgency to Civil War*, Institute for the Study of War, Middle East Security report 8, March 2013, 12.

[15] Although other divisions also covered the same areas of Damascus, Darʿa and Homs, only those divisions, their command structures and ranks were deemed somewhat reliable. See Holliday, *The Assad Regime*, 12–19; Human Rights Watch, 'By All Means Necessary', 82–7.

[16] Holliday, *The Assad Regime*, 42–53; Human Rights Watch, 'By All Means Necessary', 82–7; Holliday, *The Assad Regime*, 12–19.

on multiple fronts at the same time.[17] In addition, defections, most common amongst low-ranking conscripts, did not result in the collapse of the army but were common enough to prevent mobilisation of the estimated 220,000-strong army due to the possibility of further defections.[18] As early as the siege of Darʿa in April 2011 and the killings that ensued, defectors from different divisions and areas of Syria reported witnessing soldiers being ordered to kill civilians, as well as killings by intelligence officers of soldiers who hesitated to carry out commands to attack civilians.[19]

The specific constellation of forces mobilised by the Assad rule was determined according to two primary factors: geography and command structure. Forces available in close proximity to areas of civil unrest were mobilised in segments with preference given to sub-units that were most intimately and directly connected to Assad's handpicked and trusted commanders, who had either overseen the recruitment process within their ranks or were given command over already closely vetted subordinates.[20] For instance, the decision-making and planning of the first killings of civilians in Darʿa on 29 and 30 April 2011, resulting in at least ninety-eight deaths, involved Assad's most trusted military henchmen: Major General Jamil Hassan, director of Air Force Intelligence at the time; Colonel Suheil Hassan from Special Operations; and his deputy Fawaz Qubair.[21] In total, estimates suggest that even at the onset of the militarisation of the Syrian conflict, when territorial control and state capacity were not significantly contested or strained, only a third of Syrian armed forces could be mobilised by the Assad rule.[22]

The constellation of mobilised forces reflected the same mistrust, as an organising principle, that shaped institutional arrangements within the military field before the uprising. The operational features of each distinct security

---

[17] Hokayem, *Syria's Uprising*, 58.
[18] Ibid., 58–60.
[19] See Human Rights Watch, 'By All Means Necessary', 48, 63.
[20] For a detailed report on the early mobilisation of armed forces, see Holliday, *The Assad Regime*, 27–40.
[21] These details are based on the first-hand accounts of defectors who witnessed the conversations in person. See Human Rights Watch, 'By All Means Necessary', 60. The patterns of mobilisation, composition of forces, operational features and the nature of violence deployed followed the same patterns witnessed in Darʿa in early 2011 and al-Bayda in 2013.
[22] The total number of conscripts in the Syrian military, excluding the intelligence and security apparatus, were estimated around 220,000. Holliday, *The Assad Regime*, 7.

branch during mobilisation were reflective of pre-existing arrangements in place within the military domain, specifically between the army and the security apparatus (intelligence). As the army was deployed on frontlines, intelligence agencies orchestrated the exercise of state violence against civilians. The Assad rule also needed additional extra-judicial armed actors, unrestrained by formal linkages that implicate those in power, to provide rapid deployment and slow down the expansion of oppositional armed groups. It is in this context that paramilitary formations proliferated within the military field.

The paramilitary landscape

In an effort to depict the emergent institutional order, Ariel Ahram points out that rather than looking at pro-government militias from a narrow functionalist perspective as mere by-products of diminished state capacity or state absence, pro-government militias in Syria and beyond play a crucial role in processes of state (trans)formation.[23] His approach is one that rightly blurs categorical distinctions between state and non-state pro-government armed actors. In other words, the rise of paramilitary groups does not by default imply the end or the absence of the state, but rather introduces new modalities of governing and deploying violence. Reinoud Leenders and Antonio Giustozzi take this a step further to interrogate the specific relationship between the state and paramilitary formations, specifically centring the question around the state's regulatory capacity with regards to Syria's primary pro-government paramilitary group – the National Defence Forces.[24] Similar to Ugur Ungor's remarks on paramiltarism in Syria and beyond, the emergent consensus seems to be that rather than operating on the spectrum of state absence and presence, the rise of pro-government paramilitary groups represents shifts in state-military relations from dyadic and hierarchical, to multipolar and heterarchical.[25] Heterarchical institutional orders stand for multiple hierarchical arrangements tying a multitude of armed groups to a variety of sponsors and

---

[23] Ariel Ahram, 'Pro-Government Militias and the Repertoires of Illicit State Violence', *Studies in Conflict and Terrorism* 39, no. 3 (2016): 207–26.

[24] Reinoud Leenders and Antonio Giustozzi, 'Outsourcing state violence: The National Defence Force, "Stateness" and Regime Resilience in the Syrian War', *Mediterranean Politics* 24, no. 2 (2019): 157–80.

[25] Leenders and Giustozzi, 'Outsourcing state violence', 157–80; Ugur Ungor, *Paramilitarism: Mass Violence in the Shadow of the State* (Oxford: Oxford University Press, 2020), 118–38.

constituencies. At times, these networks intertwine to cooperate or compete, and at times, remain distinct.[26] This heterarchy in the military field opens up possibilities for strategic as well as forced shifts between state sponsorship and withdrawal depending on leverage, and strategies of violence on behalf of emergent military formations as well as those directing state violence.[27]

The earliest quasi-military formations that broke onto the Syrian scene between the years 2011 and 2012 were the popular committees (*lijan sha'biyyeh*), often referred to by opposition groups as '*shabbiha*'.[28] The early tasks of these groups were to establish checkpoints within key neighbourhoods and mobilise against perceived threats (protestors, militants or improvised explosive devices) when needed. Often comprised of neighbourhood residents and locals, the purpose of these groups was to serve as vigilantes; they were the eyes, ears and sometimes arms of the security forces. The specific composition of these groups varied depending on their specific region and location. Overall, the groups were comprised of small networks of trust, only informally connected to the personnel of security agencies. Although many members were not individually instructed to join the groups by intelligence officers, they did not operate without the knowledge, consent and intermittent supervision of intelligence agencies.[29] Checkpoints were not propped up whimsically by these groups but were strategically established in coordination with official security forces in place.[30] In an effort to maintain order, security forces did not tolerate random checkpoints organised by residents unless mechanisms of regulation and channels of communication were established.[31] The weapons at the disposal of the popular committees in 2011 were limited to medium weaponry (semi- and fully automatic rifles) and light weaponry (pistols, knives, batons

---

[26] Reinoud Leenders and Antonio Giustozzi, 'Foreign sponsorship of pro-government militias fighting Syria's insurgency: Whither proxy wars?', *Mediterranean Politics* (24 November 2020), https://doi.org/10.1080/13629395.2020.1839235.
[27] Leenders and Giustozzi, 'Outsourcing state violence', 157–80; Ungor, *Paramilitarism*, 157–60; Ahram, 'Pro-Government Militias', 207–26.
[28] Aron Lund, 'Chasing Ghosts: The Shabiha Phenomenon', in Michael Kerr and Craig Larkin (eds), *The Alawis of Syria: War, Faith and Politics in the Levant* (London: Hurst, 2015), 254–6.
[29] Detailed case study features in Chapter Five.
[30] Thanassis Cambanis et al., *Hybrid Actors: Armed Groups and State Fragmentation in the Middle East* (New York: The Century Foundation Press, 2019), 58–9.
[31] This often involved civilian intermediaries and power brokers with pre-existing connections to local authorities (civilian or security). For more, see Chapter Five for a case study.

and other blunt weapons) individually possessed by group members. At the onset, there were no salary structures in place and individuals volunteered personal time and alternated shifts to operate checkpoints.[32]

By 2012–13 a number of popular committees had amalgamated to form the *Quwat al-Difa' al-Watani* (National Defence Forces) as an official and state-backed paramilitary group in support of the Assad rule and mobilising alongside the Syrian army. Although the NDF ended up becoming officially linked to the Syrian state through the Syrian Ministry of Defence, the state reined in those groups only by fending off Iranian influence and using Russian support to keep the NDF within the Ministry of Defence's overall chain of command.[33] Upon semi-formalisation, salary structures were introduced and a limited amount of weapons was made available to militants.[34] The effort to quasi-formalise the popular committees maintained a modicum of regulatory capacity on behalf of the state over the broader military domain upon the proliferation of armed actors. Reportedly, during the early period of paramilitary mobilisation, Lebanese Hezbollah forces and the IRGC took the lead in promoting the increased amalgamation of paramilitary groups into a unified force.[35] However, given that such paramilitary formations eventually serve as post-conflict foundations of military and ultimately political power, losing control of the popular committees to other sponsors, even if they were allies during the war, was equivalent to the Assad rule losing military control in the country. The military outcome of the war with opposition forces would have been inconsequential for the Assad rule had the popular

---

[32] Author's interview with a member of NDF forces in Kasab, interview conducted in Beirut, Lebanon on 2 March 2020.

[33] Cambanis et al., *Hybrid Actors*, 56. For a detailed exploration of the role of the Iranian Revolutionary Guard Corps and the Lebanese Hezbollah with regards to the NDF see Leenders and Giustozzi, 'Foreign sponsorship', 4–7; For information on Russian and Iranian competition, see Minahl Barish, 'Private Security Companies in Syria: New Contractors in service of the Regime' (in Arabic), *Robert Shuman Foundation: Wartime and Post-Conflict in Syria* (WPCS), 28 July 2020, 22–3: https://medirections.com/images/dox/Security%20Companies%207282020-last.pdf.

[34] Salaries and weapons varied from region to region depending on the strategic significance of each region and armed group. Overall, salaries were nowhere near sufficient to serve as a means of subsistence and weapons made available were AK47s and a limited number of rounds of ammunition either as one-time or monthly handoffs. For specific details, see the case study on Kasab in Chapter Five. Samer Abboud also reports that the NDF received designated training facilities and other formal features. See Samer Abboud, *Syria* (Malden, MA: Polity Press, 2016) 126.

[35] Cambanis et al., *Hybrid Actors*, 58–9.

committees been effectively co-opted by other actors such as Iran or Russia.[36] At the same time, those groups operated and committed crimes in ways that would distance top commanders directing institutions of state violence from incrimination.[37] The Assad rule's strategies to quasi-integrate the NDF within state structures did not stem from concerns for state integrity or state authority, despite official government rhetoric framing efforts as such.[38] Aside from the NDF, foreign-backed paramilitary groups, such as the Lebanese Hezbollah, the Iraqi Asa'ib Ahl al-Haq and Abu Fadl al-Abbas Brigades, operated around the country, both independently and in coordination with the Syrian army but without any meaningful restriction or dependency upon the Syrian state.[39]

Informality, networks of violence and war economies

Informal networks played a crucial role during the war in expanding the reach and influence of the Assad rule – specifically in areas or operational spaces that are beyond the institutional reach of state structures. Even before the conflict in 2011, a complex web of informal networks and associates created various social, economic, religious, political, military and intelligence groups that served the Assad rule in numerous ways. Informality as a framework of government operation is not unique to Syria but is a strong feature of post-Soviet contexts as well.[40] As Solnick explains, post-Soviet states, specifically in the last ten years of the Soviet Union, were informally compartmentalised at various levels of state bureaucracies to reinforce patronage networks and exchanges that not only hijacked the state but also created 'inner states' within state bureaucracies.[41] With the atrophy of the Soviet Union's coercive capacity,

---

[36] Leenders and Giustozzi, 'Foreign sponsorship'; Ahram, 'Pro-Government Militias', 207–9.
[37] The massacre of Houla is a case in point.
[38] See, for instance, the remarks of Luna al-Shibl, advisor to Bashar Assad, in an interview with Russian state-owned RT News, broadcasted on 18 January 2022: https://www.youtube.com/watch?v=64ctRtHZ97s.
[39] Leenders and Giustozzi, 'Foreign sponsorship', 5.
[40] Steven L. Solnick, *Stealing the State: Control and Collapse in Soviet Institutions* (Cambridge, MA: Harvard University Press, 1998); Vladimir Gel'man, 'Subversive Institutions, Informal Governance, and Contemporary Russian Politics', *Communist and Post-Communist Studies* (2012): 300.
[41] Solnick, *Stealing the State*.

pre-existing informal associations and networks emerged to define new heterarchical systems.[42]

In Syria, informal economies (smuggling, monetary transactions, barter systems for goods and services, and transportation taxes) existed before 2011 and expanded thereafter parallel to the expansion of private militias, paramilitary groups and unhinged security agencies.[43] Networks of violence, within the state and beyond, gained growing economic functions throughout the conflict. The economic functions and activities of the Syrian army's Fourth Division, headed by Bashar Assad's brother, Maher Assad, are a case in point.[44] The Fourth Division, one of the most privileged and utilised instruments of repression in Syria, controlled the maritime ports of Latakia and Tartus for extended periods of time during the conflict and was involved in convoy protection services, scrap trade and levying taxes on checkpoints.[45] The growing might of the Fourth Division also led to the creation of private security companies linked to members of the Fourth Division and associates of Maher Assad.[46]

On 5 August 2013 a new presidential decree by Bashar Assad (decree 55) granted licensing prerogatives and supervision tasks of private security companies to the Ministry of Interior.[47] Prior to increased formalisation during the conflict, private security companies, networks of violence and informal economic operations were active in Syria and were still closely associated with the Assad rule. The difference is that, prior to 2011, those who had access to state institutions were able to expand their informal economic activities, whereas after 2011 the military field expanded independent of state institutions, pushing the Assad rule to try and co-opt or absorb these actors through the state. Foreign sponsorship and economic incentives were amongst the decisive factors that led to the expansion of such networks beyond the

---

[42] David Hoffman, *Oligarchs: The Wealth and Power in the New Russia* (New York: Public Affairs Books, 2002).
[43] David Woodruff, *Money Unmade: Barter and the Fate of Russian Capitalism* (Ithaca, NY: Cornell University Press, 1999); Vadim Volkov, *Violent Entrepreneurs: The Use of Force in the Making of Russian Capitalism* (Ithaca, NY: Cornell University Press, 2002).
[44] Ayman al-Dassouky, 'The Economic Networks of the Fourth Division During the Syrian Conflict', *European University Institute*, 24 January 2022, https://doi.org/10.2870/95105.
[45] Ibid.
[46] Barish, 'Private Security Companies in Syria'.
[47] Ibid., 4.

framework of the state.⁴⁸ The Ministry of Interior has been unable to absorb all private security companies, however those who evade state regulation are not autonomous from the Assad rule. In fact, as Minhal Barish suggests, immunity from state regulations takes place due to intimate links with the intelligence services, the Fourth Division or other influential associates of the Assad rule.⁴⁹

Prior to the conflict, informal networks of violence, known as *shabbiha*, were also characterised by their economic functions. The *shabbiha* were individuals with varying levels of access to intelligence agencies or key figures within the institutions of violence that were granted access to illicit cross-border movement of goods at a significant profit due to economic protection measures that limited the import of foreign products during the rule of Hafez Assad.⁵⁰ The Syrian–Lebanese border, for instance, provided significant economic opportunities for the *shabbiha* operating off the Syrian coast and in Damascus. This was facilitated through the Syrian occupation of Lebanon until 2005. Other *shabbiha* groups, such as the Berri clan in Bab el-Nerab on the outskirts of Aleppo City, similarly funnelled smuggled goods, such as alcohol, cigarettes and weapons through the Syrian–Turkish borders. The original *shabbiha* are infamous for their immunity even when aggressing state institutions such as local police. The term *shabbiha*, rooted in the Arabic word *shabah* (ghost), refers to the fluidity of these groups, referring to their illusive form as well as their terrorising practices, including murder, kidnappings and rape.⁵¹ The word *shabah* is also a colloquial designation (specifically in Syria and Lebanon) for Mercedes Benz Series S320 cars that close associates of the Assad rule drove across the Syrian–Lebanese borders, having chosen this model in part for the large size of its trunk. Many of these individuals, known as the original *shabbiha*, emerged as leaders within the ranks of the NDF and some died fighting for the Assad rule.⁵² The self-sustaining and

---

⁴⁸ Barish, 'Private Security Companies in Syria', 19.
⁴⁹ Ibid., 22–3.
⁵⁰ For the role of Moustafa Tlass in developing these networks and the internal competition over official customs enforcement see Barout, العقد الأخير, 36, fn 16.
⁵¹ Yassin al-Haj Saleh, *The Impossible Revolution* (C. Hurst, 2017), 45–8.
⁵² Aron Lund, 'Assad's Broken Base: The Case of Idlib', *The Century Foundation*, 14 July 2016, https://tcf.org/content/report/assads-broken-base-case-idlib/ (accessed 18 March 2017); senior members of the al-Berri clan were executed by Liwa' al-Tawhid in 2012. Hilal al-Assad, a second

predatory economic functions of these networks of violence were critical in light of the economic pressures of the Syrian war. At the same time they also incentivised further militarisation for predatory purposes or for protection from it.

The new order

The use of state violence against civilians in early 2011 initiated a devolutionary process, which saw the proliferation of armed actors and violence in Syria. Pre-2011 institutional arrangements within the military field consisted of fragmented institutions and networks, overlapping in function and joined through a central node composed of the president and his close associates heading the most privileged and endowed sections of the military and security apparatuses. The weakness of this structure was its inadequacy for expansive mobilisation on multiple fronts. The limited capacities of the institutions of violence in response to widespread anti-government military mobilisation saw the transformation of institutional arrangements from fragmented networks connected through a central node, to a structure with multiple nodes of varying centrality and density of exchanges.

After 2011, the state's compromised regulatory capacity over the broader military domain had significant consequences for the Assad rule and for other sponsors such as Iran and Russia alike. Civilian armed mobilisation and regional competition over sponsorship by powers such as Russia and Iran saw the military domain proliferate in ways that threatened the capacity of the Assad rule to emerge from the war with any meaningful military or political power, regardless of the outcome of the conflict with opposition groups. Despite its informal and formal capacities to permeate the paramilitary landscape, the Assad rule continues to contend with paramilitary groups to re-establish its influence. However, the Syrian state has neither the coercive capacity nor the resources needed to grant the Assad rule a blanket prominence. The Assad rule must therefore compete with other sponsors,

cousin of Bashar Assad, was amongst the original *shabbiha* that emerged in the 1970s upon the ascent of Hafez Assad. He died in the area of Kasab on the north coast of Syria in 2014. See Mohammad D., 'Who is Hilal al-Assad?', *Syria Comment*, 5 April 2014, https://www.joshualandis.com/blog/hilal-al-assad-mohammad-d/#:~:text=Hilal%20al-Assad%20was%20the%20commander%20of%20al-Difa%E2%80%99%20al-Watani,parents%20of%20an%20Alawi%20soldier%20fighting%20with%20him.

while competing for sponsorship in order to generate the resources needed for establishing patronage or reinstating the state's regulatory capacity where needed. Given that state regulatory capacity, once effectively established, would automatically undermine the role of foreign sponsorship, the Assad rule will find ample sponsors supporting its survival but only in ways that continue to undermine the state.

Devolution of Territorial Control

Prior to the takeover of Aleppo in 2017, the Assad rule's reign was limited to a narrow patchwork of territories extending from the Syrian coast to Damascus with inroads into Aleppo City. At this time, the Syrian army had demonstrated an overall lack of capacity to 'conduct joint armored-infantry operations or coordinating ground-air operations'.[53] The technologies of warfare at the disposal of the Assad rule and opposition forces along with the pre-2011 geographies of socio-economic marginalisation determined the political landscape of the Syrian conflict until 2017. State forces were deployed to secure static assets and supply routes in areas most crucial for the survival of the Assad rule. As full deployment on the frontlines was impossible, state violence was increasingly limited to distanced attacks through air power and artillery forces in opposition-held areas. This not only targeted civilians in opposition-held areas but also rendered civilian infrastructures such as hospitals and bakeries casual targets of explosive projectiles launched by government forces.[54] Opposition forces, on the other hand, were limited to mortar attacks that did not have the same destructive capacity as the state's violence.

The Assad rule deemed the cities of Aleppo, Damascus, Hama and Homs the most crucial areas for its survival.[55] Opposition forces relentlessly targeted supply lines and connections (highways and villages) between these cities as they represented weak points in Assad's military strategy. In addition to supply lines, Aleppo City and Damascus witnessed sustained skirmishes. Besides the fact that these two cities are the most populous and economically significant of all Syrian cities, opposition groups intensified their operations in those areas

[53] Hokayem, *Syria's Uprising*, 58.
[54] Jose Martinez, 'Stifling Stateness: The Assad Regime's Campaign Against Rebel Governance', *Security Dialogue* 49, no. 4 (2018): 235–53.
[55] Hokayem, *Syria's Uprising*, 59.

for two strategic reasons: (1) government-held areas of Aleppo were the most stretched and deprived of supplies, and (2) Damascus represented the logistical hub of the Assad rule and state violence. Pinning pro-government forces on these two fronts would geographically stretch its military capacities and restrain its military mobilisation in other areas. The mobilisation of Hezbollah and Russian forces, however, rendered the equation obsolete and resulted in a government takeover of Aleppo City in 2017, which decisively reversed the tide of war.[56]

The first city to be captured by opposition groups was Raqqa in early 2013, followed by the capture of Idlib City in 2015 and the intermittent capture of the city of Dar'a during 2016.[57] Prior to discussing the military constituents of opposition forces it is important to state that, until 2017, urban–rural socio-economic divides largely delineated emerging military frontlines between opposition and pro-government forces. Opposition groups mobilised and operated in the vast but less populated Syrian countryside around urban centres. The constituents of opposition groups were diverse and their processes of formation were not uniform. Some groups emerged from localities, and others, specifically hardline Salafi-Jihadi groups such as Daesh and Jabhat al-Nusra, were localised throughout the war.[58] Raqqa, the first city under the rule of opposition groups, was captured by the Free Syrian Army (FSA), which was comprised of defected soldiers, local militias formed upon the retreat of government forces and rebel groups formed to contest the Assad rule.[59] Soon after, Salafi-Jihadi groups, including Jabhat al-Nusra and the Islamic State of Iraq and Syria (Daesh), began to dominate the military scene amongst opposition ranks. The military history of those groups, their localisation in different areas, foreign sponsorship, ideological framing, strategies of government and public administration is rich and complex.[60] Territorially, however, the outcome of the military contests amongst these groups, and between the Assad rule and these groups, yielded four different territorial zones: the northwest (Idlib and

---

[56] Abboud, *Syria*, 95.
[57] Ibid., 129, 133–4.
[58] Jerome Drevon and Patrick Haenni, 'How Global Jihad Relocalises and Where it Leads: The Case of HTS, the Former AQ Franchise in Syria', *Robert Schuman Centre for Advanced Studies: The Middle East Directions Programme, European University Institute* 2021, 2, 8–10.
[59] Abboud, *Syria*, 97–104.
[60] Hokayem, *Syria's Uprising*, 67–104.

surroundings under the rule of Hay'at Tahrir al-Sham – the rebranded and localised al-Qaeda known as Jabhat al-Nusra);[61] the northeast (popularised as Rojava) under the command of the Syrian Democratic Forces (SDF);[62] northern territories under the command of Turkish-sponsored armed groups (northern Aleppo and nearby borderlands known as 'Euphrates Shield');[63] and the areas once contested by the Free Syrian Army in the south in and around Dar'a.[64]

Geographies of state atrophy: a spatial analysis

Geographies of atrophy within the military domain in Syria were not only manifest along urban–rural divides that in broad strokes demarcated the territorial zones controlled by pro- and anti-government factions. The reconfiguration of institutional ecologies manifested in borderlands as well. Throughout the Syrian conflict, borderlands became centres of political contestation, contested from within, and competing with a multitude of other areas over greater autonomy and influence.[65] The devolution of state capacity to control borders led to novel ways of instrumentalising borders and creating alternative political economies that determined cross-border exchanges as well as the circulation of wealth and power at the local level. Under conditions of state atrophy, borderlands emerged as strategic sites for projecting and contesting power; in some instances, this lead to the growth of peripheral areas demographically and economically, but more often eventually leading to destructive militarisation and state return even if through foreign, rather than Syrian, capacity.

---

[61] Abboud, *Syria*, 175–8.
[62] Abboud, *Syria*, 163–70, 204; Knapp, Flach and Ayboga, *Revolution in Rojava*, 133.
[63] Asya El-Meehy and Haid Haid, *Mapping Local Governance in Syria: A Baseline Study* (Beirut: ESCWA, 2020), 33–5.
[64] The rise and fall of Daesh's territorial control is integral to the devolutionary process that shaped the political geography of the Syrian conflict. This will be the focus of the next section on the use of violence as a generative force. For more on the dynamics of the south, see Abdallah Al-Jabassini, 'From Rebel Rule to a Post-Capitulation Era in Daraa Southern Syria: The Impacts and Outcomes of Rebel Behaviour During Negotiations', *European University Institute: Wartime and Post-Conflict in Syria Project*, June 2019, 18–25; Abdallah Al-Jabassini, 'Dismantling Networks of Resistance and the Reconfiguration of Order in Southern Syria', *European University Institute: Wartime and Post-Conflict in Syria Project*, October 2021.
[65] Victor Konrad, 'Toward a Theory of Borders in Motion', *Journal of Borderlands Studies* 30, no. 1 (2015): 1–17.

Three modalities of border control emerged, based on the various constellations of armed forces in place after 2011: (1) state actors on one side and non-state actors on the other, (2) non-state actors on both sides and (3) hybrid administration. It is important to note that non-state actors do not include pro-government paramilitary groups that are associated with the Syrian state (such as the NDF and remnants of Popular Committees). Non-state actors are those that fall outside the scope of the Syrian state including anti-Assad forces that contest the state's territorial control as well as pro-government forces that fall entirely outside the scope of the Syrian state (formally associated with other regional states, such as the Lebanese Hezbollah). The emergent border schemes depicted here did not necessarily endure. Nonetheless, the typology captures snapshots of transformational change in the military field in its territorial dimensions, specifically in borderlands.

The northern and western borders of Syria provide examples of non-state and state actors on either side of the border. Here, the border systems in place are characteristically asymmetric. The Turkish government, for instance, could unilaterally decide whether any border crossing is accessible and determine the limits and restrictions of movements therein. Motivated by its own security concerns and strategic interests, the Turkish government's position varied according to the non-state actors it dealt with and the risk models in place. For instance, Ankara offered a safe haven in the north for anti-government forces and even turned a blind eye to the movement of Jihadis into Syria through Turkey.[66] Turkey's alliance with opposition groups ensured a robust Turkish presence (and influence) in Syria while also counterbalancing the Kurdish Democratic Union Party (PYD). Ankara considers the armed wing of the PYD, known as the People's Protection Units (YPG) and operating as a dominant group within the broader SDF (Syrian Democratic Forces), as part of the separatist Kurdistan Workers' Party (PKK), a designated terrorist organisation in Turkey.[67] Vignal argues that Turkey's implementation of new border control technologies (walls, fences, trenches and surveillance mechanisms) sought to effectively control all movement in eastern border regions

---

[66] Hokayem, *Syria's Uprising*, 115–19.
[67] Abboud, *Syria*, 204

with a Kurdish presence.[68] On the other hand, Syrian borderlands in Idlib and northern Aleppo had periods of controlled porosity, with the Turkish–Syrian border providing a vital lifeline for opposition forces and borderland populations in those areas.

The second type of border administration is composed of non-state actors on both sides of the border. Examples here include the Syrian–Iraqi border after the rise of Daesh and the Lebanese–Syrian border before 2014. There are multiple non-state groups present within these contexts: on the Iraqi–Syrian border, the Kurdish PYD developed a working relationship with the Kurdish Regional Government (KRG) in Iraq. It is strategically allied with the PKK, which has a growing presence in northern Iraq and continues to operate through networks of support across Iraqi–Syrian borders.[69] Meanwhile, Daesh controlled wide stretches on both sides of the Syrian–Iraqi border prior to being dislodged as part of the international military campaign against the group that began in 2014. On the eastern Lebanese–Syrian border along the Qalamoun mountain range, Lebanese Hezbollah forces effectively control the area (with a minor presence of the Lebanese army) while opposition groups had a limited presence on the Syrian side until they were pushed out in mid-2014. Additionally, Iranian-backed Shi'a militias deployed on both sides of the Syrian–Iraqi border upon the territorial defeat of Daesh.[70] These forces regularly crossed the borders to support pro-government forces, and even controlled smuggling routes (weapons, diesel, and so on), benefiting from the closure of formal border crossings.[71] Prominent non-state actors, despite being institutionally disconnected from the Syrian state, are in fact intimately connected to other regional states (such as Iran or Turkey). Those who received less commitment and sponsorship on behalf of regional powers, such as Daesh

---

[68] Operations Olive Branch and Euphrates Shield are also clear illustrations of asymmetric power relations; Leila Vignal, 'The changing borders and borderlands of Syria in a time of conflict', *International Affairs* 93, no 4 (2017): 821.

[69] Particularly the case through the informal Smeilka crossing between Syria and Iraq. Workshop on 'Iraqi-Syrian borders after Daesh' organised under Chatham House Rules by Carnegie, Middle East Center and Konrad Adenauer Stiftung, 11–12 June 2019, Beirut.

[70] Shelly Kittleson, 'Iraq's Qaim border open to nonlocal PMU fighting in Syria', *Al-Monitor*, 25 April 2019, https://www.al-monitor.com/pulse/originals/2019/04/iraq-anbar-qaim-pmu-shiite-militia-iran-syria.html#ixzz5yU18RCZy.

[71] Workshop on 'Iraqi-Syrian borders after Daesh' organised under Chatham House Rules by Carnegie, Middle East Center and Konrad Adenauer Stiftung, 11–12 June 2019, Beirut.

or SDF forces upon the retreat of American troops, were in a far more precarious condition than those who found committed support. It is for this reason that this model of border administration, with non-state actors on both sides of a border, did not last long and gave way to hybrid administrations.[72]

Hybrid administrations of border control combine state actors and non-state actors. This arrangement is visible in southern Syria, where a truce was reached between the Assad rule and armed opposition groups in mid-2018. The agreement saw the Syrian state formally regain control over the border while the Russian military effectively maintained control over internal security matters.[73] As part of the deal, some opposition groups surrendered their heavy weaponry and were allowed to remain in their cities, while some parties opposed to the deal were evacuated to northern Syria.[74] In hybrid border administrations, formal state presence, be it Syrian or otherwise, remains visible. Prior to the Russian military presence in southern Syria, Jordan maintained diplomatic ties with the Syrian state while also managing border crossings controlled by opposition groups and permitting the movement of humanitarian aid into Syria. Furthermore, Jordan also hosted military camps for some Syrian opposition groups, backed and supported by the United States.[75] However, as the number of Syrian refugees entering Jordan increased, the Jordanian government implemented stricter levels of border control by limiting, for instance, the free movement of Syrian-Palestinians, before ultimately closing both official and unofficial crossings for the movement of people.[76] Jordan's approach to its borders is a case of a neighbouring state negotiating diverse interests. On one hand, the Jordanian government preferred not to take a directly hostile stance against the Assad government and even maintained a level of diplomatic engagement; on the other hand, it did not take an antagonistic position against

---

[72] Out of thirty-three border crossings, Vigal identifies the Lebanese–Syrian borders (five border crossings) under the control of the Syrian government in 2015. By 2020, all border crossings with Jordan, Lebanon and Iraq, with the exception of the Iraqi Kurdistan areas and border crossings with Turkey, were under the control of the Syrian government. See Leila Vignal, *War-Torn: The Unmaking of Syria 2011–2021* (Oxford: Oxford University Press, 2021), 73–4.

[73] Jabassini, 'From Rebel Rule', 18–25.

[74] Al-Tamimi, A. (2018). The post-rebellion south: Interview. Aymenn jawad Al-tamimi's blog (13 August), available at: http://www.aymennjawad.org/2018/08/the-post-rebellion-south-interview.

[75] Vignal, 'The changing borders', 821.

[76] Ibid.

non-state groups either, allowing the movement of humanitarian aid and hosting military camps for brief intervals.[77]

Armed actors on borderlands have instrumentalised borders to consolidate their presence, promote their interests and those of their allies. They have also attempted to create dependencies and asymmetric relations of influence between one another. These were pursued by soft (minimal and limited regulations) and hard (considerable restrictions and controls on exchanges and movement) measures of border control. The same border may be deemed soft regarding certain exchanges and hard for other types, as strategies and methods of control shift based on military developments in nearby areas. The Syrian–Jordanian borders have fluctuated from soft to hard, but also included elements of softness and hardness at the same time. This can be seen in the relatively free movement of humanitarian aid, contrasted with restrictions on the movement of people across the border. The same can be said of Iraqi–Syrian borders where refugees from the two sides fled to the other side at various points after 2014.[78]

The political economy of state atrophy: the view from borderlands

Borders generally refer to the political and jurisdictional limits that separate states from each other and mark the acknowledged territorial boundaries of state authority.[79] They perform a variety of functions depending on the regulations and enforcement mechanisms regarding cross-border ties and exchanges.[80] Since 2011, the Assad rule prioritised internal military frontiers and, in comparison, neglected its international borders.[81] When on the offensive, the go-to military tactic of the Assad rule has been a war of attrition to

---

[77] Vignal, 'The changing borders', 821.
[78] By 2018, about 11,000 Iraqis were still in the Hol camp on the Syrian side of the border. While PKK, Shi'a militias and Daesh fighters (to a lesser extent today) regularly crossed the borders, access to most parts of these borders has become heavily restricted. Furthermore, on the Iraqi side (except Kurdistan) there is what is officially called al-Ardh al-Haram (prohibited land); about 10 km of buffer zone inside Iraqi borders where a curfew is in place for unlicensed movement; Workshop on 'Preventing the reemergence of Violent Extremism in Northeast Syria' organised under Chatham House Rules by the National Agenda for the Future of Syria, UN: ESCWA, 10–11 December 2019, Beirut.
[79] James R. Crawford, *The Creation of States in International Law* (Oxford: Oxford University Press, 2006), 46–8.
[80] Ibid.
[81] The Syrian–Turkish borders for instance did not have any official Syrian army forces deployed.

cut off enemy supply lines coupled with indiscriminate shelling of the enemy space altogether. The areas most resilient to such tactics have been borderlands. Access to borders and border crossings make it harder to besiege territories without cooperation from forces on the other side of the border. Thus, borders acted as decisive resources for the survival of non-state armed groups while simultaneously providing outlets of influence for neighbouring states and forces. Amidst the devolution of the state's monopoly of violence, states, militant groups and other local and transnational actors all responded in different ways to circumstances of short-lived political vacuums and peripheral autonomy around borderlands. Borderlands emerged as desired sites for their economic and strategic functions, which eventually invited fierce territorial contests.

Borderlands became strategically important for humanitarian considerations as well. By 2014, as the Assad rule sought to prevent aid and relief efforts from reaching opposition-controlled areas, the UN humanitarian system and private international organisations, such as Mercy Corps, bypassed the Syrian state entirely and established cross-border operations in partnership with non-state armed groups and entities in control of border areas.[82] Similarly, neighbouring states with a political stake in the ongoing conflict, such as Turkey, set up military camps along the border and permitted, at various intervals, the movement of people, combatants, weapons and medical supplies, as well as cross-border access for medical treatment.[83] In the short periods of stability around borders and active border crossings, some villages have prospered and grown to become towns with new industries and capital, which attracted a host of unemployed and displaced labour, and became a lifeline for surrounding areas as well. This was evident in the northern border town of Azaz where informal economies prospered.[84]

In this context, economic opportunities due to proximity to other jurisdictional spaces and access to illicit cross-border activities expanded

---

[82] Martin Chulov, and Emma Beales, 'Aid group Mercy Corps forced to close Damascus operations', *The Guardian*, 23 May 2014, https://www.theguardian.com/world/2014/may/23/aid-group-mercy-corps-forced-to-close-damascus-operations-syria.

[83] Vignal, 'The changing borders', 809–27.

[84] Armenak Tokmajyan, 'The war economy in Northern Syria', *The Aleppo Project*, December 2016, https://theblueshield.org/wp-content/uploads/2018/06/Tokmajyan_War-Economy_N-Syria.pdf.

beyond associates of the Assad rule. Such opportunities are most prevalent in borderlands where privileged networks enjoy considerable access on both sides of the borders.[85] Despite its propaganda campaigns declaring the end of colonial ('Sykes-Picot') arrangements by bulldozing random sand dunes along the Syrian–Iraqi border, Daesh used highways to extract rent either by kidnapping, plundering or establishing checkpoints to tax economic exchanges and transportation activities across formal and informal border crossings.[86] Informal networks and pathways for cross-border movement and exchanges are invaluable for state actors and non-state actors alike to secure the resources and logistics needed for survival or expansion during conflict. On the Syrian–Iraqi border, decades of informal economic exchanges intertwined with Jihadi networks, first in the aftermath of the US invasion of Iraq and later in the aftermath of the 2011 uprising. The overlap of Jihadi networks and informal economic networks sustained non-state militant groups before and after 2011.[87] Meanwhile, the Syrian state had purposely turned a blind eye to these exchanges after the US invasion of Iraq in 2003 as a means of increasing its political leverage in Iraq to the east and pressuring US forces based there.[88] These pre-existing networks were 'entrenched in networks of kinship between Deir el-Zor [Syria] and Anbar [Iraq]' who became more active after the Gulf War sanctions on Iraq, Syria's economic woes after 2000, post-invasion developments in Iraq and the devolution of the Syrian state's regulatory capacity over the military domain after 2011.[89] Previously, the Assad rule guided informal networks through its dominance over the institutions of violence. With the level

---

[85] For instance, subsidised fuel smuggled and sold in territories beyond national borders is a profitable market niche (as in Syrian fuel sold in Lebanon). The smuggling of livestock was also common practice across the Iraqi–Syrian border, often conducted by tribal groups whose members reside on the two sides of the border (such as the case with the Shumar tribe).

[86] Carter Malkasian, *Illusions of Victory: The Anbar Awakening And The Rise of The Islamic State* (Oxford: Oxford University Press, 2017), 150.

[87] Peter Neumann, 'Suspects into collaborators', *London Review of Books*, vol. 36, no. 7, 3 April 2014, 19–21.

[88] Peter Harling and Alex Simon, 'Erosion and resilience of the Iraqi-Syrian border', *EUI Working Papers*, 2015, 1–10, http://cadmus.eui.eu/bitstream/handle/1814/37015/RSCAS_2015_61.pdf; Further discussed in Chapter Four.

[89] Ibid.

of influence gained by actors involved in the military domain and in borderlands, the Assad rule faces unprecedented constraints to control cross-border informal exchanges going forward.[90]

Violence as a Generative Force

The instrumentality of violence in generating instability or order in conflict zones is a well-researched niche of civil war studies. Rebel formations involved in armed conflict across the globe face somewhat similar challenges, operate in comparable conditions of limited resources and options, and share similar objectives of improving their chances of surviving a protracted war. Scholars agree that territorial control improves the chances of rebel groups to sustain their presence and operations against other groups. As argued by Arjona, the stronger the control of armed groups in localities, the better the chances of eliciting material resources, recruits and local cooperation.[91] Effective control and local cooperation with armed factions do not necessarily depend on the local population's ideological agreement with the forces in place.[92] Rather, displays of violence against dissidents and extreme retributive practices

---

[90] Harith Hasan and Kheder Khaddour, 'The Transformation of the Iraqi-Syrian Border: From a National to a Regional Frontier', *Carnegie Middle East Center*, 31 March 2020, https://carnegie-mec.org/2020/03/31/transformation-of-iraqi-syrian-border-from-national-to-regional-frontier-pub-81396.

[91] Ana Arjona, *Rebelocracy* (Cambridge: Cambridge University Press, 2016), 9.

[92] Robert Sampson and Per-Olof Wikstrom conclude that even beyond circumstances of systemic collapse, in places such as Chicago and Stockholm, there is a strong correlation between violence and order. See Robert Sampson and Per-Olof Wikstrom, 'The Social Order of Violence in Chicago and Stockholm Neighborhoods: A Comparative Perspective', in Stathis Kalyvas, Ian Shapiro and Tarek Masoud (eds), *Order, Conflict, and Violence* (Cambridge: Cambridge University Press, 2008), 98, 116–17. Their findings are based on surveys of 8,872 Chicago residents and a longstanding study of violence and social ecology in Stockholm. The comparative analysis evidently shows that even in these two relatively stable areas (compared to that of Syria today) the rate of violence is decisively determined by the level of contestation over control (by formal structures such as the state, or informal structures such as gangs and turfs) rather than disadvantage, poverty or social cleavages. Methods of social organisation applied by Colombian militias in Medellín after the 1980s qualify and further develop this proposition. According to Francisco Gutierrez-Sanin, self-described leftist militias in Medellín established a 'modicum of order' through public displays of brutality, exemplary executions and 'harsh punishments of deviants', and not due to leftist ideological appeal as claimed by the militias at the time. See Francisco Gutierrez-Sanin, 'Organization and Governance: The Evolution of Urban Militias in Medellin, Colombia', in Ana Arjona, Nelson Kasfir and Zachariah Mamphily (eds), *Rebel Governance in Civil War* (Cambridge: Cambridge University Press, 2017), 246.

against defiance and non-compliance restrain opposition (potential or real), consolidate control and may contribute to an eventual ideological congruence between armed forces and local populations.

Violence and order

Organised violence can be instrumental for establishing control through terror and elimination of opponents. However, Stathis Kalyvas argues in his classic *The Logic of Violence in Civil War* that organised violence alone, especially when instruments of coercion are scarce, limited in reach, and contested by a multitude of armed factions, is insufficient for such a purpose.[93] For example, William Reno relates how, during Charles Taylor's rule in Liberia between 1990 and 1992, the ruling NPFL (The National Patriotic Front of Liberia) constructed administrative bodies and courts to create an alternative order while simultaneously displaying brutality and violence, leading to an intricate new system of patronage and loyalty networks.[94] The courts of Liberia are comparable to the Shariʻa courts of al-Nusra, which controlled the issuance of permits for cross-border activities, defined the educational content of local schools and carried out public displays of punishments and court sentences. In protracted armed conflicts where the monopoly of violence has devolved at various rates in different areas, administrative bodies, social services and displays of order are complementary to violence in establishing order and encouraging the cooperation of the local population.[95]

Interlinkages between violence and order are contingent upon technologies of violence as well as the ability to maintain conditions of liveability for the local population through the provision of supplies (medical, fuel, food and other basics). Kalyvas further suggests that indiscriminate and random violence during civil wars is rare and incidental. He reveals that incidents of indiscriminate communal violence are the outcome of

---

[93] Stathis Kalyvas, *The Logic of Violence in Civil War* (Cambridge: Cambridge University Press, 2006), 147.

[94] William Reno, 'Predatory Rebellions and Governance: The National Patriotic Front of Liberia, 1989–1992', in Ana Arjona, Nelson Kasfir and Zachariah Mamphily (eds), *Rebel Governance in Civil War* (Cambridge: Cambridge University Press, 2017), 265–86.

[95] Arjona, *Rebelocracy*, 9.

a 'steep imbalance of power' or 'desperation'.[96] Weinstein adds, based on the cases of Uganda, Mozambique and Peru, that disorganised rebel groups comprised of recruits lacking discipline and organisation in pursuit of short term and narrow objectives are more likely to commit indiscriminate predatory violence.[97] Organised rebel groups engaged in sustained warfare are more often selective with their resources and efforts.[98] Thus, expressions of exaggerated violence are calculated rather than random. Even the deployment of seemingly indiscriminate violence may serve a strategic function. Kalyvas's empirical data also highlights local responses to rebel behaviour. His work is based on comparative evidence ranging from the Shining Path in Peru in the late 1980s, to the Mau Mau rebellion in Kenya against the British between 1952 and 1964 and the Davao area of the Philippines as it transitioned from communist rule to an anti-communist autocracy after the late 1980s. He points out that expressions of a shift in ideological positioning and cooperation on behalf of the local populace is a function of effective control.

Borders and borderlands in Syria witnessed mass population strategies that altered demographic realities in specific areas to eliminate potential dissidents and bring about swift ideological congruence.[99] For example, this was witnessed in the 2014 battle between Daesh and Kurdish forces in Kobani (Ain al-Arab), a strategic city on the Syrian–Turkish border. While Daesh attacked the border town with genocidal intent, Turkey shut its borders, practically besieging the local population and militants alike in the face of Daesh. Areas on the Syrian–Turkish border with a strong SDF presence presented a serious security concern for Turkey – these northern borderlands once again became the site of executions, displacement, deportations and resettlement initiatives, which reconfigured the demographic reality in the area in the wake of the withdrawal of US troops in late 2019.[100]

---

[96] Kalyvas, *The Logic of Violence*, 147.
[97] Jeremy Weinstein, *Inside Rebellion: The Politics of Insurgent Violence* (Cambridge: Cambridge University Press, 2006), 203.
[98] Kalyvas, *The Logic of Violence*, 210–329.
[99] Edith Szanto, 'Sayyida Zaynab in the State of Exception: Shi'i Sainthood as "Qualified Life" in Contemporary Syria', *International Journal of Middle East Studies*, 44, no. 2 (May 2012): 285–99.
[100] For more on organised destruction and displacement as population strategies, see Vignal, *War-Torn*, 105–56.

Sectarian formations

René Girard, most renowned for *Violence and the Sacred*, discusses at great length specific population strategies to bring about ideological shifts, namely through ritualistic spectacles of violence and sacrifice, and their correlations with local consent towards violent groups.[101] From a historical standpoint, Girard's observations are most poignant in the pre-Colombian context of meso-America, specifically throughout the Aztec empire where stylistic elements of the exercise of violence, similar to the splendour of violence projected by ISIS, was central to the organisation of social and political life.[102] For instance, the Toxcatl Ceremony is a well-studied Aztec public ritual of sacrifice with elaborate archaeological evidence regarding the details of its nature and its application. Archaeological evidence shows the ritual took place during Aztec rule from the early fourteenth century until even after the invasion of the Spaniards in the sixteenth century.[103] The ritual was usually carried out on a 'sacrificial stone (techalt)' in elevated and central locations.[104] The sacrificed had their chest cut open with a ritual knife called a *tecpatl* and the heart was removed while the individual was still alive.[105]

The crucial element reinforcing in-group solidarity in the sacrificial process was that the sacrificed was always presented as someone deemed an outsider and of symbolically significant status, for example through 'physical excellence' or political status.[106] The sacrificed were mostly prisoners of war

---

[101] René Girard, *Violence and the Sacred* (New York: W. W. Norton & Co., 1972), 255. This point is also discussed in Pierre Bourdieu, *Pascalian Meditations* (Cambridge: Polity Press, 2000), 138–78; Émile Durkheim, *The Elementary Forms of Religious Life* (Oxford: Oxford University Press, 2008), 303–91.

[102] For detailed examples of such brutal displays targeting social others by ISIS, see Jean-Louis Comolli, *Daesh, Le Cinema et la Mort* (Lagrasse: Verdier, 2016), 14. Examples include but are not limited to the Jordanian pilot captured and burnt alive in a cage, foreign captives decapitated, homosexuals thrown off buildings or towers and public amputations of thieves.

[103] The archaeological evidence shows that the ritual was carried out even before Aztec rule, dating back to the third century CE; Madeline Nicholson, 'Public Ritual Sacrifice as a Controlling Mechanism for the Aztec', Honors Scholar Theses, University of Connecticut, 2017, 5.

[104] Ibid.

[105] Nicholson also details other similar systemically carried out (regularly and routinely pre-organised) rituals. Ibid.

[106] Ibid., 5–6.

who symbolised the social other, and rituals were staged on top of pyramid-shaped temples (such as the Templo Mayor) located in city centres.[107]

Girard argues that through the dramatisation and splendour of violence, victims *become* structured and identified as the social other in the process of the sacrificial ritual, and 'the entire community can be reborn in a new [. . .] cultural order' with new bonds.[108] In other words, the social other is defined through the sacrificial ritual. The spectacular violence also reminds 'citizens (both in the city and outside) what will happen if rebellion occurs'.[109] In line with the expansionist course of Daesh, archaeological evidence showcases that the number of people sacrificed during Aztec rule increased with the expansion of the empire. Excavations of burial sites revealed that eighty per cent of entombed collections came from peripheral towns and city-states.[110] Spectacular violence and exclusionary measures such as sacrificial rituals were employed for the purpose of socio-political integration: political integration of newly annexed peripheral areas through terror and displays of unrestrained power; social integration through the definition of otherness during and through the sacrificial act. The continuation of such rituals, even after the advent of Spanish conquistadores, forced Christianisation and prohibition of such rituals is only proof of the efficacy of such measures.[111] In other words, even if local cooperation does not depend on ideological positioning or convictions, exclusionary discourses and practices may eventually lead to ideological realignment and a change of convictions.[112]

Throughout the war in Syria, Jabhat al-Nusra (currently known as Hay'at Tahrir al-Sham), the Islamic Front (and its most significant faction, Ahrar al-Sham) and Daesh emerged as the most potent contenders for territorial control. Vast territories and oil fields fell under the control of these

---

[107] When the Templo Mayor was completed, its inauguration included the sacrifice of a staggering 20,000 captives. Ibid., 8.

[108] Girard, *Violence and the Sacred*, 255.

[109] Ibid.

[110] David Carraso, *City of Sacrifice: The Aztec Empire and the Role of Violence in Civilization* (Boston, MA: Beacon Press, 1998), 65.

[111] These rituals retreated to peripheral communities as the centres were occupied by the Spanish. See Nicholson, 'Public Ritual Sacrifice', 11. Furthermore, Nicholson argues that such rituals were even upgraded and Christianised by adding crucifixion elements. Ibid., 13.

[112] James Fearon and David Laitin, 'Violence and the Social Construction of Ethnic Identity', *International Organization* 54, no 4 (2000): 847.

groups. Their organisational structures evolved and ultimately shrank, but unremittingly relied on religious councils, Islamic theologians and Islamic courts. Hay'at Tahrir al-Sham for instance was fully committed to a network of Islamic courts called Dar al-Qada'.[113] Before Dar al-Qada', the Nusra Front and other factions of the Islamic Front subscribed to 'Shari'a Commissions', which implemented religious rules and regulations.[114] These 'Shari'a Commissions' served as authorities controlling the police, judiciary and *hisbah*.[115] The institution's objective was to become a comprehensive body that regulates judicial, executive, educational and various other societal functions.[116] As a result of factional disputes amongst the members of the 'Shari'a Commissions', disagreements between its theologians, and the success of the Islamic State in providing a functional competing religious structure, the Nusra Front withdrew its membership, spearheading its own religious authority, the still active Dar al-Qada'.[117] In a recording, the leader of al-Nusra, Abu Muhammad al-Jawlani, claimed that the new religious judiciary aims to establish 'an alternative to the Shari'a commissions with stricter rules'.[118] The debate between theologians Mu'tasim Billah al-Madani and Abu Azzam al-Najdi reveals that, despite disagreements amongst Syria's radicalised groups, extreme interpretations of Islamic law gradually emerged as common denominator across the board. After defecting from the Nusra Front to the Islamic State, Abu Azzam al-Najdi praised the latter for implementing the *hudud* – ancient brutal punishments for crimes committed within territories under Islamic rule. In response, Nusra Front theologian al-Madani noted a

---

[113] Matthew Barber, 'Al-Qaeda's Syrian Judiciary – is it really what al-Jolani makes it out to be?', *Syria Comment*, 9 November 2014, http://www.joshualandis.com/blog/al-qaedas-syrian-judiciary-really-al-jolani-makes/?utm_source=feedburner&utm_medium=email&utm_campaign=Feed%3A+Syriacomment+%28Syria+Comment%29 (accessed March 2018). Still active to date based on local reports and author's interview with local contacts from 6 March 2017.
[114] Barber, 'Al-Qaeda's Syrian Judiciary'.
[115] Religious police monitoring behavioural aspects of society and enforcing Islamic norms and practices. See Aleppo Shari'a Commission – The ASC Branch Commission Document, 'Primary Source: The Structure of an Aleppo Sharia Commission Branch in the Countryside', *Goha's Nail*, 14 May 2014, https://gohasnail.wordpress.com/2014/05/14/primary-source-the-structure-of-an-aleppo-sharia-commission-branch-in-the-countryside-2/ (accessed March 2018).
[116] Ibid.
[117] Barber, 'Al-Qaeda's Syrian Judiciary'.
[118] Ibid.

judicial sentence of stoning carried out by his faction in Saraqeb, Idlib.[119] As Heller points out, for both theologians, stoning became the measure of prowess and piety.[120]

Radicalised factions other than Daesh also provide numerous examples of exemplary executions and displays of brutality. For instance, when Jaysh al-Fateh (coalition of the Nusra Front and the Islamic Front's Ahrar al-Sham) captured the city of Idlib in early 2015, suspected government collaborators were lynched, including the infamous Jamal Suleiman, former commander of the Popular Committees.[121] In addition, around a month after the city was captured, the group reportedly issued a list of 750 individuals who had closely collaborated with the government.[122] By mid-2015 many of those on the list were declared missing and others had been publicly executed.[123]

The use of religious labels aimed at dehumanising and excluding opponents serves the function of establishing control through the identification and subordination of opponents and dissidents. The executions and beheadings of members of the al-Sheitaat tribe in Deir el-Zor by the Islamic State, which took the lives of more than 700 of its members as the tribe had revoked a pledge of allegiance, is a case in point.[124] The excavation of mass graves in the town of Abu Haman near Deir el-Zor has shown that more than 300 of those killed were executed after the battles: many casualties were shot at point blank range.[125] The number of casualties is reportedly much higher as new mass graves continue to be discovered.[126]

---

[119] Sam Heller, 'Jeish al-Muhajireen wal-Ansar Shar'i: "I bring you good news...", *Abu al-Jamajim*, 25 October 2014, https://abujamajem.wordpress.com/2014/10/25/jeish-al-muhajireen-wal-ansar-shari-i-bring-you-good-news/ (accessed March 2018).

[120] Ibid.

[121] Naji Abu Bakr, إدارة التوحش: أخطر مرحلة ستمر بها الأمة (Syria: Dar al-Tamarrud, n.d.).

[122] Ibid.

[123] Ibid., 7–11, Quoted originally by Ahmad Dallal, *The Political Theology of ISIS: Prophets, Messiahs, and 'the Extinction of the Grayzone'* (Tadween Publishing: George Mason University, 2017), 16.

[124] Oliver Holmes and Suleiman Al-Khalidi, 'Islamic State killed 700 people from Syrian tribe: monitoring group', 17 August 2017, https://www.reuters.com/article/us-syria-crisis-execution/islamic-state-executed-700-people-from-syrian-tribe-monitoring-group-idUSKBN0GG0H120140817. Haian Dukhan, 'The ISIS Massacre of the Sheitat Tribe in Der ez-Zor', August 2014, *Journal of Genocide Research* (2021).

[125] Ibid.

[126] Kareem Shaheen, 'Up to 15,000 Isis victims buried in mass graves in Syria and Iraq – survey', *The Guardian*, 30 August 2016, https://www.theguardian.com/world/2016/aug/30/up-to-15000-bodies-may-be-buried-in-mass-graves-in-syria-and-iraq-survey.

Religious idioms went hand in hand with displays of violence to identify and eliminate non-conformists, regardless of their religious belonging. For instance, after a May 2012 suicide attack in Deir el-Zor, Jabhat al-Nusra declared that 'these blessed operations will continue until the soil of al-Sham is cleansed from the filth of the *noseiris* and the Sunnis are relieved of their oppression'.[127] On 4 August 2013 opposition fighters launched a large-scale offensive in the Latakia countryside, capturing more than ten Alawite villages.[128] Government forces regained control over the area on 18 August. According to a Human Rights Watch report, during this time fighters from the Islamic State (previously known as Islamic State of Iraq and Syria), al-Qaeda's Nusra Front (currently Hay'at Tahrir al-Sham) and Ahrar al-Sham (the biggest faction and founding member of Islamic Front) among others, killed 190 civilians, of whom 57 were women and 17 children.[129] During the offensive, an Alawite shrine was reportedly destroyed and its sheikh killed. In addition, according to the report by the Human Rights Watch, many of the victims had been beheaded or shot at close range. Some Christians from Homs, particularly in Talkalakh, received similar treatment from Islamic militants.[130] Another report by the Syrian Observatory for Human Rights documents killings by Jihadis of sixty Shi'ites, including women and non-armed civilians, in the rebel-held eastern town of Hatla, Deir el-Zor.[131] Although the persecution of social groups branded as others in such circumstances is often portrayed as instinctive savagery or the expression of religious hatred, persecution served the strategic purpose of depopulating areas of previous administrative personnel whose loyalty and administrative

---

[127] The term *noseiri* refers to the Alawite sect. For more on the attack, see A. Y. Zelin, 'New Statement from Jabhat al-Nusrah: "Bombing of the Headquarters of the Military Security and Air Force Intelligence in Dayr az-Zor (Deir el-Zor)"', *Jihadology*, May 20, 2012, www.jihadology.net/2012/05/20/new-statement-fromjabhat-al-Nusrah-bombing-of-the-headquarters-of-the-militarysecurity-and-air-force-intelligence-in-dayr-az-zur-deir-al-zour/.

[128] Anne Barnard, 'Syrian Civilians Bore Brunt of Rebels' Fury, Report Says', *New York Times*, 11 October 2013, http://www.nytimes.com/2013/10/11/world/middleeast/syrian-civilians-bore-brunt-of-rebels-fury-report-says.html?pagewanted=1&_r=1.

[129] Human Rights Watch, 'You Can Still See Their Blood'.

[130] Paul Wood, 'Christians Targeted by Foreign Jihadis in Syrian War', *BBC*, 18 July 2013. http://www.bbc.com/news/world-23361938 (accessed 27 August 2014).

[131] Hania Mourtada and Anne Barnard, 'Dozens of Shiites Reported Killed in Raid by Syria Rebels', *New York Times*, 12 June 2013. http://mobile.nytimes.com/2013/06/13/world/middleeast/syria.html?from=global.home.

experience were deemed threatening. Examples include the persecution of Christian and Druze villages in Idlib by the Nusra Front and Ahrar al-Sham as well as the persecution of the Yezidis on Mount Sinjar, near the Syria-Iraq highway, which was key for the organisation's military and economic operations.

Despite recurrent attacks targeting 'other' social groups, the Sunni Muslim population residing under the control of radicalised groups was by far the biggest casualty that suffered from their methods.[132] Through the common use of theologically loaded and dehumanising labels such as *kuffar, murtaddin, mushrikin* or *khawarij* Islamic groups targeted each other (and Sunni Muslims) more than other religious groups in Syria.[133]

The spectacle of brutality in Syria, including public punishments and displays of violence such as stoning, went hand in hand with efforts to create organisational and administrative structures for establishing social order and controlling educational and ideological channels. In other words, management of violence in Syria during the conflict was an instrument of social organisation. The Islamic State's discourse and commentaries regarding its own violence support this proposition. Daesh explicitly claimed that the aim of increased brutality and overall chaos was to create a vacuum that could then be 'filled' and 'managed' and become the foundations of a 'full-fledged state'.[134] Thus, Daesh affirmed the instrumentality of its violence. It also affirmed that even indiscriminate violence (such as suicide bombers or car bombs) was deployed strategically so as not to antagonise compliant or sympathetic segments of the population. This is evident in the organisation's Jihadi discourse, echoing the

---

[132] Zeina Karam, 'Hundreds of bodies exhumed from mass grave in Syria's Raqqa', *Associated Press*, 27 November 2018, https://www.apnews.com/01c50935854b425295ef8731cdfc42a4.

[133] *Kafir* is widely translated as the excommunicated and the unbelievers; *murtad* refers to apostates who have abandoned Islam; *mushrik* refers to idolaters and polytheists; *khawarij* are those who have endorsed Islam and pledged allegiance to the relevant religious authority followed by their withdrawal and breaking of allegiance. These terms are expressed through declarations, statements, manifestos, policies, practices and religious institutions of Syria's largest Islamic armed factions, namely Jabhat al-Nusra, Daesh and the Islamic Front. See Aron Lund, 'The Politics of the Islamic Front, Part 1: Structure and Support', 14 January 2014, *Carnegie Endowment for International Peace*, http://carnegieendowment.org/syriaincrisis/?fa=54183 (accessed April 2015). See also Joshua Landis, 'Zahran 'Alloush: His Ideology and Beliefs', *Syria Comment*, 15 December 2013, http://www.joshualandis.com/blog/zahran-alloush. For examples of interfactional disputes and killings, see Charles Lister, *The Syrian Jihad: The Evolution of an Insurgency* (London: Hurst, 2015), 151–218.

[134] 'From Hijrah to Khilafah', *Dabiq* 1, no. 38 (June–July 2014).

widely circulated notion of *idarat al-tawahush* (the management of savagery). This management of savagery is explicitly referred to as an instrumental stage consisting of areas of exaggerated brutality and mayhem where existing societal structures utterly collapse. Daesh was well aware that creating neglected, marginal areas would provide ideal circumstances for creating administrative bodies and performing basic administrative tasks to appeal to large segments of the population with great effect (such as through establishing Shari'a courts, the provision of salaries, providing social services). Daesh fully understood the power and potential of exaggerated brutality: 'And if we fail [to establish the Islamic State through savagery] this does not mean that the struggle is over, but the failure (of savagery) will lead to more savagery', which would in turn strengthen the conditions for establishing an alternative order. This does not imply that all violence exhibited by Daesh was indiscriminate. Rather, when Daesh commited indiscriminate violence against non-combatants, it did so with a strategic outlook.

The violence in areas under the control of radicalised groups by the groups in charge was aimed at power consolidation, not only through the elimination of incumbents but also through the suppression of civilian dissent – manifest or potential. In fact, once effective control was attained, these groups have shown greater restraint with their use of force.

For instance, in February 2014, the Christians of Raqqa saw the first formal *dhimmi* pact offered by the Islamic State. The signed agreement purported to protect *ahl al-kitab* (the people of the book) under the newly established Islamic rule. The pact claimed the following:

> This is what the servant of God, Abu Bakr al-Baghdadi, the Commander of the Faithful [. . .] has given to the Christians concerning the pact of protection. He has given them security for themselves, their wealth, their churches and the rest of their property in the province of Raqqa: their churches should not be attacked, nor should anything be taken [by force] from them, nor from their domain, nor anything from their wealth, and there should be no compulsion against them in religion, and none of them should be harmed.[135]

---

[135] Aymenn al-Tamimi, 'The Islamic State of Iraq and ash-Sham's dhimmi pact for the Christians of Raqqa province', *Syria Comment*, 11 February 2014, http://www.joshualandis.com/blog/assad-regime-jihadis-collaborators-allies.

The agreement included other stipulations aimed at segregating and subjugating these groups through denigrating measures such as the marking of Christian houses with specific signs.[136] The example of *dhimmitude* illustrates how in areas where control is already established, taxation and economic extraction were prioritised.[137] This exploitation, however, was simultaneously instrumentalised for redefining social solidarities. The system of *dhimmitude* aided the reconfiguration of social relations by antagonising communities that coexisted peacefully before the conflict. The function of exclusionary discourses and practices by radicalised groups has been the reconfiguration of social solidarities through the active promotion of distinct modes of self-perception as well as the perception of others through exclusionary practices – identification and subordination.[138]

---

[136] The letter 'n' in Arabic was painted on Christian houses for identification and even confiscation of property where the agreement does not apply. The conditions mentioned in the agreement of *dhimmitude* are the following: (1) That they must not build in their town or the periphery a monastery, church or monk's hermitage, and must not rebuild what has fallen into disrepair; (2) That they must not show the cross or any of their scriptures in any of the roads or markets of the Muslims and they must not use any means to amplify their voices during their calls to prayers or similarly for the rest of their acts of worship; (3) That they must not make Muslims hear recital of their scriptures or the sounds of their bells, even if they strike them within their churches; (4) That they must not engage in any acts of hostility against the Islamic State, like giving housing to spies and those wanted for a reason by the Islamic State, [. . .], they must not aid such persons in concealing or moving them or other such things. If they know of a conspiracy against the Muslims, they must inform them about it; (5) That they must not engage in any displays of worship outside the churches; (6) That they must not stop any of the Christians from embracing Islam if he so wishes; (7) That they must respect Islam and Muslims, and not disparage their religion in any way; (8) The Christians must embrace payment of the jizya – on every adult male: its value is four dinars of gold. . .on the Ahl al-Ghina [the wealthy], and half that value on those of middle income, and half that on the poor among them, on condition that they do not conceal anything from us regarding their state of affairs. And they are to make two payments per year; (9) They are not allowed to bear arms; (10) They are not to deal in selling pork and wine with Muslims or in their markets; and they are not to consume it [wine] publicly – that is, in any public places; (11) They should have their own tombs, as is custom; (12) That they must accept the precepts imposed by the Islamic State like modesty of dress, selling, buying and other things.

[137] For examples of the changing levels of violence and their connections to changing circumstances and the local balance of powers between a multitude of armed groups, see Ahmad Abazeid and Thomas Pierret, 'Les Rebelles Syriens d'Ahrar al-Sham: Ressorts Contextuels et Organisationnels d'une Déradicalisation en Temps de Guerre Civile', *Critique Internationale* 78, no. 1 (2018), 63–84.

[138] Martin A. Nome and Nils B. Weidmann, 'Conflict Diffusion via Social Identities: Entrepreneurship and Adaptation', in Jeffrey Checkel (ed.), *Transnational Dynamics of Civil War* (Cambridge: Cambridge University Press, 2014), 173–201.

Population strategies through administrative structures under state atrophy

States and non-state actors alike pursue power consolidation, including through population strategies intended to alter demographic realities as a means of extending presence and control.[139] Population strategies include systemic efforts to reconfigure social perceptions and worldviews as well as strategies of demographic engineering.[140] Demographic strategies have been and continue to be employed throughout the conflict, in contentious borderlands and beyond.[141] For instance, following a truce in the area of Qalamoun on the Syrian–Lebanese borders, 2,500 rebel fighters, along with their families, were transferred to rebel-held Idlib.[142] Meanwhile, the PYD's shutting down of schools and remodelling of educational curricula to promote ethnic narratives of nativism, indigeneity and territorial entitlement have marginalised a variety of social groups living in northeast Syria.[143]

The main motive behind efforts of demographic engineering stems from the following premise: the relative size and loyalty of a population has implications for establishing effective control and government.[144] In other words, in conflicts where identity is politicised as a method of mobilisation and recruitment, demographic engineering is usually geared towards

---

[139] John McGarry, 'Demographic engineering: The state directed movement of ethnic groups as a technique in conflict regulation', *Ethnic and Racial Studies* 21, no. 4 (1998): 613–38; Paul Morland, *Demographic engineering: Population strategies in ethnic conflict* (Burlington: Ashgate, 2014).

[140] Myron Weiner and Michael Teitelbaum, *Political demography, demographic engineering* (New York: Berghahn Books, 2001); Milica Z. Bookman, *The demographic struggle for power* (London: Frank Cass & Co., 1997); Haroutioun Akdedian, 'Ethno-religious subjectivities in the Syrian war: Dynamics of sectarianism and sectarianization', *The Middle East Journal* 73, no. 3 (2019): 408–30.

[141] Vignal, *War-Torn*, 133–56.

[142] Mohammad A. Ibrahim and Tariq Adely, 'Last rebel faction leaves mountains on Syrian-Lebanese border alongside displaced', *Syria direct*, 14 August 2017, https://syriadirect.org/news/last-rebel-faction-leaves-mountains-on-syrian-lebanese-border-alongside-displaced.

[143] 'Assyrians in Syria protest PYD's closure of schools in Qamishli', *Assyrian Policy Institute*, 28 August 2018, https://www.assyrianpolicy.org/news/assyrians-in-syria-protest-pyd-s-closure-of-schools-in-qamishli; Samuel Dolbee, 'After ISIS: Development and demography in the jazira', *Middle East Brief* (2018), 121, available at: https://www.scribd.com/fullscreen/385677257; Max J. Joseph and Mardean Isaac, 'Romancing Rojava: Rhetoric vs. Reality', *Syria Comment*, 31 July 2018, https://www.joshualandis.com/blog/romancing-rojava-rhetoric-vs-reality/.

[144] Bookman, *The demographic struggle for power*, 8.

creating a greater overlap between military frontlines against enemy spaces and social boundaries in an effort to create a bounded sovereign space.[145] This is an effort not only pursued by the Assad forces, but also by those militarily contesting it.

Administrative structures that emerged in opposition-held areas represent efforts of re-establishing state-like regulatory structures to improve conditions of liveability and maintain order. When the local council of Azaz appointed new members of municipal government in July 2018, as newly appointed municipal official (*mukhtar*) Mawas Danun affirmed, the Turkish state micromanaged these appointments. Appointees, new to their posts, had never occupied local positions before.[146] Turkey's role in administrative matters in the north of Syria came about after its offensive, upon the withdrawal of US troops, in partnership with Syrian rebel formations targeting the Kurdish population in borderlands to drive them out and resettle Syrian refugees from Turkey to these areas.[147] Besides active efforts to alter demographic realities, the war brought with it new dynamics that wrought radical and unexpected demographic changes. Before Turkey's invasion, the population of the northern Syrian town of Azaz on the Syrian–Turkish border had skyrocketed from 30,000 in 2011 to more than 200,000 as of 2017, as a result of the battle of Aleppo, its proximity to the Turkish border and the cross-border resources it provided.[148]

As the case of Azaz suggests, not all local administrative structures were created by the armed forces in place. Armed groups rarely had the resources and capacity needed to be able to create full administrative cadres for local service provision. This applies even to sizable groups such as Hay'at Tahrir al-Sham in Idlib, where officials have explicitly stated that they must work with

---

[145] Benedict Anderson, *Imagined Communities: Reflections on the origin and spread of nationalism* (London: Verso, 2016).

[146] Mawas Danun, interview with a *mukhtar* of Azaz (interviewed by Aymenn Jawad Al-Tamimi, 13 August 2018, http://www.aymennjawad.org/2018/08/interview-with-a-mukhtar-of-azaz.

[147] Author's interview with Alva Ali, project Director of PEL Civil Waves, a non-profit organisation operating in borderland areas in northeast Syria including Sari Kani (*ras al-'ein*) and Tal Abyad. Beirut, 11 November 2019.

[148] Umar Farouq, 'Turkey puts down roots in a corner of war-torn Syria', *Los Angeles Times*, 13 July 2018, http://www.latimes.com/world/la-fg-turkey-syria-20180713-story.html.

existing societal actors to fulfil administrative needs.¹⁴⁹ It is in this context that civilian networks such as the Local Coordination Committees (LCCs) played an important role due to local shortages.

During the onset of the uprising, LCCs were primarily dedicated to citizen journalism and organising protests. These functions shifted as territorial control shifted. Finding themselves under opposition rule, many LCCs expanded and were somewhat formalised into Local Councils (LCs) becoming service providers. The LCCs represent social spaces of solidarity that encapsulate brave and creative expressions of human agency under conditions of state atrophy.¹⁵⁰ LCCs however never amalgamated into a unified structure across all opposition-held areas and their influence remained limited.

LCCs and LCs worked with whatever was at their disposal to be able to ease the deprivation and suffering of those residing in opposition-held areas. The sectors they were involved in included health, education, law, transport, humanitarian aid and waste management.¹⁵¹ Despite their crucial role for local residents, LCCs and LCs both government forces and opposition groups placed them under different kinds of pressure. As Samer Abboud notes, for activists, 'the space between regime and rebel violence has indeed been very limited'.¹⁵² Many local councils, such as the local council in Aleppo City, despite not having any capacity to undermine armed groups in place, were marginalised by them all the same.¹⁵³

Areas that returned to government control were either entirely depopulated of such actors, as in Aleppo City, or were absorbed and co-opted within state structures, as in Raqqa since governmental return.¹⁵⁴ Dominant armed factions had an active role in the selection of positions in councils, while they

---

¹⁴⁹ This also applies to the management of the religious field. See Drevon and Haenni, 'How Global Jihad Relocalises', 17–18.
¹⁵⁰ The case of Deir Hafer in Chapter Five provides a glimpse of the challenges that the local councils faced before and after Daesh. For a more comprehensive and personalised perspective, see Yassin-Kassab and Leila al-Shami, *Burning Country: Syrians in Revolution and War* (London: Pluto Press, 2016), 57–76.
¹⁵¹ Abboud, 75; al-Meehy and Haid, 30–8.
¹⁵² Abboud, 77.
¹⁵³ For a detailed discussion of such dynamics, see Chapter Four about developments in the religious domain in opposition held areas. See also Abboud, *Syria*, 77–8.
¹⁵⁴ See Chapter Four on Aleppo City; see also al-Meehy and Haid, 25–8.

lacked accountability towards local residents and imposed hierarchical structures of supervision.[155]

This model of centralised and hierarchical accountability in a context of devolved functions in service provision resembles decentralisation measures and devolution of state functions in social services witnessed after Bashar Assad came to power in the year 2000. Since 2011, a series of laws and decrees have been passed that further formalise this devolutionary process under the 'National Decentralisation Plan', doubling the number of administrative units in the country at the city, town and township levels, and devolving the competencies of ministries to local administrative units that lack the fiscal and technical capacities needed to fulfil such services.[156] Local councils under opposition-held areas too do not possess sufficient fiscal capacity to raise local revenues and ultimately depend upon decision-making at the level of central authorities.[157] Eventually, armed groups prevailed over LCCs and LCs along with their population strategies, with the exception of a handful of pockets of resistance that managed to push back and temporarily maintain a measure of civilian autonomy through rarely attained bargaining capacity.[158]

Conclusion

The devolution of violence in Syria left the state but one player in the competition for power in a context in which different groups sought influence and presence. In light of the erosion of territorial control, separatist and radicalised tendencies were galvanised, and violence emerged as the ultimate tool of political power and social control. Similar to processes of civilisational decline described in Ibn Khaldoun's *al-Muqaddima* and Joseph Tainter's *Collapse of Complex Societies*, the Syrian contexts are manifestations of decaying sociopolitical order.[159] In other words, as societies grow more dependent on the

---

[155] See al-Meehy and Haid, 24–40.
[156] For a detailed discussion of the specific measures and decentralisation policies see al-Meehy and Haid, 20–3.
[157] Ibid., 45–9.
[158] See Chapter Five for case studies on Kasab and Deir Hafer for details of such bargaining processes. For bargaining processes between HTS and local religious actors, revisited in Chapter Four, see Drevon and Haenni, 'How Global Jihad Relocalises', 17–18.
[159] Joseph Tainter, *The Collapse of Complex Societies* (Cambridge: Cambridge University Press, 1988); Ibn Khaldun, *The Muqaddimah: An Introduction to History* (Princeton, NJ: Princeton University Press, 2015), 165–72.

concentration of resources, centralised institutional arrangements and modes of operation, the weakening of the main organising force, such as the state, unleashes a process of devolution and localisation where society breaks into 'smaller, less differentiated and heterogeneous, and . . . fewer specialized parts'.[160] When the superstructure shrinks to the scale it has in Syria, localities are left to their own fate and to new patrimonial devices of communal organisation and government.

In the face of extravagant levels of savagery and uncertainty, for the local population to survive it must reciprocally display spectacular obedience and cooperation, for the cost of disobedience (real or speculated) is tremendous. This applies to both government- and opposition-held areas. Local narratives and comparative studies suggest that displays of obedience and cooperation are often mimetically expressed by intentionally reproducing the discursive and behavioural attributes of those in power. These displays do not necessarily reflect successful socio-political engineering. Rather, such displays reflect the local population's methods of survival and adaptation strategies.

It is the religious self-validation, along with absolutist operational and constitutive features of radical theology endorsed by rebel groups in Syria, which ultimately rendered them comparable to the Syrian government. Rather than a political agenda addressing structural inequities, prominent rebel groups endorsed absolutist operational and constitutive features to function as self-validating political sovereigns.[161] In the midst of developments triggered by the devolution of violence, perceptions of the social other took on an existential meaning; because, in such a situation, the decision regarding the identity of friend or enemy is assumed to be over life and death. In such circumstances, friend/enemy political distinctions become broader communitarian terms of us/them, engulfing and defining the social and initiating a new process of communitarianism. The new communitarianism is thus a field of human judgement that, in the presence of potent antagonising forces, engendered a process of intensifying dehumanisation in the form of sectarianism.

---

[160] Tainter, *The Collapse of Complex Societies*, 38.
[161] Hans Maier, 'Political Religion: A Concept and its Limitations', *Politics, Religion & Ideology* 8, no. 1 (2007), 5–16.

3

Ethno-religious Subjectivities: Dynamics of Communitarianism and Sectarianisation*

When discussing Syria's general situation in Aleppo City by late 2011, interlocutors often used the term *fawda* to refer to surrounding events in the country, a term that has wide-ranging connotations, extending from a small kerfuffle to mayhem and chaos. With almost a full year of unrest, *fawda* was no longer an abstract term that expressed uncertainty. Rather, it reflected a reality that people were living with on a day-to-day basis. Between 2011 and 2013, I spent an extended period of time accompanying Hovsep in Aleppo and later in Beirut after he left Syria. At the time, he was a student at the University of Aleppo. 'The revolutionaries called it the University of Revolution', with continuous anti-government rallies that reached 'at least 10,000 students when the UN observers were in the country'. Based on his experiences, *fawda* was related to both the Assad rule's willingness to use violence to suppress demonstrations, and of protest dynamics by anti-government student activists.

> *There used to be multiple demonstrations in different faculties to divide the security forces. The ones I saw, let's say at 1.30pm, one person yells* 'allahu akbar' *and people quickly rally around him. It only lasts five to ten minutes before the security forces get there and start beating people up and detaining them. If the demonstration grows too big, security forces start throwing tear gas and firing rounds*

---

* An earlier version of this chapter was presented at the Middle East in Transition conference at Deakin University in Melbourne in 2017. Parts of this chapter are also published in Harout Akdedian, 'Ethno-Religious Belonging in the Syrian Conflict: Between Communitarianism and Sectarianization.' *The Middle East Journal*, vol. 73 no. 3, 2019, pp. 417–37

of live ammunition in the air or even at the demonstrators. It happened once that [I saw] they started firing at people. The demonstration ends, a few students are detained. The following day, you'd get a bigger demonstration demanding the release of the detained students. The students who were only watching after seeing their friends beaten and detained end up joining the next protest.

The pattern of these events was predictable: protesters rallied, security forces attacked and detained a number of students, then another anti-government rally took place, and then government supporters responded to the new protests because 'government supporters knew that these demonstrations were going to take place . . . they were always ready to mobilise too'. When I suggested that the situation was far too organised and orderly to be considered an example of *fawda*, he replied,

Fawda is in the overall situation. There is no room for reason or neutrality anymore. It's insanity and partisanship. For instance, the pro-government demonstrators would chant stuff like 'whoever doesn't join us is a traitor'. Or 'whoever doesn't join us his mother is from Qatar', 'The shabbiha *are hungry we want to eat the infiltrators'. And both sides were cursing each other and trying to be as offensive as possible. It's madness. It's* fawda.

Other people also consistently spoke of mayhem, even if they characterised the meaning in different ways. Some reflected on the contrast between what was portrayed on television and what was happening on the ground, for there was a huge discrepancy in the way local and international media agencies reported events. 'People don't know what to believe anymore,' said one interviewee, 'and we don't know what's really happening. We live in the country and don't know what's happening.'[1] Some reflected on their experiences with the growing militarisation and armed presence in their areas.[2] Both the official army and the opposition groups appeared unpredictable in their treatment of local inhabitants. Hovsep explained:

I was pulled over by a Syrian army checkpoint manned by three soldiers in Aleppo [city]. [. . .] One of the soldiers demanded my papers, looked at them

---

[1] I23, Author's interview in Aleppo City, August 2011.
[2] I21, Author's interview in Aleppo City, August 2011; I22, Author's interview in Aleppo City, August 2011

and told me that we are wanted by the government. I told him fine. He asked us to open the trunk; he wanted to search the car. I opened the trunk and he asked me to pull the driver's seat forward. During this, I don't know what exactly he did but when I came back to see him, he was still looking and shuffling the stuff I had in the trunk. When I got there he pulled aside a rag that was in the trunk and there was a hand grenade underneath. He asked me where this came from. I was terrified. I swore to God that I had no idea where it came from. I told him it's not mine, that I have no idea. He started asking me questions such as who are you working for? Who are you taking this to? He told me we should be ashamed of ourselves that we are residents of Suleymaniye and Sheikh Taha and were behaving like this. These areas are entirely pro-government. I told him it's not mine and if he wanted to confiscate the car he should do so but I have nothing to do with the hand grenade. I told him maybe someone did it on purpose to set me up. In the end, he told me they'll confiscate the car and take me with them for interrogation. I agreed to it. Then they started laughing all of a sudden. They told us to come along and started teaching us how to use a hand grenade. Then they told me that they will forgive us but they will have to confiscate the hand grenade. I didn't say anything I just nodded. I knew he put it there. Because the other soldier had the exact identical hand grenade in his chest pocket.

Hovsep and his father had worked for almost a decade to be able to afford the Kia Cerato that he acceded to give up out of utter fear and as a desperate attempt to avoid detention despite being innocent. It had taken so long to acquire the car due to restrictions on imported cars that were gradually reduced when trade protection measures and government regulations were eased.

> Author: *So he didn't tell you that he put it there. He just told you that he forgives you?*
> Hovsep: *He indirectly told me that they were just testing me. And then he let me go.*
> Author: *How did you feel after this?*
> Hovsep: *Some people take this lightly. I don't take it lightly. That's a sign of lack of respect and lack of intelligence. They are disrespecting the people who still have a bit of loyalty to them. They know that we can't do anything that we're peaceful. So this is just an expression of the mayhem I told you about. But people can see how these people [regime] have absolutely no respect and*

don't deserve any respect or loyalty. The regime would do anything to stay in power. They would sell their brother even. The army that is supposed to bring in stability are the ones who bring in chaos. They are doing random things. They don't know what they're doing. [. . .] We used to say that the safety and stability of Syria is unequalled in the Middle East, it's all a myth. It was an illusion enforced by fear.

Hovsep often spoke about how being neutral or distanced from the conflict was becoming less of an option. By December 2012, it was evident that the silent majority, those who identified as neutral and came to be known as '*ramadiyyin*' (the grey ones), found the country in a transition from one social order to another, with the new social order described as being about 'us' against 'them' with limited space in between. Identity was becoming increasingly politicised and ethno-religious relations were becoming more and more antagonistic:

> Author: *Do you feel like the different religious sects are starting to hate one another?*
> Hovsep: *[. . .] I think the regime hijacked the Alawi community, as if they represent the Alawi community. It was because of the regime's activism that the Sunnis got the wrong impression of Alawis. I'll give you an example. One of my professors at the university, everybody knew that he is Alawi, and he was loved by everyone. The vast majority of the attendants were Sunni Muslims. About eighty per cent were Sunni Muslims. [. . .] Sectarianism wasn't that strong. Sectarian extremism grew stronger gradually because of the radicalised foreign fighters and the minority discourse and profile of the regime – the regime presenting itself as if it's defending minority groups. They hijacked all minority groups this way. The opposition forces turned towards the sectarian discourse because they know that the majority of the Syrian population is Sunni Muslim and they wanted to mobilise them and delegitimise the representational capacity of the Asad regime.*

The politicisation of ethnicity and religion was intensifying and undermining notions of national unity.

> Hovsep: *I went to an Armenian School. They told us since we were kids to identify ourselves as Syrian Arabs out of fear. They told us you have to*

mention Arab Syrian. Syrian on its own is not enough. Although we were in Armenian schools and we were all Armenians, they told us to always identify ourselves as Syrian Arab. This was mostly evident during the ninth grade and twelfth grade official exams.

Author: *How so? What do you mean during official exam?*

Hovsep: *You have to write your name at the beginning of the official national exams. Before your name you must write the initials A and S for Arab Syrian followed by first and last names.*

Author: *So why do you think they did that?*

Hovsep: *I don't know. In my opinion, they used to teach us in school that the Syrian regime is based on Arab nationalism. And Arab nationalism is based on the idea that everyone is Arab before being Syrian. That's why they kept indoctrinating us as Arab Syrians.*

Author: *So how about now? Do you feel like you're Arab Syrian?*

Hovsep: *Look, when I used to write in the exams that I am Arab Syrian, I wasn't writing because I believed in it or because I wanted to. Even my friends, they are the same. We simply had to.*

Author: *So you don't feel like you're Arab Syrian?*

Hovsep: *Of course I'm not Arab Syrian. I'm Armenian. I'm Armenian Syrian you could say. But to say that I'm Arab Syrian, It's wrong, it's false. Are Kurds Arabs? They're not. The Kurd is a Kurd. The same with the Armenians and the Tcharkaz and others.*

Author: *Isn't Arab nationalism the foundation of Ba'thist Syria? If people don't identify themselves as Arab Syrians, then it means nation-building has failed. That there is no nation.*

Hovsep: *Look, you can't generalise. You're speaking to a Syrian Armenian. Perhaps you can find someone else, an Armenian that may identify as Arab Syrian. They would say stuff like, we have Armenian origins, but now we are Syrian Arabs because Syria gave us citizenship and protection and so on.*

Author: *So how do you see it? Is it a success or a failure?*

Hovsep: *The project [nation-building] was successful for a long time. But after the events started after 2011, it's obvious that the entire population [started] think[ing] this was a game. A veneer of Arab nationalism that everybody was affirming out of fear, but not belief. Even the government didn't believe in it. It was just a way of forming a seemingly unified nation formed out of many nations.*

By late 2012 the Ba'thist version of national unity, or whatever was left of it, had been thoroughly undermined. This brought questions about identity to the forefront of politics. I asked Hovsep about his opinion on Syria's future. His answer highlighted the politicisation of ethno-religious identity, but more dramatically, he foresaw a sectarian existential struggle looming:

> *Despite all that is happening, it's still the beginning. I see both sides fighting for their survival and as long as foreign intervention will not stop supporting them we'll get there for sure. I don't see any hope for things to change. I think it'll take a very long time. I want to tell you the last story about my friend. He's from Tartous. I don't know his sect. I swear to you we have never asked about people's sects before! I swear to God, we didn't care. We found out that he was kidnapped and tortured by the government. We think they might have confused the name. He was killed and his body returned to his family. How do you think his family feels about the regime? And this is happening on both sides. Things will escalate.*

There was a sharp contrast between Hovsep's disposition towards the uprising in 2011 compared to his views in late 2012. By early 2011, Hovsep was a sceptic and somewhat of an Assad sympathiser. By late 2012, he was a fervent oppositionist. Defiant and eloquent, he was never intimidated out of taking on much older staunch supporters of the Assad rule including immediate family members. Those intellectual clashes were more than mere academic disagreements. Most of the exchanges were heated, escalated to shouting matches and sometimes led to estrangement within the family. By 2013, Hovsep and his family members left Aleppo for good, leaving every valuable possession behind, including the brand new Kia Cerato. They took a twelve-hour bus ride with limited luggage as it was the safest, tried and tested route compared to venturing in a convoy of private cars with valuables and crossing every checkpoint from Aleppo to Tripoli in Lebanon through the Khanaser route. Eventually, a trusted contractor, who made a profitable living out of transporting personal cars and belongings for people who left the country in a hurry, reported that the Nusra Front had seized the car as it was pulled over on a checkpoint. Hovsep received an invitation to appear in front of Nusra's local court to reclaim his car. He never considered it.

Besides mass violence and massacres against civilians during the war, day-to-day incidents, such as Hovsep's experiences, made it more and more difficult to maintain distance from the dynamics of state atrophy and devolution of violence. Religious and cultural sites with significant heritage and symbolic value were not spared from harm either. The approximately 148 ft (45 m) high minaret of the Great Umayyad Mosque of Aleppo that was erected in the eleventh century was destroyed in late April 2013.[3] Ten days prior, on 13 April 2013 in the southern Province of Dar'a, the minaret of the Omari Mosque, built in the seventh century by the Caliph Omar Ibn al-Khattab, was razed to the ground.[4] Such incidents were followed by the ritualisation of heritage destruction under Daesh, which created the appropriate environment for the continuous politicisation of identity and the relentless sectarianisation of the conflict.[5] In addition to the institutional sectarianism instilled by the Assad rule, as mentioned, a number of armed groups showcased agendas of sectarianisation during the conflict, after 2011. The Nusra Front (NF), currently operating as Hay'at Tahrir al-Sham, the Islamic State (Daesh), Ahrar al-Sham, Faylaq al-Rahman, Jaysh al-Islam and Liwa' al-Tawhid have all affirmed these agendas through public manifestos, declarations and policies that set out to exclude variations of Islam or other religious groups.[6] Similarly notable are Shi'a armed factions with sectarian profiles such as Liwa' al-Baqr, Liwa' al-Imam Zein al-Abidin and Iran's Islamic Revolutionary Guards Force,

---

[3] Abdul Qadir Rihawi, *Arabic Islamic Architecture: Its Characteristics and Traces in Syria* (Damascus: The Ministry of Culture and National Leadership, 1979); 'Minaret of Historic Syrian Mosque Destroyed in Aleppo', *The Guardian*, 24 April 2013, https://www.theguardian.com/world/2013/apr/24/minaret-historic-syrian-mosque-destroyed-aleppo.

[4] 'Historic Mosque in Daraa Destroyed in Syrian Army Shelling', *Al-Arabiya*, 14 April 2013, https://english.alarabiya.net/News/middle-east/2013/04/14/Historic-mosque-in-Daraa-destroyed-in-Syrian-army-shelling-.

[5] Sofya Shahab and Benjamin Isakhan, 'The ritualization of heritage destruction under the Islamic State', *Journal of Social Archaeology* 18, no. 2 (2018): 212–33.

[6] Liwa' al-Tawhid, 'البيان رقم واحد حول الائتلاف والحكومة المفترضة', [Communique Number One About the Coalition and the supposed Government], *leuaaltawheed.com*, 24 September 2013. http://leuaaltawheed.com/ال-الحكومة-و-الائتلاف-حول-1-رقم-البيان/; Aymann J. al-Tamimi, 'The Islamic State of Iraq and ash-Sham's Dhimmi Pact for the Christians of Raqqa Province', *Joshua landis blog*, 26 February 2014, http://www.joshualandis.com/blog/islamic-state-iraq-ash-shams-dhimmi-pact-christians-raqqa-province/.

The Quds Brigade, previously under the command of one infamous Qasem Soleimani.[7] Whether or not the social environment is subdued by dynamics of sectarian mobilisation, the extent to which it remains impervious to such processes, or the different ways the phenomenon is socially experienced, interpreted and redefined, remain legitimate questions, subject to scholarly debate and requiring continuous research.

Locating Sectarianisation through Narrative Analysis

The outcome of sectarian influences depends upon individual modes of interpretation, internalisation and reconstruction of meaning. In other words, the impact of sectarianisation on society is not self-evident and can never be assumed.[8] Agency cannot be reduced to a matter of receptive and reactive device without autonomous potential over itself or the structures at play. Similarly, it cannot be isolated from material conditions that play a structuring role. In other words, social perceptions are the product of both subjective and structural processes. This means that exploring the dynamics of sectarianism and sectarianisation in the Syrian conflict cannot omit subjective processes of internalisation and socially derived languages and cognitive strategies that shape socio-cultural perceptions, cognitive strategies for constructing meaning and discursive habits or modes of representation.

The narratives highlighted in this chapter challenge causal or linear conceptions of correlations between alleged pre-existing sectarianism and post-2011 sectarianisation: where one either created the other or intensified and inevitably became the other.[9] The two are outcomes of distinct processes and therefore must be analysed separately to qualify the nature of their linkages. Ethno-religious subjectivities are not decisively defined by sectarian political strategies (before the conflict or throughout), and there

---

[7] Aymann J. Al-Tamimi, 'The Syrian Civil War & Demographic Change', *aymennjawad.org*, 15 March 2017. http://www.aymennjawad.org/19745/the-syrian-civil-war-demographic-change; Aziz al-Azmeh, 'Civil War in Syria', interview by Ardeshir Mehrdad, *Middle East for Change*, 20 November 2016. https://www.strikingmargins.com/news-1/2017/3/6/interview-with-prof-aziz-al-azmeh-civil-war-in-syria.

[8] Rex Hudson, *The Sociology and Psychology of Terrorism: Who Becomes a Terrorist and Why?* (Washington, DC: Library of Congress: Federal Research Division, 1999).

[9] This refers to the argument whether sectarian mobilisation during the conflict created an unprecedented ethno-religious communitarianism in Syria, or pre-existing 'primordial' sectarianism hardened and manifested during the conflict.

is no evidence to suggest that the sectarianisation that emerged during the conflict is the outcome of hardening 'primordial hatreds' that led to sectarian mobilisation.[10]

Despite the lack of causality or linearity between the two, dehumanising narratives and discourses that were constructed throughout the conflict towards social others were bifurcated along the dual lines of ethno-religious markers and political allegiances during the conflict. Where those two distinctions met to define the same social other, novel notions of antagonistic ethno-religious communitarianism emerged. In contrast, pre-existing notions of ethno-religious communitarianism were defined by the immediately preceding histories and experiences of social coexistence. The narratives reveal that notions of coexistence not only persisted until the period of data collection (late 2014), but also acted as a counter narrative that effectively resisted the emergent ethno-religious dehumanisation and antagonism. This is apparent in the tensions found in narratives voiced by participants where contradictions commonly featured between and within narratives voiced by participants.

The narratives reveal a post-2011 Syrian context of contradictory and competing subjectivities, reflecting a society negotiating and clashing over what unites and/or divides it in a moment of political and, for many, existential crisis. The plurality of narratives and contradictions therein further illustrate the limits of sectarianisation and demonstrate its inability to homogenise social subjectivities in the first few years of the conflict as it neither eliminated the fluidity between different ethno-religious communities, nor homogenised the diversity within each group. Nonetheless, despite being a non-hegemonic social construct, the emergent sectarianism cannot simply be reversed by changing the conditions that led to it. Once it commands a prevalent stance as a dominant code and output of emergent institutional arrangements, it 'becomes deposited in persons in the form of lasting dispositions, or trained capacities and structured propensities to think, feel and act in determinant ways, which then guide them'.[11] Therefore, to depict an emerging habitus of

---

[10] Christopher Phillips, 'Sectarianism and Conflict in Syria', *Third World Quarterly* 36, no. 2 (2015): 371; Joshua Landis, 'The Great Sorting Out: Ethnicity and the Future of the Levant', *Qifa Nabki*, 18 December 2013, https://qifanabki.com/2013/12/18/landis-ethnicity/.

[11] Loïc Wacquant, 'Habitus', in Jens Becket and Zafirovski Milan (eds), *International Encyclopedia of Economic Sociology* (London: Routledge, 2005), 316.

sectarianism as an outcome of state atrophy, this article presents data regarding the meanings behind both dehumanisation and ethno-religious differentiation in the same sectarian categories and terms used by the parties of the conflict itself. The reason for this is that categories act as powerful cognitive channels and tools to conceptualise and classify complexity that may otherwise be inconceivable to human cognitive abilities, especially under conditions of overwhelming violence and complex trauma. To understand such language, categorical reasoning and communication need to be unpacked and elaborated as they encapsulate 'maximum information with the least cognitive effort'.[12]

Conceptual Framework

The narratives presented were collected in the form of semi-structured interviews with Syrians from different regions, ethnicities, religions, genders, age groups and levels of education. These narratives provide a sample of local perspectives, worldviews and modes of thinking regarding ethno-religious relations in a context of heightened violence. The first two fieldwork sessions were conducted in Syria between the months of July and August 2011. Interviews were obtained from the province of Aleppo. Between December 2012 and August 2014, further interviews were conducted intermittently in suburban Beirut with Syrians residing in Lebanon, who left Syria as a result of the war. Given that topics such as sectarianism were generally taboo in Syria, Syrians who fled the conflict for the short-lived and relative security of Lebanon were less pressured by these factors, something that encouraged active participation.[13] These enabling circumstances in Lebanon changed as the civil war in Syria and growing government-led xenophobia in Lebanon intensified after 2014, negatively affecting the responsiveness of participants approached after February 2014.[14] To ensure as much as possible that respondents' testimonies

---

[12] Rogers Brubaker, *Ethnicity without Groups* (London: Harvard University Press, 2006), 71.
[13] Information such as interviewees' place of residence in Syria, departure date and conditions of departure were elicited and confirmed through third parties. Respondents participated in interviews as civilians. Some have explicitly identified themselves on record as being supporters of certain armed factions, and others have even alluded to participating in military activities during the conflict. All respondents have expressed their opinions and shared their narratives in their capacities as civilians without formal affiliation with armed groups.
[14] The security situation in Lebanon deteriorated significantly after 2014. Multiple suicide attacks targeted both the Lebanese army and Hezbollah strongholds. See Dana Khraishe, 'Car bomb in Beirut kills four, wounds 77', *The Daily Star*, 2 January 2014. http://www.dailystar.com.lb/News

were relevant and not misinterpreted, the chapter focuses mostly on data gathered between December 2012 and February 2014 when the Syrian conflict witnessed the prominence of sectarian factions.[15]

A total number of sixty-three interviews were obtained from different Syrian ethno-religious groups, including individuals who identify as Alawite, Sunni-Arab, Sunni Kurdish, Armenian, Greek Orthodox and Assyrian. Interviewees came from different parts of Syria including Aleppo, Damascus, Hasakah, Raqqa, Deir el-Zor, Tartous, Latakiah, Hama and Homs. Despite the relatively small number of interviewees, the diversity amongst the participants enables a discussion of salient features and dominant cognitive strategies across different positionalities.[16]

Narratives are outlined under three salient thematic foci: (1) dehumanisation, (2) oppression and (3) intermarriage. Through these themes, sampled

---

/Lebanon-News/2014/Jan-02/242913-huge-explosion-rocks-beiruts-southern-suburbs.ashx. The attacks were a reply to Hezbollah's growing involvement in Syria and the Lebanese army's stance. Lebanese government officials also released multiple statements about the country's inability to host Syrian refugees. See Najib Mikati, 'My country cannot cope with the Syrian refugee crisis', *The Telegraph*, 21 January 2014. https://www.telegraph.co.uk/news/worldnews/middleeast/lebanon/10587174/Lebanon-PM-My-country-cannot-cope-with-the-Syrian-refugee-crisis.html.

[15] The Lebanese Hezbollah's and other Shi'a militias' presence in Syria started in 2012 and had increased significantly by 2013. This further fuelled the sectarianism of factions such as Nusra and IS who reached their peak in 2013 and 2014 with multiple sectarian attacks, statements and policies. See Rania Abouzeid, 'The Jihad Next Door: The Syrian Roots of Iraq's Newest Civil War', *Politico Magazine*, 23 June 2014. https://www.politico.com/magazine/story/2014/06/al-qaeda-iraq-syria-108214. See also, 'Deadly Experience', *The Economist*, 20 August 2015. https://www.economist.com/middle-east-and-africa/2015/08/20/deadly-experience; al-Tamimi, 'The Islamic State of Iraq and ash-Sham's Dhimmi Pact'.

[16] As a researcher, my profile as a Lebanese-Armenian with Syrian-born parents almost certainly meant that many interviewees attributed to me a certain bias, with consequences for the data gathered. During initial field visits, my Lebanese Armenian profile seemed, to many, to be an indication of neutrality and impartiality. This, in a context in which identity and ethno-religious belonging were not as politicised as they would soon become, interviewees were generally responsive in the usual context of caution and scepticism when discussing politics and identity in Syria. With minority groups, I was aware of the possibility that they perceived me as biased towards them. For interviewees from the Sunni-Arab communities (and to an extent those from the Kurdish population), I believe, I was typically perceived as a distant individual who was interested in a cause that a lot of Syrians were passionate about, but very few outside Syria were actually informed about. In the later stages of the research, these attitudes and perceptions changed. The politicisation of ethno-religious belonging, combined with the involvement of neighbouring countries such as Lebanon in the Syrian conflict increasingly stigmatised my role as a researcher, diminishing my perceived neutrality and the responsiveness of interviewees. My Lebanese accent revealed my identity to interviewees. Most interviews were conducted in Arabic and some in Armenian. I personally translated all data into English.

narratives highlight processes of intensifying sectarianism characterised by ethno-religious differentiation as well as lack of trust and increased animosity towards social others. While ethno-religious differentiation and communitarianism is affirmed as present before the conflict, dehumanising notions of ethno-religious others are stated as emergent, unprecedented, provoked and/or contingent. The term communitarianism describes perceptions of communal relations in Syria before the conflict with more accuracy and sensibility to the diversity and fluidity of inter-communal relations than the term sectarianism. Communitarianism, defined as the individual's sense of belonging and responsibility to a perceived community, considers the importance of communities as categories of dynamic social structuration without predetermining communal relations to predefined markers of identity such as ethnicity, religion or confessional belonging.[17]

Subjectivities
Dehumanisation

The narratives presented here are divided amongst those who attributed all exclusionary outlooks in society to exclusionary opposition groups and those who attributed them to government forces. Either way, the data indicates a shift in perceptions of ethno-religious relations from 'normal' to antagonistic. More than half of interviewees felt that relations amongst Syria's ethno-religious communities used to be 'normal', 'neighbourly' and 'amicable'. For example, a staunch opponent of Islamic groups identifying as Alawi from Hama claimed that, in his area, Sunni-Arabs made up around ninety per cent of the population, and his community, along with other Christian communities, made up the remaining ten per cent.[18] When asked about the social interactions between the Sunni-Arab majority and the other groups he said, 'The relations were perfect. There was nothing wrong.'[19] Another interviewee identifying as Alawi from Tartous claimed that in his area where almost ninety

---

[17] Shlomo Avineri and Avner De-Shalit, *Communitarianism and Individualism* (Oxford: Oxford University Press, 1992); Aziz al-Azmeh, 'Sectariansm and Anti-Sectarianism', *Striking from the Margins*, 1 December 2017. https://www.strikingmargins.com/news-1/2017/12/20/prof-aziz-al-azmeh-sectarianism-and-antisectarianism.
[18] I42, Author's interview, Lebanon, December 2013.
[19] Ibid.

per cent are Alawis, with Sunni-Arabs making up about five per cent of the general population,

> *Everything was just fine, there was nothing happening between us. We were all fine. Not only between these two towns [Banyas and the rest of Tartous] but even with Darʻa [Sunni-Arab majority], there were no issues at all before the 'events'. Before the events nobody asked about sect or religion.*[20]

It is worth considering that as respondents express their views about how enviable relations were prior to the conflict, they are modifying their assessment of these relations based on the conditions in place at the time of the interview. In other words, the same respondents who have described pre-war communal relations as 'normal' or 'perfect' could have expressed different opinions had they been asked prior to the conflict. In other words, these narratives do not assert that communal relations were perfectly harmonious prior to the conflict in Syria. Rather, what these narratives illustrate are the mechanisms and factors that have influenced respondents' narratives about communal relations throughout the war. According to respondents, the primary stated factor that transformed perceptions of communal relations from 'normality' to antagonistic or even a state of enmity was a perceived existential threat, which necessitated isolationism as a safety measure. Relative to how things were prior to the escalation of the conflict, respondents deemed relations to have become far worse. In fact, many respondents have acknowledged that oppressive arrangements targeted certain communities before the conflict to express their awareness of communal issues. Prior to focusing on the theme of oppression, it is important to elaborate on the state of dehumanisation and antagonistic othering that developed during the course of the war. This helps us distinguish narratives of post-war dehumanisation and those of pre-war ethno-religious discrimination and oppression.

An Assyrian interviewee from Hasaka working as a concierge in suburban Beirut described his region as fifty per cent Sunni Muslims and fifty per cent other minorities (mostly Kurds, then Assyrians and Armenians). According to him, these different groups never had issues: 'in fact, all the different sects were very close to one another. Everyone would invite each other to weddings

---

[20] I45, Author's interview, Lebanon, December 2013.

or funerals regardless of religious belonging.'²¹ When interview questions turned toward ethno-religious relations after the onset of the conflict, most interviewees from the Alawi and Sunni communities considered each other as social others, rarely refraining from expressing scepticism and lack of trust towards individuals from the other group. Given the nature of the conflict in Syria and the brutal power struggle between sectarian armed factions, the antagonisation of ethno-religious communities is an indication of successful strategies of mobilisation.

An Alawi interviewee working as restaurant manager said he truly believed that there were alternatives to the Assad government: 'no one believes, including me, that if Assad is gone, the country will be dead or will be destroyed. There are alternatives, I'm sure.'²² The problem, as he saw it, was that the other groups could not be trusted:

> *In Banyas when they took to the streets and organised rallies they were yelling right in front of us that they want to send the Alawis to the coffin and the Christians to Beirut. Nowadays that's no longer the case, even the Christians will be sent to the coffin.*²³

The person was not in Banyas to witness those expressions and was not able to validate them, yet believed such a narrative to be true. A Sunni-Arab interviewee commenting about the Alawi community mentioned, 'They only believe in power, self-interest. They are in power and that's all they want to do – mostly represented by the existing government. They have enslaved our society.'²⁴ This statement is highly representative of the logic of dehumanisation during the war – respondents did not distinguish between combatant parties and the general populace; most Alawis were deemed one and the same as those in power, and most Sunnis were deemed affiliates of Jihadi groups.

Antagonistic views about other ethno-religious communities were not limited to Alawi and Sunni communities. An Armenian from Aleppo explained that there were no longer any mixed areas, with different communities having withdrawn to their own strongholds. He said that the conflict

---

[21] I52, Author's interview, Lebanon, January 2014.
[22] I42, Author's interview, Lebanon, December 2013.
[23] Ibid.
[24] I50, Author's interview, Lebanon, January 2014.

between the different communities had become existential, a battle for survival: 'There were areas where people [from different communities] have been living together for a long time. After the events they started killing each other.'[25] Another interviewee identifying as Armenian from Aleppo said, 'if Assad falls we'll be stamped on. The Muslims won't let us live.'[26] She spoke of how Armenians were targeted by theft and kidnappings for blackmail. The reason, she said was that 'they [affiliates of Sunni-Arab opposition groups] are the filthiest people you can ever meet'.[27] Dehumanising views towards the Sunni Muslim population circulated widely. A Sunni-Arab from Hama told this story:

> I 54: *I can give you a personal example. When I went to my barber in Hama, he is an Isma'ili guy, he refused to cut my hair. He refused to take me in.*
> Author: *Why is that?*
> I 54: *He recognised me as a Sunni Muslim.*
> Author: *How did he do that?*
> I 54: *When I'm home I usually grow a beard and shave my moustache. And they can also tell from the silver ring on your finger. So he rejected me. They are afraid [. . .]*[28]

A Sunni-Kurdish university graduate from 'Afrin remarked how '*Conservatism and radicalisation are increasing not only amongst the Sunni Muslims, but also in all sects. Let's say Bashar is gone, it doesn't stop there. The war will continue. The war of sects. The war will be sectarian.*'[29]

It is noticeable that interviewees expressed scepticism and hostility towards social others regardless of specific ethno-religious markers. For instance, an Armenian tradesman from Aleppo said the same of the Kurdish population as he did of Sunni-Arabs: 'you can't trust them'.[30] When asked about the Kurds and what their religious views were, he answered confidently: '*Do they have a religion? They don't have a religion. They worship fire. Just because of interest*

---

[25] I40, Author's interview, Lebanon, December 2012.
[26] Ibid.
[27] I41, Author's interview, Lebanon, December 2013.
[28] I54, Author's interview, Lebanon, January 2014.
[29] I39, Author's interview, Lebanon, December 2012.
[30] I40, Author's interview, Lebanon, December 2012.

they claim to be Sunnis [. . .] At the end of the day, they're all the same. Kurds are similarly irrational. You can't reason with them.'[31]

A similar narrative on the Kurds came from an Assyrian interviewee from Hasaka. When asked about the situation in Hasaka he said that Kurdish forces were defending their area. However, when asked about the Kurds' hostility towards the government and the fact that, for example, they were barred from teaching Kurdish history in schools, he quickly replied saying, '*What history? What are you talking about? Do Kurds have history? They have no history*'.[32] The same interviewee had this to say about the Sunni Muslim population: '*These people can only function with dictatorships and strong rulers. Uncivilised bunch. How do you expect democracy and freedom to work in a society like this?*'[33]

Nearly all narratives surrounding social relations after the conflict expressed a heightening of distrust and often an open dehumanisation of the ethno-religious social other. The most important finding in this regard was that hostile or dehumanising opinions after 2011 engulfed even groups somewhat distant from the armed conflict and expressed similarly dehumanising perspectives on one another. According to interviewees, the fact that such dehumanising views were rarely expressed prior to the conflict reveals the respondents' awareness of the differences in their views before and throughout the conflict. The next section explores notions of ethno-religious relations prior to the conflict to highlight reflections on perceptions of ethno-religious relations before and after 2011.

Oppression

When asked why they were resentful towards other groups, many interviewees pointed to the existential implications of the struggle for power as well as the history of their sect as victims of oppression and injustice. This sense of unfair treatment of one's sect informs narratives of communal relations even prior to the conflict. In other words, some of those who expressed that relations were 'normal' also acknowledged pre-existing issues directly or indirectly.

---

[31] I40, Author's interview, Lebanon, December 2012.
[32] I52, Author's interview, Lebanon, January 2014.
[33] Ibid.

Expressions of strong pre-existing ethno-religious solidarity can be seen in an Alawi interviewee's claim about Alawi and Sunni in-group solidarities that, based on lived experience, did not imply hostility prior to the conflict:

> *The Alawi would never deny being Alawi. They would never claim being something different or not being Alawi. It's engrained in us. With the Sunnis too, that's how they are. They do the same. And we do the same. This is how we are. We don't get scared. We say it. But now that everything is based on sectarian discrimination, if you hire someone you don't trust they might put a bomb in your house or something of the sort.*[34]

Responses reveal that the transition from 'normal' to antagonistic relations came about through a self-reinforcing cycle of dehumanisation between individuals from different communities. Perceived lack of trust and animosity on the part of the social other reinforced the lack of trust and animosity extended towards the social other. This cyclical pattern is the pyscho-social mechanism that provides the emergent antagonistic and dehumanising sectarianism a degree of autonomy to reinforce themselves in circumstances of state atrophy, and devolution of violence and lack of a unifying structure.

Narratives about social relations prior to the conflict, including those who affirmed that communal relations were amicable and 'normal', explicitly acknowledged and affirmed pre-existing oppressive arrangements. Slightly less than half of respondents argued that communal relations in Syria included asymmetric and oppressive elements. Here, there seems to be a contradiction: how could communal relations be deemed normal and oppressive at the same time? Pre-existing oppressive arrangements were hardly ever projected towards other communities as such, but rather attributed to the nature of state–society relations. In other words, the oppressive state of affairs, specifically regarding the Kurdish population and the Sunni-Arab population, was not a matter of one ethno-religious community oppressing another, but rather a political configuration imposed by those in power. Hence, while ethno-religious relations were deemed 'normal' and even 'perfect' between communities themselves, some communities perceived themselves as marginalised and oppressed by the power structures in place. The dehumanising sectarianism that was expressed

---

[34] I45, Author's interview, Lebanon, December 2013.

after wartime mobilisation, on the other hand, was directed towards individuals and communities as such and distinctions between armed groups and civilians were blurred.

Interviewees who were sympathetic to exclusionary Islamic groups, for instance, spoke of Syria before the conflict as a severely divided country, characterised by formal and informal structures that divided the population into first-class and second-class citizens. They spoke of being treated as second-class citizens, and of being treated as such because of their ethno-religious affiliation. Similar narratives were more broadly echoed by Kurdish and Sunni-Arab interviewees. An interviewee identifying as Sunni-Kurd from 'Afrin explained:

> *We [Kurds] are second-class citizens [. . .] they don't treat us like the rest of them. For instance, if you want to get married you need to have a security clearance from the government. This only happens in Kurdistan [Northern Syria]. Meaning if you want to sleep with your wife you need to have the government's approval. Otherwise they won't issue a licence, a permit. You'll have to pay a ton of money and a few sacks of sugar. We don't get government jobs. They don't give us any political freedoms. Because we have these rights taken from us and to prevent us from taking these rights back we are oppressed.*[35]

When it was mentioned that other communities shared the same sense of victimhood and oppression, he remarked,

> *Armenians or the Turkmens are not persecuted for example, because they have no claim to land in Syria. Armenians have their churches and schools and what not. Our leaders, on the other hand, have been imprisoned for decades, because they talked about self-governance.*[36]

Another interviewee identifying as Sunni-Kurd from Kobani detailed the social oppression he had experienced:

> *In school, the history teacher was Alawi, and during history lessons he had never mentioned about the Kurds at all – as if we never existed. One day, I told him that this isn't right and these history books are misleading. They*

---

[35] I46, Author's interview, Lebanon, January 2014.
[36] Ibid.

called the police on me and detained me for interrogation. They were trying to instil fear in me to give away information about who is educating me in these matters related to Kurds in Syria. They ended up telling me not to talk about such things any more. It's the same in universities. You can learn Hebrew in Syrian universities, but you can't learn Kurdish. My brother complained about this, they told him they would kick him out if he brings this up again.[37]

The sense of being oppressed by the political system in place was common amongst other communities as well. Nevertheless, it was Kurdish and Sunni-Arab interviewees who felt most strongly that their communities were singled out and systematically targeted. '*For example, we in Dar'a pay more taxes than other areas, the extra money goes to Alawis to have them stay loyal to the regime,*' claimed an interviewee identifying as Sunni-Arab.[38] Another interviewee also identifying as Sunni-Arab from Deir el-Zor said,

A very close friend of mine was detained for three years and then imprisoned under charges of terrorism for being a Shari'a student. Is that fair in your opinion? He is now a member of the Nusra. You can also tell from the way in which the Sunnis are treated in the army. Sunni Muslims are always relegated to lower ranks in the army. The Alawis on the other hand are all generals and commanders. The Alawi officials consider Sunnis as outsiders. The Sunni Syrians are considered strangers in the Syrian army. We are strangers in our own country's army. What do they think they are doing? How long do you think they'll get away with this? And that's why people had started gathering weapons from before. The state and the police were no longer there to protect us. So our tribes had weapons just in case they need it. And now it turns out we need these weapons against the regime itself.[39]

As interviews focused on topics of social and political oppression, interviewees increasingly revealed that the defining features of 'us' and 'them' had already been presented before the conflict but were limited to relations between

---

[37] I55, Author's interview, Lebanon, February 2014.
[38] I50, Author's interview, Lebanon, January 2014.
[39] I58, Author's interview, Lebanon, February 2014.

oppressor and oppressed. In other words, sectarianism was imposed by an oppressor driven by sectarian motives.

For interviewees identifying as Sunni-Arab with a sympathetic view of radicalised Islamic groups and who felt a strong sense of victimhood, the crucial antagonistic social 'other' was often specified as the group in charge of decision-making, the state and the security apparatus. This was the Assad family and the political elite surrounding them. The Assad family however, especially after the conflict, was often deemed an extension of the Alawi community:

> I 53: *I have to say the Sunnis used to get annoyed by the Shi'a.*
> Author: *Why is that?*
> I 53: *Well they didn't allow us to teach the Qur'an for instance.*
> Author: *The Shi'a didn't?*
> I 53: *Yes, the ruling class.*
> Author: *You mean the Alawis?*
> I 53: *Well, Shi'a and Alawis are the same thing.*
> Author: *So why didn't they allow you to teach the Qur'an?*
> I 53: *They wanted to transform society in their own image. They all believe in secularism and consider themselves secular. They wanted to have everybody be the same. But the fact is, secularism is supposed to allow all religions. This is not the case in Syria. If you're a Sunni you have less religious freedom than others.*[40]

Notions of pre-existing sectarian segregation and discrimination voiced by interviewees in this chapter are founded on the different ways different social groups were deprived of opportunities compared to others. Those notions speak directly to institutionalised sectarianism, as highlighted in the previous chapters. However, the Assad rule's sectarian modes of operation neither confirm the sectarian motives of those in power nor deny the sectarian facets of power structuration. In other words, sectarian modes of government, as discussed in the previous chapter, may be strategically used without being decisively informed and determined by sectarian ambitions or motivations.

---

[40] I53, Author's interview, Lebanon, January 2014.

While the sectarian constituency of state institutions is evident, it is reductionist to portray that the Assad rule was motivated and guided by sectarian ambitions in the sense that it strove to improve the situation of Alawi communities and blindly trusted Alawis, whereas Sunnis were deemed untrustworthy and intentionally marginalised on the grounds of their religious beliefs or belonging.[41] The power structuration within the institutions of violence was based on loyalty networks. Appointments within the military were not necessarily based on the segregation of different ethno-religious denominations. Rather, appointments were based on an assessment of loyalty and asymmetric dependencies. In this sense, the sectarian aspects of state institutions were an outcome of expanding networks of loyalty and kinship within state structures rather than the actual motivation, structuring logic and organising principle behind appointments.

Perceptions of sectarianism were based on an account of political processes of power structuration and were not defined or solely informed in any decisive measure by an already existing predominant social reality of sectarianism. This is yet another indication that the political and the social should be studied as somewhat distinct. This does not, however, deny that there are correlations between political and social aspects of sectarianisation. Institutional nepotism, predominantly within the institutions of violence, led those who did not enjoy equal opportunities and access to government positions to mistrust those behind the state and perceive them as sectarian. In turn, this mistrust led to increased mistrust and scepticism on behalf of those in power who continued to rely on their networks of trust and loyalty. As the interviews suggest, this notion of sectarianism before 2011 applies to state–society relations and is political in essence rather than a comprehensive socio-cultural reality found in perceptions of inter-communal relations or interactions between social groups.

This point is also evident from respondents that deemed the oppression against their communities not limited to local matters and linked with regional or global questions. An interviewee identifying as Sunni-Kurd from 'Afrin explained: *'Kurdistan is stolen by Turkey, Jordan, Iraq, a part of Russia and*

---

[41] The last chapter on civilian efforts towards community protection elaborates on the marginalised status (socio-economically and institutionally) of the 'Alawi population in Latakia countryside.

Saudi Arabia. This is called Grand Kurdistan. Mesopotamia is us. We were here since the beginning [. . .] We are oppressed in Turkey, in Iran, in Iraq, in Syria.'[42]

An interviewee identifying as Sunni-Arab from Deir el-Zor, a staunch supporter of Islamic groups, spoke of the labels used to refer to the Islamic groups. This man saw al-Qaeda as friends: '*they are the good guys who stand up for the Muslims. They stand for the oppressed.*' During our conversation it became clear that his understanding of al-Qaeda, much like those who expressed apologetic views, was based on the organisation's performance in a local context, not on al-Qaeda's international profile. '*Who else was there to fight for us against the government? There was nobody,*' he said.[43]

The interviewee went as far as denying accusations of the oppressive theological outlook of these exclusionary groups when it came to other ethno-religious communities. When asked about the massacres that had been perpetrated by Islamic groups, his answer was that these crimes must have been committed by the government's secret services and their militias. He said that Islamic organisations don't commit such crimes, as they are prohibited in Islam. He situated these accusations in the context of propaganda against Sunni Muslims. '*They want to finish us,*' he said. He provided this last statement on the innocence of exclusionary Islamic groups when it came to such acts:

> *They label us as extremists as terrorists because they are targeting us. None of these accusations are true. They are against us because we don't follow the US and we don't follow secularism. Let me ask you a question. When the Christians come from Europe to Africa and preach Christianity and spread their message, nobody seems to notice or care about it. But when we talk about our religious rights and spreading the message of Islam, the entire world goes crazy and it's deemed unacceptable. How do you explain this? Isn't this oppression?*[44]

---

[42] I46, Author's interview, Lebanon, January 2014.
[43] I53, Author's interview, Lebanon, January 2014.
[44] Ibid.

Intermarriage

The topic of intermarriage clarifies the already explored themes of ethno-religious relations prior to the conflict, specifically narratives about 'normal' relations and what the 'normal' state of affairs had been for respondents. It was noticeable that, while interviewees claimed good neighbourly relations between different ethno-religious communities, nearly all said that intermarriage was uncommon, even intolerable. The function of ethno-religious sectarianism appears to be social differentiation on personal and collective levels. However, ethno-religious distinctions were never an obstacle to social coexistence or interaction. In addition, the operational space of social sectarianism was notably limited to private life in the context of personal values and family values. In other words, ethno-religious differences only mattered according to interviewees in the context of marriage, the role of women in family and society, and childhood education and early upbringing. As evident from narratives about intermarriage, these differences only came up at the private level and were never consequential in any public domain such as in economic exchanges or in the context of work. The narratives around intermarriage further accentuate the distinct features of pre-existing communitarianism and its fundamental difference from the emergent dehumanisation.

An interviewee from Hasaka noted that intermarriage between the different communities of his area was impossible.[45] An interviewee identifying as Armenian from Aleppo similarly claimed that intercommunal relations were excellent, but that contemplating intermarriage was a step too far:

> I 55: *We have plenty of Sunni Muslim friends. My husband works with Sunni Muslims and he has Sunni work partners.*
> Author: *Are you OK for your kids to intermarry with a Sunni Muslim?*
> I 55: *Impossible. Impossible. That's unacceptable.*
> Author: *How about before the events?*
> I 55: *Before or after. It doesn't matter. We don't intermarry. We might intermarry with other Christians. But not with Muslims.*

---

[45] I52, Author's interview, Lebanon, January 2014.

Author: *Why not?*

I 55: *We are very different. We have different values. We're incompatible.*

Author: *How come you're incompatible? You just said you have a lot of friends who are Sunni Muslims.*

I 55: *We're incompatible when it comes to family matters and social issues. It's easy to be friends and respectful with people. But to marry someone who is different with different values, with opposite values in fact, that's impossible. How do you raise your kid? We would marry Christians because we have similar views regarding women and things like that.*[46]

The same rejection of intermarriage between different religious denominations was expressed by a Sunni Muslim from Hama: '*In general, different sects do not intermarry,*' he said, '*we attend other people's weddings, people from different religion. But we don't intermarry.*'[47] Similarly, an interviewee identifying as Assyrian from Aleppo stated firmly, '*no way, there's none of that*'.[48]

Despite claims of amicable relations between different sects, almost all interviewees agreed that communities always maintained a certain distance from one another. An interviewee identifying as Sunni-Kurd from Kobani insisted that there was very little interaction between the different sects.[49] He said that people only came into contact in the context of work: '*other than that there's not much in common between these people. For instance, there is no intermarriage or family bonds.*'[50] He went on to say that Syrian nationalism was once unquestioned because of this distance. Perceived social differences were never an impediment to coexistence or notions of national belonging. As he saw it, sectarian and regional loyalties had always been strong in Syria, and for this reason '*it's always socially preferred to marry someone from the same town and religion*'.[51]

A second interviewee and university graduate identifying as Assyrian from Aleppo said that in her residential area, where the majority of people were either Christian or Kurd, there were no issues between them. There was 'total

---

[46] I55, Author's interview, Lebanon, February 2014.
[47] I54, Author's interview, Lebanon, January 2014.
[48] I49, Author's interview, Lebanon, January 2014.
[49] I43, Author's interview, Lebanon, December 2013.
[50] Ibid.
[51] Ibid.

harmony' between them, at least when they interacted, which was in the context of work. Otherwise, 'they stayed in their neighbourhoods and we stayed in ours'.[52] Another interviewee identifying as Sunni-Arab in Deir el-zor said,

> *There were no interactions between the different sects in Deir el-Zor. The same way that people in the countryside never interacted with people from the cities either. The same applies to genders across families. In our communities, I would never interact with women neighbours or even distant women relatives for instance.*[53]

Intermarriage between different communities came up in almost every interview, sometimes through direct questioning, but often as something the interviewees themselves brought up. Intermarriage is a significant and revealing topic when it comes to inter-communal social relations because of the symbolic value and social implications of marriage. The assumption that intermarriage between different groups is taboo rests on the prior conviction that other groups are fundamentally different, thus making it impossible to join them together as a single social unit. Those who felt that communal relations were amicable but rejected or denounced the idea of intermarriage implicitly acknowledged the place of social sectarianism in Syrian society. This does not mean that the social divisions between Syria's different ethno-religious communities were the same before and after the rise of radicalised groups. As the interviewees made clear, while 'us/them' perceptions had always been present, they had not been pervasively antagonistic in lived experiences and in interactions with the social other. Furthermore, although most interviewees were opposed to intermarriage, examples of intermarriage did come up. One interviewee went on to tell of the personal experience of his uncle's wife, a Sunni Muslim who had never been exposed to Alawi communities before:

> *My uncle is married to a Sunni woman for example; she comes from a Sunni family. When they got married, my uncle had to 'kidnap' her; they fled together because her parents didn't want to allow it, because my uncle is Alawi. Her family [denounced her]. So they moved all the way to our areas in Tartous.*

[52] I49, Author's interview, Lebanon, January 2014.
[53] I53, Author's interview, Lebanon, January 2014.

> *The first four to five days she wouldn't sleep at night. Because they've told her that we kill people in their sleep. That's what they think of us. Her family is mostly with Bashar. She only had one brother who went on a demonstration. So imagine what the ones who oppose the government think of us.*[54]

Despite antagonistic narratives of social relations and the social 'other', the majority of interviewees expressed that not all members of other social groups were the same. This was based on recollections of social interactions, exchanges and lived experiences that defy the logic of sectarianism. As is the case with the respondent above, even those affirming their or the social other's sectarian outlook do not live up to their sectarian language (in the case above, despite an avowed sectarian outlook, intermarriage and coexistence did take place). Narratives of lived experiences are inconsistent with notions of sectarianism as both were voiced by the same respondents.

As discussed, political action and behaviour are not necessarily an indication of belief and conviction. Similarly, personal beliefs or convictions do not necessarily define behaviour. In other words, the decision to side with the forces in place or oppose them is not necessarily derived from beliefs (sectarian or otherwise), rather from immediate circumstances in place and available options. This, however, does not negate the presence of sectarian modes of cognition nor does it necessitate that behaviour agrees with the dominant modes of cognition. In a context of devolving violence on the scale witnessed in Syria, necessities frequently shaped behaviour more than principles or convictions. This is the crux of the thesis on sectarianism's limits and the limits of its capacity of causation, be it before or throughout the conflict.

Most respondents made contradictory statements during their interviews, expressing both antagonistic and amicable views about the social other. While nearly all interviewees expressed a mistrustful hostility towards the ethno-religious social 'other', they also expressed some positive opinions premised on trust, empathy and notions of national belonging or unity. The reason that such contradictory opinions co-exist can be attributed to contradictory influences and factors, which compete to shape each respondent's perspectives and narratives.

---

[54] I45, Author's interview, Lebanon, December 2013.

Conclusion

In summary, narratives elicited about ethno-religious relations were shaped around two central topics: (1) perceptions of ethno-religious relations prior to the conflict and (2) perceptions of social relations after the conflict. On the first topic, narratives were divided between notions of normal, neighbourly, amicable relations, and others that avowed asymmetric, exploitative and oppressive arrangements. Even those who perceived relations prior to the conflict as 'normal' affirmed that Syrian society was comprised of different ethno-religious groups. Nevertheless, perceived ethno-religious divides were never an impediment for different ethno-religious communities to interact or coexist. Perceptions of 'normal' relations were based on the common perception of distinct communities that attempted to maintain a degree of internal cohesion and communal individuality without compromising coexistence.

Overall, sectarianism as an explanatory and analytical lens seems to take inspiration and grounding from sectarian discourses and vocabularies voiced by Syrians. Syrians, however, have voiced accounts affirming, undermining and/or denying that the conflict in Syria is sectarian. The Syrian conflict has included both sectarian and non-sectarian aspects. Social reality and social subjectivities remained pluralistic due to the unique ways different areas and communities experienced the conflict. Even when the situation in Syria lapsed into a civil war and sectarian factions became widespread and prominent, interviewees' perceptions and narratives were still diverse and shaped by exposure to myriad factors. Furthermore, the discrepancies between narratives of lived experience and discourses about social others reveal that not even those avowing a sectarian outlook (through voiced stereotypes or dehumanising vernacular) live up to that language when they are in contact with the social other.

In theory, dehumanisation, as a sociological process with its unique cognitive and social mechanisms for eliciting antagonistic and exclusionary perceptions and behaviour, is distinct from ethno-religious differentiation, which is similar to any other cognitively active but not behaviourally consequential category of social differentiation. The data reveals, however, that the two are correlated. Given that dehumanisation manifested through ethno-religious, but not theological, codes of the armed groups, it reinforces ethno-religious differentiation. Pre-existing ethno-religious communitarianism plays a contradictory role. On one hand, pre-existing notions of structural discrimination and victimhood are reproduced to reinforce post-2011 dehumanisation. On the other, notions and experiences of peaceful coexistence between communities undermine it. The contradictory influences result in pluralistic narratives that expose the limits of dehumanisation and sectarianisation. The process of dehumanisation primarily entails the reconfiguration of the ethno-religious social other by attributing additional and novel exclusionary meanings and values to ethnic and religious belonging. As shown by the interviews, given that notions of communitarianism and dehumanising sectarianism remained distinct and simultaneously at work until 2014, dehumanising notions had not evolved into unassailable belief systems – assuming such a thing could exist. The extent to which the pre-existing communitarianism has become subsumed by dehumanisation since 2014 requires further research. However, if the emergent dehumanisation is the outcome of conflict dynamics, then it is bound to eventually morph and change, even if without disappearing. How the emergent dehumanisation will change or be instrumentalised is a question that can only be answered by looking forward.

This episode of sectarianisation could have an enduring and influential presence in cognitive realities, imaginaries and memories without being an impediment to coexistence. It could also continue to be reproduced and play a structuring role in a post-conflict context, in the same way other episodes of strife and victimhood have been reproduced. The war, it seems, not only promoted ethno-religious scepticism, but also reinforced demographic isolationism and sectarian power structures with expanded dependent constituencies. Going forward, these structural elements, such as the reconfiguration of the role of the religious domain discussed in the next chapter, promise to perpetuate and reinforce, rather than undermine, factional solidarities.

4

Institutional Ecologies during State Atrophy: The Religious Field as Case Study*

The devolution of the monopoly of violence and the shrinking of the state's regulatory capacity have repercussions that are beyond the military field. The prominence of the religious field illustrates this reality. This chapter looks at the socio-economic place and political role of religion as an institutional domain under conditions of state atrophy. The religious domain witnessed significant transformations in the variety of functions it fulfilled. At the same time, the capacity and presence of religious actors increased, in terms of fulfilling socio-economic and political functions.

The prominence of the religious domain is connected to institutional developments in other domains.[1] The endowment of structuring, regulating and mobilising functions to religion in Syria after the year 2000 materialised through its expansion in public services such as aid, relief and other forms of municipal services, while the state's civic (citizenship-based modelling of political community) and developmental (equitable economic development and social welfare) functions continued to diminish. The devolution in state functions was not initiated by the state atrophy witnessed after 2011. Devolution of socio-economic public functions, from state institutions

---

* Parts of this chapter were previously presented at the 2017 Arab Council for Social Sciences Conference in Beirut, Lebanon. A more advanced draft was presented in a closed workshop at the Carnegie Middle East Centre in Beirut, Lebanon in 2018. Findings were also shared at the Striking form the Margins conference at the American University of Beirut in 2019. Parts of this chapter are published under Harout Akdedian, 'Stifling the Public Domain in Syria: Religion and State from Neoliberalism to State Atrophy' in *Striking from the Margins: State, Religion and Devolution of Authority in the Middle East*, edited by Aziz al-Azmeh et al., 91–118. London: Saqi Books, 2021.

[1] Seth Abrutyn, 'Reconceptualizing the dynamics of religion as a macro-institutional domain', *Structure and Dynamics* 6, no. 3 (2013): 1–31.

towards private interest, was underway in economic and religious forms since the neoliberal changes after the year 2000. The reconfiguration of the religious field throughout the Syrian conflict is therefore the outcome of the intersection of two sets of conditions: (1) neoliberal modes of government between 2000 and 2011 and (2) state atrophy under conditions of armed conflict since 2011. The first represents government policy to withdraw the state from public functions without compromising its regulatory capacity over other domains and the latter constitutes a period of significantly diminished capacity in service provision. Despite the fact that the two periods represent distinct processes of state atrophy, they nevertheless yielded comparable outcomes. Both periods led to a singular and uni-directional trajectory of a more limited role for the state and an increased role for the religious field in public functions. This translated to a growing strategic significance of religion for the Assad rule.

The specific roles of individual religious actors and organisations in government-controlled and opposition-controlled areas are too vast to be covered in a single chapter. The aim here is to identify shifts in institutional roles rather than present a comprehensive review of the religious domain per se. Overall, the religious field in government-controlled areas, as it did in the period before 2011, continued to remain apologetic and subservient to the political powers in place. By doing so, the religious field took on further structuring capacity in relation to the public domain. This trend of an expanding and more capable formal religious field continued to reinforce the Assad rule in a variety of ways, both symbolic and material, while further undermining the state's public functions. Although politically apologetic functions towards military and political structures in place were present in opposition-controlled areas as well, the focus of the chapter is predominantly on areas where territorial control shifted but eventually returned to government control. Looking at points when power transitioned back and forth reveals a great deal about strategies of power consolidation, institutional arrangements and the place and role of religion in what is today a government-controlled area.

State-religion relations are continuously renegotiated as the Assad rule, in its attempts to rebuild its power and capacity, specifically in the aftermath of costly military ventures, surrenders state functions to the religious field to generate influential clients and offset diminished state capacity to perform public functions.[2] While the Assad rule remains uncompromising regarding the state's regulatory capacity over the religious field, it offers prerogatives to provide public functions as a reward to co-opt new religious partners. The outcome is a continuous and more comprehensive reconfiguration of state–society relations defined by the deregulation of state functions with regard to the public.[3]

After a brief background on state-religion relations in Syria highlighting the interplay of coercion and clientelism, the chapter focuses on the religious field in Syria between 2000 and 2011. Two case studies then examine the micro-dynamics of religious actors and their social actions at the grassroots level after 2011. The case of Aleppo City highlights the differences between adjacent government-held western Aleppo and opposition-held eastern Aleppo in a diverse urban setting. The roles of religious actors in both areas provide examples of religious actors taking on municipal tasks and socio-economic distributive functions. The mass displacement of religious actors upon government takeover of eastern Aleppo, followed by the takeover of government-sanctioned actors, highlights the population strategies pursued by the Assad rule through the religious field. The case of Kassab, a provincial town on the Syrian coast where the religious field is almost exclusively comprised of Armenian religious actors, illustrates the variety of political functions, in addition to socio-economic functions, that religious actors fulfilled within government-held areas under conditions of increased militarisation and devolution of violence. The two case studies are then followed by an overview of formal (legal-rational) state-religion arrangements in government-held areas, as well as those in Idlib, Turkish-backed 'Euphrates Shield' areas and areas under the control of the SDF.

---

[2] Thomas B. Hansen and Finn Stepputat, 'Sovereignty revisited', *Annual Review of Anthropology* 35, no. 1 (2006): 295–315.

[3] The public sphere as institutional domain stands for the domain controlled by the state, which is at the general service of a given population and body politic (citizens). State control, in the sense of protection from privatisation, as well as the public function of that domain, are the determinant features that constitute the public domain. This definition is elaborated on in the Conclusion as it is analytically central for projections about state–society relations.

State–Religion Relations in Syria: The Interplay of Violence and Clientelism

The Assad rule's informal networks are composed of local clients, dependents and affiliates in areas that are more or less beyond the dictatorship's immediate reach.[4] For instance, Syria's rural periphery, from Rif Dimashq to the countryside of Aleppo, included networks of relationships that provided the Assad rule with considerable connection, access and influence.[5] These relationships developed over decades through partnerships with influential local families, business communities, tribal formations and religious leaders.[6] Some members of these networks were officially connected to the state through membership to the army, the municipality offices, governorate level institutions, intelligence offices and the Ba'th party.[7] Others were educators, relatives of officials and members of tribes without official affiliation to the state, but who enjoyed the backing of the security apparatus.[8]

Since Bashar al-Assad's ascension to power and the introduction of neoliberal policies after the year 2000, the religious field emerged as a primary site for intensifying and expanding informal and formal clientelistic arrangements. Informal networks within the religious establishment operated in the public domain, often with the direct knowledge of state bureaucracy, and served an extension of the Assad rule. With a degree of autonomy, influential members within such networks gained bargaining power vis-à-vis the Assad rule for the local services and dependencies they generated.[9] Overall, the government remained the patron due to its instruments of coercion, and religious figures and entities were clients gaining privileges in return for their loyalty and services.

---

[4] Stephen Heydemann, *Networks of Privilege in the Middle East: The Politics of Economic Reform Revisited* (London: Palgrave, 2004); Radwan Ziadeh, السلطة والاستخبارات في سوريا (Power and intelligence services in Syria) (Beirut: Riad El-Rayyes, 2013).

[5] Haian Dukhan, *States and Tribes in Syria: Informal Alliances and Conflict Patterns* (London: Routledge, 2018); Aron Lund, "Assad's broken base: The case of Idlib," *The Century Foundation*, 14 July 2016, https://tcf.org/content/report/assads-broken-base-case-idlib/.

[6] Dukhan, *States and Tribes in Syria*; Heydemann, *Networks of Privilege*; Thomas Pierret, *Religion and State in Syria: The Sunni Ulama from Coup to Revolution* (Cambridge: Cambridge University Press, 2013).

[7] Pierret, *Religion and State*.

[8] Lund, *Assad's Broken Base*.

[9] Fabrice Balanche, 'Les municipalités dans la Syrie Baathiste: Déconcentration administrative et contrôle Politique', *Revue Tiers Monde* 193, no. 1 (2008): 169–87.

The Assad rule thus gained instruments of power and influence aside from its institutions of coercion and was able to mobilise these networks for purposes of social control in various forms.[10] Informal networks provided top-down visibility and accessibility in localities while shaping horizontal resource extraction and circulation. These resources are economic through financial and profitable exchanges; social in the services they provide and social dependencies they reinforce or undermine; and cultural through their function of producing and disseminating symbols, norms and values which inform subjectivities and shape public expressions – such as expressions of religiosity or political legitimacy.

Before expanding on post-2000 developments, it is important to mention that state-religion relations in Syria were decisively shaped in the aftermath of violent confrontations between the Syrian Muslim Brotherhood and Hafez al-Assad's forces between 1982 and 2000. For the Assad rule, the 1982 Hama uprising was an existential threat – if not dealt with effectively and decisively, it threatened a nationwide uprising. Protests were taking place in locations beyond Hama, such as Aleppo. The outcome of state repression of the religious field, specifically for Sunni Islam, was its effective removal from the political field altogether. In the aftermath, the Assad rule developed and nurtured its own religious authorities in the public domain though religious figures such as the late Sheikh Muhammad Sa'id Ramadan al-Buti (prolific scholar and sheikh of the Umayyad mosque in Damascus between 2008 and 2013) and Sheikh Badreddin Hassoun (Grand Mufti of Syria from 2005 until 2021). The confined religious activism of religious figures and organisations, coupled with the explicit loyalty of the remaining religious figures, reinforced the Assad rule by neutralising ideological and political contenders.[11]

In the aftermath of the Hama uprising, the state continued its coercive policies towards the religious domain. For instance, as Pierret notes, mosques were left closed in between prayer times and religious lessons or ceremonies were virtually non-existent.[12] Simultaneous to efforts to keep religious observance and activities at bare minimum, the state prevented the growth of independent

---

[10] Stephen Heydemann, *Syria: Revolution from Above* (New York: Routledge, 2002); Bassam Haddad, *Business Networks in Syria: The Political Economy of Authoritarian Resilience* (Palo Alto, CA: Stanford University Press, 2012).

[11] This includes active unions that mobilised along with the MB in the 1980s.

[12] Pierret, *Religion and State*, 70–1.

religious networks by co-opting and supporting a new cadre of influential religious figures.[13] Rather than relegating religion to grassroots-level activism and pushing for its complete omission from the public sphere, the state kept the religious domain visible, and filled it with dependent figures, while monitoring their activities closely. For example, the Ministry of Awqaf, the official state branch dealing with religious matters and endowments, received the full backing of the state to expand its reach within the religious domain. According to the Bureau of Statistics, the budget of the ministry tripled between 1980 and 1984.[14] State-related religious institutions largely refrained from religious interpretation and issuance of religious decrees. In fact, religious decrees, fatwas and the opinions of clergymen were visibly neglected. For instance, in an interview with Pierret, 'Abd al-Qadir al-Za'tari, the fatwa secretary in 2005, noted that the position he held was vacant for a decade prior to his appointment and fatwas were limited to local level religious establishments and their constituencies.[15]

The Assad rule's efforts to contain the religious field clearly manifested in Aleppo. In the 1980s the most influential figures of the Islamic religious field in Aleppo were from the same generation as Suhayb al-Shami, the head of the Aleppo Directorate of Awqaf; all in their thirties and closely associated with the religious networks of the Nabhaniyya in rural Aleppo.[16] Al-Shami determined key appointments in the Islamic religious field in Aleppo.[17] His father, Muhammad al-Shami, associated with Muhammad al-Nabhan, the founder of the Kiltawiyya institute, was closely linked with the authorities and was assassinated by the Fighting Vanguard in 1980.[18] The Nabhaniyya's domination, along with its rural religious constituency, enjoyed the backing of the state. For instance, the brother of Suhayb al-Shami, Abdel al-Aziz became a Member of Parliament in 1990.[19] Upon his death in 2007, the seat was passed to his brother Anas.

---

[13] Sawsan Zakzak, 'القبيسيات في السياق المجتمعي السوري', *Jadaliyya*, 5 July 2018: https://www.jadaliyya.com/Details/377308.
[14] Pierret, *Religion and State*, 72; Khatib, *Islamic Revivalism*, 137–8.
[15] Pierret, *Religion and State*, 76.
[16] Ibid., 82.
[17] 'The director of religious inspection until the end of the 1990s, Ahmad Taysir Ka'ayyid and his successor Muhammad al-Hamad. Mufti of Manbij Ahmad Isa Muhammad. The teachers and representatives of western Aleppo's largest mosques.' Pierret, *Religion and State*, 83.
[18] Ibid., 83.
[19] Ibid., 84.

Leading up to the crisis in the 1980s, central plans for industrialisation alienated Aleppo's textile sector, which led urban merchants and syndicates to align with the Muslim Brotherhood's anti-Assad stance, leading in turn to one of the longest strikes in pre-2011 Syrian history during March 1980.[20] On 14 April 1980 the government dissolved professional associations and detained thousands of people.[21] The Assad rule's efforts to clear out the Muslim Brotherhood from urban areas was coupled with efforts to fill the resultant vacuum in the religious field through the rural strata of religious establishments such as the Nabhaniyya group in Aleppo. This rural strata within the Sunni religious domain was not a unified monolith. In fact, rival entities within the Sunni religious field were supported by political and security authorities. For instance, in 1984 Suhayb al-Shami oversaw the closing down of the al-Furqan Shari'a institute founded by Adib Hassun, a rival of al-Shami.[22] The balance of power started shifting toward the Hassun family as Adib Hassun's son Ahmad Badr al-Din became a Member of Parliament in 1990 and later became Mufti of Aleppo in 1999.[23] Despite its permissive stance towards the elements of the religious field that were deemed loyal, the Assad rule's mistrust of religious establishments (specifically in urban centres) never dissipated and the threat of force remained the major organiser of state–religious relations even when not exhibited. Clientelist arrangements with the religious field in Syria, similar to other neo-patrimonial arrangements in the country, are based on the same three pillars: (1) scarce rewards (often access to the state; the state as a reward or resource), (2) internal competition (amongst religious actors) and (3) the coercive capacity or the threat of the use of force by the security apparatus. These three elements combine to reward, discipline, punish and ultimately create self-censorship and self-policing in the religious field.

Devolution of State Functions and the Religious Field under Bashar Assad

Between 1963 and 2000 the number of religious associations was stagnant. In 1963 the number of associations was 596 whereas in 2000 the number of

---

[20] Most notably Aleppo's Syndicate of Engineers. See Khatib, *Islamic Revivalism*, 63.
[21] Ibid., 77.
[22] Pierret, *Religion and State*, 84–5.
[23] Ibid., 85.

registered associations was 513.[24] These numbers reflect the nature of state–society relations at the time. After the Ba'thist takeover, social services were a state responsibility and those in need received assistance through unions and state institutions. What used to be an economy based on the public sector, with primary investments in infrastructure and industry, sharply switched to private capital after the year 2000. Before then, economic policy and social responsibility were largely in the hands of the state.[25]

Religious social institutions and the neoliberal turn

After the year 2000, the state expanded the operational space for religious social institutions while simultaneously surrendering socio-economic responsibilities to private interests and withholding subsidies, increasing tax cuts, waiving the protection of domestic products, allowing foreign imports and minimising the provision of social services.

Official registration patterns reveal that the rise in the number of formal associations in Syria is not due to the establishment of new organisations per se. Many associations were in fact active in an informal capacity prior to their registration in the given period. With the new permissive stance of the Assad rule, formalisation allowed new partnerships within the state framework where social organisations could acquire further capacity to carry out their activities. On the other hand, by registering, they faced legal restrictions and more transparent and visible operational conditions, which could lead to a decrease in autonomy and freedom.[26] In addition, without formalisation, they would be subject to penal codes and legal repercussions should the state mobilise against those not abiding by its framework. Within the state bureaucracy, the process of formalisation provides the state access, information and indirect influence through regulations over those associations and the people who work in them,

---

[24] Laura Ruiz de Elvira and Tina Zintl, 'The end of the Ba'thist social contract in Bashar al-Assad's Syria: Reading sociopolitical transformations through charities and broader benevolent activism', *International Journal of Middle East Studies* 46, no. 2 (2014): 332.

[25] Shamel Azmeh, *The Uprising of the Marginalized: A Socio-Economic Perspective of the Syrian Uprising*, London: LSE Middle East Centre Paper Series, issue 6, November 2014.

[26] The Ministry of Social Affairs and Labour was established in 1955 and law number 93 was passed in 1958 requiring all associations to register with the MSAL. Private methods of regulating charity associations came through initiatives such as the Damascus Charities Union established in 1957 and the Aleppo Charities Union established in 1961. De Elvira and Zintl, 'The end of the Ba'thist social contract', 332.

in addition to a level of visibility over those who receive their services. The religious field was becoming more and more integrated within state structures and, by doing so, reinforcing the Assad rule's reign over the field by extending its reach through state institutions.

Since the neoliberal changes, religious activism has grown through expanding economic exchanges and networks. The transition came about through the professionalisation of the religious field, acquisition of resources and attainment of increased autonomy in the public field. This is apparent in the type of services provided by religious social institutions. For example, as de Elvira shows, charity associations shifted from traditional short-term aid distribution to the provision of more permanent services, functioning as stimulators of economic development at a local level: provisions of livelihood, trainings and workshops, employment opportunities, literacy courses, granting microcredits and even channelling international relief and humanitarian aid.[27] The immediate outcome was that religious networks could expand their local reach through direct interpersonal exchanges within local communities. Gradually, the redistributive functions of the state were passed to religious actors and entities who collected funds as intermediaries between local and international networks.[28]

Throughout this transition, the state either turned a blind eye to the growth of religious actors or directly encouraged it. This is best illustrated in the fact that, out of 8,731 mosques in 2007, 7,162 were informal and not registered with the Ministry of Awqaf.[29] The crucial point is that these numbers come from the Ministry of Awqaf itself. In other words, the state had full awareness of the growing religious field and favoured this expansion until it realised the challenges of curbing the growth. For example, as reported by Line Khatib, in 2006, eighty per cent of the charitable associations in Damascus were Sunni Islamic, serving a network of 73,000 families with a budget of approximately 28 million USD/year.[30] Overall in Syria, by

---

[27] De Elvira and Zintl, 'The end of the Ba'thist social contract'.
[28] Local business networks played a major role in this as donations to religious entities were a profitable marketing strategy to gain access to religious networks and develop a pious image within localities. See Pierret, *Religion and State*.
[29] Khatib, *Islamic Revivalism*.
[30] Khatib, *Islamic Revivalism*, 137.

the same year, there were 976 Islamic schools and institutes with over 9,000 active mosques, which according to Khatib offered over 400,000 lessons a week.[31] Furthermore, Khatib also reports that, despite the secular impositions of the Ministry of Education, religious networks operated within educational institutes (both private and public) and influenced the curriculum and extra-curricular religious classes.[32] In addition to the sheer number of religious social institutions, the methods of outreach (print, telecommunication, social media and other virtual platforms) employed by religious networks also demonstrate an unprecedented reach and followership between 2000 and 2011.[33]

The financial capacity of religious networks played a key role in the ability of religious social institutions to professionalise and expand when the opportunity to do so arose. According to Pierret, Islamic charity associations financially relied on religious gatherings and local business networks, with some having links to Gulf capital (through donors from the Gulf, Syrians residing and working in the Gulf or those who have amassed wealth in the Gulf and returned to Syria). Pierret also observes that the 'sheikh' and the 'merchant', as occupational roles, not only share a similar socio-economic middle class but, in many cases, share kinship ties.[34] In other words, prominent religious families, such as the Rifaʿi family in Damascus, operated profitable businesses and encouraged financial autonomy as a method of avoiding reliance on exogenous sources including the state. Furthermore, local business communities improved their image within their community and accessed religious networks in order to expand their clientele, by donating and enjoying intimate links with religious networks.[35] Christian charity organisations had similar resources, combining both local and international networks through connections to private capital in the business sector, as well as faith-based, religious and other international networks of funding.[36]

---

[31] Khatib, *Islamic Revivalism*, 137.
[32] Ibid., 138–9.
[33] Ibid., 154–5.
[34] Pierret, *Religion and State*, 144–62.
[35] For instance, the Zayd movement in Damascus, through the one who actually established the movement, 'Abdelkarim al-Rifaʿi, worked on establishing and developing such relations. Ibid., 144–62.
[36] Such as UNHCR and UNDP. See de Elvira and Zintl, 'The end of the Baʿthist social contract'.

Christian entities, however, enjoyed a disproportionate level of political permissiveness, which allowed them to tap into international religious networks, unlike Islamic institutions.[37]

The Assad rule promoted the religious field as a contested space through sect-based privileges as well. Considering the relative size of the Christian population in Syria, Christian organisations feature more prominently than one would expect, compared to Islamic organisations.[38] Furthermore, Christian organisations were allowed to operate more freely and had access to sources of funding that were not available to Muslim organisations. This was evident during the influx of Iraqi refugees in Syria after 2005. The Greek Orthodox Patriarchate of Antioch, for instance, partnered with the UNHCR and UNICEF, which were not listed amongst the foreign donors allowed to operate in Syria.[39] Christian entities thus had access to unique sources of funding unavailable to others.[40]

Overall, since the year 2000, socio-economic activism on behalf of religious networks witnessed growth and expansion in multiple fields – religious, educational, social and economic. These developments gave religious organisations an expanded social presence and influence. Given that the Assad rule ultimately controlled the institutions of violence and coercion, and determined who had access to privileges; relations between the power centre and the religious field was that of patronage and clientelism. Although the Assad rule remained in control of the religious field, the religious field had managed to expand. They had direct interpersonal relations within their localities, with face-to-face exchanges and follow-ups, in addition to more frequent and expanded gatherings within churches, mosques or informal neighbourhood gatherings.

As explicitly stated in the tenth Five-Year Plan, the government aimed to 'encourage civil society organisations' contributions to local

[37] Laura Ruiz de Elvira and Tina Zintl (eds), *Civil Society and the State of Syria: The Outsourcing of Social Responsibility* (Boulder, CO: Lynne Rienner, 2012).
[38] Twenty per cent of 2002 charity organisations were Christian (equivalent to ten per cent of the population). De Elvira and Zintl, 'The end of the Ba'thist social contract'.
[39] De Elvira and Zintl, 'The end of the Ba'thist social contract'.
[40] Other examples include, and are not limited to, Catholic Relief Services, the Jesuit Refugee Service or the ACT alliance, which is a global network of more than 145 churches working on fundraising and leasing with local churches to distribute aid.

development efforts, and provide incentives to developmental processes based upon collective efforts, and offer them financial, technical and human resources'. In other words, the authoritarian state used the provision of economic privileges and the opening of socio-economic operational spaces as instruments to politically integrate the religious field and to reinforce and expand existing authoritarian power relations. The reconfiguration of the religious field into religious social institutes, transferring state services to private entities, specifically in light of direct government contracts (*'uqud tasharuqiyya*) came as an alternative to the state but not the governing power groups. Eventually, by 2008, only 0.2 per cent of the Syrian yearly budget was spent through the Ministry of Social Affairs and Labour, and 1.2 per cent through the Ministry of Health.[41] After 2011, as the monopoly of violence was contested and both the state and the Assad rule's abilities shrank significantly, the religious field transformed radically. Nevertheless, the religious field in Syria continued to be subservient to hierarchies in place while consolidating its role as an indispensable intermediary through an increased presence in the public domain. The resultant bargaining power of the religious domain with regards to the state did not extend to the government that had captured the state or its political/military constituents. In fact, the trend of an expanding and more capable formal and informal religious field continued to reinforce neo-patrimonial power relations in government-held areas after 2011, while continuously undermining the state in its civic and developmental roles.

The Religious Domain during Conflict
The case of Aleppo

The 2011 uprising created space for the clergy, who were less favoured, or those who were utterly marginalised from local power structures, to voice their discontent or mobilise to contest existing systems of hierarchy. A growing cadre of religious clergy – specifically within the Sunni religious field – mobilised against the Assad rule even before state violence and repression

---

[41] De Elvira and Zintl, 'The end of the Ba'thist social contract', 337. The source of these numbers is the Central Office of Statistics, *Majmu'a Ihsa'iyya* (Damascus: Central Office of Statistics, 2009), ch. 14.

was deployed. Others within the religious field not only remained loyal but actively mobilised to support it. The specific political role of individual religious actors depended on the nature of the clientelistic arrangements in their locality. Regardless of political positioning, the fact that the mosque and Friday prayers emerged as the equivalent of the public square where demonstrators, including those who considered themselves secular, would gather to join a protest, is the ultimate illustration of how the religious field effectively absorbed the public sphere in developments leading up to 2011. This was not a matter of religiosity – this was the outcome of a stifled public domain.

This reality perpetuated in opposition-held areas after the militarisation of the uprising. Religious actors and associations emerged as primary actors providing social services in opposition-held areas. They were the only actors with relevant experience to take on functions of social organisation. Furthermore, as the case of Aleppo demonstrates, religious entities that gained patronage and protection from armed groups out-survived and out-competed those who did not.

By the end of 2016, opposition forces in the Syrian city of Aleppo had been overwhelmingly defeated, raising serious doubts about their ability to endure the fight against the Assad rule, the Russian government and miscellaneous Shi'i militias. The Battle of Aleppo, much like the Battle of Stalingrad in the Second World War, was decisive in determining the outcome of the Syrian conflict and was characterised by close-quarters combat, massive displacements, great destruction and recurring air raids on civilian populations and infrastructure. Given the city's demographic plurality and geostrategic importance, developments in Aleppo and its religious field illustrate the situation of a variety of religious actors during state atrophy.

By 2015, having taken over much of Aleppo's countryside and half the city, opposition forces could credibly claim effective control over a sizeable territory bordering Turkey with prospects of economic viability. In the long term, uncontested control of Aleppo by opposition forces would have provided the platform to contest Damascus as Syria's centre of power. As early as September 2012, when opposition forces entered Aleppo, local and independent initiatives of self-government, such as the Free Independent

Judiciary Council, established themselves.[42] The organisation's Aleppo branch was the most organised and influential as it provided a blueprint of local government beyond government-controlled areas. The Free Judiciary applied Syrian state law, and although lawyers and judges in the organisation considered these laws in desperate need of reform, the use of an existing legal framework ensured a consistency of judgements.[43] Syrian state law is based on a combination of sources, such as civil codes in relation to property, sales, acquisitions, rent, mortgage and trading disputes, as well as religious codes in matters pertaining to personal status law.

The Free Judiciary's legal practices were primarily based on civil law, and religious courts were only consulted at need, rather than as the default reference for legal matters. In other words, the secular character of the lawyers and judges that founded the organisation overshadowed the religious aspects or components of their judicial practice. As armed factions with a religious profile became dominant, the Free Judiciary and the independent lawyers and judges came under pressure either to be co-opted or leave and vacate the judiciary.[44] According to executive members of the Free Judiciary, armed factions deemed their efforts unacceptable. Islamic factions utterly rejected Syrian state law, considering it secular and inappropriate.[45] In addition, the Free Judiciary was considered a local competitor due to its autonomy and local constituency. Eventually, Islamic factions created their own judiciaries comprised of Shari'a courts.[46]

In the early stages of the conflict in Aleppo, Shari'a courts were needed to mediate and adjudicate disagreements between different armed factions. These arbitration or mediation cases were headed by 'sheikhs' that contenders agreed on. Gradually, however, Shari'a courts became comprehensive bodies in charge of social organisation. The religious courts resembled Assad's rule as the separation between the executive (armed factions) and judiciary (legal system) was blurred. With the proliferation of Shari'a courts with various

[42] Enab Baladi, 'Free Independent Syrian Judiciary Council', *Enab Baladi*, 26 January 2016.
[43] Ibid.
[44] Author's interview with Ali al-Jassem, member of the local council of Deir Hafer's Office (Aleppo countryside) of Relief and Aid (2012–13), Utrecht, September 2018.
[45] Author's interview with Ali al-Jassem, September 2018.
[46] The Tawhid Brigade, for instance, refused to be a part of the Free Judiciary Council and the Council was formally dissolved in October 2013.

affiliations to armed groups, judicial sentences by clerics were inconsistent and unreliable.[47] Two different courts in adjacent neighbourhoods adjudicating over the same case would provide different and possibly contradictory judgements.

In Aleppo, as early as October 2012, al-hay'a al-shar'iya was operating under the guidance and patronage of the Tawhid Brigade, the Nusra Front and other influential factions in Aleppo and Idlib.[48] Its main office was in Aleppo City.[49] Operating through a network of courts, this structure served as the main local authority controlling the police, judiciary and *hisbah*.[50] The institution's objective was to become a comprehensive body regulating judicial, executive, educational and various other societal functions.[51] As a result of disputes amongst sponsoring factions of the al-hay'a al-shar'iya, disagreements between its theologians, the blacklisting of al-Nusra as a terrorist organisation and the success of Daesh in providing a functional competing religious structure, the Nusra Front withdrew its membership, spearheading its own religious authority – the Dar al-Qada'.[52] Thus, a multitude of religious courts with varying affiliations to armed factions were active by late 2014. These Shari'a courts were responsible for all government tasks including the provision of services, food supplies, transportation and education.[53]

Aleppan sheikhs exiled in the aftermath of the unrest in the 1980s also tried to play a role in the opposition movements after 2011.[54] However,

---

[47] Author's interview with Ali al-Jassem, September 2018.
[48] 'Statement of the formation of the Shariah Committee in Aleppo and its countryside', *AMC* 11 November 2012, https://www.youtube.com/watch?v=XvH0iRsucBE.
[49] Author's notes from a closed workshop on Sunni Islam with community organisers and researchers from Syria, organised by Carnegie Middle East Centre, May 2018, Beirut. Other branches were located in al-Fardos, al-Sukari, al-Hareitan, al-bab and Azaz.
[50] Religious police monitoring behavioural aspects of society and enforcing Islamic norms and practices. See Aleppo Shari'a Commission, Branch Commission Document, 'Primary source: The structure of an Aleppo Sharia Commission branch in the countryside', *Goha's Nail*, 14 May 2014, https://gohasnail.wordpress.com/2014/05/14/primary-source-the-structure-of-an-aleppo-sharia-commission-branch-in-the-countryside-2/, accessed March 2018.
[51] Barber, 'Al-Qaeda's Syrian judiciary'.
[52] Barber, 'Al-Qaeda's Syrian judiciary'; Pierret, *Religion and State*.
[53] Author's notes from a closed workshop on Sunni Islam with community organisers and researchers from Syria, organised by Carnegie Middle East Centre, May 2018, Beirut.
[54] This is linked to the League of Syrian Ulema, which is affiliated with the Muslim Brotherhood and was overshadowed by other entities with direct reach within Syria.

their estrangement from Syria for almost three decades rendered their efforts untenable. The most serious entity to claim representation of the Sunni religious field within the opposition was the Syrian Islamic Council (2014), which included a sizeable number of sheikhs still active within Syria.[55] Aleppan Islamic scholars were barely represented.[56] As in the case of the Free Judiciary, the challenge to the Syrian Islamic Council was cooperation between the armed factions on the ground. For instance, the main factions of the Islamic Front (Ahrar al-Sham, Jaysh al-Islam), similar to the Nusra and Daesh, had established their own judiciaries and rejected the Syrian Islamic Council's calls for the separation of armed factions from local judiciaries. In line with this, Aleppo's main factions had their own respective religious authorities, which were independent of other religious authorities such as the Syrian Islamic Council. At one point, local factions in Aleppo proved to be closer to the League of the Syrian Ulema and its chair Muhammad al-Sabuni, an Aleppan sheikh exiled in the aftermath of the 1980s crackdown against the Muslim Brotherhood and other dissenting groups. In a public statement on October 2012, the leaders of the Tawhid Brigade commissioned al-Sabuni to take charge of humanitarian and relief efforts in the areas where the group operated, considering him a religious authority and reference.[57] Al-Sabuni's role diminished as the Tawhid Brigade became a shadow of its former self, and sources of funding became increasingly scarce. This was due to US sanctions and anti-terrorism laws, which restricted Gulf-based financiers and donors,[58] Sisi's takeover in Egypt, which nullified the

---

[55] Thomas Pierret, 'The Syrian Islamic Council (CIS)', *Diwan*, 13 May 2014, http://carnegie-mec.org/diwan/55580; AlJazeera, April 4, 2014, الإعلان عن تأسيس المجلس الإسلامي السوري.

[56] The most prominent figure who was also a member of the Syrian Islamic Council's executive board in 2014 was Abdallah al-Salqini, the brother of outspoken Mufti of Aleppo, Ibrahim al-Salqini, who died under mysterious circumstances in September 2011. Author's field observations, September–October 2011. The funeral of the late sheikh marked one of the first instances of anti-government protests in Aleppo, see: Yousefl Halabi, "جنازة الشيخ ابراهيم سلقيني.mpg," *YouTube*, 27 June 2012, https://www.youtube.com/watch?v=lpW5A0PkQiI; Ugarit News – Syria, "6 9 Aleppo 2ج الأموي الجامع في السلقيني إبراهيم الشيخ تشييع جنازة في المشيعين أعداد , حلب أوغاريت," *YouTube*, September 6, 2011, https://www.youtube.com/watch?v=iu162V1_PBo.

[57] Shabasy, "نداء قادة لواء التوحيد للشيخ الصابوني," *YouTube*, 22 October 2012, https://www.youtube.com/watch?v=055Izzq66JI.

[58] Most significantly in Qatar and Kuwait. The US pressure led to the resignation of Kuwait's justice minister Nayef al-Ajami, a Salafi fundraiser for multiple factions. See Elizabeth Dickinson, 'Playing with fire: Why private Gulf financing for Syria's extremist rebels risks igniting sectarian conflict at home', *The Brookings Project on US Relations with the Islamic World*, 6 December 2013, https://

Egyptian Muslim Brotherhood's support,[59] and the protracted nature of the conflict, which created fatigue amongst donors.[60]

The impact of networks of funding on armed factions, rebel alliances and ideological framing is important to point out. For instance, a previous member of Aleppo's local council's relief office recounted hosting delegations from the Egyptian Muslim Brotherhood in Aleppo that brought suitcases of cash with them.[61] The formation of the Islamic Front, and the alliance between the Tawhid Brigade (previously a part of the Syrian Islamic Liberation Front) and Ahrar al-Sham (previously a part of the Syrian Islamic Front), was motivated by efforts to frame armed factions in a manner that would attract potential donors.[62] Amongst the sources are the Turkish charity organisation IHH, which has close ties to the AKP government, the Sham Islamic Committee (Saudi-based organisation combining humanitarian and religious/missionary activism) and the global Qatari 'id Charitable Foundation.[63] Similarly, Kuwaiti charity networks became a central node in funnelling Gulf capital into Syria.[64] These charity networks were religious in nature and their donors seemed to understand the conflict in purely religious terms. Therefore, the more religiously observant an armed group proved itself to be on the ground, the more trustworthy it was deemed by donors. In fact, formal state officials in the Kuwaiti government were even involved in these transactions and clearly expressed their economic activities and support in religious and often sectarian terms.[65] Armed factions on the ground, however, were strategic about their framing and statements regarding their religious agenda. Both Ahrar al-Sham and Tawhid made ambiguous and somewhat contradictory statements about

---

www.brookings.edu/research/playing-with-fire-why-private-gulf-financing-for-syrias-extremist-rebels-risks-igniting-sectarian-conflict-at-home/.

[59] Author's in-person interview Utrecht, Netherlands, with member of the local council in Aleppo countryside, 18 September 2018.

[60] Thomas Pierret, 'Salafis at war in Syria: Logics of fragmentation and realignment', in Francesco Cavatorta and Fabio Merone (eds), *Salafism After the Arab Awakening: Contending with People's Power* (Oxford: Oxford University Press, 2017), 275–313.

[61] Author's in-person interview Utrecht, Netherlands, with member of the local council in Aleppo countryside, 18 September 2018.

[62] Pierret, 'Salafis at war', 275–313.

[63] Aron Lund, 'Syria's Salafi insurgents: The rise of the Syrian Islamic Front', *Swedish Institute of International Affairs*, March 2013, 25; Pierret, 'Salafis at war', 275–313.

[64] Dickinson, 'Playing with fire', 21–2.

[65] Ibid., 22.

their religious agendas based on the expectations of potential donors and political sponsors.⁶⁶

Alongside religious courts, religious networks, associations and charity groups linked to armed factions emerged as comprehensive bodies of local government in charge of the public field through various social services as well as relief distribution, the administration of refugee camps and other humanitarian functions. In some cases, religious indoctrination accompanied social services. Examples vary from the standardisation of veiling, to the distribution of the Qur'an, to running orphanages with life arranged around religious teachings and the memorisation of the Qur'an.⁶⁷ Of seventy-seven social and humanitarian associations surveyed in opposition-controlled areas in the province of Aleppo, forty-nine (sixty-four per cent) were religious. Twenty-one of the aforementioned organisations were outright religious through their dedication to religious activism such as proselytisation or provision of religious education. The other twenty-nine were faith-based organisations (FBOs) that provided non-religious services but were either run by religious actors and operated through religious networks or framed their organisational aims as explicitly inspired by religious principles and beliefs. According to the UNHCR, FBOs are 'a broad range of organisations influenced by faith. They include religious and religion-based organisations/groups/networks; communities belonging to a place of religious worship; specialised religious institutions that have a religious character or mission'.⁶⁸

The UNHCR also affirms that FBOs have consistently been amongst 'UNHCR's top ten implementing partners'.⁶⁹ The aforementioned organisations do not represent an exhaustive list of all organisations that have been active in opposition-held areas in Aleppo. There may be other organisations, religious or otherwise, that were not identified. Nevertheless, the

---

⁶⁶ For a detailed account regarding ideological framing and its correlations with sources of funding, see Pierret, 'Salafis at war', 275–313.
⁶⁷ Examples of such entities include and are not limited to al-Jam'iyya al-Khayriyya lil-Qur'an al-Karim, Shabab li'ajl Sourya, Jam'iyyat al-Bunyan al-Marsus al-Khayriyya, al-Jam'iyya al-Khayriyya lil-musanada al-insaniyya and Jam'iyyat sham sharif.
⁶⁸ UNHCR, *On Faith-Based Organizations, Local Faith Communities and Faith Leaders* (Geneva: UNHCR, 2014), 8.
⁶⁹ UNHCR, *On Faith-Based Organizations*.

operational methods and nature of services provided by the surveyed entities indicate an unprecedented expansion of the religious domain. Religious social institutions in the province were quickly formed in the post-2012 period of violent conflict, acting as the primary responders to the needs and hardships of local communities. In this way, religious actors emerged as trusted networks with significant capabilities through humanitarian and relief exchanges. Out of the twenty-one outright religious entities, only four were purely dedicated to proselytisation and religious education and mostly refrained from social or humanitarian services.[70] Al-Jami'iyya al-Khayriyya lil-Qur'an al-Karim, for instance, defines its mission as 'to connect all societal sectors to the holy Qur'an by memorisation, understanding, and activism through high quality methods, specialised expertise and comprehensive programmes'.[71] The organisation's activities include the direct supervision of Qur'anic activities in opposition-held areas, liaising and connecting all classes of Qur'anic memorisation in such areas, providing logistical support and achieving financial stability to schools of *hifz*.[72] In pamphlets released in early 2016, the organisation stated that in March 2016 it printed and distributed 35,515 books of the Qur'an, assisted twenty-nine Qur'anic institutes and centres as well as 32,467 Qur'anic students, and provided teacher education, professional training and other types of support to 1,487 Qur'anic educators.[73] The organisation stated that in the following month of April, it had published and distributed 19,058 books of the Qur'an, reached out to thirty Qur'anic institutes and centres (19,320 students) and supported 934 Qur'anic educators.[74]

Purely religious organisations played a key role in collaborating and coordinating with a multitude of other organisations that combined social, humanitarian and relief services with religious activism.[75] For example, Al-Jami'iyya

---

[70] Al-Jami'iyya al-Khayriyya lil-Qur'an al-Karim, Mu'assasat jil al-Qur'an, Mu'assasat al-Aqsa al-Qur'anniyya and Mu'assasat Bara'im al-Islam al-ta'limiyya.
[71] According to the organisation's website. Dead link: http://www.quransyria.org/ar/117.html (accessed 14 November 2017).
[72] Ibid.
[73] Pamphlet released by the organisation in March 2016 (author's hard copy).
[74] Pamphlet released by the organisation in April 2016 (author's hard copy).
[75] The organisation's primary activities took place in their own centres inside Syria such as Markaz Abu Obaida Bin Al-Jarrah Al-Qurani in Kafarnuran, Aleppo.

al-Khayriyya lil-Qur'an al-Karim partnered with Jam'iyyat Othman bin Afan al-Tanmawiyya, which combines relief and developmental activities with educational endeavours and proselytisation and its presence extends from Idlib to Aleppo. In one of the organisation's Qur'anic centres, Markaz Othman Bin 'afan AlQur'aniyya in Aleppo's Atarib, the two organisations consistently worked together to organise social activities. In a clear attempt at religious indoctrination, the centre targets impressionable segments of society by combining memorisation courses with entertainment events aimed at children and adolescents. Jam'iyyat Othman Bin Afan's activities include relief and aid for winter preparations, financial assistance, food rations, administration of bakeries, distribution of bread and establishing mosques and refugee camps. The organisation was amongst the most active in the besieged Aleppo City from 2015 until 2016.[76] The organisation also explicitly strove to standardise the plain black *niqab* covering the entire face including the eyes.[77]

Entities that were able to establish themselves in opposition-held areas could not operate without the consent and active support of the armed groups in place. In the case of Harakat Al-Shabab Al-Muslim in Aleppo and Idlib, for instance, the organisation was directly established by the Nusra Front around the end of 2012.[78] The organisation acted as a comprehensive social institution addressing the needs of local populations, including transportation services, through shuttles from Tarik Al-bab to Al-mashhad in Aleppo. Not all entities operating in opposition-held areas were locally housed, as some only visited to provide services and left thereafter. Regardless of the degree of affiliation with the armed forces in place, relief and social efforts acted as primary resources for the establishment of alternative forms of government and the maintenance of basic standards of liveability, without which armed groups were unable to maintain control and establish a viable political order. Furthermore, religious networks were predominant channels for social and relief services. As the UNHCR acknowledges, religious communities and actors in various

---

[76] The organisation's Youtube channel posted details on the following link which is no longer accessible: https://www.youtube.com/watch?v=nVIS MGdOI (accessed 27 February 2018).
[77] Pamphlet released by the organisation for the year 1437 AH (October 2015/October 2016) (author's hard copy).
[78] In the case of Harakat Al-Shabab Al-Muslim in Aleppo and Idlib, for instance, the organisation was reportedly established by the Nusra Front by the end of 2012. See the following statement: https://www.zamanalwsl.net/readNews.php?id=33711.

capacities proved to be key local partners, without which their access and reach within Syria would be extremely limited. Through local knowledge and grassroots connections, religious networks played a vital role for both local populations and donor entities. The head of the Syria Relief Network (SRN), Dr Kais al-Dairi, affirms that even organisations that were not religious or faith based, such as the SRN, often had to work with local religious networks to establish knowledge and local networks of aid distribution.[79]

Religious social institutions in government-held areas tended to share the same function. On one hand, given the inability of the state or municipalities to provide basic social services, religious entities began to professionalise and expand in unprecedented ways. Local religious entities, specifically from none-Sunni groups, took on a vast array of responsibilities including medical and health services, livelihood and financial assistance, administration of schools, provision of water, electricity and sanitary services, reconstruction, developmental services and employment opportunities. Religious actors deemed trustworthy in government areas were granted unprecedented prerogatives within their communities. For instance, the Aleppo Charities Union in Aleppo remained moderately active after 2011, as its board of directors were directly assigned in 2009 by Diala al-Haj Arif, the head of the Ministry of Social Affairs and Labour at the time.[80] Religious entities amongst minority groups also took on large-scale municipal tasks to offset disintegrating state structures and services.[81] For instance, religious entities sponsored the distribution of electricity through privately owned and operated electricity generators.[82] In addition, artesian water wells were dug on church premises to provide locals with access to water and offset water shortages.[83] Furthermore, the Latin Church of Aleppo, for instance, helped initiate many economic

---

[79] Author's phone interview with Kais al-Dairi, July 2017.
[80] Laura Ruiz de Elvira, 'State/charities relation in Syria: Between reinforcement, control and coercion', in Laura Ruiz de Elvira and Tina Zintl (eds), *Civil Society and the State of Syria: The Outsourcing of Social Responsibility* (Boulder, CO: Lynne Rienner, 2012).
[81] Examples include and are not limited to the Greek Orthodox Patriarchate of Antioch, the Latin Church and Syriac Orthodox Patriarchate of Antioch and All the East.
[82] Author's interview with Revd Haroutioun Selimian, the head of the Armenian Evangelical Community in Syria, Beirut, October 2017.
[83] Author's phone interview with Aleppo residents, May 2017.

projects proposed by residents, either to renovate damaged workplaces or restart businesses that were shut due to the circumstances at the time.[84]

International religious networks played a key role in funnelling aid and resources to different churches. For instance, the International Orthodox Christian Charities and the Middle East Council of Churches were able to work through the networks, churches and associations of the Greek Orthodox Patriarchate of Antioch, which enjoyed unmatched privileges in Syria.[85] The ACT alliance operates with a similar model. It is the largest coalition of Protestant and Orthodox churches and church-related organisations engaged in humanitarian, development and advocacy work in the world, and has more than 130 members (churches) from 120 countries.[86] According to their monthly and annual reports from 2017, the coalition was able to provide an annual total of USD 9,117,605.00 in direct assistance through local partners. The aid included shelters and renovation efforts, livelihood, food security and education, amongst others.[87] The cumulative sum of the aid funnelled to entities operating in government-controlled areas contributed to the maintenance of social order and upheld basic standards of liveability in those areas. Herein lie the political functions of aid distribution through religious entities during the Syrian conflict. Aid, relief and religious actors were instrumental for alleviating the impact of war and aiding in the maintenance of social order.

The case of Kasab

The case of religious organisations in Kasab illustrates the instrumentality of the religious field during conditions of militarisation. In the case of Aleppo City and its surrounding areas, territorial control shifted and military developments continuously changed local circumstances. The dynamics of the religious field in Kasab, on the other hand, illustrate bargaining processes, internal competitions and privileges at play in an area that predominantly remained under government control, except for a brief period of opposition control from 23 March 2014 until 15 June 2014. Even in a seemingly stable area such as Kasab, the role of religious actors at the level of localities has been paramount.

---

[84] Assistant researcher's interview with H.M. June 2018, Aleppo City.
[85] Author's interview with members of the Secretariat of ACT Alliance, June 2017, Geneva.
[86] 'About', *ACT Alliance*, https://actalliance.org/about/ (accessed 28 February 2022).
[87] Author's copy of internal reports at ACT Alliance (2016–17).

Religious actors in Kasab played a key role in maintaining social order, not only through relief and aid distribution, but also through their role in shaping recruitment patterns within paramilitary formations in the area.

The town of Kasab is situated in the province of Latakia on the Syrian coast, east of the Mediterranean and bordering Turkey. Although it was not until March 2014 that the area came under direct attack, the broader turmoil in the Syrian Arab Republic had been transforming Kasab since 2011. By the end of 2012, the town already lost its economic productivity and faced the possibility of being besieged.[88] Conflict dynamics brought tourism to a halt, depriving locals of their main revenue streams.[89] As a result, remittances, charity and aid played a crucial role in maintaining basic standards of liveability. These circumstances reinforced the importance of religious organisations within the locality.

On 21 March 2014 a coalition of opposition groups initiated a three-pronged attack on Kasab, coming from the east, north and northwest.[90] The incessant gunfire from all directions and the number of militants in opposition ranks overwhelmed local military formations. Al Nusra Front, Sham al-Islam and Ansar al-Sham took over the city in a matter of days.[91] Casualties were minimal among the civilian population, as locals managed to flee the area before armed opposition groups took over.[92] After government forces took control of the area in June 2014 almost half of those displaced from the community returned to their homes.[93]

---

[88] Hagop Tcholakian, *The Three Days of Kessab: 21–23 March, 2014* (Middletown: self-published, 2015).

[89] Tcholakian, *Three Days of Kessab*; Shogher Ashekian, 'Տեղահանութիւն, Հասարակական Յիշողութիւն և Անձնական Փորձառութիւն (Քեսապի Պարագայ)', in Antranik Dakessian (ed.), *Armenians of Syria: Proceedings of the Conference (24–27 May 2015)* (Beirut: Haigazian University Press: Armenian Diaspora Research Center, 2018), 509–38.

[90] Numbering around 3,000 with the frontline extending from the western villages of al-Samra, to the north of Kasab in the vicinity of Jabal al-Aqraʻ on the Turkish border and around the eastern areas of Tal 45 and Nabʻ al-Murr. 'Syrian Armed Opposition Coastal Offensive', *The Carter Center*, 1 April 2014, https://www.cartercenter.org/resources/pdfs/peace/conflict_resolution/syria-conflict/2014CoastalOffensive-April1.pdf.

[91] Tcholakian, *Three Days of Kessab*; Aymenn Jawad Al-Tamimi, *The Latakia Front: An Interview on the Rebel Side*, 6 April 2014, retrieved 14 May 2020 from *Syria Comment*; Ashekian, 'Տեղահանութիւն, Հասարակական Յիշողութիւն և Անձնական Փորձառութիւն'; The Carter Center, 'Syrian Armed Opposition'.

[92] Tcholakian, *Three Days of Kessab*; Ashekian, 'Տեղահանութիւն, Հասարակական Յիշողութիւն և Անձնական Փորձառութիւն'; Sevan Manjikian, *Քեսապ 2014: Տեղահանութիւն և Վերադարձ* (NA: Arevelk, 2017).

[93] Author's interviews (4A and 20A) with locals from Kasab, March 2020, Beirut.

Kasab's main, official community organisers were the Armenian Evangelical Church, the Armenian Apostolic Church and the Armenian Catholic Church. It is notable that members of the Alawi community did not have access to local culturally specific charitable or relief-providing associations in Kasab. Social and economic assistance was available to them outside of Kasab, specifically in Latakia City. In fact, it was not until 2019 that the first non-religious and non-Armenian charity organisation was created in Kasab, named 'al-jam'iyya al-khayriyya fi Kasab'.[94] The area's relief and aid infrastructure was therefore entirely in the hands of religious organisations. The Kasab branch of the Emergency Relief and Rehabilitation Committee (Relief Committee) was formed of representatives of existing Armenian ecclesiastic bodies in Kasab.[95] However, aid distribution was largely devised by the central committee in Aleppo City, which was comprised of the official heads of Armenian churches Syria-wide.[96] Alongside these religious organisations, as Tcholakian describes, the Tashnak, a quasi-official Armenian political party in Syria, 'effectively had the national, ecclesiastic, educational and cultural life of the region's Armenians under its control'.[97] In Kasab, the Tashnak operated through the dominant Armenian Orthodox Church.[98] Although other religious entities operated independently of the Tashnak, their constituencies were small, less organised and less cohesive.

The prominence of sect-based religious actors within this community is the outcome of overall demographic specificities in the area, as well as the institutional landscape that the Assad rule had nurtured before 2011. Demographically, before 2011, the population of the area was approximately

---

[94] Author's interview with a church representative from Kasab, March 2020, Beirut.
[95] Author's interview with the head of the Armenian Evangelical Church in Kasab before 2015, March 2020, Beirut.
[96] Ashekian, 'Տեղականութիւն, Հալաքական Յիշողութիւն և Անձնական Փորձառութիւն', 516.
[97] Tcholakian, *Three Days of Kessab*, 40; Nicola Migliorino, 'Kulna Suriyyin? The Armenian community and the State in contemporary Syria', *Revue des mondes musulmans et de la Méditerranée*, 2006, 115–16. The fact that the Tashnak, otherwise known as the 'Armenian Revolutionary Federation' or 'Tashnagtsoutiun' exists in more than twenty-four different countries provides the branch in Syria with organisational and membership structure despite not having officially recognised structures within Syria as such. In addition, the organisation acts through cultural and religious organisations that have formal recognition.
[98] The head of the church was a self-avowed member of the political party. Author's interview with the head of Armenian Orthodox Church of Kasab at the time of the attack, March 2020, Anjar, Lebanon.

seventy per cent Armenians.⁹⁹ Within Armenian communities in Syria in general, ecclesiastic bodies and religious leaders operated as official community representatives in relation to the state and the Assad rule.¹⁰⁰ Religious actors were official intermediaries between their constituents and the state under the country's personal status laws. Simultaneously, religious actors functioned as informal intermediaries between their constituents and the operatives of the Assad rule such as local intelligence agencies or other privileged cronies. Despite the history of mistrust between the Assad rule under Hafez al-Assad and Armenian sect-based organisational structures, Armenian organisations, specifically the Tashnak, were able to forge significant clientelistic arrangements that guaranteed privileges unavailable to other sect-based or religious organisations in the country. The fact that the overall number of Armenians in Syria does not pose a threat to the Assad rule, even if mobilised against it, is amongst the factors that facilitated such arrangements. A more critical driving force behind these arrangements is the fact that Armenian clerical and non-clerical representatives within the Tashnak provide access, knowledge and self-policing when needed in a community that is often deemed insular and difficult to access. Lack of access for the security apparatus translates into automatic mistrust on their behalf. Transparency and access, on the other hand, yield favours and privileges.

The symbolic benefits of such arrangements for the Assad rule are significant, specifically in bolstering the self-ascribed image of the dictatorship as protector of minorities. On the other hand, by granting access and closely collaborating with the security apparatus, religious organisations gained privileges such as running culturally specific institutions, including schools, charities and cultural associations that only served Armenians.¹⁰¹ These arrangements granted Armenian community organisers with bargaining capacity within the state apparatus while the Assad rule gained access and influence through neo-patrimonial arrangements where the welfare and prosperity of community

---

⁹⁹ Sevan Manjikian, *Թեսապ Շրջանի Հայրիթեան Աիեակագործութիւն: 2006–2007*. (Aleppo: Hamazkayin Press, 2010), 40; J. B. Khedra, مجلة خطة لتنمية السياحة البيئية في منطقة كسب واستثمارها طبيعياً. جامعة تشرين للبحوث والدراسات العلمية *1* 31, (2009): 113–31.

¹⁰⁰ For instance, the heads of Armenian churches in Syria travelled with a diplomatic passport as state representatives. Author's interview with the head of Armenian Evangelical Churches in Syria, Haroutioun Selimian, June 2018, Beirut. See also Migliorino, 'Kulna Suriyyin?'.

¹⁰¹ Migliorino, 'Kulna Suriyyin?'.

organisers and their constituents depended on maintaining the status quo and the power structures in place. In addition, bearing witness to the Assad rule's coercive capacity and the marginalisation of other communities in cultural, political and economic forms, Armenian community organisers continuously offered the loyalty of a small but resourceful and politically useful segment of Syrian society. These characteristics and arrangements were put to the test during the dynamics of state atrophy in Kasab.

There were two permanently stationed paramilitary formations in Kasab: one that fell under the umbrella of the National Defence Forces,[102] and another entirely comprised of Armenians who did not receive weapons or salaries from the NDF and had their own sources of funding. The latter's military equipment was light weaponry and hunting rifles, and the group patrolled the borders to provide surveillance and a measure of protection around the area. The first factions that formed in the area were the Lijan Shaʻbiyyeh (*shabbiha*) under the umbrella of the NDF. In March 2014 their forces in Kasab numbered approximately fifty militants containing an overwhelming majority of recruits from the Alawi community.[103] According to locals with intimate knowledge of the Armenians who joined these ranks, the total number of Armenian recruits was around five.[104] Both of the paramilitary formations in Kasab were under the overall command of Hilal al-Assad, who was killed in the clashes of Kasab in March 2014. The superintendent of forces in Kasab was the mayor, Vazken Chaparian.[105] However, the two factions operated under distinct local command structures and did not have a locally unified operational system. The limited Armenian presence in the NDF was not a spontaneous expression of societal structures. Religious actors had a key role in designing, mediating and facilitating these arrangements. Prior to 2014, local power rested in the hands of the Armenian Orthodox Church and its head, Father Muron Avedisian, who had a leading role in local arrangements including in relief distribution, recruitment patterns, coordinating with central religious figures in Aleppo and bargaining for approvals with the security

---

[102] Lijan Shaʻbiyyeh, otherwise known as *shabbiha*.
[103] Tcholakian, *Three Days of Kessab*; Interview 14A.
[104] Author's interview with the head of Armenian Orthodox Church of Kasab before 2015, March 2020, Anjar, Lebanon.
[105] Tcholakian, *Three Days of Kessab*.

apparatus.[106] For instance, multiple community meetings were held under the auspices of local churches to discuss such arrangements and address concerns about having a unified local structure with the NDF, which threatened to mobilise local combatants beyond the parameters of self-defence.[107]

In addition to recruitment patterns, religious actors in Kasab were able to mobilise regional and trans-local institutional ties to provide resources and aid during circumstances of urgent need. A week after the evacuation of Kasab, 1,151 Armenians were registered as displaced in Latakia by the Relief Committee.[108] Only displaced people of Armenian origin stayed in the Armenian Apostolic Church of Latakia. Having access to the church in Latakia City provided the infrastructure needed to maintain cohesion in exile and preserve the possibility of voluntary return when circumstances changed. Members of the Alawi community who moved to Latakia City received aid and support through separate organisations such as Jam'iyat Bustan al-Khayriyah, which belonged to Rami Makhlouf at the time.[109] Others were displaced to nearby towns and villages. The displaced also relied on kinship ties and extended family members who resided elsewhere.

While in exile, Armenian community organisers in Kasab were able to mobilise international networks, specifically in the diaspora and in the Republic of Armenia, for fundraising as well as other purposes. For example, a social media campaign with the hashtag #savekesab saw the likes of Kim Kardashian and United States Congress representative Adam Schiff bring the small area's circumstances to global platforms. Throughout the period of displacement in Latakia, many local and international, secular, faith-based and religious aid agencies were allowed to aid the displaced.[110] This included entities such as the Syrian Red Crescent, International Red Cross, UNRWA, UNHCR, the Greek Orthodox Patriarchate of Antioch and other churches

---

[106] Manjikian, Բուսալ 2014.
[107] Tcholakian, *Three Days of Kessab*. This arrangement of having a separate paramilitary formation was unique to Kasab and did not happen in Aleppo City, for instance, where the same Armenian organisational structures also had a presence. In Aleppo City the mobilisation of Armenian recruits was directly within the NDF even when funnelled by Armenian organisations.
[108] Manjikian, Բուսալ 2014.
[109] Author's interview with members of the Relief Committee overseeing relief operations in Latakia City, March 2020, Beirut, Lebanon.
[110] Author's interview with the head of the Armenian Evangelical Church in Kasab before 2015, March 2020, Beirut, Lebanon.

from the region, such as the Armenian Evangelical Church in Beirut and the Armenian Catholicosate of Cilicia based in Beirut. The aid that the displaced received was comprehensive and included livelihood allowances, accommodation, food, clothing, hygiene kits and other packages. A prominent community leader commented, 'our people in Kasab were more comfortable in displacement than they were in their homes'.[111]

The fundraising efforts and lack of transparency in aid distribution created significant friction between the various religious and sect-based organisations during and after displacement. The funds collected for the small community were deemed far greater than the needs of impacted individuals. Donations were often collected elsewhere and centralised with community leaders in other locations, primarily in Aleppo City. The primary religious centre for all bodies in Kasab, ecclesiastic or civil, was Aleppo City. As the situation in Aleppo worsened, and specifically during the siege of Aleppo until 2016, the salaries and funds that community organisers in Kasab had become accustomed to receiving, came to a halt. This centre-periphery dependency diminished the decision-making capacity of local religious entities. Even in the midst of displacement, donations to Kasab were funnelled through the Relief Committee in Aleppo City, which determined the resources allocated to Kasab and the resources directed to fulfilling existing needs elsewhere, predominantly based on a comparison with the level of need in Aleppo City. Some local needs in Kasab, such as heating during winter, were deemed secondary and nonessential.[112] Lack of transparency about donations gathered for Kasab created frictions within the community, such as between the Armenian Catholic Church in Kasab and the Relief Committee. The Relief Committee in Kasab excluded the head of the Armenian Catholic Church in Kasab from decision-making processes. There were frictions even between the Armenian Catholicosate of Antioch in Lebanon and the Tashnak leadership in Lebanon over the collection and distribution of aid in Kasab.[113] Furthermore, having

---

[111] Author's interview with the head of Armenian Orthodox Church of Kasab before 2015, March 2020, Anjar, Lebanon.
[112] Author's interviews with local residents and with heads of churches in Kasab, March 2020, Beirut, Lebanon.
[113] Focus Group Discussion with community representatives from Kasab and Beirut, 3–4 March 2020, Beirut, Lebanon.

full understanding of the social power behind aid distribution, religious entities refused to share databases about local residents or coordinate relief operations as a matter of policy.

When the population began to return, missing furniture and electrical appliances were widespread in residences.[114] Locals reported that the vandalism and looting of properties in Kasab had been carried out by opposition groups and pro-government forces alike.[115] Some of the summer residences that did not belong to locals were stripped of everything of value: furniture, tiles, electrical wiring and so on.[116] This type of looting has been dubbed '*ta'fish*' throughout the Syrian conflict and was directly associated with pro-government forces and the *shabbiha*. The widespread reports of local property being looted by pro-government security personnel created further tension between the local *mukhabarat* (specifically *Amen Dawle*) and religious representatives in the community.[117] Eventually, and throughout the period since the attacks, central community representatives from Aleppo with direct access to centres of power in Damascus utilised their channels to put pressure on local officials to halt such acts as they were impacting permanent residents. The matter was also brought up in a meeting in 2014 between Armenian community representatives and the governor of Latakia at the time, Riyad Hjab, who later became prime minster and the highest-ranking political dissident and defector to date.[118] Upon hearing the complaints of local representatives during the meeting, the governor threatened to throw the mayor in jail if adequate steps were not taken to address these concerns. Similarly, power-shortage concerns were addressed during such meetings. 'Right after we had those meetings, power was back almost most of the time. We had less outage than Latakia City for a while,' expressed the head of one the churches present in the meetings.[119] Such preferential treatment was not

---

[114] Author's interviews with resident from Kasab, March 2020; Manjikian, Քեսապ Շրջանի Հայորթեան Վիեակագրութիւն, 19.
[115] Tcholakian, *Three Days of Kessab*, 71; confirmed by local residents through author's interviews with resident from Kasab, March 2020.
[116] Author's interviews with multiple heads of churches in Kasab, March 2020, Beirut and Anjar, Lebanon.
[117] Ibid.
[118] Author's interview with representatives from Kasab present in those meetings, March 2020, Beirut, Lebanon.
[119] Author's interview, March 2020, Beirut, Lebanon.

solely due to the power of religious actors in Kasab or their central leadership in Aleppo City. The image of the Nusra Front attacking Christian communities provided a specific example of the narrative that the Assad rule had been promoting since the onset of peaceful protests. Every assistance that Armenians received under the circumstances projected the image of the Assad rule as a protector of minorities and portrayed the opposition as exclusionary and intolerant.

The role and function of Armenian religious organisations illustrates how, regardless of demographic reality, the relative size of sect-based constituencies does not necessarily reflect the power structures in place. Institutional arrangements reflect how power and wealth could be concentrated within small but highly organised and resourceful networks of associates. It is for this reason that assessing the overall religious field in Syria to reveal the power dynamics at play requires observation beyond the Sunni religious field. The restraints imposed on Islamic religious associations by the Assad rule can only be fully understood when compared to the privileges of non-Muslim organisations. This does not mean that the Assad rule is driven by sectarian ambitions. In Kasab, the Alawi population's institutional marginalisation both locally, compared to Armenian institutions in Kasab, or regionally, compared to institutional arrangements in the province of Latakia, is evidence that sectarianism is not a driving force. Rather, sect-based strategies are used as an effective instrument of control where and when they aid power consolidation or extend the influence of the Assad rule or the local intelligence apparatus, regardless of the specific sect or type of social formation in question.

The Armenian Evangelical Church of Kasab emerged as the primary leadership within the Armenian institutional landscape after 2014, despite the fact that the population designated as Armenian Evangelical is less than ten per cent of the local Armenian population. The performance of the Armenian paramilitary group and the arrangements in place under the auspices of the Armenian Orthodox Church and the Tashnak were deemed unsatisfactory by the intelligence apparatus and the NDF.[120] This ultimately resulted in an overhaul of the local hierarchies in place, as two of the three representatives of Armenian religious organisations were removed and only

---

[120] A detailed discussion of these dynamics features in the next chapter.

one of them was replaced by a new representative. The head of the Armenian Orthodox Church left for Lebanon and never returned. Until 2020, his seat remained vacant. The Armenian Evangelical Church in Kasab then effectively emerged as the new local authority. All local religious and social functions were transferred to the new representative of the Evangelical Church. For instance, the 2019 Christmas mass at the Orthodox Church of Kasab was carried out by the head of the Armenian Evangelical Church. The Assad rule also allowed the Armenian Republic, which competes with the Tashnak over local influence, to support the new leadership in Kasab. In 2015 the Armenian ambassador came to Kasab in person to hand over Armenian passports to residents of Kasab alongside representatives of the Armenian Evangelical Church. This bolstered the image of religious representatives from the Armenian Evangelical Church while also further depopulating the area of Armenian inhabitants.

State atrophy and the religious field in Syria: an overview

On 12 October 2018 a new legislation, Law 31, redefined the prerogatives of Syria's Ministry of Awqaf. The legislation imposed greater state control over the religious field.[121] For example, Article 49 of the law stipulated the creation of a Central Council directed by the head of the ministry of religious endowments, with sub-branches spanning across every municipal and administrative centre to oversee religious rituals and celebrations and to evaluate implementation of the ministry's plans. In addition, Article 5 established a Jurisprudential and Scholarly Council (*al-majlis al-ilmi al-fikhi*) with the power and authority to define appropriate religious discourse.[122] The minister also has the authority to penalise religious figures who deviate from standards set by the council. These institutional arrangements followed a centralised regulatory model that reasserts the authority of the state over the religious field. A close examination of the document, however, reveals a variety of models at work, specifically in relation to the role of the religious domain with regards to socio-economic functions.

---

[121] Azzam Al-Kassir, 'Formalizing regime control over Syrian religious affairs', *Sada: Middle East Analysis*, 14 November 2018, https://carnegieendowment.org/sada/77712.
[122] Ibid.

For instance, Section 5 of the legislation is dedicated to the economic and financial aspects of the Ministry of Awqaf and includes multiple stipulations regarding the usage and development of lands and properties belonging to the ministry, which is one of the biggest landowners in Syria. Economic investments, activities and budgetary expansions also feature in Section 5. The expanding economic prerogatives of the ministry rendered the budget of the ministry more independent and granted the ministry greater autonomy to collect and organise its own funds. This increased institutional and fiscal autonomy, featured in Article 89 of Section 5, allows the ministry to establish businesses and financial corporations with the purpose of generating funds. The ministry is also capable of repurposing and developing its properties for residential, touristic or commercial purposes as stipulated in Article 91. In this way, Law 31 formalised the proposition that the Ministry of Awqaf and the religious domain more broadly do not operate as religious and social establishments per se. Rather, religious establishments officially operate as influential economic actors. Such functions have a direct bearing on power relations between state and religion as well as in terms of the broader presence that the religious field has in public functions.

While the Assad rule utilises the state to regulate the religious field, it does so in ways that undermine the socio-economic role of the state with regards to the public. The 'public', as opposed to the private, stands for that space, societal, organisational or service provision, which in principle ought not to be withdrawn, discrete, exclusive, inaccessible or privileged.[123] From an institutional standpoint, the 'public domain' stands for (1) the domain controlled by the state, which is (2) at the general service of a given population and body politic (citizens). State control, in the sense of protection from privatisation, as well as the 'public' function of that domain, are both determinant features that constitute the 'public domain'.[124] With the neo-patrimonial institutional arrangements that constitute state capture by the Assad rule, public and private distinctions are blurred. The public domain does not enjoy the protection

---

[123] Raymond Williams, *Keywords: A Vocabulary of Culture and Society* (Oxford: Oxford University Press, 2015), 184–5.
[124] Seth Abrutyn and Jonathan H. Turner, 'The old institutionalism meets the new institutionalism', *Sociological Perspectives* 54, no. 3 (2011): 283–306.

of the state and is vulnerable to capture by private or factional interests, such as religious actors.

Institutional arrangements in legal-rational forms under the Assad rule are not products of uniform strategies or visions by the Assad rule regarding the role of the state with regards to the public sphere. Rather, the Assad rule pursues seemingly contradictory measures of simultaneous centralisation and decentralisation, on occasion undermining the state's regulatory capacity and at others leading to consolidating it, but always aiming towards consolidating state capture and eliminating opposition (real or potential). However, even in circumstances when the state's regulatory capacity is reaffirmed, it is reaffirmed in ways that ensure the inability of state institutions (ministries and administrative branches alike) to hold decision-making capacity beyond procedural matters. For example, soon after Article 35 of Law 31 brought the office of the Grand Mufti under the authority of the Ministry of Awqaf, the entire position of the Grand Mufti was annulled altogether through another presidential decree in November 2021.[125] Competition within the religious field between the head of the Ministry of Awqaf, Abd el-Sattar al-Sayyed, and that of the previous Grand Mufti, Hassoun, may have led to the sidelining of Hassoun as a sign of al-Sayyed's growing stature and Hassoun's fall from Assad's favour.[126] This explains the sidelining of Hassoun but not the reason why the position of the Grand Mufti was annulled altogether. The religious functions of the position of the Grand Mufti were effectively transferred to the *majlis al-ilmi al-fikhi* in Law 31, making the position redundant. However, the position of Grand Mufti carries significant symbolic and cultural values, especially when it can be deployed to bolster the image of the Assad rule, within Syria and beyond. The elimination of the position follows the same transition from a predominantly hierarchical to heterarchical power structuration witnessed in the military field, which is becoming more and more essential for establishing patronage in institutional domains that are now characterised by a multitude of hierarchies

---

[125] Thomas Pierret, 'An Excommunication in Damascus', interview with Michael Young, 19 November 2021, Carnegie Middle East Centre.
[126] Ibid.

competing and cooperating to gain greater privileges and sponsorship. The replacement of a solitary post such as that of the Grand Mufti with a multi-member council such as *the majlis* brings the religious domain within the same institutional modelling that reinforces the Assad rule by integrating a greater number of hierarchies through the state apparatus.

The cases discussed in this chapter predominantly focus on religious actors with a sizeable presence in public functions. The religious field, however, does not enjoy a dominant position in every part of Syria. It is therefore crucial to qualify the analysis by saying that it is only in places where religious actors have emerged as primary actors during processes of state atrophy that their prominence in both socio-economic and political arenas increased. In the case of Kasab, the three main Armenian churches had been continuously active without interruption for multiple generations.[127] The individuals occupying the institutional ranks were either known in the areas they served or were familiar with charitable and relief work. Such institutional privileges, trans-local linkages and local bargaining capacity translated into significant material benefits and advantages during state atrophy.

In terms of ethno-religious subjectivities, religiosity and sectarianism are not inherently correlated as they represent distinct imaginaries. Religiosity is not bound to express itself in sectarian terms, the same way that sectarianism may express itself in areligious terms. Institutionally however, sect-based and religious actors can be almost indistinguishable. Armenian organisations in Kasab avowed to aiding the non-Armenian population regardless of denominational belonging. Similarly, religious entities in Aleppo City also documented aiding anyone in need, regardless of religious belonging. However, since the onset of the conflict, religious and faith-based organisations explicitly stated that when donors earmark their aid for a certain population exclusively, that aid is strictly reserved for that population alone.[128] Furthermore, given that most of the charity and relief efforts relied on local religious partners, aid and relief distribution was structurally designed to prioritise religious constituents, which reinforced sect-based actors in the process.

---

[127] Khedra 'خطة لتنمية السياحة البيئية في منطقة كسب واستثمارها طبيعياً'.
[128] Focus Group Discussion with community representatives from Kasab and Beirut, 3–4 March 2020, Beirut, Lebanon.

In contrast, after the government took over opposition-held areas in Aleppo City, entities and individuals that had any role in local government within opposition-held areas were deemed terrorists and rooted out during the displacements in the aftermath of the battles.[129] These areas, once deprived of their local societal structures through the armed factions in place, were again deprived of any functional local networks after government takeover. Furthermore, entities operating in government-held areas were allowed to operate in areas previously held by opposition groups.[130] During these transitions, the religious field was weaponised as an instrument of social control. Overall, areas that have remained under government control possessed more resilient and better connected religious networks, which translated into more favourable conditions of liveability in surrounding areas. Areas that returned to government control after lengthy rebel rule, on the other hand, were deprived of such conditions.

In areas recaptured by the government, trusted local religious figures or institutions were co-opted and those whose allegiances were questioned were replaced. Clientelistic arrangements based on the same three pillars of internal competition, limited state rewards and coercion were reinstated, even as the state as a resource became utterly depleted in the given economic circumstances. Even those who had a role in reconciliation agreements during transitions of power, in the model of Adnan al-Afyouni in Damasacus or Bassam Dafda' in Ghouta who were later assassinated, are not necessarily guaranteed continuous state favouritism or survival. This illustrates how the state or state access as a reward is not an award for a track-record of loyalty, rather it is a forward-looking instrument of maintaining allegiance and drawing clientelist services. The rise and fall of Grand Mufti Hassoun is a case in point. The value of allegiances and services in the eyes of the Assad rule depend on current and future performance and not previous acts of loyalty. Even in places

---

[129] Even religious entities that operated in rebel-held areas and contributed to 'reconciliation agreements' that handed control to pro-government forces are at risk of harassment and arrest by security forces. Author's soft copy of arrest warrants and orders to cease religious activities issued to local religious authorities in Dar'a.

[130] Author's interview with Cedric Prakash, regional advocacy and communications officer of the Jesuit Refugee Service, Middle East and North Africa, Beirut, November 2017; See also 'Our Living After Surviving', *JRS Syria*, 2018, https://jesuitmissions.org.uk/wp-content/uploads/2018/03/JRS-Al-Sakhour-2018.pdf.

that remained mostly under government control throughout the war, such as Kasab, loyal religious actors were dispensable and only those who were best suited to extend the reach and reinforce the Assad rule and the security apparatus were deemed trustworthy and were granted prerogatives within their areas and beyond.

Some areas have continuously evaded the control of the Syrian government and pre-existing state structures have atrophied, such as in Idlib in the northwest and the SDF-controlled areas of Syria's northeast. In these areas the religious field emerged as a contested site where local religious actors, both pre-existing and those that emerged after state atrophy, found themselves either resisting or competing for the patronage of dominant political and military forces in place.[131] In all of these regions, emerging arrangements replicate mechanisms of state-centred institutional modelling. Examples include the *wizarat al-awqaf wa-l-da'wa wal-Irshad* under the rule of Hay'at Tahrir al-Sham in Idlib, or the various local Directorates of Endowments, Fatwa and Religious Affairs in Turkish-controlled areas reporting to the Turkish state's Diyanet, or the SDF's (Syrian Democratic Forces) *hay'āt diniyya*. In each of those cases, the question of religious management and government follows the same model of state authority, where power to regulate over other domains, including religion, is deferred to the political powers in place and those who have established the capacity to coerce.[132] In this sense, while the authority of the Syrian state under the Assad rule is undermined, state atrophy did not yield the collapse of state structures altogether. Developments in the religious field throughout the Syrian conflict further demonstrate that even where the Syrian state or the Assad rule lost effective control or meaningful presence, state-based models of institutional arrangements were pursued to varying levels of success, regardless of the ideological affiliation of the armed forces in place.[133]

---

[131] Thomas Pierret and Laila Alrifaai, 'Religious Governance in Syria amid Territorial Fragmentation', in Frederic Wehrey (ed.), *Islamic Institutions in Arab States: Mapping the Dynamics of Control, Co-optation, and Contention* (Beirut: Carnegie Endowment for International Peace, 2021), 53–72.

[132] Ibid.

[133] These state-like arrangements paralleled the neo-patrimonial arrangements that transformed religious actors into clients of the military/political powers in place.

Conclusion

Prior to 2011, the state's coercive capacity, selective favouritism and local competition between religious networks over rewards and resources offered by the Assad rule ensured a competitive internal configuration, which reinforced clientelist arrangements. Since 2011, in government and opposition areas alike, the religious field emerged as a primary actor in the public domain through social and economic activities, while state and municipal structures effectively atrophied. Although the growing presence of religious actors in the public domain began with the neoliberal shift after the year 2000, the devolution of state functions after 2011 exacerbated this process.

Religious entities played a crucial role in alleviating the suffering of local inhabitants throughout the conflict, however, by doing so, they played a significant political role as well. As the outcome of the wars of attrition in areas such as Aleppo and Damascus were largely determined by capacities of procurement, religious entities were functionally weaponised throughout the Syrian conflict to counteract policies of death, sieges, economic degradation and the severe conditions of scarcity and deprivation in government- and opposition-held areas alike. As the state's economic capabilities remained weak, the growing reliance on the religious domain for economic and social purposes continued, and the expansion of the religious field in the public sphere proceeded without interruption.

The religious field as a broad and uncoordinated social and organisational network, regardless of internal divisions, emerged as a central node for the circulation of socio-economic resources. At the intersection of the two processes and histories, of (1) neoliberal modes of economic management and (2) state atrophy, emerged a religious field that serves as an alternative distributive system reorganising both society and state–society relations. The religious field emerged as a primary site of social influence and concentration of social power. Through its impact on the quality of life of populations in need, it is on par with the state, if not superseding it, as a social regulator. However, given the coercive capacities of the Assad rule, the religious domain and the actors therein remain dependent on the permissive stance of existing power structures. In government-held areas, while the religious field presents a challenge and an alternative to the state, it continuously remains, voluntarily or otherwise, subservient to neo-patrimonial and authoritarian power structures. In opposition-held areas too, local religious networks either served local forces in place (directly or indirectly) or were sidelined. Finally, areas that returned to government control were either vacated of previous religious networks or saw the co-optation of religious actors by the Assad rule.

Typological distinctions between social services and religious activism are difficult to maintain in practice. Through social institutions, religious actors play a structuring and regulating role, and so do accompanying notions of religiosity, piety and sanctity. Religiosity and religious observance are not inherent features of society. They are contingent upon the broader role of the religious field in the public domain. The ability to become interwoven with socio-economic exchanges provides the religious field with wide ranging influence over everyday life. Through expanding socio-economic exchanges, sect-based structures are also reinforced depending on the intensity of exchanges between religious or confessional authorities and their local constituents. Such structures and solidarities have expanded and promise to have an enduring presence. Their specific roles will largely depend on the nature of the clientelistic arrangements at the local level. Overall, however, the religious field remains apologetic to political powers in place, as it has no capacity to directly mount a challenge. Through its politically apologetic stance, the religious field harnesses a broader presence in the public domain and reinforces itself while also reinforcing the political powers in place.

5

Civilian Agency and its Limits: Community Protection in Deir Hafer and Kasab*

Civilian agency during state atrophy did not express itself in sectarian terms alone despite processes of sectarianisation and the consolidation of sect-based organisations in the military and religious domains. Often dismissed as inconsequential, civilians and civilian organisations were actively involved in efforts of community protection during the conflict. Community protection efforts by civilians at the local level are also expressions of civilian agency that often defied and sometimes reinforced processes of sectarianisation. Either way, political action did not stem from sectarian predispositions or objectives alone. Despite its discursive prevalence, sectarianism was not a primary organising principle for collective mobilisation in efforts of community protection.

Community protection efforts by civilians stemmed in response to local conditions of state atrophy and security threats. This chapter provides a documentation of such examples in Deir Hafer and Kasab, and focuses on four main variables that shaped the nature and outcome of civilian community protection efforts: (1) modalities of violence against civilians, (2) organisational capacity of civilian community organisers, (3) their local autonomy and (4) social trust within the areas examined. The chapter answers the following key questions: (1) What are the range of threats and

---

* A detailed report based on the datasets informing findings in this chapter was provided to UN-ESCWA – National Agenda for the Future of Syria programme. All interviews for the case study on Kasab were conducted in Lebanon during the month of March 2020. All semi-structured interviews or the case study on Der Hafer were obtained remotely throughout April 2020.

shocks that civilians confront under conditions of state atrophy as witnessed in Deir Hafer and Kasab? (2) What strategies for community protection were employed by civilians in an attempt to protect themselves and their communities from dynamics of state atrophy? (3) What conditions limited civilian efforts of community protection? Based on the two divergent case studies, the chapter depicts variations in local circumstances, patterns of community mobilisation throughout the conflict and variables that eventually undermined efforts to resist, cope and adapt to rapidly shifting institutional landscapes.

Strategies of civilian community protection in Kasab and Deir Hafer include negotiating for safe spaces, bargaining with armed groups (state and non-state actors), developing norms of civilian non-collaboration to resist militarisation against other communities, assisting in procurement and distribution of relief and creating civilian-led bodies to adjudicate disputes amongst civilians as well as between civilians and armed actors. The experiences of these two communities reflect the broader range of threats experienced by communities across the country since the onset of violence. Specific examples of threats ranged from economic insecurity and diminished livelihoods to direct communal attacks and indiscriminate violence. While civilian community organisers initiated and led community-protection efforts, their success and level of endurance depended upon local and trans-local multilateral arrangements involving armed groups, state or state-like institutions and stakeholders within the international aid industry.

The majority of community protection efforts fall under the category of survival and coping strategies of self-preservation in the face of violence, where communities tried to evade violence and conflict-fragility. There were fewer instances of adaptive and mitigating strategies aimed at taming the impact or reducing the scale of violence. It is noticeable here that civilian arrangements and negotiated agreements to protect civilian infrastructure were not the outcome of organised negotiations by civilian organisers but rather the outcome of personal initiatives by intermediaries in positions of power. Transformative strategies, on the other hand, which aim to address structural conditions to provide more options for civilian organisers or expand the boundaries of possible social and political actions (such as community protection) hardly featured at all. This predominance of reactive approaches to community protection reveals the conditions that undermined and restrained expressions of civilian agency during state atrophy.

Community Protection in Theory

Community protection efforts take on a variety of forms and require detailed observation of how civilians react when faced with various threats.[1] The literature points out that efforts of community protection can be categorised into three strategies: (1) survival and coping strategies, (2) adaptive and mitigating strategies and (3) transformative strategies.[2] Survival and coping strategies are aimed at self-preservation in the face of violence and threats. Survival methods stand for efforts of escaping from violence.[3] Adaptive and mitigating strategies are aimed at taming and reducing the impact or scale of violence. Unlike coping strategies, which seek to avoid violence, adaptive strategies require *engaging* with sources or manifest forms of violence in an effort to reduce the level of harm.[4] Transformative strategies aim towards preventing violence or enhancing local preparedness for future shocks. Transformative strategies can take on different forms: (1) addressing structural sources of conflict and violence towards preventing conflict and achieving justice, (2) recovery steps such as reconstruction and trauma-informed psycho-social support to address experiences of harm and (3) reinforcing capacities of resilience by learning from past experiences and

---

[1] Ken Menkhaus, 'Making Sense of Resilience in Peacebuilding Contexts: Approaches, Applications, Implications', *The Geneva Peacebuilding Platform*, 2013, 2; UNDRR, 'Resilience', *United Nations Office for Disaster Risk Reduction*, 18 March 2015, https://www.undrr.org/terminology/resilience (accessed 23 March 2020).

[2] UNDRR, 'Resilience'; Oliver Kaplan, *Resisting War: How Communities Protect Themselves* (Cambridge: Cambridge University Press, 2017); David Cadier, Matteo Capasso and Karoline Eickhoff, 'Researching Resilience: Implications for Case Studies in Europe's Neighbourhoods', *EU-LISTCO*, January 2020, 140, https://www.eu-listco.net/publications/researching-resilience.

[3] These include developing early warning systems, avoiding casualties, evacuation plans and managing shelters and sanctuary spaces; Kaplan, *Resisting War*.

[4] Such strategies include establishing dialogue channels with armed opposition groups, organising protests against local aggression, shaming the security apparatus, coordination committees and solidarity norms, organisational structures based on local networks that resist outside policing, operating local justice systems and managing links and interactions with external non-governmental or inter-governmental organisations (NGOs and IGOs) for various purposes such as humanitarian and relief efforts; Ibid.

improving preparedness based on existing weaknesses in strategies, capacities and structural conditions.[5]

Specific measures and strategies of community protection vary based on prevailing conflict dynamics and circumstances such as geostrategic location, local socio-economic conditions, presence of armed forces (including number of armed groups and balance of power), local resources and patterns of militarisation and recruitment.[6] Despite obstacles facing civilian efforts of community protection, civilians do have capacity – albeit limited – during armed conflicts to save lives, mitigate mass and permanent displacement and maintain community cohesion.[7] Armed groups need the support and cooperation of local communities as effective control is contingent upon broader ability to draw civilian cooperation and elicit material resources, recruits and information.[8]

With the ability to coerce by deploying violence, armed groups have greater capacity to influence and impose themselves than civilian entities or community organisers. Weinstein argues that 'rebel groups that emerge in environments rich in natural resources or with the external support of an outside patron tend to commit higher levels of indiscriminate violence; movements that arise in resource-poor contexts perpetrate far fewer abuses and employ violence more selectively and strategically."[9] This pattern, according to Weinstein, is decisively influenced by the armed groups' level of need for local cooperation and resources.[10] In circumstances of protracted conflict, similar to that of Syria, where resources are scarce, foreign support

---

[5] Transformative strategies include negotiating peace zones void of weapons, restrictions on recruitment, collaborative agreements between different towns, addressing local grievances and relative deprivation, ensuring greater inclusivity and representation in local decision-making, redistribution of wealth and aid and developing equitable labour to capital relations such as between labourers and landowners in pastoral and agricultural areas; Cadier, Capasso and Eickhoff, 'Researching Resilience'; Kaplan, *Resisting War*; Menkhaus, 'Making Sense of Resilience'.

[6] Stathis N. Kalyvas, *The Logic of Violence in Civil War* (Cambridge: Cambridge University Press, 2006).

[7] Ibid.; Ana Arjona, *Rebelocracy: Social Order in the Colombian Civil War* (Cambridge: Cambridge University Press, 2016).

[8] Kalyvas, *The Logic of Violence*, 147; Francisco Gutierrez-Sanin, 'Organization and Governance', in Ana Arjona, Nelson Kasfir and Zachariah Mampilly (eds), *Rebel Governance in Civil War* (Cambridge: Cambridge University Press, 2017), 246–63; Arjona, *Rebelocracy*, 11.

[9] Jeremy Weinstein, *Inside Rebellion: The Politics of Insurgent Violence* (Cambridge: Cambridge University Press, 2007), 7.

[10] Ibid.

Community Protection Measures	Deir Hafer	Kasab	Description
Shelters	Limited Presence	Limited Presence	Limited presence in both cases – not on par with the scale and nature of threats and scale of violence.
Evacuation (organised)	Limited Presence	Limited Presence	Lack of organised evacuation jeopardised vulnerable members of the community such as the elderly and those without property or kin in safer areas.
Cohesion in exile (organised)	Limited Presence	Present	The displaced from Deir Hafer face numerous obstacles to voluntary return. The displaced from Kasab face fewer but persisting obstacles.
Early Warning Systems (organised)	Absent	Absent	There were no organised early warning systems.
Warning signals of imminent threats (unorganised)	Present	Present	Kasab's geographic and natural landscape amplified warning signs. No technology or communication channels were used to inform civilians about threatening developments. Similarly, Deir Hafer predominantly relied on personal observations of military movements.
Mobilisation of international networks	Limited Presence	Present	Civilian entities in Kasab were able to mobilise international networks consistently – although aid procurement and distribution lacked strategic or long-term planning. Deir Hafer enjoyed less connections and the aid was inconsistent and insufficient.
Bargaining and negotiating with opposing armed groups (state and non-state) for safe spaces	Present	Absent	Deir Hafer managed to protect vital infrastructure from conflict for prolonged periods, despite the fact that underlying agreements were precarious. Kasab's civilian population had very limited channels of communication with armed opposition groups.
Non-violent conflict resolution mechanisms	Present	Limited Presence	Informal mediation took place in Kasab through ad-hoc intermediaries deemed reputable. Deir Hafer's civilian council had an office dedicated to arbitration and mediation.
Civilian autonomy (vis-à-vis armed groups)	Limited Presence	Limited Presence	Greater space for civilian administrative and operational autonomy in Deir Hafer post-2011 – prone to the interference of armed factions. Existing armed groups in Kasab did not intervene in the everyday life of civilians except for the looting that took place when residents were displaced. Local surveillance by the security apparatus was uninterrupted and pre-existing environment of limited space for civilian initiatives continuously restrained post-2011 civilian operational spaces.
Armed protection (self-defence)	Limited Presence	Limited Presence	Insufficient capacity to resist violence against civilians despite increased militarisation.

is conditional and limited and armed groups need local cooperation, there are possibilities for local communities to take independent measures of community protection, depending on the level of organisational capacity within respective communities. Civilian entities, with the minimal leverage they possess, may also try to expand the space for civilian autonomy, protection and bargaining mechanisms in various ways.[11] The cases of Kasab in Latakia province and Deir Hafer in Aleppo province help us understand these processes and discern opportunities and challenges for civilian community protection during conflict.

Deir Hafer in Focus

Deir Hafer, situated in Aleppo province approximately 50 km east of Aleppo City, is among the major cities of Aleppo's countryside, along with Manbij and al-Bab. Deir Hafer emerged as a fiercely contested area with significant geostrategic position due to its proximity to the military airport of Kweiris, the air force academy within its premises, and the thermal power plant, located halfway between Aleppo and Deir Hafer, which provided electricity province-wide.[12] The city is at the entrance of a primary corridor connecting the coast, Aleppo City and the major highway M5 (Damascus–Aleppo) to Raqqa, practically granting access to both Syria's northeast and the vast *badiya* (desert) extending across the Syrian–Iraqi borders. As a result of these geopolitical qualities, the city witnessed multiple episodes of violence and was contested by multiple military actors until government takeover in 2017.[13] Different armed opposition groups controlled the town and its vicinities for various intervals and each period brought new patterns of violence and vulnerabilities.

---

[11] Kaplan, *Resisting War*.
[12] Anab Baladi (2019, 7 11). بمحطة كهرباء حلب في عهدة عقد إيراني مرتقب للمزيد: *https://enabbaladi.net/archives/340690#ixzz6LDaRWpNv*. Retrieved April 30, 2020, from Anab Baladi: https://www.enabbaladi.net/archives/340690; Enab Baladi; Hamimo, M. M. (2019). لا يوجد حالياً تقنين في سورية. Al-Watan.
[13] Abdullah Hasan, 'الحرس الثوري من داعش الى حافر: دير' 'Deir Hafer: From Daesh to the Revolutionary Guard', *A'ayn al-Madina*, 14 September 2018, https://ayn-almadina.com/public/details/%D8%AF%D9%8A%D8%B1%20%D8%AD%D8%A7%D9%81%D8%B1..%20%D9%85%D9%86%20%D8%AF%D8%A7%D8%B9%D8%B4%20%D8%A5%D9%84%D9%89%20%D8%A7%D9%84%D8%AD%D8%B1%D8%B3%20%D8%A7%D9%84%D8%AB%D9%88%D8%B1%D9%8A/4627/ar.

Conflict dynamics

By the second half of 2012 a local armed faction was formed in Deir Hafer under the name 'Katibat Abu Dujana'. According to residents, no significant clashes were recorded. Government forces vacated the city by mid-2012 to concentrate their presence in the city of Aleppo.[14] In the period prior, however, the city witnessed multiple clashes between protestors and the local security apparatus, specifically by the personnel of the Political Security Directorate in the city, in addition to local intelligence offices and other branches from nearby towns such as Maskana's Military Security that were mobilised to suppress demonstrations.[15] In terms of violence and threats, by the end of 2012, kidnappings and extortion had become widespread.

Prior to the withdrawal of government forces in 2012, kidnappings and detentions by the local security apparatus aimed to suppress activists and protestors. Other acts of kidnapping targeted those with known wealth, in order to collect ransom. Such incidents continued to take place after the local faction took over.[16] '*Kidnappings had become more rampant unfortunately,*' declared a previous resident who supported the local faction.[17] Participants also revealed how ransom was a factor in both government detentions and kidnappings by militiamen alike as multiple respondents described how friends or family members detained by militants or the security apparatus were released in return for large sums of money.[18] There were also mentions of additional kidnapping incidents motivated by vengeance for previous acts of injustice or against potential government collaborators[19].

When the Syrian government's security forces vacated the city of Deir Hafer, they left behind a sizeable governance and security vacuum for the approximately 40,000 residents in the city proper and its surrounding

---

[14] Interviews 2B, 6B; Hasan, 'Deir Hafer'; The state security apparatus in Aleppo countryside prioritised Aleppo City and concentrated its presence there.
[15] Interview 10B.
[16] Interviews 16B, 21B.
[17] Interview with Majlis personnel.
[18] Interviews 10B, 21B.
[19] Interview 14B.

villages in the *nahiya* (district).[20] As armed opposition groups in the area ramped up operations against the military airport of Kweiris between 2012 and 2013, the city of Deir Hafer came under heavy fire.[21] Violence towards civilians shifted considerably. According to residents in the area, along with every attack on the Kweiris airport by opposition groups, air raids by government forces targeting the civilian population of Deir Hafer intensified significantly.[22]

'*The bombing was aimed at punishing civilians, to push them against the local faction [participating in besieging and attacking the Kweiris airport],*' declared a local activist.[23] He continued, stating, '*air raids against the city not only did not discriminate between combatants and non-combatants, but intentionally targeted residential areas and city centres.*'[24]

The range of missiles that were used varied and included artillery attacks and barrel bombs. According to local activists in support of opposition groups, however, '*without besieging Kweiris, the city would have been more easily and more repeatedly targeted*'.[25] Attacks on Kweiris rendered the airport un-operational and air raids came from military airports further away, such as the T-4 airbase in Homs.[26]

Lack of internal security drove many civilians to join existing military factions for protection. By late 2012 and early 2013 the broader area of Deir Hafer, Maskaneh and al-Bab had multiple military groups that were organised and active on significant fronts, such as the Kweiris airport. Amongst the most noteworthy were Liwa' al-Tawhid's Eleventh Division in Maskaneh and Deir Hafer, the Islamic State of Iraq and the Levant (Daesh) predominantly in al-Bab, and Harakat Ahrar al-Sham.[27]

---

[20] Central Bureau of Statistics, *Census for Nahiyat Der Hafer* (Damascus: Government of Syria, 2009). The *nahiya* includes Hmeyme Koubra and Hmeyme Soughra, 'akoula, Mab'ouja, Southern Rasm el-Hermel, Tal Ayoub, Oum al-Mura, Oum Zalila and Zoubeida.

[21] Hasan, 'Deir Hafer'; Interview 17B.

[22] Interview 21B.

[23] Ibid.

[24] Ibid.

[25] Interview 17B.

[26] Ibid.

[27] Centre for Documenting the Syrian Revolution (2012). حلب | دير حافر • بيان تشكيل لواء رايات النصر. YouTube https://www.youtube.com/watch?v=wBMVHbqnMRI&t=1s; Lund, A. (2013, Feburary 28). Syria's Salafi insurgents: the rise of the Syrian Islamic front. Swedish Institute of International Affairs; Al Jazeera. (2017). "الباب".. مفتاح الشمال السوري. Retrieved 10 May 2020, from Al

By the first half of 2013, despite the expansion of Daesh in nearby areas such as al-Bab, the area of Deir Hafer and its local factions remained largely under the banner of the Free Syrian Army and maintained amicable relations with all factions.[28] As explicitly declared by one of the most high-ranking representatives of Katibat Abu Dujana at the time, Atallah al-Wasmi, the faction repeatedly refused fighting against other armed opposition groups, including Daesh.[29] According to interviewees, '*Daesh, at the time, was similar to any other armed group in the region*' and did not show signs of brutality towards the populace.[30] Moreover, the organisation prided itself for providing social services and fighting corruption in areas held by armed opposition groups.

Economic vulnerability in the area was one of the main reasons why Daesh was eventually capable of taking over Deir Hafer with great ease. The decline of local employment opportunities created ideal circumstances for Daesh's takeover, specifically after its expansion in Iraq and the resources it commanded as a result.

After Daesh clashed with Ahrar al-Sham in Maskaneh in early 2014, taking over Deir Hafer in the process, the local faction of Abu Dujana split with many of its members joining Daesh while others remained with Ahrar al-Sham but withdrew from the area.[31] Throughout retransitions and shifts in local military powers, social mistrust and tribal divisions became more prominent. Sudden transitions in local military hierarchies and sudden shifts in exclusionary leadership structures continuously fuelled competing networks of trust and kinship.

With the takeover of Deir Hafer, Daesh renamed the town to Dār al-Fateh as a symbolic expression of the organisation's ambitions to radically reconfigure the city. Deir Hafer's circumstances under Daesh were not different from those of Raqqa, the declared capital of so-called Islamic State.

Jazeera: https://www.aljazeera.net/encyclopedia/citiesandregions/2017/2/13/%D8%A7%D9%84%D8%A8%D8%A7%D8%A8-%D9%85%D9%81%D8%AA%D8%A7%D8%AD-%D8%A7%D9%84%D8%B4%D9%85%D8%A7%D9%84-%D8%A7%D9%84%D8%B3%D9%88%D8%B1%D9%8A%D8%A7.

[28] Ugarit News Syria. (5 January 2013). أو غاريت دير حافر حلب كتيبة أبو دجانة , تشكيل سرايا النشامى. YouTube https://www.youtube.com/watch?v=ny6jlUOYkv4.

[29] alWasmi, A. (2013). الغرب يشترط للتسليح مقاتلة الكتائب الإسلامية. YouTube https://www.youtube.com/watch?v=5UK5L4p6jgk&t=4s.

[30] Interviews 2B, 4B, 8B, 20B.

[31] Interviews 8B, 21B.

Daesh transformed its approach from cooperative and submissive to locals, to coercive and brutal.[32] Aside from brutal punishments and exclusionary practices, Daesh transformed the local infrastructure through the introduction of field hospitals, improvised military factories and a public platform in the centre of the city to stage punishments. The scale of violence upon the community escalated with the annulment of previous arrangements (which were made through intermediaries to save local infrastructure from aerial bombardment). As a result, the local surgical hospital, for instance, was bombed in April 2015.[33]

Furthermore, Daesh used both coercive and enticing methods to create its new local cadres.[34] *'Their salaries were significantly high compared to salaries at the time and they could provide privileges and clout to those they wanted to co-opt'*.[35] The organisation also tried to make an example of those who were difficult to co-opt and abused them with either coercion or punishment for their stance.[36] Local actors with previous administrative experience or expertise faced such alternatives.[37] Extortion by Daesh recruits was rampant. Media activists feared for their lives and all satellite routers and Internet equipment were confiscated. The need for protection as well as financial incentives motivated some locals to join.[38]

Government forces replaced the reign of Daesh in February 2017 after a week-long siege and intense aerial bombardment by Russian forces. Daesh fighters abandoned their positions. Since then, the government issued multiple statements calling for the return of local residents to Deir Hafer.[39]

---

[32] Interviews 2B; 4B; 8B; 20B.
[33] 'Victims are among the dead and wounded in the bombing of Deir Hafer Hospital, and among the victims is a doctor', *Mu'asasat Taht el-Mjhar*, 23 April 2015, http://www.almjhar.com/ar-sy/NewsView/2212/92467.aspx.
[34] Interviews 2B; 4B; 8B; 20B.
[35] Interview 21B.
[36] Interviews 4B; 6B; 13B.
[37] Abbas al-Deri, 'داعش تقتحم قرية"تل أيوب"بريف حلب وتعدم الثوار بتهمة مرتدين', *Orient News*, 21 May 2014, https://orient-news.net/ar/news_show/79180.
[38] Interview 21B.
[39] 'Hundreds of residents of Deir Hafer area and its surroundings return to their homes in the eastern countryside of Aleppo', *SANA*, 20 July 2017, http://www.sana.sy/?p=593189.

Community protection

There were a few skirmishes between Katibat Abu Dujana and government forces during the withdrawal of government forces. The artillery and air force of Kweiris airport started targeting the city, specifically in late 2012 and early 2013, when opposition groups ramped up operations against the military airport of Kweiris.[40] As a result of the reciprocated violence targeting civilians, many residents vacated their homes and moved to safer areas. The countryside was targeted less than the city.[41] Given the limited means of self-protection against such scales of violence, most efforts consisted of personal measures such as people abandoning the central areas of the Deir Hafer township and moving to the countryside, to relatives or family farmlands.[42]

When violence struck, those unable to leave would either run to the basement of their houses or towards a centrally located room away from balconies, windows or outermost façades of their buildings.[43] As bombardments reoccurred, most locals became familiar with the sounds and patterns of bombings. As helicopters or fighter jets were heard approaching, residents would identify their trajectory and head towards areas away from their path.[44] Residents and first responders also learned the bombing patterns, in which the same target was often attacked twice in a brief interval.[45] In the face of indiscriminate mass violence, these basic and personal initiatives were all that locals could do for self-protection.[46] Interviewees expressed that civilian councils and military factions either did not pay attention to them or simply could not do anything in the face of such violence. '*No one asked about us, there were no shelters, there was nothing*,' echoed multiple participants.[47]

---

[40] Hasan, 'Deir Hafer'; Interview 17B.
[41] Interviews 6B, 10B.
[42] Interviews 6B, 8B, 10B.
[43] Interviews 8B, 10B.
[44] Interview 8B.
[45] Interview 8B.
[46] Interview 19B.
[47] Interviews 14B, 19B.

The most targeted areas were those closest to the Kweiris military airport on the western side of the *nahiya* (district).[48] Some residents, who had no safe place to go to, remained in their houses,[49] but towns, such as Rasm Abboud, were usually vacated during attacks on the Kweiris airport by armed opposition groups. These evacuations were temporary and uncoordinated; families simply learned the pattern of violence and noticed military preparations ahead of time and vacated beforehand, temporarily leaving their homes.[50]

Permanent mass displacements took place in Deir Hafer during transitions of power and shifts in territorial control between armed opposition groups. Displacement patterns for Deir Hafer were uncoordinated and depended upon military developments in the area. For instance, when the local armed group took over in 2012, many of those who vacated headed westward towards Aleppo City.[51] Those displaced later, when the situation in Aleppo City had also deteriorated, headed north (within the Syrian Arab Republic and beyond).[52] During the rule of Daesh, the organisation did not allow people to leave for extended periods of time, and planted mines along the road to the northeast towards areas controlled by the SDF to prevent people from leaving.[53] Upon government return, those who left headed towards SDF controlled areas in the northeast.

Among the most noteworthy community protection efforts throughout the violent episodes of the conflict were focused on the city's most vital infrastructures. For instance, the only surgical hospital in Deir Hafer was owned by Member of Parliament Fahmi al-Hasan at the time.[54] Reportedly, the owner received a part of the hospital's income, which incentivised him to protect the building from bombardment utilising his position within the government.[55] This implicit, de facto agreement remained in place even after Katibat Abu Dujana pledged allegiance to Ahrar al-Sham. Furthermore,

---

[48] Interviews 2B, 21B.
[49] Interview 21B.
[50] Interviews 2B, 5B, 6B, 21B.
[51] Interviews 5B; 6B; 20B.
[52] Interviews 1B; 21B.
[53] Interview 21B.
[54] Interviews 1B, 14B.
[55] Interview 1B.

some residents living close to the hospital would go there for protection from shelling.[56] What is noteworthy here is that the protection of the hospital was not only incentivised for purposes of community protection but also through the positionality and personal financial gains of those who had authority and power to ensure the safety of the facility. In other words, given that Fahmi al-Hasan had a level of influence within state structures and in opposition-held areas, he was in a position to broker such arrangements.

The situation of the local industrial bakery (*al-furn al-āli*) was similar as it was not bombed and its diesel and flour were provided by the government in return for local wheat and a portion of the bakery's revenues.[57] The employees (those employed before the withdrawal of government forces in 2012) continued to receive their salaries provided that they travelled to areas held by the government to receive their pay cheques.[58] Interviewees also shared how those who did travel to collect their pay cheques were interrogated by government forces.[59] When they returned to their areas '*they also received harassment from local factions because their loyalty was questionable. It was suspected that they were working as informants but the truth is they were working at the bakery and had nothing to do with the armed factions.*'[60]

To address issues of widespread kidnappings at the time, local notables, such as elderly tribesmen, were reportedly asked to intervene and mediate in efforts of releasing the kidnapped. These mediations however neither provided protection nor addressed drivers behind the kidnappings. The efforts of tribal notables remained limited to mitigating harm and attempting to mediate with kidnappers who were willing to negotiate or engage.

Civilian-led initiatives enjoyed more freedoms after 2012 and took on leading roles in organising the locality and address arising vulnerabilities. The most notable initiatives came about through the structures of the post-2012 local civilian council, which included multiple offices and branches directly aimed at addressing local needs and safety concerns. The most noteworthy

---

[56] Interview 19B.
[57] Interviews 1B, 8B, 11B, 21B.
[58] Interviews 11B, 21B.
[59] Interview 11B.
[60] Interview 21B.

branch for the purpose of this study is the 'reconciliation committee' (Lijnat al-Musalaha), which worked on diffusing tensions and addressing local disagreements to prevent conflict escalation. The committee was active between 2012 and 2014 as a civilian conflict-resolution and de-escalation body.

Between 2012 and 2014 a number of unprecedented media initiatives were employed by local youths. They formed local newspapers (*al-bayan*) and relied on social media, specifically Facebook pages such as *Tansiqiyet Deir Hafer*, to raise awareness and provide safety guidelines in the area.[61] For instance, according to one of the administrators, the Facebook page would post information about recent attacks and advise residents to avoid areas under attack or in danger of potential air raids.[62] In addition, new local civilian structures were formed under the umbrella of the civil councils.

Deir Hafer's council, similar to other local councils in areas beyond the control of the government, comprised multiple specialised offices, such as the relief office and the judiciary office. The judiciary included both a religious council and a legal office that was composed of religious judges, as a well as lawyers and judges from public law. The Lijnat al-Musalaha (the 'reconciliation committee' mentioned above) was also within the legal office, with its main office in the centre of the town.[63] The committee's mode of operation was such that when disagreements arose amongst local citizens it would mediate and try to help find adequate solutions.[64] Often, when the religious court received a case, it immediately forwarded it to the committee.[65] As an informal arbitration court of first instance, the court *'always preserved the right to forward the case to [the formal court] al-mahkama al-Shar'iyya that had the backing and enforcement provided by armed forces in the area'*.[66]

According to members of the committee, eighty-five per cent of cases brought before the committee were solved without the need to forward the file to the court.[67] Cases brought before the committee included issues

---

[61] Interviews 4B, 16B, 21B.
[62] Interview 21B.
[63] Interviews 7B, 16B, 19B.
[64] Interviews 1B, 6B, 7B.
[65] Interview 7B.
[66] Interview 19B.
[67] Interview 19B.

and disagreements of inheritance, divorce and marriage, payment of debt, property rights, agricultural matters of land and labour management, and rentals.[68] Many interviewees expressed how the committee prevented conflict escalation and avoided potential violence in the city: *'they [the committee] did a great job and they were much needed. They did the best they can'.*[69]

The committee was headed by local notables from a variety of tribes in the area – namely, representatives from the al-Hadidiyin, al-Kharraj and Bani Jamil. Professionally, the individuals who formed the group were renowned teachers and esteemed tribal and religious figures.[70] The committee members, comprised of a lawyer, a judge, a religious judge and two other reputable members from the community, were among those viewed as neutral and fair regardless of tribal affiliation.[71]

Amongst the many challenges that the committee faced was that air raids made its office inoperational, although its personnel remained active and visited people in different places.[72] According to a high-ranking member of the committee, one of the glaring challenges the committee faced was that armed factions intervened in its operations and competed for influence within.[73] This took place despite the committee's structure, which was designed to protect it from interference. Ultimately, the religious court was the primary authority in judicial matters and it was directly appointed and enforced by the armed factions in place. Given its relative distance from armed factions, compared to the religious court, the committee enjoyed relative leeway and autonomy. However, individuals accepting the mechanism and outcome of the process of the committee might have done so to avoid standing before the religious court and not due to a satisfactory performance by the committee. For the people in Deir Hafer's silent majority, for instance, who had frictions with the armed groups in place, the reconciliation committee was the best option around, and many avoided such processes altogether assuming

---

[68] Interviews 6B, 7B.
[69] Interviews 1B, 3B, 6B, 7B.
[70] Interview 6B.
[71] Interview 1B; 7B; 19B.
[72] Interview 21B.
[73] Interviews 3B; 7B.

they would not find justice. This also influenced local perceptions of the committee, who despite the avowed reputable standing of its personnel, was perceived by many as lacking autonomy.[74] Many of those who welcomed the idea behind the reconciliation committee also hypothetically projected its restricted autonomy due to the influence of local armed forces even when they had no experience interacting with the committee.[75]

As mentioned, the local military faction later integrated with Ahrar al-Sham in 2013, before effectively dissolving in the aftermath of the takeover by Daesh in 2014. Daesh had been in charge of al-Bab since late 2013 and had a broad presence in Deir Hafer as well.[76] It did not, however, attempt to exclude other factions and establish hegemonic rule, and its military presence was limited. With its complete takeover of Deir Hafer and beyond in 2014, the situation of the city and local power relations changed dramatically. Until then, civilian-led institutions enjoyed more freedoms than before and took on leading roles in organising the locality and addressing vulnerabilities.

Economic vulnerability

Dire economic circumstances in the area were one of the city's most notable local vulnerabilities. Even local agricultural production became expensive as irrigation and transportation required fuel and diesel, which became more expensive with the fluctuation of the Syrian pound, the decline in local oil extraction and refinement, and extortionist trade practices, which drove prices up. Food produce in the area witnessed an exponential spike in prices and efforts to impose a price ceiling on essentials proved futile.[77] Beyond greed, farmers and traders were also genuinely unable to pin their prices due to the Syrian pound's fluctuations, and many trade centres such as in al-Bab or in Turkey started trading in United States dollars (USD).[78]

---

[74] Interviews 13B; 14B; 15B; 16B.
[75] Interviews 13B; 14B; 19B. Only two interviewees out of twenty-one explicitly stated they did not know about the committee at all.
[76] Al Jazeera. (2017). "الباب.. مفتاح الشمال السوري".
[77] Shabakat Halab News, 'جولة ميدانية في مدينة دير حافر', Retrieved 5 May 2020, *YouTube*, 24 September 2013, https://www.youtube.com/watch?v=Bfx9mZSV_To.
[78] Interviews 2B; 11B; Shabakat Halab News, 'جولة ميدانية في مدينة دير حافر'.

Despite these challenges, there was sufficient autonomy for locals to organise peaceful protests against the inflated rates imposed by traders within Deir Hafer.[79] The relief office and other charity organisations in the city were barely capable of providing food supplies (oil, rice, sugar, etc.) and basic necessities (such as milk for infants) to maintain the most elementary conditions of liveability for families in need.[80] These efforts, however, were no match to the needs and socio-economic vulnerabilities in place.

In light of this situation, Deir Hafer grew more dependent on the neighbouring city, al-Bab, as a gateway to relief and humanitarian organisations in Turkey. This reinforced pre-existing dependencies between the two cities, which intensified regional tensions. According to interviewees who had a role in the local council's relief office, most humanitarian aid came through al-Bab.[81] It had become common practice for al-Bab officials to withhold part of Deir Hafer's aid.[82] Furthermore, many kidnappings, according to interviewees, were traced to individuals and factions from al-Bab.[83] As local agricultural produce declined in winter in Deir Hafer, al-Bab became the centre for merchandise and goods coming through Turkey.[84] Prices soon increased along with Deir Hafer's dependency on al-Bab's markets, and Deir Hafer residents bore the brunt, while those in al-Bab with access to trade routes in Turkey benefitted. It was in the given economic circumstances and after expanding into Iraq and securing capital and military equipment that Daesh was able to not only impose itself militarily on other factions, but also recruit more people with enticing salaries and create more capable administrative structures.

Stifling civilian-led community protection efforts

Before taking over Deir Hafer in 2014, Daesh had already established itself in the city in all ways except militarily. Its strategy in Deir Hafer was similar to its strategies elsewhere east of Syria: wherever it lacked military capacity

---

[79] Interviews 6B; 21B.
[80] Shabakat Halab News, 'جولة ميدانية في مدينة دير حافر'.
[81] Interviews 12B; 21B.
[82] Interviews 12B; 21B.
[83] Interview 16B; 21B.
[84] Shabakat Halab News, 'جولة ميدانية في مدينة دير حافر'.

and found itself in areas contested by multiple factions, Daesh adopted a cooperative stance to help alleviate local conditions, fight corruption and establish order through services and administrative structures. It made itself useful to civilians and military factions alike. The local Da'wa (proselytisation) office explicitly aimed at improving the organisation's image. Given the massive lack of capacity and personnel in civilian structures, Katibat Abu Dujana welcomed the organisation provided that it limited its operations to administrative matters and respected its local authority. By late 2013, Daesh recruits ran the local 'Islamic police', Da'wa office, local clinics and other services in the city, and explicitly stated their membership to Daesh in a civilian capacity.[85] After Daesh clashed with Ahrar al-Sham in early 2014 in Maskaneh, it turned towards Deir Hafer and took over the area without any notable clashes.[86]

The biggest tribal group in the area was the Hadidiyin. Before 2012, the Assad government provided privileges and access to power to the tribe's senior figures due to their wide networks and expansive social ties.[87] This harked back to Assad senior's policies of creating a broad coalition of farmers, peasants and tribesmen in rural areas to extend his reach and power.[88]

The Hadidiyin remained in power with Daesh as the organisation capitalised on a sense of relative marginalisation that had been festering since 2012. With the broad coalition of cross-tribal representation within Katibat Abu Dujana, the Hadidiyins' previous clout diminished between 2012 and 2014. Daesh successfully appealed to members of the tribe by providing the opportunity for a return to its previous stature.[89] Before 2012, many members of the Hadidiyin and al-Kharraj had joined the Ba'th party and filled security branches locally as well as in other parts of the Aleppo province, such as Aleppo City.[90] Locals from Deir Hafer were often recruited and filled the state apparatus elsewhere. For instance,

---

[85] Shabakat Halab News, 'جولة ميدانية في مدينة دير حافر'.
[86] Interviews 8B; 21B.
[87] Interview 18B; Haian Dukhan, *State and Tribes in Syria: Informal Alliances and Conflict Patterns* (London: Routledge, 2019).
[88] Dukhan, *State and Tribes in Syria*.
[89] Interview 3B; 8B.
[90] Interviews 3B; 10B; 15B; 18B.

Abd al-Hanan Hajjo – from Deir Hafer and the tribe of Bani Saʿid – was appointed chief of police in Idlib City and later in Aleppo City.[91] Member of parliament, deputy vice president and owner of Deir Hafer's only surgical hospital, Fahmi Hasan was also from the region of Deir Hafer (born in Rasm Abboud) and from the Hadidiyin tribe.[92]

From the standpoint of Deir Hafer's political economy, the state and the Baʿth were the biggest employers, either through direct government positions or through subsidiary entities such as the farmers' union and other centralised agricultural planning initiatives. Through clientelistic distribution of wealth, services, privileges and positions, the Assad government captured the state and established neo-patrimonial relations even beyond its immediate reach. Locally privileged tribal figures nurtured their own clientelist networks by employing and appointing their kin and tribal affiliates within state departments and institutions under their influence.[93] This created a system of social hierarchy where tribal affiliation became a factor in the residents' opportunities and privileges.

Within tribal networks, varied groups and topographies of power existed depending on nature of kinship and proximity to those recruited in significant positions within the state apparatus. In 2012, when Deir Hafer effectively joined the opposition, it was rebelling against an older generation of local tribal leaders as much as it was against the government. These two classes of authority were intimately linked. Katibat Abu Dujana was composed of various tribes, but the majority hailed from a younger generation that created new local leadership and put aside the old guard. The conflict from a local standpoint was a struggle between these classes.

After Daesh took over, many of the Hadidiyin who were members of Katibat Abu Dujana joined Daesh, whereas the majority of Bani Jamil tribesmen remained with Ahrar al-Sham.[94] According to those who closely witnessed the transition of power from Abu Dujana to Daesh, the local

---

[91] Interview 21B.
[92] People's Council of Syria, 'حسن فهمي: عضو مجلس الشعب', *Syrian Arab Republic: The People's Council*, http://www.parliament.gov.sy/arabic/index.php?node=211&nid=1162&RID=26&Last=252&First=0&CurrentPage=0&FName=&LName=&City=&Cat=&Mem=&Com=&Aso=&or=& (accessed 20 May 2020).
[93] Dukhan, *State and Tribes in Syria*; Interviews 3B; 10B; 15B; 18B.
[94] Interviews 1B, 2B, 4B, 6B, 7B, 8B, 10B, 14B, 15B.

CIVILIAN AGENCY AND ITS LIMITS | 191

Daʻwa office and Daesh personnel grew more acquainted to local tensions through their presence in the city prior to the organisation's military takeover.[95]

With the takeover of Deir Hafer by Daesh, the primary difference in patterns of violence impacting the community was that all previous arrangements through intermediaries to save local infrastructure from aerial bombardment were annulled; as a result, the local surgical hospital was bombed in April 2015.[96] Among the casualties was the city's famous doctor, Dr Radwan al-Umar, who died in the raid. Before his death, Daesh held the doctor in detention for denouncing its methods.

Daesh used both coercive and enticing methods to create its new local cadres.[97] Every interviewee from Deir Hafer had personal stories about their suffering under Daesh. The events of Tal Ayoub in 2014 represented the point of no return for civilian autonomy and those who opposed the organisation.

May 2014 saw a series of clashes, detentions and killings by Daesh forces in and around the town of Tal Ayoub.[98] The incident began with Daesh attempting to co-opt a local military commander with the *nom de guerre* of Aba ʻaʼisha – a farmer who had mobilised and commanded less than thirty friends and family members, such as his sons, to fight against government forces in the region.[99] After refusing to join Daesh, surrender weapons, or vacate the area, a large number of Daesh troops with approximately forty military vehicles, equipped with medium-to-light weaponry, surrounded the village from all directions and conducted a terror campaign against residents.[100] Aba ʻaʼisha's house was attacked and clashes ensued, ending with the capture of his son, who was later executed in the centre of Deir Hafer where his body was displayed.[101] At the same time, Daesh troops proceeded with a campaign of detentions in the wider area including the town of Rasm al-Abed where the renowned medical doctor Khamis

---

[95] Interview 21B.
[96] Taht elMjhar, 'Victims among the dead'.
[97] Interviews 2B; 4B; 8B; 20B.
[98] al-Deri, 'داعش تقتحم قرية تل أيوب'.
[99] Interview 6B.
[100] Interviews 5B; 6B; 21B.
[101] Interview 6B.

al-Yousef was detained, tortured and interrogated.[102] Dr al-Yousef himself reveals how Daesh during the time had brought a detainee from Tal Ayoub and decapitated him in Rasm al-Abed.[103] The terror campaign was similar to other extreme measures and spectacles of violence adopted by the organisation to establish control and domination.[104]

In February 2017 government forces took over the area. Daesh fighters abandoned their positions. Since then, the government issued multiple statements calling for the return of local residents to Deir Hafer.[105] The city featured regularly on state TV channels, showing local development and investment in rehabilitating the infrastructure of the city and promoting agricultural activities.[106] The government also continued its efforts to reorganise tribal groups and create new networks of patronage. Such efforts are widely condemned by the Majlis al-Qaba'il wal-Wujaha' Fi al-Dakhel al-Souri through statements signed by more than fifteen local tribes and clans.[107] Tribal leadership continues to be contested and organisational capacity continuously shifts based on the patronage in place. Many who were previously connected to the government and did not take part in any civilian or military activism between 2012 and 2017 reportedly returned to local leadership positions.[108] Upon return, those who had any role in local organisational and administrative efforts during opposition control face uncertainties and existential threats.

Kasab in Focus
Conflict dynamics

Kasab remained mostly under government control throughout the conflict. Despite its relative isolation, the area faced multiple threats. In August 2012 the Kasab–Latakia highway was cut off, and at the same time there were skirmishes on the Latakia–Basit road.[109] These two roads were the only

---

[102] Interviews 5B; 6B; 21B.
[103] Interview 6B.
[104] Akdedian, 'On Violence and Radical Theology', 361–80.
[105] SANA, 'Hundreds of residents of Deir Hafer area and its surroundings return to their homes'.
[106] Ibid.
[107] 'Syrian Tribes and Clans Deny Participation in "Deir Hafer" Meeting', *Syria Call*, 5 June 2018.
[108] Interviews 15B; 21B.
[109] Tcholakian, *The Three Days of Kessab*.

connections to Latakia – the closest city to Kasab and its main connection to Damascus and Beirut throughout the war.[110] The economic vulnerabilities in the wake and throughout the conflict in Kasab had major implications for civilian community organisers and their capacity to protect their community from harm and recover from shocks. Between 2012 and 2014 the youth comprised the biggest portion of those who had left, agricultural production dwindled and tourism came to a halt, resulting in hardly any locally generated revenue streams to sustain the local population.[111]

The loss of youth left the agricultural sector lacking operational capacity – specifically Armenian landowners who already relied on labour from nearby towns, which was no longer available as these areas were held by armed opposition groups across the frontlines towards Idlib. Pre-existing economic disparities influenced by patterns of militarisation in the region. Many labourers from the Turkmen communities in neighbouring areas were among the ranks of the armed opposition groups that attacked the area where landowners had aligned with the government.[112]

Heavy reliance on tourism in the period preceding the turmoil also created economic vulnerability due to diminished self-sufficiency. Despite the economic vulnerabilities in place, until the 2014 attack, locals lived with a relative sense of isolation and distance from the direct reach of violence.[113] There was an attack on the town of Nabʿ al-Murr, 4 km south of Kasab, on 8 August 2012. The town is located in close proximity to the Syrian–Turkish border crossing. Although the attack was halted, the town of Nabʿ al-Murr was almost entirely vacated by families who ended up relocating to Kasab.[114] It was only when three mortars were launched on Christmas day, 25 December 2012 (as celebrated by Catholic Armenians), the town of

---

[110] Ibid.; Shoghig Ashekian, 'Տեղահանութիւն, Հալաքական Յիշողութիւն և Անձնական Փորձառութիւն (Քեսապի Պարագայ)', in Antranik Dakessian (ed.), *Armenians of Syria: Proceedings of the Conference (24–27 May 2015)* (Beirut: Haigazian University Press: Armenian Diaspora Research Center, 2018), 509–38.

[111] Tcholakian, *The Three Days of Kessab*; Ashekian, 'Տեղահանութիւն, Հալաքական Յիշողութիւն և Անձնական Փորձառութիւն'; Interview 15B.

[112] Interviews 4A; 8A; 10A; 14A.

[113] Interviews 15A; 20A.

[114] Tcholakian, *The Three Days of Kessab*; Ashekian, 'Տեղահանութիւն, Հալաքական Յիշողութիւն և Անձնական Փորձառութիւն'; Interview 18A.

Kasab itself recorded the first attack against it.[115] For residents, they were a clear message that they were now a target.[116] Despite the occasional mortar attacks and limited skirmishes on the eastern front of Nabʿ al-Murr, the area of Kasab remained relatively stable until 2014.

On 21 March 2014 the attack on Kasab was from three frontlines: east, north and northwest. The incessant gunfire from all directions and the number of attacking factions was overwhelming. Armed opposition groups (Al Nusra Front, Sham al-Islam and Ansar al-Sham) took over the city by attacking Kasab through multiple fronts along the Turkish border in March 2014.[117] Armed opposition forces numbered around 3,000 and the frontline extended from the eastern villages of Samra, to the north of Kasab in the vicinity of Jabal al-Aqraʿ and around the western areas of Tal 45 and Nabʿ al-Murr.[118] Multiple calls for support were sent out to the official Syrian army, who did not oblige. In fact, the superintendents of the Armenian forces made multiple calls for artillery forces around Kasab to open fire with the specific coordinates of the attacking forces, to no avail.[119]

Before the conflict, the presence of the Syrian Arab Army around the Syrian–Turkish borders was limited, and the army did not patrol the border with Turkey under the official pretext that the Syrian Arab Republic considers the borderline illegitimate.[120] The presence of official Syrian Arab Army troops along the border stayed minimal after 2011 as well. According to local residents, Turkish authorities facilitated cross-border military operations

---

[115] Ashekian, 'Տեղահանութիւն, Հալաքական Յիշողութիւն և Անձնական Փորձառութիւն'.
[116] Ashekian, 'Տեղահանութիւն, Հալաքական Յիշողութիւն և Անձնական Փորձառութիւն'; interviews 1A–20A; Tcholakian, *The Three Days of Kessab*.
[117] Tcholakian, *The Three Days of Kessab*; Aymenn J. Al-Tamimi, 'The Latakia Front: An Interview on the Rebel Side', *Syria Comment*, 6 April 2014, https://web.archive.org/web/20171105235553/http://www.joshualandis.com/blog/latakia-front-interview-rebel-side/ (accessed 14 May 2020); Ashekian, 'Տեղահանութիւն, Հալաքական Յիշողութիւն և Անձնական Փորձառութիւն', 509–38.
[118] The Carter Center, 'Syrian Armed Opposition'.
[119] Sevan Manjikian, *Քեսապ 2014: Մեղահանութիւն և Մերադարձ* (NA: Arevelk, 2017); Ashekian, 'Տեղահանութիւն, Հալաքական Յիշողութիւն և Անձնական Փորձառութիւն', 521.
[120] Tcholakian, *The Three Days of Kessab*.

amidst the 2014 attacks.¹²¹ These factors effectively rendered the border a source of danger and vulnerability.

Casualties were minimal among the civilian population, as members of the community managed to flee the area before armed opposition groups took over.¹²² Some community members were displaced to Latakia and returned to their homes after the withdrawal of armed opposition groups by mid-2014. Others relocated to other countries such as Lebanon, and from there some moved on to Armenia, Canada and Australia.¹²³ Since the attack, almost half of the community's inhabitants returned to the area.¹²⁴ Upon their return, the displaced found considerable damages to ecclesiastic and private property, as many houses were looted and churches were desecrated.¹²⁵ The community's infrastructure has been revived but the area lost its most vital components such as local tourism, a significant portion of the youth, and many of those with higher education and agricultural skills.

It is noticeable that the attack, which started on 21 March 2014 by a coalition of forces from the Al Nusra Front, Sham al-Islam and Ahrar al-Sham, was labelled 'Ma'rakat al-anfal' – which alludes to religiously motivated 'war of spoils'. The name itself highlights the contradictory and confusing statements from the attacking forces in the eyes of local inhabitants. '*They named the operation "Ma'rakat al-anfal", and uploaded videos of looting, desecrated and mocked religious symbols, they [the attacking forces] were at the same time portraying themselves that they were protecting our religious establishments,*' declared a local clergy.¹²⁶ In line with this, it is also important to note that during the early stage of the attack, mortars and attacks took place in the territories of the border town of Nab' al-Murr, the villages of al-Dilbeh and

---

¹²¹ Interviews 4A; 7A; 8A; 10A; Fabrice Balanche, 'Latakia Is Assad's Achilles Heel', *The Washington Institute*, 23 September 2015, https://www.washingtoninstitute.org/policy-analysis/view/latakia-is-assads-achilles-heel (accessed 21 April 2020).
¹²² Tcholakian, *The Three Days of Kessab*; Ashekian, 'Տեղահանութիւն, Հալապական Յիշողութիւն և Անձնական Փորձառութիւն'; Manjikian, *Թեսապ 2014*; Sara E. Williams, 'The invasion of Kassab: "We were evicted"', *Al Jazeera*, 30 April 2014, https://www.aljazeera.com/news/2014/4/30/the-invasion-of-kassab-we-were-evicted.
¹²³ Manjikian, *Թեսապ 2014*.
¹²⁴ Interview 4A.
¹²⁵ Ashekian, 'Տեղահանութիւն, Հալապական Յիշողութիւն և Անձնական Փորձառութիւն'.
¹²⁶ Interviews 4A; 20A.

Kurkuna and the vicinity of the town of Kasab.[127] All of these areas housed the Alawite population of the area. Armed opposition groups attempted to frame their operations to target the Alawite community alone. From the perspective of the local population, however, there was no sense of reassurance or safety regardless of ethno-religious belonging.[128] Furthermore, combatants from opposition groups after arriving in Kasab expressed strong supremacist views with regards to other religious and denominational groups, Armenians and Alawis alike.[129]

Upon return, many citizens found their belongings to be missing.[130] It is difficult to assess the extent to which the damage and looting of properties in Kasab was done by armed opposition groups or government forces. Both were reported.[131] *'Some of the summer residences [that did not belong to locals] were completely looted, everything – furniture, tiles, electric wirings, anything of value'*.[132] The widespread reports of local property being looted by pro-government security personnel created tension between the local *mukhabarat* (specifically *Amen Dawle*) and religious representatives in the Armenian community.[133] Upon return to their homes in late July 2014 many locals noticed or heard from neighbours that appliances and furniture were in different houses.[134] Belongings had moved while locals were away. Given that such matters were never redressed even after their halt, trust issues lingered amongst the population.[135] The area lost half of its inhabitants, the vast majority of its youth, its economic self-sufficiency and residents consider the region under continuous threat of recurrent violence for its proximity to opposition-controlled Idlib.[136]

---

[127] Tcholakian, *The Three Days of Kessab*, 71
[128] Interview 18A.
[129] Ibid.; Al-Tamimi, 'An Interview on the Rebel Side'.
[130] Interviews 14A; 18A; Manjikian, Թաաա *2014*, 19.
[131] Interview 18A; Tcholakian, *The Three Days of Kessab*, 71.
[132] Interview 18A.
[133] Interview 14A.
[134] Ibid.; Interviews 4A; 8A.
[135] Interviews 4A; 18A; Manjikian, Թաաա *2014*.
[136] Mehmet A. Aksoy, 'Syrian Turkmen: Fighting to Survive', *Al Jazeera World*, 16 August 2017, https://www.aljazeera.com/programmes/aljazeeraworld/2017/08/syrian-turkmen-fighting-survive-170806082405511.html (accessed 20 May 2020); Government of Turkey 'Bayirbucak Turkmens take refuge in Turkey', *Relief Web*, 1 February 2016, https://reliefweb.int/report/turkey/bayirbucak-turkmens-take-refuge-turkey; Jack Stubbs and Humeyra Pamuk, 'Russian raids

Community protection

Civilian strategies of community protection evolved and changed based on the scale and intensity of violence impacting Kasab since 2011. In early 2012 and during the early phase of the militarisation of the uprising, many representatives of the Armenian community called for a position of neutrality. As Kaplan indicates in his seminal book *Resisting War*, the three representatives of Armenian churches in the Syrian Arab Republic issued public statements that called for neutrality.[137] Unlike other areas, such as Aleppo City where Armenian neighbourhoods at close proximity to actively contested frontlines ended up mobilising through pro-government paramilitary forces, Armenian community organisers maintained distinct security arrangements that were separate from the local National Defence Forces in Kasab. Despite being under the unified regional command of the NDF at the time of the March 2014 attack, the NDF and the Armenian paramilitary formation under the auspices of the Tashnak did not have a unified operational structure.[138]

Between 2012 and 2013, as the Syrian unrest became more widespread and military developments in rural Latakia and Idlib disrupted the local economy further, personal connections to community members abroad and remittances became vital income streams. When the two roads connecting Kasab to Latakia were compromised and locals realised it was possible for Kasab to become intentionally or unintentionally besieged, even if it was not to be directly attacked, they intensified their efforts to store preserved food in safe areas.[139] Furthermore, there were safe areas designated within the town for civilians to congregate in case of a sudden attack.[140]

---

repeatedly hit Syrian Turkmen areas, Moscow's data shows', *Reuters*, 27 November 2015, https://www.reuters.com/article/us-mideast-crisis-russia-turkey-airstrik-idUSKBN0TG1YQ20151128 (accessed 20 May 2020).

[137] Martin Armstrong and Lauren Williams, 'Armenian Christians Torn in Syria's Civil War', *Beirut: The Daily Star*, 1 October 2012, https://hetq.am/en/article/19046; Kaplan, *Resisting War*, 296–7.

[138] Tcholakian, *The Three Days of Kessab*; Ashekian, 'Տեղահանութիւն, Հաւաքական Յիշողութիւն և Անձնական Փորձառութիւն'; Manjikian, *Քեսապ 2014*.

[139] Ibid.

[140] Ashekian, 'Տեղահանութիւն, Հաւաքական Յիշողութիւն և Անձնական Փորձառութիւն'.

Before the 2014 attacks, Kasab's demographic reality had already shifted due to economic circumstances in place and mandatory conscription laws, which drove many of the young Armenian male population with opportunities abroad to leave.[141] Common destinations for Armenians before 2014 were Latakia, Beirut and Yerevan, whereas migrating members of the Alawi community moved predominantly to Latakia city and its nearby towns to be near extended family members.[142] The loss of the youth left the agricultural sector lacking operational capacity. Furthermore, labourers from nearby towns were no longer available for hire as they resided in opposition-held areas across the frontlines towards Idlib.

When Kasab's Armenian population evacuated and arrived at the Armenian Church in Latakia by May 2014 the number of registered displaced individuals, according to the Armenian Diocese of Beroea (responsible for Armenian Apostolic Churches in Syria including the host Holy Mother of God church in Latakia), was 1,395 individuals.[143] The number of Armenian inhabitants in Kasab in early 2020 was around 900 according to the Emergency Relief Committee and the Armenian Evangelical Church in Kasab.[144] The numbers reveal that the Armenian presence had diminished disproportionately since the conflict began. Patterns of militarisation followed suit as recruits from the Alawi community in the NDF were twice as many as all the Armenian recruits combined, in big part due to possibilities for external migration or lack of. Sources of livelihood and access to trans-local networks and institutions impacted trajectories of internal and external displacement or migration, and by doing so, also impacted patterns of militarisation in the process.

Since the March 2014 offensive and throughout the clashes with opposition forces, paramilitary groups such as Ali Kayyali's National Resistance and Lebanese Hezbollah forces were also active on the front lines in addition

---

[141] Interviews 10A; 16A.
[142] Interview 18A.
[143] Armenian Diocese of Beroea, 'The Crisis of Syrian Armenians and the Displacement of Kessab's Armenians: A Brief Report', *Horizon*, 24 June 2014, https://horizonweekly.ca/en/41718-2/ (accessed 13 May 2020).
[144] Interviews 4A; 10A.

to local paramilitary forces.[145] In his book, *The Three Days of Kessab*, Hagop Tcholakian attributes the position of Armenian communities to not enlist with the NDF to an overall and nationwide community stance under the banner of 'positive neutrality'.[146] The notion of positive neutrality, however, is highly contested within Armenian leadership structures as the language of neutrality was quickly abandoned after 2012. Nonetheless, leading community organisers, ecclesiastic and civil, predominantly continued to air on the side of neutrality and autonomy vis-à-vis paramilitary actors wherever possible. In Aleppo City, for instance, some community representatives hold meetings with members and representatives of oppositionist groups.[147] As the conflict spread to Aleppo and the city was ravaged by war, different neighbourhoods mobilised in different ways depending on where the front lines fell. Armenian community representatives calling for neutrality and rejecting the enlisting of the local youth in the NDF in Kasab, advocated for the opposite in Aleppo where the danger was imminent and local demographic features and urban frontlines did not allow the maintenance of organisational autonomy.[148]

A series of measures were enacted by Armenian organisations to maintain a level of autonomy and organisational distinction from military and paramilitary forces. In Kasab, between 2012 and 2014, Armenian and Alawi community members participated in local consultations and town meetings to discuss matters related to community protection.[149] The military formations under Armenian command numbering less than two dozen armed men remained separate.[150] Despite the fact that many decided neutrality was impossible in the face of hostile military formations and the dangers ahead, the majority refused enlisting the young male population under the command structure of the National Defence Forces and receive funds and

---

[145] Al-Tamimi, *An Interview on the Rebel Side*, 2014; The Carter Center, 'Syrian Armed Opposition'; Interview 8A.
[146] Tcholakian, *The Three Days of Kessab*; Kaplan, *Resisting War*, 296–7; Armstrong and Williams, 'Armenian Christians Torn'.
[147] Interview 11A.
[148] Interview 14A.
[149] Ashekian, 'Տեղահանութիւն, Հաւաքական Յիշողութիւն և Անձնական Փորձառութիւն', 517.
[150] Interview 17A.

weapons accordingly.[151] Armenians who ended up enlisting out of personal volition received, like other recruits, a monthly salary, a Kalashnikov rifle and from sixty to one hundred bullets.[152] Neither the weapons provided nor the payrolls were deemed sufficient for self-defence and the command structure of the paramilitary group would have eroded the authority and structure of the Armenian leadership: ecclesiastic (local churches) and civil (predominantly the Tashnak). In addition, the National Defence Forces were not solely for self-defence mechanisms and did mobilise into areas beyond Kasab.[153] Armenian representatives were pressured to express and demonstrate loyalty to the Assad rule. At the same time, the majority, including dominant parties and organisers, such as the Tashnak, along with the leading churches, deemed the prospects of the local youth joining the ranks of paramilitary formations with command structures that are independent of Armenian communities a matter that would have effectively mobilised the entire community as mercenaries beyond the parameters of self-defence.[154]

Although Armenian and Alawi community representatives participated in local consultations between 2012 and 2014, such consultations never translated to cooperative actions, unified plans or coordinated activities. Besides procedural matters, no strategic plans or mutual self-defence mechanisms were developed.[155] There were neither coordinated military plans nor unified evacuation plans or early warning systems in place. As the head of one of the Armenian churches in Kasab asserts, it happened that prior to the 2014 attacks, suddenly and without notice, the entire Alawi community had vacated their areas: *'perhaps they received news of an imminent attack,'* the clergy proclaimed, *'but they didn't tell us.'*[156] Each community relied on its own channels and capacities.

The Armenian forces were deployed along the border but had very limited surveillance equipment that did not allow tracking movement beyond

---

[151] Tcholakian, *The Three Days of Kessab*; interviews 18A; 20A.
[152] Tcholakian, 2019; Ashekian, 'Տեղահանութիւն, Հալաքական Ցիշողութիւն և Անձնական Փորձառութիւն'.
[153] Interviews 14A, 18A.
[154] Tcholakian, *The Three Days of Kessab*; Ashekian, 'Տեղահանութիւն, Հալաքական Ցիշողութիւն և Անձնական Փորձառութիւն'.
[155] Tcholakian, *The Three Days of Kessab*; interview 7A.
[156] Interview 15A.

immediate areas, specifically at night. Armenian forces under the informal leadership of the Tashnak used hunting rifles and light weapons to provide monitoring and surveillance, and occupied strategic posts along the border. The other forces too, despite also having limited and basic equipment, had cross-border relations inside territories under Turkish control. These were primarily based on cross-border illicit trade relations and smuggling ties developed throughout the years.[157] Such connections included few members from the Armenian community.[158]

There were no coordinated early warning systems for evacuation plans developed throughout the conflict.[159] According to community leaders who took part in community meetings, there were always ideas and proposals about evacuation plans but they always remained hypothetical and never translated to actual plans.[160] The population relied on the state and security apparatus in place. The reliance on security organisms was reinforced in light of pre-2014 overall sense of relative protection from the conflict.

Economic vulnerability

The nature of labour-capital relations in Kasab was such that the vast majority of landowners belonged to the Armenian community. Most Armenian landowners in the area either rented out portions of their land to members of the Alawi community or relied on labourers residing outside of Kasab (predominantly from the Turkmen community). Some Armenian landowners continued cultivating their own land, relying on family relations and networks of kinship.[161] Between 2000 and 2011, the latter category became scarcer as revenues from tourism far outweighed the income from agriculture.

Class divisions and land ownership was in fact one of the vulnerabilities manifesting in the 2014 attacks, as many labourers from the Turkmen communities in the Kasab vicinity were among the ranks of the armed groups that attacked the area.[162] In fact, after those groups had taken over

---

[157] Interview 7A.
[158] Ashekian, 'Տեղահանութիւն, Հասարակական Յիշողութիւն և Անձնական Փորձառութիւն'; interview 7A.
[159] Interview 14A.
[160] Ibid.
[161] Interviews 10A; 18A; 20A.
[162] Interview 4A; 8A; 10A; 14A.

the area, some Armenian landowners received phone calls from those who had worked on their lands promising to take care of the property.[163] After becoming displaced, many Armenians contacted their acquaintances from Turkmen community members who were previously hired as labourers to receive news and updates about their properties in Kasab.[164] Some of those also expressed joy to have taken over the lands of the previous landowners and the opportunity of profiteering. In addition to class divisions, heavy reliance on tourism in the period preceding the turmoil created much economic vulnerability due to diminished self-sufficiency. According to the municipality's declared numbers, visitors and tourists between the year 2000 and 2005 expanded from a year-round total of 300,000 to more than one million.[165]

In light of this, agricultural productivity was no longer a necessity prior to the conflict. Traditional production of pomegranate molasses, wine, laurel soap, dried fruits, sweets and vinegar dwindled and were reframed as traditional local skills aimed at bolstering the area's image as an attractive tourist site. A by-product of such rapid shifts in economic modes of production towards tourism was the price of properties, rentals and real estate. Given the high demand for temporary residences during summer, rentals became a profitable niche. According to the Central Bureau of Statistics, in 2004 the town of Kasab and its villages contained 1,360 residences out of which 805 were vacant and only 460 were occupied.[166] Furthermore, there were an additional 109 residences under construction in the same year.[167] According to locals, the spike in local property prices and demand led many residents to sub divide their lands and either sell a part of it or develop it as a rental property.[168] In light of this, many buyers from Aleppo or the Syrian coast bought properties or land as summer residences, investments or both.[169] The economic shifts changed the local mindset towards

---

[163] Interview 10A.
[164] Ibid.
[165] Municipality of Kasab, 2005; Jalal B. Khedra, '31', 'خطة لتنمية السياحة البيئية في منطقة كسب واستثمارها', مجلة جامعة تشرين للبحوث والدراسات العلمية, "طبيعياً", no. 1 (2009): 113–14.
[166] Central Bureau of Statistics, 2004.
[167] Ibid.
[168] Interviews 8A; 20A.
[169] Interviews 8A; 20A.

less appreciation of the labour-intensive agricultural activities specifically amongst the youth.[170] Naturally, as new property owners emerged, the area's demographic and cultural features also relatively changed.[171] After 2011, when the community was forced to find avenues other than tourism, agricultural productivity was not only insufficient but also lacked capacity. Efforts to revamp agricultural production faced myriad emergent obstacles and challenges such as shortages in fuel, exorbitant prices and currency deflation. Due to these local circumstances, most members of the community relied on a combination of relief, charities and remittances.[172] With the turmoil and instability that came after 2011, the community increasingly relied on remittances and fundraising from abroad, whether through organisations or through personal connections.

Stifling civilian-led community protection efforts

The 2012 attack on Nab' al-Murr represented a warning but at the same time created the impression among locals that the town was well protected and the self-defence mechanisms in place were efficient as no casualties were recorded. In March 2014, however, the attack was from all three sides: east, north and northwest. The incessant gunfire from all directions and the number of attacking factions was overwhelming. Although there were no early warning mechanisms in place, the mountainous landscape of Kasab amplified the sounds of live ammunition and explosions.[173] The scale of the attack was unlike any other that Kasab experienced throughout the conflict. Locals, who throughout the conflict had grown accustomed to the sounds of war, were quick to realise that this was an attempt to overtake the area. The lack of evacuation plans, drills or delegation of neighbourhood responsibilities to carry out a comprehensive evacuation created massive panic in the community.[174] In addition, a number of false alarms and precautionary evacuations prior to the 2014 attacks led many residents to believe that the evacuation would be temporary and that in a matter of hours they would

[170] Interview 10A; 20A.
[171] Interviews 8A; 13A; 20A.
[172] Interviews 9A; 10A.
[173] Interview 4A.
[174] Tcholakian, *The Three Days of Kessab*; interview 18A; Williams, 'The invasion of Kassab'.

return to their homes. The majority of those who vacated carried minimal belongings and left without knowing what direction to go, where to congregate, and who to ask questions of.[175] Although the evacuation ensued in the hour immediately after the onset of the attacks in the morning of 21 March 2014, it was not until the end of the next day that rebel forces entered Kasab.

The community remained largely cohesive in Latakia city and mobilised support through its local, national and international links. Media campaigns by local, international and social media channels brought the situation to the attention of international actors. Many media outlets, however, were falsely circulating reports about massacres occurring in Kasab.[176]

Most inhabitants evacuated without belongings. Some were left behind, specifically elders of the Armenian community who either needed assistance or refused to leave altogether.[177] The Alawi community vacated the area separately and had its own channels of information.[178] Nonetheless, there were still many of those community members who were similarly unaware of developments and what course of action to take. For example, an Armenian community leader who drove a school bus from Kasab, picking up residents along the way, picked up individuals and families from the Alawi community who, otherwise, had no means of vacating the area.[179] It is striking how, after more than two years of uncertainty, community organisers had still not developed a comprehensive early warning system that would notify residents about the movement of attacking troops. Without an organised evacuation plan, vulnerable members of the community were left more exposed than others. According to Shoghig Ashekian, a pro-Tashnak historian and a local of Kasab, those on the front lines notified their supervisors and family members of the attack and the need to evacuate, and some of them stayed on the front lines until 22 March 2014.[180] With so many

---

[175] Interview 18A; Tcholakian, *The Three Days of Kessab*.
[176] Tcholakian, *The Three Days of Kessab*, 151; Hania Mourtada, 'Rebels Reassure Christians After Capturing Key Syrian Border Town', *Time*, 27 March 2014, https://time.com/40378/syria-kessab-christians/ (accessed 15 May 2020).
[177] Tcholakian, *The Three Days of Kessab*.
[178] Interview 18A.
[179] Ibid.
[180] Ashekian, 'Տեղահանութիւն, Հասարակական Յիշողութիւն և Անձնական Փորձառութիւն', 519; interview 18A.

community members relying on informal and uncoordinated channels to learn about specific developments, where the danger was, and where to head, it is safe to say beyond reasonable doubt that the community was not organised nor prepared for the situation. Beyond those on the front lines, civilian community leaders who could have organised the community were not consulted, and were unprepared and overwhelmed by the scale and intensity of the attack in its early instance.

The final destination of the evacuation was also unclear. As time passed on the day of the attack, the head of the Relief Committee, who was also the head of the Armenian Apostolic Church of Kasab at the time, arrived at the Armenian Apostolic Church in Latakia. Later, those who were stationed outside of Kasab learned about the destination and proceeded there.[181] Even some of the heads of other churches from Kasab were not made aware of this destination and learned about developments and plans throughout the day.[182] This placed as many as hundreds of community members, unaware of their potential destination congregating near the town of Badrousiyeh on the coastal road, in unnecessary and avoidable risk as there were clashes raging in the vicinity.[183] Many community organisers who could have played a crucial role in their civilian or ecclesiastic capacities trusted the security organisms in place, which did not consult with them or prepare for such an eventuality. The assumption and overall environment was such that with the variety of forces present, measures would surely be in place by those in charge, and that if the need ever arose, those forces would know what to do. The immediate chaotic evacuation along with the fact that self-defence mechanisms did not succeed in halting the advances on Kasab, shocked the community, damaging public confidence and leading to trust issues, particularly among those who felt excluded from decision-making processes or have not found space for cooperative actions in organising the community.

A week after the evacuation of Kasab, 1,151 people were registered as displaced in Latakia by the Relief Committee.[184] In addition, there was a large number of families who did not stop in Latakia and headed straight

---

[181] Interview 18A.
[182] Ibid.
[183] Interview 15A; Tcholakian, *The Three Days of Kessab*.
[184] Manjikian, Բեսսաց 2014.

to Lebanon and twenty-five families who, in the midst of the chaos, had moved from village to village, with some moving outside of the Syrian Arab Republic.[185] The number of the registered was only based on the displaced of Armenian origin who stayed in the Armenian Apostolic Church of Latakia. As mentioned, members of the Alawi community who moved to Latakia received aid and support through separate organisations.[186] Others were displaced to nearby towns and villages. Both communities relied on pre-existing kinship ties or joined those who had left before the attack for employment or to continue their studies abroad.

The majority of the displaced were able to congregate in one place, maintain cohesion in exile and were able to return home less than three months after displacement, helping restore the community. One of the first restorative efforts by the Emergency Relief and Rehabilitation Committee was repairs to windows, doors and locks of homes.[187]

While in exile, the aid that the displaced received was comprehensive.[188] However, the lack of transparency in the aid received and distributed during and after displacement, led to mistrust in the community.[189] Informal mediation processes were used and a renowned community representative with reputable standing was asked to intervene to mediate informally.[190]

Since the community's return, most damages to infrastructure as well as properties were repaired through separate church funds as well as donations funnelled through the Relief Committee. Despite the fact that Kasab did not witness further military developments, the areas around Kasab, known as Jabal Turkman, housing members of Syrian Turkmen community, underwent drastic transformations. In the aftermath of the Turkish downing of Russian jets in late 2015, Russian offensives upon the Turkmen communities housing opposition groups increased and resulted in a reported displacement of 300,000 Turkmen from Northern Latakia.[191] Demographic

---

[185] Ibid., 10–11.
[186] Interview 18A.
[187] Manjikian, *Քեսապ 2014*.
[188] Interviews 9A; 14A.
[189] Interview 18A.
[190] Ibid.
[191] Aksoy, 'Syrian Turkmen'; Government of Turkey, 'Bayirbucak Turkmens take refuge in Turkey'; Stubbs and Pamuk, 'Russian raids'.

transformations are not limited to Kasab – the region of Northern Latakia witnessed drastic demographic transformations. Inequitable labour-capital relations and relative deprivation remain broader regional issues that impact Kasab as well.

Community Protection in Kasab and Deir Hafer: A Synthesis

Kasab and Deir Hafer represent 'influential cases' as they provide examples of community protection efforts at the local level against specific threats and instances of violence.[192] Both areas gained geostrategic significance throughout the conflict and were directly targeted by violence. Both experienced mass displacement and are peripheral areas with regional administrative dependencies on centres of power beyond the locale. Simultaneously, both cases depict contrasting conflict dynamics and divergent efforts, strategies and experiences of civilian community protection.[193]

Kasab remained mostly under the control of the government whereas various groups controlled Deir Hafer for extended periods. This had significant implications for patterns of continuity and change in local civilian actors, civilian autonomy, as well as levels of harm and patterns of violence within the two communities. Despite both communities having faced existential threats, the violence and destruction that Deir Hafer experienced was more relentless and sustained. Kasab has remained under threat but only sustained one episode of direct communal attack. This attack drove the entire community away but recorded few civilian casualties and a sizeable portion of those displaced remained cohesive and returned to their homes in less than three months. In this sense, Kasab presents a relatively positive case compared to Deir Hafer, which sustained more civilian casualties, more scattered trajectories of evacuation, dispersed displacement and existential threats to potential returnees. Initiatives in Kasab and Deir Hafer offer examples of local efforts to maintain autonomy, develop non-violent conflict-resolution mechanisms and procure the necessities for preserving

---

[192] John Gerring, 'Case Selection for Case-Study Analysis: Qualitative and Quantitative Techniques', in Janet Box-Steffensmeier, Henry Brady and David Collier (eds), *The Oxford Handbook of Political Methodology* (Oxford: Oxford University Press, 2010), 567.
[193] Alexander L. George and Andrew Bennett, *Case Studies and Theory Development in the Social Sciences* (Cambridge, MA: MIT Press, 2005), 67.

living conditions. The contrasting experiences across the two locations are indicative of the range of threats and vulnerabilities faced by communities across the Syrian Arab Republic.

Threats to both communities have been shaped by a combination of local circumstances and vulnerabilities as well as broader conflict patterns and dynamics in the Syrian Arab Republic. The year 2014 witnessed significant shifts in the balance of powers and patterns of violence in the Syrian conflict, which negatively impacted civilian community organisers. Preceding this period – between 2012 and 2013 – both Deir Hafer and Kasab exhibited many examples of community protection. In Deir Hafer there was no major factional in-fighting, civilian initiatives flourished (albeit in a limited capacity, such as local newspapers, conflict resolution committees and peaceful protests) and vital infrastructures were protected from destruction through informal agreements and arrangements with government forces. For Kasab, the period between 2012 and late 2013 presents a period of community alertness, social cohesion and preparedness. There were multiple community meetings and discussions about possible risks and actions, new civilian committees were formed for relief efforts, residents had taken personal measures for evacuation and the majority of the locality avoided being mobilised against other communities.[194]

By late 2013, however, it is evident that in both areas civilian initiatives gradually diminished and armed groups increasingly emerged as the sole security and safety providers. As discussed, a sense of fatigue increased, manifesting in different forms, including the normalisation of threats and vulnerabilities by civilian community organisers and increased sense of detachment from risks and responsibilities.[195] Furthermore, in the first half of 2014, both areas witnessed unprecedented levels of active contests over territorial control, which introduced new shocks, increased the level of violence in the respective areas, exposed pre-existing vulnerabilities and created additional vulnerabilities that diminished civilian capacities of community protection. As an interviewee from Kasab summarised: *'those who were left*

---

[194] Tcholakian, *The Three Days of Kessab*.
[195] Sabine Sonnentag, 'Recovery from fatigue: The role of psychological detachment', in Philip L. Ackerman (ed.), *Cognitive Fatigue: Multidisciplinary Perspectives on Current Research and Future Applications* (Washington, DC: American Psychological Association, 2011), 253–72.

[in the community] after 2014 have surrendered to the reality as is . . . without any initiative or willingness to cooperate, or try to change their circumstances. Everyone became aid dependent.'[196]

This resonates with statements from community organisers in Deir Hafer as well:

> *As soon as [Daesh] took over, the campaign against us [activists] escalated to an unprecedented level – the majority of us were either coerced out of activism, were intimidated and fled or ended up being co-opted. We had no means to resist or organise ourselves [. . .] They [Daesh] took away Internet routers and monitored social media channels closely. On top of that, public executions spread fear amongst everyone; even their [Daesh] followers. From then on, every one of us was just trying to survive. There was no room for activism or to organise ourselves.*[197]

It is a challenge to retrospectively examine, quantify and provide scientific measurement of social trust, fatigue and trauma levels, specifically while conflict fragility and vulnerability remain uninterrupted and baseline studies are unavailable.[198] However, findings from interviews and focus group discussions suggest that Deir Hafer's armed factions and civilian structures welcomed Daesh's charitable activities and much needed assistance in local administrative matters before its military takeover. This was due to local fatigue from constant bombardment, lack of resources and limited administrative capacity. Although it was impossible for anyone to predict the forthcoming brutality of Daesh, it is clear in retrospect that the growing reliance on its cadres diminished the role and centrality of local civilian structures. Similarly, Kasab residents had entirely surrendered vital disaster preparedness efforts, such as evacuation plans and early warning systems, to the security apparatus in place, which proved insufficiently and inadequately prepared for such an eventuality.

---

[196] Interview 20A.
[197] Interview 21B.
[198] Miro Klarić, Branka Klarić, Aleksandra Stevanovic, Jasna Grkovié and Suzana Jonovska, 'Psychological Consequences of War Trauma and Postwar Social Stressors in Women in Bosnia and Herzegovina', *Croatian Medical Journal*, 48, no. 2 (2007), 167–76.

Both communities exhibited similar dynamics of susceptibility to growing threats, economic fragility, diminished resources, inflation, displacement and existential shocks. However, the direct violence the two communities confronted varied in scale and nature. Throughout the period between 2011 and 2017, Deir Hafer witnessed kidnappings, aerial attacks by artillery and warplanes and violence by armed factions against the population. The direct violence that Kasab sustained was more contained, but the community was susceptible to greater harm and damage than what actually occurred. Furthermore, despite sharp differences in exposure to harm, the overall impact of the conflict on the social fabric of both communities was comparable in nature and scale. Both communities witnessed the loss of more than a third of their populations, increased social mistrust, a diminished sense of safety and the exacerbation of pre-2011 elements, such as limited civilian autonomy, that contributed to diminished civilian capacity to self-organise.

The communities' experiences of displacement and evacuation present sharp contrasts and provide differing obstacles to recovery. In the case of Kasab, a large part of the community was able to remain cohesive abroad, leading to the return of a sizeable section of the community and maintaining cohesion in exile among those who have remained outside. In contrast, evacuation patterns for Deir Hafer were uncoordinated and depended upon military developments in the area. For instance, when the local armed group took over in 2012, many of those who left headed westward towards Aleppo City.[199] Those displaced later, when the situation in Aleppo City had also deteriorated, headed north (within the Syrian Arab Republic and beyond).[200] After government takeover, many residents left to the northeast towards SDF-controlled areas.[201] The obstacles to the voluntary return of the displaced are also somewhat different for each case. Economic challenges and mandatory military service and conscription apply to both. However, mass destruction, security concerns and fear of vengeance or punitive actions by state security apparatus are not applicable for Kasab.

---

[199] Interviews 5B; 6B; 20B.
[200] Interviews 1B; 21B.
[201] Interview 21B.

By 2014, both communities experienced heightened episodes of violence, which effectively overpowered and overwhelmed local capacity for community protection. The experiences of the two areas reflect the need to maintain and expand civilian-led spaces for efforts of community protection. Both cases suggest that regardless of how 'native' or 'local' the armed forces and security apparatus are, such features do not always translate into effective protective measures for the civilian population. Further, both cases also suggest that, despite emerging socio-political divides within the areas studied, social trust and cooperative dispositions for purposes of community protection persist at the neighbourhood level but are inconsequential without organisational structure and autonomy to mobilise. That said, the case studies also reveal that community resilience has its thresholds – which are determined by the scale of violence faced and the limitations posed to civilian capacity (which easily becomes overburdened and overwhelmed during protracted armed conflicts). In fact, efforts of community protection in both cases consist of strategies aimed at survival against threats. The lack of transformative strategies or capacities is a direct indication that civilians under conditions of state atrophy operate within the options available to them but are unable to bring about structural changes that can introduce new pathways or options. The conflict prevented vital opportunities for transformative strategies to address local sources of conflict and fragility, and to recover from shocks. This was primarily due to the relentless pressures of the broader conflict, which local actors had little influence over. Other factors that drained civilian capacities in both cases included forced displacement due to mass violence, economic hardship and economic/educational immigration opportunities beyond the locale. Community protection in both cases gradually and increasingly depended upon conditions that were beyond the influence of civilians.

Limits to Civilian Agency

Centre-periphery dependencies provided shifting opportunities and restraints based on conflict dynamics, but ultimately restrained the autonomy of local actors in Der Hafer and Kasab. Especially during moments of geographic isolation and lack of local resources, centre-periphery dependencies proved detrimental. As explained later in this section, repercussions of centre-periphery dependencies during conflict were compounded by pre-existing economic vulnerabilities and lack of disaster-informed and sustainable models of economic development in both areas. This significantly harmed and exacerbated the fragility of local communities and their capacity to withstand threats. This section expands on some of the structural conditions that shaped the outcome community protection efforts listed.

Local autonomy

Local autonomy for civilian community actors in Deir Hafer and Kasab is directly linked to prevailing institutional structures and power relations in both communities. Institutional structures and power relations between key societal, military and political actors and community-based organisations delimited the level of autonomy and decision-making capacity for local civilian actors. Power dynamics between civilian community organisers and non-civilian power groups in place (military groups within localities and centre-periphery dependencies between neighbouring areas) have delimited the space for civilians to plan, mobilise and/or implement community protection measures. In Deir Hafer, civilian autonomy was shaped by the level of intervention of military groups in the work of civilian community organisers, whereas Kasab's civilian community organisers were also constrained by broader military and paramilitary structures in the region of Latakia, political power in Kasab, as well as the institutional hierarchies within which civilian actors mobilised. These factors diverted decision-making responsibilities to central authorities located outside of civilian capacity.

In the period between 2012 and 2014, civilian entities in Deir Hafer had unprecedented operational space to organise and take initiatives such as publishing new local magazines and engaging in social media activism. The local Shoura Council emerged as a contested space amongst local notables to express different ideas and compete for influence in local matters.[202] Undoubtedly, such civilian spaces were not entirely accessible to everyone, as activists who mobilised and filled such ranks were concerned about infiltration. Given the dangers in place and the possible eventuality

---

[202] Interview 21B.

of government return, many also decided not to join these ranks out of fear of guilt by association, or of any sign that might incriminate them in the eyes of the Syrian government. After the marginalisation of the old tribal leadership, relations of kinship were used as trust networks to fill local administrative structures. These two combined factors determined the cross-tribal but narrow cadre of emergent civilian structures. Given the co-dependencies between local factions and civilian structures in matters of administration, enforcement and protection, the two bodies were closely linked, not only operationally but also through kinship ties between the two organisms.[203] This further increased the influence of armed groups over civilian structures.

In addition, Katibat Abu Dujana often intervened in civilian matters – as in the case of Lijnat al-Musalaha. Nevertheless, given that the local faction did not have the capacity to run administrative or civil institutions, a level of de facto autonomy and operational space existed despite interventions and pressures from armed opposition groups. When Daesh took over, the landscape changed drastically, as all civil institutions were replaced by Daesh offices and recruits.

For Kasab, local autonomy, in terms of maintaining organisational distinction, was of clear significance for the Armenian community. However, there were two fundamental dependencies and power structures that significantly limited the capacity of local civilian structures. On one hand, the overall power and decision-making capacity in the province of Latakia was in the hands of close associates of the Assad family, such as Hilal al-Assad. Despite representing the demographic majority in the area of Kasab, the Armenian presence in administrative state structures was severely limited, in Kasab and the province of Latakia alike. For example, according to a census conducted between 2006 and 2007, the public hospital/clinic had only one Armenian employee out of a total of twenty; the water company had one Armenian employee out of a total of nineteen; the central telecommunication and post office had one Armenian employee out of twenty. Perhaps the area of most representation was in the local municipality board, which comprised ten members – before the conflict, seven of those were Armenians,

---

[203] Interview 21B.

including the head of the municipality, and only three were members of the Alawite community.²⁰⁴ The number in 2020 was at six Armenians and four Alawite members.²⁰⁵ Although the head of the municipality is Armenian, it is customary that the person is a member of the Ba'th and acts in their role as such.²⁰⁶ Demographic representation in the municipality is rather symbolic and does not necessarily reflect decision-making power. Besides its executive board, the municipality had thirty-nine employees of which only three were Armenian in 2007.²⁰⁷ Although most of the employments, except for the municipality board, are low-paying technical and professional positions, the lack of presence in state institutions creates not only a level of detachment and disempowerment but also limited resource circulation and information sharing. The overall environment was such that security branches were the ultimate authority and anything unauthorised or not initiated by them was viewed suspiciously. As a result, local initiatives were often self-censored and self-restrained to narrow cultural and social initiatives. From a local standpoint, security branches override the autonomy and influence of the Tashnak within the Armenian population.

Organisational capacity

Organisational capacity and local autonomy are interdependent, specifically with regards to decision-making capacities. Regardless of resources at hand, without the autonomy to carry out decisions and strategies, resources have little consequence. Similarly, without organisational resources, decisions and strategies are impossible to carry out and implement regardless of the nature and limits of local autonomy. Organisational capacity refers to the internal organisational conditions that enable or constrain protective strategies and shape their outcomes. These include organisational reach within localities and beyond, resource availability and procurement ability, organisational size (number of employees or members), institutional knowledge and memory in relation to areas of operation and information

---

²⁰⁴ S. Manjikian, *Բեսաք Շրջանի Հայոթեան Միեակագրութիւն: 2006–2007* (Aleppo: Hamazkayin, 2010), 40.
²⁰⁵ Interviews 4A; 10A.
²⁰⁶ Interview 19A.
²⁰⁷ Manjikian, *Բեսաք Շրջանի Հայոթեան Միեակագրութիւն*, 40.

processing mechanisms to inform strategies and methods. According to the UNDP's Capacity Assessment Methodology, leadership structures, knowledge accountability and institutional arrangements, such as budget management, 'define the scope of [organisational capacity] assessment'.[208] Despite the flexibility and variations in assessment models, organisational capacity ultimately depends upon the objectives and deliverables of specific initiatives and efforts.[209] Organisational capacity is measurable only in relation to the efforts and objectives of each specific organiser and each initiative.[210]

The primary distinction between civilian entities in Deir Hafer and Kasab was that most entities in Kasab existed before the conflict, whereas those that were active in Deir Hafer post-2012 emerged in response to local needs. This has influenced the resources and abilities of civilian organisers in these two areas, as pre-existing leadership, networks, partnerships and experiences translate into resources during conditions of heightened vulnerability. Unlike Kasab, Deir Hafer's nascent civilian entities did not have the same resources. The three main Armenian churches and the local mosque in the town of Kasab were continuously active without interruption before 2011.[211] Armenian organisations avowed to aiding the non-Armenian population since the onset of the conflict, except when donors targeted their aid for the Armenian population alone.[212] However, the Alawite community lacked charity or social enterprises in Kasab due to the small size of the community in the area as well as the availability of other accessible charities in Latakia City. The primary actors that have supported the Armenian population during the conflict were locally based, whereas the Alawite community relied on networks and associations in Latakia City. Furthermore, churches in Kasab were directly linked to their respective centres in Aleppo. Even the Armenian Relief Committee, which formally emerged in 2012, enjoyed strong pre-existing structures as its leadership was comprised of pre-existing

---

[208] UNDP, *Capacity Assessment Methodology* (New York: United Nations Development Programme, 2008), 6.
[209] Ibid.
[210] Seth Abrutyn and Jonathan H. Turner, 'The Old Institutionalism Meets the New Institutionalism', *Sociological Perspectives* 54, no. 3 (2011): 283–306.
[211] Khedra, 'خطة لتنمية السياحة البيئية في منطقة كسب واستثمارها طبيعياً'.
[212] Interviews 4A; 10A.

community representatives from each denomination. In time of need, the town was not only able to rely on its expats abroad but also on the official ecclesiastic networks and international donors. The individuals filling up the Relief Committee in Kasab were not new to the communities they served and, to an extent, were familiar to charitable work and community organising.

These pre-existing affiliations also introduced restraints for civilian organisers. As the situation in Aleppo worsened, and specifically throughout the siege of the city, all salaries and funds that Kasab used to receive came to a halt. This centre-periphery dependency was also a factor in diminished local decision-making capacity regarding the allocation of emergency funds.[213]

In Deir Hafer, most civilian structures emerged throughout the conflict and public services, such as the industrial bakery, garbage collection and the thermal power plant, continued operating with reduced personnel and capacity. Some of those who had worked in the respective institutions took on bigger responsibilities with limited experience and training. The civilian council emerged in 2012 but did not enjoy established trans-local partnerships and connections. Efforts of outreach and building connections had to be improvised and nurtured during rapidly changing circumstances and volatile conditions.

Centre-periphery dependencies also existed in Deir Hafer. Economic activities in Deir Hafer were based on agriculture and trade. Despite the area providing wheat and electricity nationwide, it only received a marginal share of the revenues. Deir Hafer, similar to the other towns of Aleppo's countryside, experienced relative deprivation of benefits or resources while urban centres, such as Aleppo City and Damascus, were further reinforced as sites of investment.[214] Nearby cities such as al-Bab and Manbij fared better than

---

[213] Interview 4A.
[214] Shamel Azmeh, 'The uprising of the marginalised: a socio-economic perspective of the Syrian uprising', *LSE Middle East Centre Paper Series 6*, 2014; Isam al-Khafaji, 'De-Urbanising the Syrian Revolt', *The Arab Reform Initiative*, 6 March 2016, 1–18, https://www.arab-reform.net/publication/de-urbanising-the-syrian-revolt/.

Deir Hafer economically during the conflict as they emerged as economic centres due to access to the Syrian-Turkish border.[215]

In 2008, Decree 445 administratively separated Deir Hafer from the region of al-Bab to form the new administrative region of Deir Hafer composed of Nahiyat Deir Hafer, Nahiyat Rasm alHirmil alimam and Nahiyat Kuweiris Sharqi.[216] As a distinct administrative area, Deir Hafer received its own security branch, whereas previously it was unified with al-Bab and effectively governed from there. As a distinct administrative area, a number of new government jobs and administrative ranks were available for distribution within Deir Hafer. This measure diminished Deir Hafer's historic reliance and administrative subordination to the city of al-Bab, while creating new positions of power locally. These arrangements created new dependencies between smaller towns in Deir Hafer, such as Hmeyme, on the city of Deir Hafer. During the conflict, Deir Hafer became a centre for other regional townships in the same way that al-Bab once again became a centre for Deir Hafer. According to interviewees from Deir Hafer's civilian council and a member of Mercy Corps' local office supporting the local bakery in Hmeyme, the local bakery in Hmeyme came under significant pressure from Deir Hafer's civilian council to relocate its operations to Deir Hafer if it was to continue to operate.[217]

Although both Deir Hafer and Kasab were dependent on other centres they were also centres in and of themselves to other peripheries, such as Hmeyme for Deir Hafer and areas of Jabal Turkman (Bayirbucak) for Kasab. This strongly points out the need for regional policy approaches that connect multiple localities to address equitable labour relations and sustainable economic planning and management. This would minimise economic deprivation during conflict, and reduce relative deprivation, which could become a source of social strife and compromise cooperative dispositions. Despite both areas being now reconnected to their previous economic and administrative centres in Aleppo City and Latakia City, neither of these

---

[215] Kheder Khaddour, 'Consumed by War: The End of Aleppo and Northern Syria's Political Order', *Friedrich Ebert Stiftung*, October 2017, 1–19, http://library.fes.de/pdf-files/iez/13783.pdf.
[216] AlJamahir, 'Events in the Regions of Der Hafer and Atarib Will Contribute to Developmental Awakening in the province', 25 February 2009.
[217] Interviews 14B; 21B.

centres function now as they did prior to the conflict, given the socio-economic and physical harm (specifically Aleppo City) they sustained throughout the conflict.[218]

Social trust

Social trust is a binding relational force defined by cooperative predispositions and favourable views towards other individuals, groups and institutions.[219] During armed conflict, social trust is consequential for collaborative action that may include sharing sensitive information, coordinating safety plans, mobilising other members of the community in high-risk contexts and maintaining organisational unity.[220] In the context of armed conflict, with ruptures and transformations to the existing social fabric, networks of social trust often serve as pathways of cooperation and mobilisation – creating what Wilson describes as 'lock-in' effects that shape pathways and strategies of community protection.[221] Wilson's point is not to condemn collaborative endeavours of community protection to predetermination. Rather, his point is that in a context of conflict fragility and radical socio-economic transformations, patterns of continuity and change in social trust and collaborative networks inform trajectories of community mobilisation at the local level. Findings from surveys conducted in Deir Hafer and Kasab tell a similar story. Perceptions of mistrust restrained collective action. However, where trust was affirmed as present, such as at the neighborhood level, it did not always lead to collective action.

Throughout the conflict, social trust, in terms of perceptions of in-group relations, relations between groups, as well as trust relations with institutions and organisations in place, reveal significant changes and transformations in outlook and predispositions.[222] The survey results show that 56.4 per cent of Kasab's respondents and 77.3 per cent of respondents from

---

[218] Khaddour, 'Consumed by War'.
[219] Cadier, Capasso and Eickhoff, 'Researching Resilience', 11.
[220] Geoff A. Wilson, 'Community resilience: path dependency, lock-in effects and transitional ruptures', *Journal of Environmental Planning and Management* 57, no. 1 (2014): 8.
[221] Ibid., 10.
[222] Tanja Borzel and Thomas Risse, 'Dysfunctional State Institutions, Trust, and Governance in Areas of Limited Statehood', *Regulation & Governance* 10 (2016): 149–160.

Deir Hafer do not consider most residents of their respective communities trustworthy. The fact that more than half of the population expressed blanket mistrust towards their own community is a strong indication that local trust is compromised. When asked whether trust amongst residents has changed throughout the conflict, 63.8 per cent of respondents from Kasab and 63.9 per cent of respondents from Deir Hafer answered that 'the level of trust amongst residents has got worse'.

The surveys indicate that the presence of communal threats and insecurity do not automatically lead community members to fuse together, trust one another and self-organise. When asked whether the level of violence or danger has changed since the major episodes of violence up until 2014, 69 per cent of respondents from Deir Hafer answered that risks increased (47.4 per cent 'increased a lot'; 21.6 per cent 'slightly increased'). Similarly for Kasab, 61.7 per cent of participants responded that risks also increased (43.6 per cent 'slightly increased' and 18.1 per cent 'increased a lot'). Despite the different experiences of fragility and violence in both communities since 2014, both datasets indicate an overwhelming sense that the two areas are still deemed unsafe despite the abatement of episodes of direct communal violence. Amongst the threats that communities face, for instance, 77.7 per cent of respondents from Kasab and 81.4 per cent of respondents from Deir Hafer answered that they are concerned about theft in their areas. Furthermore, 88.7 per cent of respondents from Deir Hafer and 91.5 per cent of respondents from Kasab declared that they keep the doors and windows of their houses locked at night.

In the daytime, however, 53.6 per cent of respondents from Deir Hafer and 47.9 per cent from Kasab declared that they keep their doors and windows unlocked. The respondents' positions from both communities reflect a level of awareness that the dangers and threats faced are contextual and contingent upon circumstantial factors and not inherent regional features. For example, in relation to specific areas of danger, 54.6 per cent of respondents from Deir Hafer declared that there are specific neighbourhoods within the area that they deem unsafe and avoid. In contrast, the data from Kasab indicates that only 33 per cent of respondents avoid certain neighbourhoods and 62.8 per cent do not deem any neighbourhood in Kasab unsafe, indicating that most participants identify the source of danger emanating from without and not within. In line with this, amongst the most noticeable areas of strengths that both communities exhibited through the surveys was the scale of trust and cooperation at the neighbourhood level. In other words, when asked if respondents would leave their children with neighbours to attend urgent matters, 73.2 per cent of respondents from Deir Hafer and 81.9 per cent from Kasab answered 'yes'. In line with findings from interviews and discussion groups, the surveys show that neighbourhood-level communities are comprised of extended family members and intimately connected acquaintances. This trust, however, did not translate into an organisational shape and was neither consequential nor integral to efforts of community protection.

When responding to what social differences often cause problems, for Deir Hafer, political opinion (19.4 per cent), ethno-linguistic (16.5 per cent) and residential status (displaced vs. original resident – 14.1 per cent) featured the highest. For Kasab too, the highest-ranking social categories that cause problems are political opinion (21.6 per cent), ethno-linguistic differences (19.3 per cent) and residential status (displaced vs. local, 19.3 per cent). In terms of wealth disparity and class divisions, 82.5 per cent of Deir Hafer's respondents either agreed or strongly agreed that people in the community mainly 'look out for their personal welfare' without much concern for 'community welfare'. Findings from Focus Group Discussions, semi-structured interviews and surveys from Deir Hafer also voiced that although there were no significant levels of poverty in the area, wealth disparity and relative deprivation on a regional level (between Deir Hafer and surrounding areas) exist. A similar analysis applies to Kasab, where 65.9 per cent agreed that people in the community mainly 'look out for their personal welfare' without much concern for 'community welfare' (37.2 per cent agree and 28.7 per cent strongly agree).

In relation to cooperative dispositions within Der Hafer, 72.2 per cent of respondents claimed that members of their community (56.7 per cent 'often'; 15.5 per cent 'sometimes') work and interact with other communities in Der Hafer. Whereas only 13.4 per cent claimed that members of their community do not interact with other groups. For Kasab, 71.3 per cent of respondents state that members of their community 'sometimes' interact or work with other communities in Kasab. In line with Der Hafer's indicators, 'trade and work relations' (26.1 per cent for Kasab and 22.5 per cent for Der Hafer) and 'common interests and goals' (20.4 per cent for Kasab and 20.6 per cent for Der Hafer) top the list of motivators for cooperation.

Furthermore, amongst all answers to the open-ended question about obstacles to the return of the displaced from Kasab and Der Hafer, the most prominent were: 'lack of security' (23.4 per cent for Kasab and 18.6 per cent for Der Hafer) and 'unemployment, poverty and lack of social services' (20.2 per cent for Kasab and 14.4 per cent for Der Hafer). Der Hafer's respondents also mentioned 'military service' (11.3 per cent) and 'regime oppression' (8.2 per cent) as additional obstacles to the return of the displaced. The primary distinction between the two surveys is concerning sources of insecurity – for Der Hafer, the Assad rule and the security apparatus remain the biggest threat for potential returnees, whereas for Kasab it is broader dynamics of insecurity and armed conflict.

Examining patterns of inclusion in accessing resources as well as trust relations with decision-makers and local leadership, the dataset indicates that participants faced exclusion when accessing services or activities essential for community protection. For Der Hafer 13.7 per cent of respondents answered yes to being excluded from 'financial aid', 13.2 per cent from 'equal employment opportunities', 12.8 per cent from 'food and relief' and 12.8 per cent from 'voting and participation in political activities'. Within the Kasab sample, the highest-ranking areas were 'financial aid' (22.6 per cent), 'food and relief' (18.3 per cent) and 'equal employment opportunities' (16.5 per cent). Despite the fact that 'voting and participation in political activities' did not feature highly in Kasab (7.9 per cent), it is noticeable that female participants comprise 77 per cent of those who affirmed such a deprivation.

When asked about the reasons behind such exclusion, respondents from Kasab mentioned three primary factors: 'level of income' (25.4 per cent), occupation (20.9 per cent) and 'ethnicity and race' (14.9 per cent). While factors such as level of income or occupation (or employment) may be deemed legitimate factors of discrimination with regard to aid distribution or financial aid, other featuring factors such as 'political views' and 'religious belief' are potentially discriminatory in a way that may create or reinforce exclusionary and antagonistic social relations. For Deir Hafer, the three highest-ranking factors were: 'level of income' (24.7 per cent), 'political views or affiliation' (18.5 per cent) and both 'religious belief' and 'occupation' at 12.3 per cent.

In communities where social exclusion and mistrust are on the rise, avenues of change and access to decision-makers are crucial to bringing about social change or act collectively. When asked whether participants are able to meet with community leaders and organisers within their locality, 22.7 per cent of participants from Deir Hafer answered 'yes, with most community leaders', 63.9 per cent answered 'no, with only few or none' and 13.4 per cent of participants refrained from answering. In tangent, participants were also asked if they thought their 'community should be organised differently': 46.4 per cent of participants answered 'very differently' and 39.2 per cent answered 'slightly differently'. Despite the desire for change, most participants expressed lack of access to local leaders and decision-makers. With the sample from Kasab, on the other hand, most participants claimed that they have 'access to most community leaders' (53.2 per cent). However, at the same time, when asked if the community should be organised differently, only 4.3 per cent of respondents claimed it should be organised the same way. The rest of respondents were divided somewhat evenly between 'very differently' (40.4 per cent) and 'slightly differently' (44.7 per cent). While this may suggest that community members have access to community leaders and expect them to eventually bring about desired changes, it can also suggest, as elaborated through the qualitative data, that despite the Armenian population's access to local Armenian leaders, this accessibility does not translate into actual change – which means that the local leadership, despite being open to members of the community, is unable to bring about effective change.

It is noticeable that with both samples, level of income and gender did not influence responses to questions about access to local leadership or expectations regarding how communities should be organised. There were, however, two categories within the Kasab dataset that showed discrepancies – place of current residence and ethno-religious belonging. In answering whether they can meet with most community leaders, out of the 36.2 per cent of respondents answering 'none, or only few', the overwhelming majority were residents of Kasab (73.5 per cent). Similarly, of the 40.6 per cent of respondents who wanted to see their communities organised 'very differently', 63 per cent identified as residents of Kasab. Furthermore, more than 90 per cent of respondents identifying as Muslim Arab Alawite answered that they can only meet few or no community leaders in Kasab. This is also in alignment with qualitative findings about societal structures within Kasab where Armenian social organisations dominate but operate as politically peripheral within the province of Latakia more broadly.

Social trust is often compromised in the aftermath of 'contentious politics and [. . .] social mobilisation based on identity'.[223] The surveys point out that despite ethno-religious divides, social trust was not primarily defined by sectarianisation alone. Furthermore, despite the prominence of sect-based and religious actors, socio-political action and behaviour was neither exclusively guided by nor exclusively manifested in sectarian terms.

Local intermediaries were crucial for intervening in cases of kidnappings or tensions that might arise between members of the community, as in the case of Kasab. In the Kasab surveys, the most trustworthy segment of the population was deemed the elderly (18 per cent). On the other hand, surveys suggested that the least trustworthy were viewed as members of other ethnic or linguistic communities (1.6 per cent), the youth (3.2 per cent) and municipality employees (4.8 per cent). For Deir Hafer, on the other hand, the most neutral category of 'shop owners' featured as the most trustworthy category at 16.7 per cent, whereas the elderly featured at 2.7 per cent. This further accentuates the possibility for community-specific and context-sensitive approaches that avoid a one-size-fits-all operational mode such as working with sect-based actors as entry-points to political, social and humanitarian solidarity.

---

[223] 'Strengthening Social Cohesion: Conceptual Framing and Programming Implications', *UNDP*, 27 February 2020, 17, https://www.undp.org/publications/strengthening-social-cohesion-conceptual-framing-and-programming-implications.

Survey Sample Characteristics: Kasab

Categories	Frequency	Per cent
Place of residence during survey		
Lebanon	14	14.9
USA	5	5.3
Canada	12	12.8
Armenia	2	2.1
UAE	3	3.2
France	1	1.1
Latakia	4	4.3
Kasab	46	48.9
Other (outside Syria)	6	6.4
Other (inside Syria)	1	1.1
Total	94	100.0
Ethno-religious belonging		
Muslim Arab Alawite	19	20.2
Armenian Catholic	19	20.2
Armenian Orthodox	48	51.1
Armenian Evangelical	6	6.4
No answer	2	2.1
Total	94	100.0
Gender		
Male	53	56.4
Female	39	41.5
No answer	2	2.1
Total	94	100.0
Age		
16–24	9	9.6
25–35	27	28.7
36–55	40	42.6
above 55	15	16.0
No answer	3	3.2
Total	94	100.0
Highest level of education		
Primary	15	16.0
Secondary	22	23.4
Tertiary	41	43.6
Postgraduate	8	8.5
No answer	8	8.5
Total	94	100.0

Survey Sample Characteristics: Deir Hafer

Categories	Frequency	Per cent
Place of residence during survey		
Deir Hafer	32	33.0
Germany	10	10.3
KSA	4	4.1
Netherlands	7	7.2
Turkey	11	11.3
Jarablus	4	4.1
Azaz	9	9.3
Al Rai	4	4.1
Al Raqqa	2	2.1
Afrin	4	4.1
Other	7	7.2
No answer	3	3.1
Total	97	100.0
Ethno-religious belonging		
Muslim Arab Sunni	90	92.8
Muslim Kurdish Sunni	1	1.0
Other	4	4.1
No answer	2	2.1
Total	97	100.0
Gender		
Male	77	79.4
Female	17	17.5
No answer	3	3.1
Total	97	100.0
Age		
16–24	5	5.2
25–35	56	57.7
36–55	31	32.0
above 55	1	1.0
No answer	4	4.1
Total	97	100.0
Highest level of education		
Illiterate	1	1.0
Primary	15	15.5
Secondary	29	29.9
Tertiary	33	34.0
Postgraduate	6	6.2
No answer	13	13.4
Total	97	100.0

Conclusion

The violence undermining civilian initiatives in kasab and Deir Hafer were shaped by a combination of local circumstances and vulnerabilities as well as broader conflict patterns and dynamics in the Syrian Arab Republic. The year 2014 witnessed significant shifts in the balance of powers in the Syrian conflict. Until late 2013 armed opposition groups were increasingly successful in mobilisation nationwide. Territorial control by government forces, specifically before the military intervention of its foreign allies, consisted of a territorial patchwork of detached urban centres, increasingly under pressure from myriad armed opposition groups in urban outskirts and the hinterland. The decisive involvement of the Russian army and Lebanese Hezbollah forces by 2014, along with the expansion of Daesh into Iraq, shifted the dynamics of the conflict considerably. Armed opposition groups shifted attention and resources towards combatting Daesh as the latter threatened and overwhelmed other factions in its areas of presence. Deir Hafer fell to Daesh in these circumstances. Simultaneously, Russian and pro-Iranian forces grew more present and effectively tilted the course of the conflict in favour of the government. The attack on Kasab was an attempt by armed opposition groups to create diversion, ease pressure from other fronts and offset losses of other strategic sites such as the town of Yabroud on the vital Damascus–Homs highway.

Threats in Kasab and Deir Hafer evolved unpredictably throughout the conflict. Overall most civilian actions and efforts were reactive in the sense that they did not have a transformative outlook to change the circumstances they operated within. Rather they worked within the conditions available to them. This is the manifest limits to collective civilian agency under conditions of state atrophy – civilians under conditions of state atrophy in Kasab and Deir Hafer operated within the options available to them but were unable to bring about structural changes that can introduce new pathways or options for civilian mobilisation.

Civilian efforts during conditions of state atrophy are often guided by norms and objectives of community protection.[224] However, the limitations

---

[224] Kaplan, *Resisting War*, 307.

in place were tied to local capacity and broader conflict dynamics and structural conditions. The predominance of reactive approaches in efforts of community protection illustrates the limited options for civilian agency and stifling institutional conditions presented by state atrophy.

Conclusion
The Future of State–Society Relations

The undermining of 'non-democratic' systems of government does not necessarily lead to the rise of democratic ones.[1] Similarly, the undermining of hierarchical state systems does not automatically lead to the rise of egalitarian systems. Systemic change depends upon institutional transformations. The military outcome of the conflict in Syria favours the Assad rule and the country's circumstances will inevitably evolve towards conflict abatement. As military contests transition towards low-intensity cycles of violence, the institutional ecology of war is likely to be increasingly formalised.[2] Institutional arrangements after 2021 are a direct extension of what preceded them. In other words, the decline in the incidences of violence in Syria marks the end of open conflict but also indicates the continuation of war through other means.

Distinctions between periods of active armed conflict and post-conflict circumstances are premised on a presumed point of rupture or transition in patterns of conflict and violence. What could be commonly considered to be an imminent post-conflict phase in Syria is, in fact, characterised by patterns of continuity in relation to dynamics of war prior to military abatement. The question of whether any form of national unity will be restored is uncertain as militarisation can still manifest through geographically limited relapse to territorial contests, insurgency movements, expanded involvement of regionally active state-actors and military forces. What is certain, however, is that

---

[1] Azmi Bishara, الانتقال الديمقراطي وإشكالياته: دراسة نظرية وتطبيقية مقارنة (Doha: Arab Center for Research and Policy Studies, 2020).

[2] As evident already from the 2012 constitution and as well as the 2020 parliamentary elections.

processes and efforts of power consolidation incentivise the avoidance of high-intensity cycles of violence and a relapse to open conflict, especially when resources and support run low. This encourages the formalisation of emergent hierarchies.

The Future of the State

Institutional transformations between 2011 and 2021 reveal a great deal about the role of the state going forward, specifically in relation to the public domain. The public functions of the state have been continuously undermined. This decline in public functions is in fact a decline in the regulatory functions of the state towards other domains – sometimes due to compromised regulatory capacity during conditions of war and sometimes by design on behalf of the ruling establishment. The public domain stands for the domain controlled by the state, but remaining at the general service of a given population. State control, in the sense of protection from privatisation, as well as the maintenance of the public function of that domain, are the determinant features that constitute the public domain. Through the blurring of private and public distinctions, and the devolution of regulatory state functions by the Assad rule, the public domain is effectively detached from the state.

With the privatisation of the state in its Assadist and neoliberal forms, the public domain is left to the whims of private interests (political, economic, sectarian, religious). This not only results in the alienation of the public from politics but also the further dissociation of the state from any notion of society, as public interest or population. The public domain is therefore institutionally outflanked and restricted by the prevailing regulatory incapacitation of the state and the prominence of private interests therein. State capture in Syria translates to the capture and privatisation of the public domain, rendering the notion of 'public domain' redundant.[3] The rise of government-sanctioned non-governmental organisations and associations between 2000 and 2011 is a

---

[3] Jürgen Habermas, *The Structural Transformation of the Public Sphere: An Inquiry Into a Category of Bourgeois Society* (Cambridge, MA: MIT Press, 1991), 177. The public domain, in its institutional forms and functions, can only bear a public service through its connecting function between state and society. For instance, the complete interlocking of state and society would relieve the public domain of its mediatory political burden of bringing state policies in line with public functions without needing to supply a new medium.

case in point.⁴ Handpicked civil society actors served intermediary functions between state and society by continuously being delegated state functions.⁵

As the state is stripped of public functions, it is institutionally encouraged to serve the functions of dominant institutional domains such as the military field. It is in this context that even apolitical institutional fields, such as the medical field, are transformed to reflect the prominence of the military domain and serve the same coercive functions that uphold the Assad rule.⁶ With the primacy of the military domain, other domains do not shed their primary functions and codes that define them, such as medical functions for the medical field or the educational functions of the educational field. Rather, those functions are instrumentalised to perform tasks required by the military field instead of being dedicated to their own codes or to a public role.

'The public domain', remains an impossibility within a context of state capture and primacy of the military domain. The cost is the population's to bear.⁷ Further austerity measures in early 2022 represent a continuation of the shrinking of both state capacity and responsibility in socio-economic regulation.⁸ The Assad rule will thus continue to produce its own opposition and will continue to anticipate it, while knowing that it is unlikely that those experiencing harm inside Syria will demand political change because of the

---

⁴ For more about GONGOs (Government Organised Non-Governmental Organisations) see de Elvira and Zintl, 'The end of the Ba'thist social contract', 333; for more about the notion of civil society, see Azmi Bishara, المجتمع المدني: دراسة نقدية (Doha: Arab Center for Research and Policy Studies, 2012), 68–71.

⁵ Aziz al-Azmeh and Faysal Darraj, 'هامش لحوار مجزوء المجتمع المدني أم أيقاظ السياسة مرة اخرى؟', in Jamal Barout and Shams alDin Kaylani (eds), سوريا بين عهدين (Amman: Dar Sindbad Lilnashr el'am, 2003), 384–9. Originally published in *al-Hayat* newspaper on Friday, 29 June 2001, no. 13984.

⁶ Annsar Shahhoud, 'Medical genocide: Mass Violence and the Health Sector in the Syrian Conflict (2011–2019)' (MA thesis, University of Amsterdam, 2020), https://t.co/gMSYf92kOq (accessed 23 February 2022); Dellair Youssef, 'In Assad's Syria School Is Prison: Mini Dictatorships and State Violence in the Classroom', *Syria Untold*, 18 November 2021, https://syriauntold.com/2021/11/18/in-assads-syria-school-is-prison/ (accessed 23 February 2022); Rahaf al-Doughly, 'Securitization as a tool of regime survival: The deployment of religious rhetoric in Bashar al-Asad's speeches', *The Middle East Journal* 75 1 (2021): 9–32.

⁷ 'Swelling As-Sweida Protests Highlight Discontent Across Government Areas', *COAR*, 14 February 2022, https://coar-global.org/2022/02/14/swelling-as-sweida-protests-highlight-discontent-across-government-areas/ (accessed 23 February 2022).

⁸ Joseph Daher, 'Expelled from the Support System: Austerity Deepens in Syria', *Middle East Directions Blog*, 15 February 2022, https://blogs.eui.eu/medirections/expelled-from-the-support-system-austerity-deepens-in-syria/ (accessed 23 February 2022).

legacy of post-uprising violence and because those experiencing harm are heavily dependent on the very system that is causing them harm.

The Future of the Assad Rule

The future of the Assad rule depends on the nature and implications of elite polarisation within the military field. Principally, the primacy of the military domain coupled with the dissociation of state from society leaves little room for bottom-up processes of institutional change. The resilience of the Assad rule resides in its ability to either absorb or eliminate potential and real contenders for power by maintaining competition over privileges. In other words, as long as elite polarisation does not involve Assad's closest associates in charge of key institutions of violence, elite polarisation will further entrench political clientelism.[9] Along with ideological flexibility, the Assad rule's strategies will include restructuring the military domain to stabilise its supremacy and balance the various sponsorships and hierarchies at work to avert direct competitors and maintain the prominence of the select branches directly controlled by Assad's most trusted associates, such as his brother Maher Assad.

Turkey, Russia, the Islamic Republic of Iran and the United States of America will have a measure of influence over Assad's strategies. The political networks of military elites and revenue sources will shape how parastate security forces exercise power and the functions they fulfil within their geographic locations.[10] In this sense, external and internal distinctions will be further blurred and more intimately enmeshed once military contests settle into low-intensity violent exchanges.

Similar to other post-Soviet contexts, it is therefore reasonable to expect that the top priority of benefactors from state atrophy in the short run will be to protect the new privileged status they have attained.[11] Given that benefactors from the ecologies of war are unlikely to accept legal or institutional arrangements that undermine their hard-earned spoils of war, the Assad rule

---

[9] Steven Solnick, *Stealing the State: Control and Collapse in Soviet-Institutions* (Cambridge, MA: Harvard University Press, 1998), 15.
[10] Louis-Alexandre Berg, *Governing Security After War: The Politics of Institutional Change in the Security Sector* (Oxford: Oxford University press, 2022).
[11] Solnick, *Stealing the State*, 251.

will continue to devolve state functions in fiscal and regulatory capacities to local clientelised subjects while also clientalising itself to foreign sponsorship.[12]

The Future of Sectarianisation

Sectarianism and political Islam forever loom as alleged destinations that are seemingly unavoidable and unavoidably incompatible, both ideologically and institutionally, with institutions of modern statehood.[13] Since the turn of the century, the topic of sectarianism in the Middle East has become increasingly politically and normatively charged.[14] As Ussama Makdisi points out, the notion of sectarianism has become tarnished by post-9/11 narratives of identity and religion in the Muslim world; narratives that frequently essentialise religious sects, endorse static conceptions of identity and ignore the historicity of sectarianism – of its transformations and different forms of expression.[15] The term has come to refer to the communal salience of factional (denominational) affiliation, distinction and antagonism within a socio-culturally diverse and plural collectivity.[16] Makdisi is amongst a series of scholars who provide scathing critiques of post-9/11 trends yet maintain that 'the notion of sectarianism can be useful in understanding the Middle East', given that its historicity as a process is acknowledged and the materiality, contingency, boundaries and limits of its forms in the given historical moment are captured.[17]

---

[12] Solnick, *Stealing the State*, 252–3.

[13] Aziz al-Azmeh, سورية والصعود الأصولي: عن الأصولية والطائفية والثقافة (Beirut: Riad El-Rayyes, 2015); Aziz al-Azmeh, 'Is Islamism the Arab Destiny?' (Globalisation Lecture at SOAS, University of London, 6 February 2013), available on YouTube: https://youtu.be/EAfLgTGWrgA (accessed 20 December 2021). The first books to come out from the onset of the uprising were characterised by a focus on sectarianism, the Muslim Brotherhood and the religious field in Syria. See Nikolaos Van Dam, *The Struggle for Power in Syria*, republished in 2011 in a third edition after the original work came about in the 1980s and 1990s, Thomas Pierret's *Religion and State in Syria*, published in 2011 and Benjamin White, *The Ashes of Hama*, published in 2013. Modern and contemporary developments were discussed in line with historical references. By default, this produced an overemphasis on processes of continuity in Syrian affairs, undermining transformation, change and rupture.

[14] Iliya Harik, 'Democracy, "Arab Exceptionalism", and Social Science', *The Middle East Journal* 60, no. 4 (2006): 664–84, https://doi.org/10.3751/60.4.12.

[15] Ussama Makdisi, 'Moving beyond Orientalist Fantasy, Sectarian Polemic and Nationalist Denial', *International Journal of Middle Eastern Studies* 40, no. 4 (2008): 559, https://doi.org/10.1017/S0 020743808081488.

[16] Azmi Bishara, *Sectarianism Without Sects* (Oxford: Oxford University Press, 2021).

[17] Makdisi, 'Moving beyond Orientalist Fantasy', 559; Suad Joseph, 'Sectarianism as Imagined Sociological Concept and as Imagined Social Formation', *International Journal of Middle East Studies* 40, no. 4 (2008): 553–4, https://doi.org/10.1017/S0020743808081464; Ussama Makdisi,

It would be 'misguided to assume that the sectarianism of wartime Syria materialised out of thin air'.[18] However, it is even more misguiding (and dehumanising) to reify notions of 'sect' and 'sectarianism' as characteristic and unchangeable essential features of any group or individual. Such inferences promote dehistoricised narratives of society and culture by projecting reified and essentialist narratives about social groups, collective mobilisation and about the role of religious or sect-based differences in the ongoing conflict. Furthermore, 'identity' as a category of enquiry into causality fundamentally conflates all practical distinctions between 'the self-ascribed or imposed identification of social, political and ideological actors with historical and social reality'.[19] In other words, discussions about identitarian politics and ideation often incorporate causal inferences about 'identity' and socio-political behaviour at personal and collective levels. However, the ideological framing and marketing strategies of armed groups or organised actors do not represent social reality or broader historical conditions by default.

The discovery of representations of the self or of others in sect-based codes and labels in the 'here and now' or at any random moment in the past cannot be considered as evidence of a much broader metaphysical force or dominant culture that informs personal and communal actions in the social, cultural and political fields. Haidar Saeed candidly points out how similar notions of sectarianism in the Iraqi context also seem to be grounded in what he describes as 'popular folklore'.[20] Public vernacular and other forms of spontaneous expressions in everyday life should rather be considered for what they are: spontaneous expressions of prevailing imaginaries and strategies to endow meaning to social reality rather than accurate representations of social reality as such. Of course, emergent antagonistic perceptions and reimagining of other groups during the Syrian conflict will inform, in tandem with other factors, socio-political behaviour at the personal level.

The Culture of Sectarianism: Community, History, and Violence in Nineteenth-Century Ottoman Lebanon (Berkeley: University of California Press, 2000).

[18] Christian Sahner, *Among the Ruins: Syria Past and Present* (Oxford: Oxford University Press, 2014).

[19] Rogers Brubaker, *Ethnicity without Groups* (Cambridge, MA: Harvard University Press, 2006).

[20] Haidar Saeed, *The sect and the nation: A theoretical attempt with references to Iraq*, Striking from the Margins Conference Presentation, 16 January 2019 (Beirut: American University of Beirut) https://youtu.be/tP1QDza28TI?t=3097 (51:36–1:20:50).

This does not imply that subjectivities end up divorced from the influence of future socio-political developments and command a static unidirectional causal capacity. It is for this reason that questions about what maintains, reproduces, reinforces or undermines such modes of perception merit special attention going forward. The role of identitarian politics and subjectivities depends upon the forces and elements that shape, promote, utilise or undermine them.

A growing body of literature already projected this line of thought onto Syria's future. Paulo Pinto's main argument in 'The Shattered Nation: The Sectarianization of the Syrian Conflict' is that pre-existing 'sectarian tensions are not the same as sectarianism'.[21] Similar to Pinto, in 'Sectarianism in Alawi Syria: Exploring the Paradoxes of Politics and Religion' Aslam Farouk-Alli challenges the explanatory paradigm of sectarianism, labelling it 'limited' and 'monolithic'.[22] He argues that the strategies used by hegemonic powers to exploit sectarian divisions are fundamental to the contemporary history of the Middle East.[23] In line with this proposition, Benjamin White in *The Emergence of Minorities in the Middle East* explores the policies of the French Mandate in Syria with regards to organising society and politics based on sectarian divisions and guidelines.[24] White focuses on the emergence of labels and categories such as 'minority' and 'majority' in the legal sphere and how this has reinforced the social standing of these terms.[25] White's work is relevant today as it reminds us that sectarian notions behind terms such as 'minority' and 'majority' are politico-legal constructs and not inherent features of social reality.[26]

This much-needed shift in scholarship represents a paradigm change in dominant frames of thought that Makdisi labelled as post-9/11 narratives.

---

[21] Paulo Gabriel Hilu Pinto, 'The Shattered Nation: The Sectarianziation of the Syrian Conflict', in Nader Hashemi and Danny Postel (eds), *Sectarianziation: Mapping the New Politics of the Middle East* (Oxford: Oxford University Press, 2017), 124

[22] Aslam Farouk-Alli, 'Sectarianism in Alawi Syria: Exploring the Paradoxes of Politics and Religion', *Journal of Muslim Minority Affairs* 34, no. 3 (2014): 207–26.

[23] Ibid., 222.

[24] Benjamin White, *The Emergence of Minorities in The Middle East: The Politics of Community in French Mandate Syria* (Edinburgh: Edinburgh University Press, 2011).

[25] Ibid., 44–5.

[26] See also Christopher Phillips, 'Sectarianism and Conflict in Syria', *Third World Quarterly* 36, no. 2 (2015): 358.

The paradigm shift is towards more nuanced and grounded approaches that examine social reality as a social construct, thus lending terms like sectarianism to epistemic questioning in the social sciences, thus resisting the reification of the subject. The shift in sectarian subjectivities in Syria is shaped by political projects and structural conditions that reinforce sect-based actors and imaginaries. Even in the context of heightened sectarian tension, political agendas for sectarianisation lack pre-defined capacity to define individual or collective behaviour.[27]

Overall, the consistency and continuity of sect-based features in social subjectivities coincide with other factors influencing perceptions of the self, the social other and communal relations – namely, class, region, ethnicity, religion, confessional belonging, occupation, linguistic specificities, kinship and tribal affiliation.[28] Communitarianism and group solidarities in Syria never crystallised along the lines of well-defined and identifiable ethno-religious markers. Rather, markers of identity remain fluid and informed by myriad factors. Before the war, a notion of distinction and distance, specifically in the private/intimate domain (matters related to personal status, family and marriage) were maintained based on religious and confessional distinctions, which were amongst other important communitarian features of pre-war Syria. Perceptions of communal relations were based on a multitude of features and layers, including ethno-religious. Going forward, despite being reinforced by institutional arrangements in place, sectarianism will not evolve into an unassailable belief system that is outside of historical processes.

---

[27] Christa Salamandra, 'Sectarianism in Syria: Anthropological Reflections', *Middle East Critique* 22, no.3 (2013): 303–6.

[28] Bernard Heyberger, *Les Chrétiens au Proch-Orient* (Paris: Manuels Payot, 2013); Leon Goldsmith, *Cycle of Fear: Syria's Alawites in War and Peace* (London: Hurst, 2015); Christa Salamandra, *A New Old Damascus* (Indiana: Indiana University Press, 2004); Maria Kastrinou, *Power, Sect and State in Syria: The Politics of Marriage and Identity Amongst the Druze* (London: I. B.Tauris, 2016); Andreas Bandak, 'States of Exception: Effects and Affects of Authoritarianism among Christian Arabs in Damascus', in Esther Fihl and Jens Dahl (eds), *A Comparative Ethnography of Alternative Spaces* (New York: Palgrave Macmillan, 2013), 197–218; Laura. R. de Elvira, 'Christian Charities and the Ba'thist Regime in Bashar al-Assad's Syria', in Christa Salamandra and Leif Stenberg (eds), *Syria from Reform to Revolt: Culture, Society, and Religion* (Syracuse, New York: Syracuse University Press, 2015), 92–109.

The Future of Religion

The rise of the Islamic State and Jihadi groups contributed to the further sectarianisation of the Syrian context through a spectacle of brutality. This has reinvigorated neo-orientalist fantasies about Islam and Muslims in public discourse. Arguments about radicalised groups range from cautiously arguing that these groups are not entirely divorced from Islam as often claimed, to explicitly stating that aggression and the subjugation of non-Muslims are intrinsic features of Islamic theology, history, tradition and therefore future.[29] Despite prevalent criticism by historians and Islamic scholars, variations of arguments attributing radicalisation to religion, Islam and even Muslims continue to find interest and proliferate.[30] The glaring tropes, emissions and elisions found in these problematic narratives pushed many commentators and scholars to respond and be distracted by oversimplified debates regarding correlations between religion and conflict, or Islam and radicalisation.[31] In the

---

[29] Tim Holland, 'We Must Not Deny The Religious Roots of ISIS', *New Statesman*, 17 March 2015, http://www.newstatesman.com/politics/2015/03/tom-holland-we-must-not-deny-relgious-roots-islamic-state (accessed 15 November 2016); Hisham Bou Nassif, 'Is Islam Truly Innocent of ISIS?', *Now Media*, 24 July 2014, https://now.mmedia.me/lb/en/commentaryanalysis/557279-is-islam-truly-innocent-of-isis. (accessed 21 November 2016); Andrew Bostom, *The Legacy of Jihad: Islamic Holy War and the Fate of Non-Muslims* (New York: Prometheus Books, 2008); Bat Ye'or, *The Decline of Eastern Christianity under Islam* (Madison, NJ: Fairleigh Dickinson University Press, 1996).

[30] For instance, Noah Feldman's *The Fall and Rise of the Islamic State*, first published in 2008, reappeared in a 2012 edition. For a similar argument, see Patricia Crone and Michael Cook, *Hagarism: The Making of the Islamic World* (Cambridge: Cambridge University Press, 1980). Through the abstraction of centuries of diverse experiences and experimentations of Islamic rule, the likes of Noah Feldman, Patricia Crone and Ernest Gellner project Islam as a quasi-monistic politico-legal orthodoxy, embodied by the Shari'a, which, according to them, serves as a comprehensive framework for social and political organisation while also enjoying a metaphysical standing. See Ernest Gellner, *Muslim Society* (Cambridge: Cambridge University Press, 1983). In other words, this Shari'a represents the embedded ethos of not only Islam but also all faithful Muslims. That Islam is unescapably political, that statehood can only be Islamic, and that all faithful Muslims are invariably Islamists in the making, are some of the predispositions found in such arguments. For a critical assessment, see Aziz al-Azmeh, 'God's Caravan', in Mehzrad Boroujerdi (ed.), *Mirror for the Muslim Prince: Islam and the Theory of Statecraft* (Syracuse: Syracuse University Press, 2013), 326–97.

[31] See political commentator Mahdi Hassan's views, in conformity with the expressed views of former Grand Mufti of Egypt Ali Gom'a and political scientist Olivier Roy – that Islamic radicalisation is not a by-product of Islam. See Mehdi Hasan, 'How Islamic Is the Islamic State?', *New Statesman*, 10 March 2015, http://www.newstatesman.com/world-affairs/2015/03/mehdi-hasan-how-islamic-islamic-state. (accessed 14 November 2016); Wael Fayez, 'داعش نبت شيطاني وتمثيلية سخيفة ضد الإسلام', *el-watan*, 21 August 2014, http://www.elwatannews.com /news/details/543055.

context of these debates, discussions regarding the nature of Islam stand out as remarkably reductionist. Such portrayals of Islam, be it as peaceful or violent, amount to nothing more than efforts to essentialise a multifaceted system of beliefs based on pre-defined functions. This debate holds limited analytical worth, if any.

Select scholars have refrained from diversions of this type, analysing instead the broader meanings and various functions of religious militancy and fundamentalism. Al-Azmeh, having long repudiated the projection of Islam as a static body of meanings or practices, proposes studying fundamentalism in its material conditions and various socio-political and socio-cultural functions.[32] With regard to the functions of contemporary radicalised groups such as Daesh, Dallal takes a further step and asks, 'why should we seek explanation of the cruelty of ISIS in some essential Islamic cultural trait, and not in the typical behaviour of gangsters who need to display spectacular cruelty and violence . . . to maintain control?'[33]

The evidence put forth in this book illustrates how armed groups engaged in protracted armed conflict act as rational actors in pursuit of strategic objectives such as establishing territorial control and undermining the influence of incumbents.[34] In the same vein, rebel formations in Syria employed various methods in pursuit of their objectives. Religious discursive and behavioural practices employed by radicalised groups, such as Daesh, served strategic

---

(accessed 14 November 2016) (in Arabic). Islamic scholars Khaled Abou el-Fadl and John Esposito further elaborate that the theology of Islam is distant from religious oppression and aggression. See Khaled Abou el-Fadl, *The Place of Tolerance in Islam* (Boston, MA: Beacon Press, 2002), 19; John Esposito, *Islam: The Straight Path* (New York: Oxford University Press, 1998). They argue that the decrees and stipulations of Jihad and religious oppression are not founded on methodologically sound Qur'anic interpretations. See Abou el-Fadl, *The Place of Tolerance in Islam*, 19. This argument assumes that Jihadis simply do not understand Islam or the Qur'an. The Qur'an contains verses for peace as well as verses calling for violence, as does the Old Testament. The neglect of the contradictory content and arbitrary focus on the peaceful content qualify the argument as apologetic.

[32] Aziz al-Azmeh, سورية والصعود الأصولي: عن الأصولية والطائفية والثقافة.
[33] Ahmad Dallal, *The Political Theology of ISIS: Prophets, Messiahs, & 'the Extinction of the Grayzone* (Tadween Publishing: George Mason University, 2017), 32.
[34] Ana Arjona, *Rebelocracy: Social Order in the Colombian Civil War* (Cambridge: Cambridge University Press, 2016), 9; Jeremy Weinstein, *Inside Rebellion: The Politics of Insurgent Violence* (Cambridge: Cambridge University Press, 2006), 198–258. For Syria specific information see Kevin Mazur, *Revolution in Syria: Identity, Networks and Repression* (Cambridge: Cambridge University Press, 2021); Megan A. Stewart, *Governing for Revolution: Social Transformation in Civil War* (Cambridge: Cambridge University Press, 2021).

functions, rather than being mere random or instinctive expressions of religious or social subjectivities.[35]

Even in cases where such discursive and behavioural practices were motivated by belief and duly expressed without awareness of their functions, this does not imply that violent practices shed their instrumentality. Through exaggerated violence and exclusionary practices, radicalised groups attempted to establish an absolutist order with hegemonic power structures enabling the suppression of dissent and the reconfiguration of communal solidarities and personal subjectivities. Ultimately, the aim of violence, as explicitly stated by the Daesh, is 'to further bring division [. . .] and destroy the grayzone everywhere'.[36] Unlike some orientalist scholars, radicalised groups understood that their 'Islamic' community does not in fact exist, and its production requires radical social and political reconfiguration of a context that is otherwise in sharp contrast with their imagined community.[37] Violence was therefore used as the decisive force, rather than religion, in the transition from an order that was contested to a new one that is consolidating.

During the Syrian uprising, the Syrian Muslim Brotherhood too attempted to harness greater local influence through the support and leverage it provided to armed groups. Nevertheless, the group remained riddled with petty quarrels and infighting within its ranks as well as with myriad other actors, within Syria and without, that were vying for political influence.[38] A great variety of religious actors are present in Syria, and even those who are not ideologically charged have a political function through their social and religious functions.

---

[35] Radicalisation in the political sense is the endorsement of violent means for uncompromising socio-political objectives in a zero sum contest. Despite their differences, these groups share the objective of establishing a theocracy to replace the current political order and exhibit similar violent practices to varying degrees.
[36] 'The extinction of the Grayzone', *Dabiq* 7, January-February 2015, https://clarionproject.org/docs/islamic-state-dabiq-magazine-issue-7-from-hypocrisy-to-apostasy.pdf (accessed 2 February 2017);
[37] ISIS also proffers a historicist argument – that of continuity with the foundational past. By claiming that re-Islamisation is not a novelty but the recovery of an essence that has been in abeyance, Jihadi groups recognise the fact that their imagined 'Islamic community' does not exist in actuality.
[38] Amongst the armed groups that the Muslim Brotherhood was associated with as sponsor or collaborator is Liwa' al-Tawhid. See also White, *The Ashes of Hama* and Dara Conduit, *The Muslim Brotherhood in Syria* (Cambridge: Cambridge University Press, 2019).

The literature on the religious field moved beyond the frameworks of revivalism or authoritarianism, which downplays the agency and political capacity of religious actors and institutions. The combination of authoritarianism and religious revivalism as frames of thought about the religious field in Syria place religiosity in a similar bracket to sectarianism in its embeddedness as an inherent and fundamental feature – bound to return as soon as repressive pressures ease. The expansion of the religious field as an institutional domain is the product of devolutionary processes in Syria before the conflict.[39] Gaps of knowledge that need to be addressed going forward are in relation to patterns of continuity and change in the transformation of the religious field after conflict abatement. The ideological output of state atrophy undermines prospects of unity, especially when emergent institutional ecologies continue to encourage factional and sectarian dispositions rather than serve civic notions of unity. The Assad rule will find a fertile ground to sow clientelist arrangements to thrive under such circumstances. It is for this reason that Jihadi groups will remain amongst the Assad rule's strategically most favourite enemies and the religious field amongst the most favoured allies, both due to their capacity to reinforce sect-based and religious factionalism.

Coda

State violence by the Assad rule is engineered and orchestrated to generate oppressive and brutally violent systems of hierarchy. While they seem robust and profoundly resilient, in the same way that they are purposefully constructed and politically engineered, they can be reverse engineered and deconstructed through targeted policies and sector-based institutional reforms. Although the Assad rule is demonstrably incapable of any reform that undermines its foundations of power, it is important to remember that despite decades of repression and fear, the Assad rule was on the brink of being toppled had it not been for the lack of adequate counterbalancing of Russian and Iranian involvement by major European powers and the US. Nevertheless, in addition to mounting a challenge against the

---

[39] Line Khatib, *Islamic Revivalism in Syria: The Rise and Fall of Ba'thist Secularism* (New York: Routledge, 2011), 137–8; de Elvira, 'Christian Charities and the Ba'thist Regime in Bashar al-Assad's Syria'.

Assad rule, Syria needs institutional arrangements that outline state–society relations in such a way that the public domain can be reclaimed. The role of the state is central for such a vision, and its dismissal, as an institutional domain, is equivalent to the dismissal of any notion of society or what is left of it.

Bibliography

Abazeid, Ahmad and Thomas Pierret. 'Les Rebelles Syriens d'Ahrar al-Sham: Ressorts Contextuels et Organisationnels d'une Déradicalisation en Temps de Guerre Civile', *Critique Internationale* 78, no. 1 (2018): 63–84.

Abboud, Samer. 'Locating the "Social" in the Social Market Economy', in *Syria From Reform To Revolt, Volume 1: Political Economy and International Relations*, edited by Raymond Hinnebusch and Tina Zintl, 45–65. New York: Syracuse University Press, 2015.

Abboud, Samer. *Syria*. Malden: Polity Press, 2016.

Abou el-Fadl, Khaled. *The Place of Tolerance in Islam*. Boston: Beacon Press, 2002.

Abou El Fadel, Khaled. 'The Pretorian State in the Arab Spring', keynote lecture at the University of Pennsylvania Law School Symposium *Democracy in the Middle East*, 11 November 2011, https://scholarship.law.upenn.edu/cgi/viewcontent.cgi?article=1041&context=jil.

Abouzeid, Rania. 'The Jihad Next Door: The Syrian Roots of Iraq's Newest Civil War', *Politico Magazine*, 23 June 2014. https://www.politico.com/magazine/story/2014/06/al-qaeda-iraq-syria-108214.

Abrutyn, Seth. 'Toward a General Theory of Institutional Autonomy', *Sociological Theory* 27, no. 4 (2009): 449–65.

Abrutyn, Seth. 'Toward a Theory of Institutional Ecology: The Dynamics of Macro Structural Space', *Review of European Studies* 4, no. 5 (2012): 167–80.

Abrutyn, Seth. 'Reconceptualizing the dynamics of religion as a macro-institutional domain', *Structure and Dynamics* 6, no. 3 (2013): 1–31.

Abrutyn, Seth and Kirk Lawrence. 'From Chiefdom to State: Toward an Integrative Theory of the Evolution of Polity', *Sociological Perspectives* 53, no. 3 (2010): 419–42.

Abrutyn, Seth and Jonathan Turner. 'The Old Institutionalism Meets the New Institutionalism', *Sociological Perspectives* 54, no. 3 (2009): 283–306.

Abrutyn, Seth and Jonathan H. Turner. 'The old institutionalism meets the new institutionalism', *Sociological Perspectives* 54, no. 3 (2011): 283–306.
Abu Bakr, Naji. إدارة التوحش: أخطر مرحلة ستمر بها الأمة. Syria: Dar al-Tamarrud, n.d.
Achcar, Gilbert. 'Hegemony, Domination, Corruption, and Fraud in the Arab Region', *Middle East Critique* 30, no. 1 (2021): 57–66.
Ackerman, Philip L. *Cognitive Fatigue: Multidisciplinary Perspectives on Current Research and Future Applications.* Washington, DC: American Psychological Association, 2011.
Adwan, Mamdouh. حيونة الانسان. Beirut: Dar Mamdouh Adwan Lil nashr wal-tawzi', 2016.
Ahmad, Eijaz. *In Theory: Classes, Nations, Literatures.* New York: Verso, 2008.
Ahram, Ariel. 'Pro-Government Militias and the Repertoires of Illicit State Violence', *Studies in Conflict and Terrorism* 39, no. 3 (2016): 207–26.
Akdedian, Harout and Aziz al-Azmeh. 'Introduction', in *Spoils of War In the Arab East: Reconditioning Society and Polity in the Arab East*, edited by Aziz al-Azmeh, Harout Akdedian and Haian Dukhan. London: Bloomsbury, 2023.
Akdedian, Harout and Harith Hassan. 'State atrophy and the reconfiguration of borderlands in Syria and Iraq: Post-2011 dynamics', *Political Geography* 80, no. 1 (2020): https://www.sciencedirect.com/science/article/pii/S09626298 1930109X.
Akdedian, Haroutioun. 'Ethno-religious subjectivities in the Syrian war: Dynamics of sectarianism and sectarianization', *The Middle East Journal* 73, no. 3 (2019): 408–30.
Aksoy, Mehmet A. 'Syrian Turkmen: Fighting to Survive', *Al Jazeera World*, 16 August 2017, https://www.aljazeera.com/programmes/aljazeeraworld/2017/08/syrian-turkmen-fighting-survive-170806082405511.html.
The Aleppo Informal Settlement Task Force, Settlements in Aleppo', *Aleppo Urban Development Project*, January 2009, http://madinatuna.com/downloads/IS-Book_en.pdf.
Aleppo Shari'a Commission, Branch Commission Document, 'Primary source: The structure of an Aleppo Sharia Commission branch in the countryside', *Goha's Nail*, 14 May 2014, https://gohasnail.wordpress.com/2014/05/14/primary-source-the-structure-of-an-aleppo-sharia-commission-branch-in-the-countryside-2/.
'Assyrians in Syria protest PYD's closure of schools in qamishli', *Assyrian Policy Institute*, 28 August 2018, https://www.assyrianpolicy.org/news/assyrians-in-syria-protest-pyd-s-closure-of-schools-in-qamishli.

al-Azmeh, Aziz. *Islams and Modernities.* London: Verso, 2009.

al-Azmeh, Aziz. 'God's Caravan', in *Mirror for the Muslim Prince: Islam and the Theory of Statecraft*, edited by Mehzrad Boroujerdi, 326–97. New York: Syracuse University Press, 2013.

al-Azmeh, Aziz. 'Is Islamism the Arab Destiny?', Globalisation Lecture at SOAS, University of London, 6 February 2013, available on YouTube: https://youtu.be/EAfLgTGWrgA.

al-Azmeh, Aziz. سورية والصعود الأصولي: عن الأصولية والطائفية والثقافة. Beirut: Riad El-Rayyes, 2015.

al-Azmeh, Aziz. 'Civil War in Syria', interview by Ardeshir Mehrdad, *Middle East for Change*, 20 November 2016. https://www.strikingmargins.com/news-1/2017/3/6/interview-with-prof-aziz-al-azmeh-civil-war-in-syria.

al-Azmeh, Aziz. 'Sectariansm and Anti-Sectarianism', *Striking from the Margins*, 1 December 2017. https://www.strikingmargins.com/news-1/2017/12/20/prof-aziz-al-azmeh-sectarianism-and-antisectarianism.

al-Azmeh, Aziz. *Secularism in the Arab World: Contexts, Ideas and Consequences.* Edinburgh: Edinburgh University Press, 2019.

al-Azmeh, Aziz and Nadia al-Bagdadi. 'Introduction', in *Striking from the Margins: State, Religion and Devolution of Authority in the Middle East*, edited by Aziz al-Azmeh Nadia al-Bagdadi, Harout Akdedian and Harith Hasan, 1–24. London: Saqi Books, 2021.

al-Azmeh, Aziz and Faysal Darraj. 'هامش لحوار مجزوء: المجتمع المدني أم أيقاظ السياسة مرة أخرى؟', in سوريا بين عهدين, edited by Jamal Barout and Shams alDin Kaylani, 384–9. Amman: Dar Sindbad Lilnashr el'am, 2003. (Originally published in *al-Hayat* newspaper on Friday, 29 June 2001, no. 13984.)

al-Dassouky, Ayman. 'The Economic Networks of the Fourth Division During the Syrian Conflict', *European University Institute*, 24 January 2022, https://doi.org/10.2870/95105.

Al-Deri, Abbas. 'داعش تقتحم قرية"تل أيوب"بريف حلب وتعدم الثوار بتهمة مرتدين', *Orient News*, 21 May 2014, https://orient-news.net/ar/news_show/79180.

al-Doughly, Rahaf. 'Securitization as a tool of regime survival: The deployment of religious rhetoric in Bashar al-Asad's speeches', *The Middle East Journal* 75, no. 1 (2021): 9–32.

Al-Jabassini, Abdallah. 'From Rebel Rule to a Post-Capitulation Era in Daraa Southern Syria: The Impacts and Outcomes of Rebel Behaviour During Negotiations', *European University Institute: Wartime and Post-Conflict in Syria Project*, June 2019, 18–25.

Al-Jabassini, Abdallah. 'Dismantling Networks of Resistance and the Reconfiguration of Order in Southern Syria', *European University Institute: Wartime and Post-Conflict in Syria Project*, October 2021.

Al Jamahir. 'ستساهم الأحداث في منطقتي دير حافر والأتارب في الصحوة التنموية في المحافظة'. 25. February 2009, https://web.archive.org/web/20120308221645/http://jamahir.al wehda.gov.sy/_print_veiw.asp?FileName=5363260872009022421 2858.

Al Jazeera. 'الباب.. مفتاح الشمال السوري'. AlJazeera, 2017: https://www.aljazeera.net/en cyclopedia/citiesandregions/2017/2/13/%D8%A7%D9%84%D8%A8%D8%A7 %D8%A8-%D9%85%D9%81%D8%AA%D8%A7%D8%AD-%D8%A7%D9%84 %D8%B4%D9%85%D8%A7%D9%84-%D8%A7%D9%84%D8%B3%D9%88 %D8%B1%D9%8A.

Al-Kassir, Azzam. 'Formalizing regime control over Syrian religious affairs', *Sada: Middle East Analysis*, 14 November 2018, https://carnegieendowment.org/sa da/77712.

al-Khafaji, Isam. 'De-Urbanising the Syrian Revolt', *The Arab Reform Initiative*, 6 March 2016, 1–18, https://www.arab-reform.net/publication/de-urbanising -the-syrian-revolt/.

Al-Tamimi, Aymann J. 'The Islamic State of Iraq and ash-Sham's dhimmi Pact for the Christians of Raqqa Province', *Joshua Landis blog*, 26 February 2014, http:// www.joshualandis.com/blog/islamic-state-iraq-ash-shams-dhimmi-pact-christia ns-raqqa-province/.

Al-Tamimi, Aymann. 'The Islamic State of Iraq and ash-Sham's dhimmi pact for the Christians of Raqqa province', *Syria Comment*, 11 February 2014, http://www .joshualandis.com/blog/assad-regime-jihadis-collaborators-allies.

Al-Tamimi, Aymann J. 'The Latakia Front: An Interview on the Rebel Side', *Syria Comment*, 6 April 2014, https://web.archive.org/web/20171105235553/http:// www.joshualandis.com/blog/latakia-front-interview-rebel-side/.

Al-Tamimi, Aymann J. 'The Syrian Civil War & Demographic Change', *aymen-njawad.org*, 15 March 2017. http://www.aymennjawad.org/19745/the-syrian-ci vil-war-demographic-change.

Al-Tamimi, Aymann Jawad. 'The post-rebellion south', Interview Aymenn Jawad Al-Tamimi's blog, 13 August 2018, available at: http://www.aymennjawad.org /2018/08/the-post-rebellion-south-interview.

Amnesty International. *Human Slaughterhouse: Mass Hangings and Extermination at Saydnaya Prison*. London: Amnesty International, 2016.

Amnesty International, *It Breaks the Human: Torture, Disease and Death in Syria's Prisons*. London: Amnesty International, 2016.

Anab Baladi. محطة كهرباء حلب في عهدة عقد إيراني مرتقب للمزيد: 11 July 2019, https://www.enabbaladi.net/archives/340690.

Anderson, Benedict. *Imagined Communities: Reflections on the origin and spread of nationalism*. London: Verso, 2016.

Arjona, Ana. *Rebelocracy: Social Order in the Colombian Civil War*. Cambridge: Cambridge University Press, 2016.

Armenian Diocese of Beroea. 'The Crisis of Syrian Armenians and the Displacement of Kessab's Armenians: A Brief Report', *Horizon*, 24 June 2014, https://horizonweekly.ca/en/41718-2/.

Armstrong, Martin and Lauren Williams. 'Armenian Christians Torn in Syria's Civil War', *Beirut: The Daily Star*, 1 October 2012, https://hetq.am/en/article/19046.

Ashekian, Shogher. 'Տեղահանություն, Հաւաքական Յիշողություն և Անձնական Փորձառություն (Քեսապի Պարագայ)', in *Armenians of Syria: Proceedings of the Conference (24–27 May 2015)*, edited by Antranik Dakessian, 509–38. Beirut: Haigazian University Press: Armenian Diaspora Research Center, 2018.

Atassi, Karim. *Syria, The Strength of an Idea: The Constitutional Architectures of Its Political Regimes*. Cambridge: Cambridge University Press, 2018.

Avineri, Shlomo and Avner De-Shalit. *Communitarianism and Individualism*. Oxford: Oxford University Press, 1992.

Awad, Ziad and Agnes Favier. 'Elections in Wartime: The Syrian People's Council (2016–2020)', *Robert Schuman Centre for Advanced Studies*, 30 April 2020, https://medirections.com/images/dox/RPR_2020_07.pdf.

Ayiq, Moris. 'الانتفاضات العربية وسؤال الدولة', *aljumhuriyya*, 7 January 2022, https://aljumhuriya.net/ar/2022/01/07/%d8%a7%d9%84%d8%a7%d9%86%d8%aa%d9%81%d8%a7%d8%b6%d8%a7%d8%aa-%d8%a7%d9%84%d8%b9%d8%b1%d8%a8%d9%8a%d8%a9-%d9%88%d8%b3%d8%a4%d8%a7%d9%84-%d8%a7%d9%84%d8%af%d9%88%d9%84%d8%a9/.

Azmeh, Shamel. *The Uprising of the Marginalized: A Socio-Economic Perspective of the Syrian Uprising* London: LSE Middle East Centre Paper Series, issue 6, November 2014.

Bakunin, Mikhail. *Statism and Anarchy*. Cambridge: Cambridge University Press, 1990.

Balanche, Fabrice. 'Les municipalités dans la Syrie Baathiste: Déconcentration administrative et contrôle Politique', *Revue Tiers Monde* 193, no. 1 (2008): 169–87.

Balanche, Fabrice. 'Latakia Is Assad's Achilles Heel', *The Washington Institute*, 23 September 2015, https://www.washingtoninstitute.org/policy-analysis/view/latakia-is-assads-achilles-heelBamyeh, Mohammad. *Social Sciences in the Arab World: Forms of Presence*. Beirut: Arab Social Science Monitor, 2015.

Bandak, Andreas. 'States of Exception: Effects and Affects of Authoritarianism among Christian Arabs in Damascus', in *A Comparative Ethnogrophy of Alternative Spaces*, edited by Esther Fihl and Jens Dahl, 197–218. New York: Palgrave Macmillan, 2013.

Bar, Shmuel. 'Bashar's Syria: The Regime and its Strategic Worldview', *Comparative Politics* 25 (2006): 353–445.

Barber, Matthew. 'Al-Qaeda's Syrian Judiciary – is it really what al-Jolani makes it out to be?', *Syria Comment*, 9 November 2014, http://www.joshualandis.com/blog/al-qaedas-syrian-judiciary-really-al-jolani-makes/?utm_source=feedburner&utm_medium=email&utm_campaign=Feed%3A+Syriacomment+%28Syria+Comment%29.

Barish, Minhal. 'Private Security Companies in Syria: New Contractors in service of the Regime', *Robert Shuman Foundation: Wartime and Post-Conflict in Syria* (WPCS), 28 July 2020, https://medirections.com/ima ges/dox/Security%20Companies%207282020-last.pdf.

Barnard, Anne. 'Syrian Civilians Bore Brunt of Rebels' Fury, Report Says', *The New York Times*, 11 October 2013, http://www.nytimes.com/2013/10/11/world/middleeast/syrian-civilians-bore-brunt-of-rebels-fury-report-says.html?pagewanted=1&_r=1.

Barnard, Anne. 'Inside Syria's Secret Torture Prisons: How Bashar al-Assad Crushed Dissents', *The New York Times*, 11 May 2019.

Barout, Muhammad Jamal. العقد الأخير في تاريخ سورية: جدليّة الجمود والإصلاح. Doha: Arab Center for Research and Policy Studies, 2012.

Barout, Muhammad Jamal and Shams alDin Kaylani (eds). سورية بين عهدين: قضايا المرحلة الانتقالية: بيانات ووثائق، حوارات وسجالات، مقالات. Amman: Dar Sindbad Lilnashr el'am, 2003.

Battatu, Hanna. *Syria's Peasantry, the Descendants of its Lesser Rural Notables and Their Politics*. Princeton: Princeton University Press, 1999.

Bayart, Jean-François. *L'État en Afrique*. Paris: Fayard, 1989.

Berg, Louis-Alexandre. *Governing Security After War: The Politics of Institutional Change in the Security Sector*. Oxford: Oxford University Press, 2022.

Bergholz, Max. *Violence as a Generative Force*. New York: Cornell University Press, 2021.

Bishara, Azmi. المجتمع المدني: دراسة نقدية. Doha: Arab Center for Research and Policy Studies, 2012.
Bishara, Azmi. الانتقال الديمقراطي وإشكالياته: دراسة نظرية وتطبيقية مقارنة. Doha: Arab Center for Research and Policy Studies, 2020.
Bishara, Azmi. *Sectarianism Without Sects*. Oxford: Oxford University Press, 2021.
Bitterlin, Lucien. *Hafez al-Assad: Le Parcours d'un Combattant*. Paris: Editions du Jaguar, 1986.
Blau, Peter. *Exchange and Power in Social Life*. New York: John Wiley & Sons, 1964.
Blom-Hansen, Thomas and Finn Stepputat. 'Sovereignty revisited', *Annual Review of Anthropology* 35, no. 1 (2006): 295–315.
Bookchin, Murray. *The Ecology of Freedom: The Emergence and Dissolution of Hierarchy*. Oakland: AK Press, 2005.
Bookman, Milica Z. *The Demographic Struggle for Power*. London: Frank Cass & Co., 1997.
Borzel, Tanja and Thomas Risse. 'Dysfunctional State Institutions, Trust, and Governance in Areas of Limited Statehood', *Regulation & Governance* 10 (2016): 149–60.
Bostom, Andrew. *The Legacy of Jihad: Islamic Holy War and the Fate of Non-Muslims*. New York: Prometheus Books, 2008.
Bou Nassif, Hisham. 'Is Islam Truly Innocent of ISIS?', *Now Media*, 24 July 2014, https://now.mmedia.me/lb/en/commentaryanalysis/557279-is-islam-truly-innocent-of-isis.
Bou Nassif, Hicham. 'Generals and Autocrats: How Coup-Proofing Pre-Determined the Military Elite's Behavior in the Arab Spring', *Political Science Quarterly* 130, no. 2 (2015): 245–75.
Bou Nassif, Hicham. '"Second-Class": The Grievances of Sunni Officers in the Syrian Armed Forces', *Journal of Strategic Studies* 38, no. 5 (2015): Appendix.
Bourdieu, Pierre. 'Social Space and Symbolic Power', *Sociological Theory* 7, no. 1 (1989): 14–25.
Bourdieu, Pierre. *Pascalian Meditations*. Cambridge, MA: Polity Press, 2000.
Brandel, Andrew and Shalini Randeria. 'Anthropological Perspectives on the Limits of the State', in *The Oxford Handbook of Governance and Limited Statehood*, edited by Thomas Risse et al., 68–88. Oxford: Oxford University Press, 2018.
Brubaker, Rogers. *Ethnicity without Groups*. Cambridge, MA: Harvard University Press, 2006.

Butler, Judith. *Bodies That Matter*. New York: Routledge, 1993.
Cadier, David, Matteo Capasso and Karoline Eickhoff. 'Researching Resilience: Implications for Case Studies in Europe's Neighbourhoods', *EU-LISTCO*, January 2020, 140, https://www.eu-listco.net/publications/researching-resilience.
Cambanis, Thanassis et al., *Hybrid Actors: Armed Groups and State Fragmentation in the Middle East*. New York: The Century Foundation Press, 2019.
Carraso, David. *City of Sacrifice: The Aztec Empire and the Role of Violence in Civilization*. Boston: Beacon Press, 1998.
Chase-Dunn, Christopher and Thomas D. Hall. *Rise and Demise: Comparing World-Systems*. Boulder, CO: Westview Press, 1997.
Chulov, Martin. 'Massacre in Tadamon: how two academics hunted down a Syrian war criminal', *The Guardian*, 26 April 2022, https://www.theguardian.com/world/2022/apr/27/massacre-in-tadamon-how-two-academics-hunted-down-a-syrian-war-criminal.
Chulov, Martin and Emma Beales. 'Aid group Mercy Corps forced to close Damascus operations', *The Guardian*, 23 May 2014.
https://www.theguardian.com/world/2014/may/23/aid-group-mercy-corps-forced-to-close-damascus-operations-syria.
Comolli, Jean-Louis. *Daesh, Le Cinema et la Mort*. Lagrasse: Verdier, 2016.
Conduit, Dara. *The Muslim Brotherhood in Syria*. Cambridge: Cambridge University Press, 2019.
Crawford, James R. *The Creation of States in International Law*. Oxford: Oxford University Press, 2006.
Crone, Patricia and Michael Cook. *Hagarism: The Making of the Islamic World*. Cambridge: Cambridge University Press, 1980.
D., Mohammad. 'Who is Hilal al-Assad', *Syria Comment*, 5 April 2014, https://www.joshualandis.com/blog/hilal-al-assad-mohammad-d/#:~:text=Hilal%20al-Assad%20was%20the%20commander%20of%20al-Difa%E2%80%99%20al-Watani,parents%20of%20an%20Alawi%20soldier%20fighting%20with%20him.
Dadoush, Sarah. 'Iran is putting down roots in eastern Syria, outcompeting Assad's regime in signing up fighters', *The Washington Post*, 28 January 2022, https://www.washingtonpost.com/world/2022/01/28/iran-syria-militias-deir-al-zour/.
Dagher, Sam. *Assad or We Burn the Country: How One Family's Lust for Power Destroyed Syria*. Boston: Little, Brown & Co., 2019.
Daghestani, Malek. 'Ya hurriyyeh', interview by Suad Qatanani, *Syria TV*, 29 March 2018, Time Stamp: 18:00–19:20, https://youtu.be/f3SiDRJj_Sk.

Daher, Joseph. *Syria After The Uprisings: The Political Economy of State Resilience*. London: Pluto Press, 2019.

Daher, Joseph. 'Expelled from the Support System: Austerity Deepens in Syria', *Middle East Directions Blog*, 15 February 2022, https://blogs.eui.eu/medirections/expelled-from-the-support-system-austerity-deepens-in-syria/.

Dallal, Ahmad. *The Political Theology of ISIS: Prophets, Messiahs, & 'the Extinction of the Grayzone'*. Washington, DC: George Mason University, 2017.

De Elvira, Laura Ruiz. 'State/charities relation in Syria: Between reinforcement, control and coercion', in *Civil Society and the State of Syria: The Outsourcing of Social Responsibility*, edited by Laura Ruiz de Elvira and Tina Zintl. Boulder, CO: Lynne Rienner, 2012.

De Elvira, Laura Ruiz. 'Christian Charities and the Ba'thist Regime in Bashar al-Assad's Syria', in *Syria from Reform to Revolt: Culture, Society, and Religion*, edited by Christa Salamandra and Leif Stenberg, 92–109. New York: Syracuse University Press, 2015.

De Elvira, Laura Ruiz and Tina Zintl (eds). *Civil Society and the State of Syria: The Outsourcing of Social Responsibility*. Boulder, CO: Lynne Rienner, 2012.

De Elvira, Laura Ruiz and Tina Zintl. 'The End of the Ba'thist Social Contract in Bashar al-Asad's Syria: Reading Sociopolitical Transformations Through Charities and Broader Benevolent Activism', *International Journal of Middle East Studies* 46, no. 2 (2014): 329–49.

'Deadly Experience', *The Economist*, 20 August 2015. https://www.economist.com/middle-east-and-africa/2015/08/20/deadly-experience.

Dean, Michael and Kaspar Villasden. *State Phobia and Civil Society: The Political Legacy of Michael Foucault*. Stanford: Stanford University Press, 2016

Di John, Jonathan. 'Conceptualizing the Causes and Consequences of Failed States: A Critical Review of the Literature', *LSE: Crisis States Working Papers* 2, no. 25 (2008): https://www.files.ethz.ch/isn/57427/wp25.2.pdf.

Dickinson, Elizabeth. 'Playing with fire: Why private Gulf financing for Syria's extremist rebels risks igniting sectarian conflict at home', *The Brookings Project on US Relations with the Islamic World*, 6 December 2013, https://www.brookings.edu/research/playing-with-fire-why-private-gulf-financing-for-syrias-extremist-rebels-risks-igniting-sectarian-conflict-at-home/.

Dodge, Toby. 'The Failure of Peacebuilding in Iraq: The Role of Consociationalism and Political Settlements', *Journal of Intervention and Statebuilding* 15, no. 4 (2021): 459–75.

Dolbee, Samuel. 'After ISIS: Development and demography in the Jazira', *Middle East Brief* (2018), 121, available at: https://www.brandeis.edu/crown/publicatio ns/middle-east-briefs/pdfs/101-200/meb121.pdf.

Donati, Caroline. *L'exception Syrienne.* Paris: La Découverte, 2009.

Drevon, Jerome and Patrick Haenni. 'How Global Jihad Relocalises and Where it Leads: The Case of HTS, the Former AQ Franchise in Syria', *Robert Schuman Centre for Advanced Studies: The Middle East Directions Programme, European University Institute* 8 (2021): https://cadmus.eui.eu/handle/1814/69795.

Dukhan, Haian. *States and Tribes in Syria: Informal Alliances and Conflict Patterns.* London: Routledge, 2018.

Dukhan, Haian. 'The ISIS Massacre of the Sheitat Tribe in Deir ez-Zor, August 2014', *Journal of Genocide Research* (2021).

Durkheim, Émile. *The Division of Labor in Society.* New York: The Free Press, 1893.

Durkheim, Émile. *The Elementary Forms of Religious Life.* Oxford: Oxford University Press, 2008.

El-Meehy, Asya and Haid Haid. *Mapping Local Governance in Syria: A Baseline Study.* Beirut: ESCWA, 2020.

Enab Baladi. 'Free Independent Syrian Judiciary Council', *Enab Baladi*, 26 January 2016.

Enab Baladi; Hamimo, M. M. (2019). لا يوجد حالياً تقنين في سورية. Al-Watan.

Enayat, Hadi. *Islam and Secularism in Post-Colonial Thought: A Cartography of Asadian Genealogies.* London: Palgrave Pivot, 2017.

Erdmann, Gero and Ulf Engel. 'Neopatrimonialism reconsidered: Critical review and elaboration of an elusive concept', *Commonwealth and Comparative Politics*, vol. 45, no. 1 (2007): 96–119.

Esposito, John. *Islam: The Straight Path.* New York: Oxford University Press, 1998.

'The extinction of the Grayzone', *Dabiq* 7, January–February 2015 https://clarion project.org/docs/islamic-state-dabiq-magazine-issue-7-from-hypocrisy-to-aposta sy.pdf.

Farouk-Alli, Aslam. 'Sectarianism in Alawi Syria: Exploring the Paradoxes of Politics and Religion', *Journal of Muslim Minority Affairs* 34, no. 3 (2014): 207–26.

Farouq, Umar. 'Turkey puts down roots in a corner of war-torn Syria', *The Los Angeles Times*, 13 July 2018, http://www.latimes.com/world/la-fg-turkey-syria-201807 13-story.html.

Fayez, Wael. '"داعش" نبت شيطاني وتمثيلية سخيفة ضد الإسلام', *el-watan*, 21 August 2014, http://www.elwatannews.com/news/details/543055.

Fearon, James and David Laitin. 'Violence and the Social Construction of Ethnic Identity', *International Organization* 54, no. 4 (2000): 845–77.
Fields, Barbara. 'Slavery, Race and Ideology in the United States of America', *New Left Review* 181, no. 1 (1990): 95–118.
Freedman, Robert. *Moscow and the Middle East: Soviet Policy Since the Invasion of Afghanistan.* Cambridge: Cambridge University Press, 1991.
Gambill, Gary. 'The Military Intelligence Shake Up in Syria', *Middle East Intelligence Bulletin* 4, no. 2 (2002), https://www.meforum.org/meib/articles/0202_s1.htm.
Gellner, Ernest. *Muslim Society.* Cambridge: Cambridge University Press, 1983.
Gel'man, Vladimir. 'Subversive Institutions, Informal Governance, and Contemporary Russian Politics', *Communist and Post-Communist Studies* 45, no. 3/4 (2012): 295–303.
George, Alan. *Syria: Neither Bread Nor Freedom.* London: Zed books, 2003.
George, Alexander L. and Andrew Bennett. *Case Studies and Theory Development in the Social Sciences.* Cambridge, MA: MIT Press, 2005.
Gerring, John. 'Case Selection for Case-Study Analysis: Qualitative and Quantitative Techniques', in *The Oxford Handbook of Political Methodology*, edited by Janet Box-Steffensmeier, Henry Brady and David Collier, 645–84. Oxford: Oxford University Press, 2010.
Giddens, Anthony. *A Contemporary Critique of Historical Materialism. Vol. 1: Power, Property and the State.* London: Macmillan, 1981.
Girard, René. *Violence and the Sacred.* New York: W. W. Norton & Co., 1972.
Goldsmith, Leon. *Cycle of Fear: Syria's Alawites in War and Peace.* London: Hurst, 2015.
Government of Turkey 'Bayirbucak Turkmens take refuge in Turkey', *Relief Web*, 1 February 2016, https://reliefweb.int/report/turkey/bayirbucak-turkmens-take-refuge-turkey.
Graeber, David. 'Foreword', in *Revolution in Rojava: Democratic Autonomy and Women's Liberation in Syrian Kirdistan*, edited by Michael Knapp, Anja Flach and Ercan Ayboga. London: Pluto Press, 2016.
Granovetter, Mark. 'The Strength of Weak Ties', *American Journal of Sociology* 78, no. 6 (1973): 1360–80.
Greico, Margaret. *Workers' Dilemmas: Recruitment, Reliability, and Repeated Exchanges — An Analysis of Urban Social Networks and Labour Circulation.* London: Routledge, 1996.
Gutierrez-Sanin, Francisco. 'Organization and Governance: The Evolution of Urban

Militias in Medellin, Colombia', in *Rebel Governance in Civil War*, edited by Ana Arjona, Nelson Kasfir and Zachariah Mamphily, 246–63. Cambridge: Cambridge University Press, 2017.

Habermas, Jürgen. *The Structural Transformation of the Public Sphere: An Inquiry Into a Category of Bourgeois Society*. Cambridge, MA: MIT Press, 1991.

Haddad, Bassam. *Business Networks in Syria: The Political Economy of Authoritarian Resilience*. Stanford: Stanford University Press, 2012.

Halasa, Malu, Zahra Omareen and Nawara Mahfoud. *Syria Speaks: Art and Culture From the Frontline*. London: Saqi Books, 2014.

Halliday, Fred. *The Middle East in International Relations: Power, Politics and Ideology*. Cambridge: Cambridge University Press, 2005.

Hansen, Thomas B. and Finn Stepputat. 'Sovereignty revisited', *Annual Review of Anthropology* 35, no. 1 (2006): 295–315.

Harik, Iliya. 'Democracy, "Arab Exceptionalism" and Social Science', *The Middle East Journal* 60, no. 4 (2006): 664–84, https://doi.org/10.3751/60.4.12.

Harling, Peter and Alex Simon. 'Erosion and resilience of the Iraqi-Syrian border', *EUI* (2015), available at: https://cadmus.eui.eu/bitstream/handle/1814/37015/RSCAS_2015_61.pdf.

Harvey, David. *The Condition of Postmodernity: An Enquiry into the Origins of Cultural Change*. Oxford: Wiley-Blackwell, 2000.

Harvey, David. 'Neoliberalism as Creative Destruction', *The Annals of the American Academy of Political and Social Science* 610 (2007): 22–44. http://www.jstor.org/stable/25097888.

Hasan, Abdullah. 'دير حافر: من داعش الى الحرس الثوري', *A'ayn al-Madina*, 14 September 2018, https://ayn-almadina.com/public/details/%D8%AF%D9%8A%D8%B1%20%D8%AD%D8%A7%D9%81%D8%B1..%20%D9%85%D9%86%20%D8%AF%D8%A7%D8%B9%D8%B4%20%D8%A5%D9%84%D9%89%20%D8%A7%D9%84%D8%AD%D8%B1%D8%B3%20%D8%A7%D9%84%D8%AB%D9%88%D8%B1%D9%8A/4627/ar.

Hasan, Harith and Kheder Khaddour. 'The Transformation of the Iraqi-Syrian Border: From a National to a Regional Frontier', *Carnegie Middle East Center*, 31 March 2020, https://carnegie-mec.org/2020/03/31/transformation-of-iraqi-syrian-border-from-national-to-regional-frontier-pub-81396.

Hasan, Mehdi. 'How Islamic Is the Islamic State?' *New Statesman*, 10 March 2015, http://www.newstatesman.com/world-affairs/2015/03/mehdi-hasan-how-islamic-islamic-state.

Heller, Sam. 'Jeish al-Muhajireen wal-Ansar Shar'i: "I bring you good news..."', *Abu al-Jamajim*, 25 October 2014, https://abujamajem.wordpress.com/2014/10/25/jeish-al-muhajireen-wal-ansar-shari-i-bring-you-good-news/.

Heyberger, Bernard. *Les Chrétiens au Proch-Orient*. Paris: Manuels Payot, 2013.

Heydemann, Stephen. *Syria: Revolution from Above*. New York: Routledge, 2002.

Heydemann, Stephen. *Networks of Privilege in the Middle East: The Politics of Economic Reform Revisited*. London: Palgrave, 2004.

Heywood, Andrew. *Politics*. London: Bloomsbury Publishing, 2019.

Hilu Pinto, Paulo Gabriel. 'The Shattered Nation: The Sectarianziation of the Syrian Conflict', in *Sectarianziation: Mapping the New Politics of the Middle East*, edited by Nader Hashemi and Danny Postel, 123–142. Oxford: Oxford University Press, 2017.

Hinnebusch, Raymond. *Syria: Revolution from Above*. New York: Routledge, 2002.

Hinnebusch, Raymond. 'President and Party in Post-Baʻthist Syria: From the Struggle of "Reform" to Regime Deconstruction', in *Syria From Reform To Revolt, Volume 1: Political Economy and International Relations*, edited by Raymond Hinnebusch and Tina Zintl, 21–44. New York: Syracuse University Press, 2015.

Hinnebusch, Raymond and Tina Zintl (eds), *Syria From Reform To Revolt, Volume 1: Political Economy and International Relations*. New York: Syracuse University Press, 2015.

'Historic Mosque in Daraa Destroyed in Syrian Army Shelling', *Al-Arabiya*, 14 April 2013, https://english.alarabiya.net/News/middle-east/2013/04/14/Historic-mosque-in-Daraa-destroyed-in-Syrian-army-shelling-.

Hoffman, David. *Oligarchs: The Wealth and Power in the New Russia*. New York: Public Affairs Books, 2002.

Hokayem, Emile. *Syria's Uprising and the Fracturing of the Levant*. London: Routledge, 2013.

Holland, Tim. 'We Must Not Deny The Religious Roots of ISIS', *New Statesman*, 17 March 2015, http://www.newstatesman.com/politics/2015/03/tom-holland-we-must-not-deny-relgious-roots-islamic-state.

Holliday, Joseph. *The Assad Regime: From Counterinsurgency to Civil War*, Institute for the Study of War, Middle East Security report 8, March 2013: https://www.understandingwar.org/report/assad-regime.

Holmes, Oliver and Suleiman Al-Khalidi. 'Islamic State killed 700 people from Syrian tribe: monitoring group', 17 August 2017, https://www.reuters.com/article/us-syria-crisis-execution/islamic-state-executed-700-people-from-syrian-tribe-monitoring-group-idUSKBN0GG0H120140817.

Hudson, Rex. *The Sociology and Psychology of Terrorism: Who Becomes a Terrorist and Why?*, Washington, DC: Library of Congress: Federal Research Division, 1999.

Human Rights Watch. *Torture Archipelago: Arbitrary Arrests, Torture, and Enforced Disappearances in Syria's Underground Prisons since March 2011*, July 2012: https://www.hrw.org/report/2012/07/03/torture-archipelago/arbitrary-arrests-torture-and-enforced-disappearances-syrias.

'Hundreds of residents of Deir Hafer area and its surroundings return to their homes in the eastern countryside of Aleppo', *SANA*, 20 July 2017, http://www.sana.sy/?p=593189.

Ibn Khaldun. *The Muqaddimah: An Introduction to History*. Princeton: Princeton University Press, 2015.

Ibrahim, Mohammad A. and Tariq Adely. 'Last rebel faction leaves mountains on Syrian-Lebanese border alongside displaced', *Syria Direct*, 14 August 2017, https://syriadirect.org/news/last-rebel-faction-leaves-mountains-on-syrian-lebanese-border-alongside-displaced.

Illing, Sean. 'The "abolish the police" movement', *Vox*, 12 June 2020, https://www.vox.com/policy-and-politics/2020/6/12/21283813/george-floyd-blm-abolish-the-police-8cantwait-minneapolis.

Ismail, Salwa. *The Rule of Violence: Subjectivity, Memory, and Government in Syria*. Cambridge: Cambridge University Press, 2018.

Jones, David, Anne Lane and Paul Schulte. *Terrorism, Security and the Power of Informal Networks*. Northampton, MA: Edward Elgar Publishing, 2010.

Joseph, Max J. and Isaac Mardean. 'Romancing Rojava: Rhetoric vs. Reality', *Syria Comment*, 31 July 2018, https://www.joshualandis.com/blog/romancing-rojava-rhetoric-vs-reality/.

Joseph, Suad. 'Sectarianism as Imagined Sociological Concept and as Imagined Social Formation', *International Journal of Middle East Studies* 40, no. 4 (2008): 553–4. https://doi.org/10.1017/S0020743808081464.

Kabe, Mariame. *We Do This Until We Free Us: Abolitionist Organizing and Transformative Justice*. Chicago: Haymarket Books, 2021.

Kalyvas, Stathis. *The Logic of Violence in Civil War*. Cambridge: Cambridge University Press, 2006.

Kaplan, Oliver. *Resisting War: How Communities Protect Themselves*. Cambridge: Cambridge University Press, 2017.

Karam, Zeina. 'Hundreds of bodies exhumed from mass grave in Syria's Raqqa', *Associated Press*, 27 November 2018, https://www.apnews.com/01c50935854b425295ef8731cdfc42a4.

Kastrinou, Maria. *Power, Sect and State in Syria: The Politics of Marriage and Identity Amongst the Druze*. London: I. B. Tauris, 2016.

Keen, David. *Useful Enemies: When Waging Wars Is More Important Than Winning Them*. New Haven: Yale University Press, 2012.

Khaddour, Kheder. 'Consumed by War: The End of Aleppo and Northern Syria's Political Order', *Friedrich Ebert Stiftung*, October 2017, 1–19, http://library.fes.de/pdf-files/iez/13783.pdf.

Khalifa, Mustafa. القوقعة. Beirut: Dar al-Adab, 2008.

Khatib, Line. *Islamic Revivalism in Syria: The Rise and Fall of Ba'thist Secularism*. New York: Routledge, 2011.

Khedra, J. B. خطة لتنمية السياحة البيئية في منطقة كسب واستثمارها طبيعياً. *Journal of Tshreen University for Research and Scientific Studies 1*, no. 31, (2009): 113–31.

Khraishe, Dana. 'Car bomb in Beirut kills four, wounds 77', *The Daily Star*, 2 January 2014. http://www.dailystar.com.lb/News/Lebanon-News/2014/Jan-02/242913-huge-explosion-rocks-beiruts-southern-suburbs.ashx.

Kittleson, Shelly. 'Iraq's Qaim border open to nonlocal PMU fighting in Syria', *Al-Monitor*, 25 April 2019, https://www.al-monitor.com/pulse/originals/2019/04/iraq-anbar-qaim-pmu-shiite-militia-iran-syria.html#ixzz5yU18RCZy.

Klarić, Miro, Branka Klarić, Aleksandra Stevanovic, Jasna Grković and Suzana Jonovska. 'Psychological Consequences of War Trauma and Postwar Social Stressors in Women in Bosnia and Herzegovina', *Croatian Medical Journal*, 48, no. 2 (2007): 167–76.

Knapp, Michael, Anja Flach and Ercan Ayboga. *Revolution in Rojava: Democratic Autonomy and Women's Liberation in Syrian Kurdistan*. London: Pluto Press, 2016.

Kolossov, Vladimir. 'Border Studies: Changing perspectives and theoretical approaches', *Geopolitics* 10, no. 4 (2005): 606–32.

Konrad, Victor. 'Toward a theory of borders in motion', *Journal of Borderlands Studies* 30, no. 1 (2015): 1–17.

Kovacs, Balazs. 'Peace-Building: From Liberal State Building Imperative to the Post-conflict Register? Perspectives from Comparison', in *Spoils of War In the Arab East: Reconditioning Society and Polity in the Arab East*, edited by Aziz al-Azmeh, Harout Akdedian and Haian Dukhan. London: Bloomsbury, 2023.

Kovacs, Balazs and Paddy Tobias (eds), 'Questioning Peace Infrastructure and Peace Formation', *Peace and Conflict Review* 9, no. 1 (2016): 1–105.

Kropotkin, Peter. *Mutual Aid: A Factor of Evolution*. New Haven: Yale University Press, 2022.

Landis, Joshua. 'The Great Sorting Out: Ethnicity and the Future of the Levant', *Qifa Nabki*, 18 December 2013. https://qifanabki.com/2013/12/18/landis-ethnicity/.

Landis, Joshua. 'Zahran 'Alloush: His Ideology and Beliefs', *Syria Comment*, 15 December 2013, http://www.joshualandis.com/blog/zahran-alloush.

Leenders, Reinoud and Antonio Giustozzi. 'Outsourcing state violence: The National Defence Force, "Stateness" and Regime Resilience in the Syrian War', *Mediterranean Politics* 24, no. 2 (2019): 157–80.

Leenders, Reinoud and Antonio Giustozzi. 'Foreign sponsorship of pro-government militias fighting Syria's insurgency: Whither proxy wars?', *Mediterranean Politics* (24 November 2020), https://doi.org/10.1080/13629395.2020.1839235.

Lister, Charles. *The Syrian Jihad: The Evolution of an Insurgency*. London: Hurst, 2015.

Liwa' al-Tawhid, 'البيان رقم واحد حول الائتلاف والحكومة المفترضة', *leuaaltawheed.com*, 24 September 2013. http://leuaaltawheed.com/ال-الحكومة-و-الائتلاف-حول-1-رقم-البيان/.

Love, Dayvon. 'Police Accountability', *Human Rights Magazine* 46, no. 2 (2021), available online: https://www.americanbar.org/groups/crsj/publications/human_rights_magazine_home/civil-rights-reimagining-policing/police-accountability/.

Lund, Aron. 'Syria's Salafi insurgents: the rise of the Syrian Islamic front', *Swedish Institute of International Affairs*, 28 February 2013.

Lund, Aron. 'Syria's Salafi insurgents: The rise of the Syrian Islamic Front', *Swedish Institute of International Affairs*, March 2013, 25.

Lund, Aron. 'The Politics of the Islamic Front, Part 1: Structure and Support', 14 January 2014, *Carnegie Endowment for International Peace*, http://carnegieendowment.org/syriaincrisis/?fa=54183.

Lund, Aron. 'Chasing Ghosts: The Shabiha Phenomenon', in *The Alawis of Syria: War, Faith and Politics in the Levant*, edited by Michael Kerr and Craig Larkin, 207–24. London: Hurst, 2015.

Lund, Aron. 'Assad's broken base: The case of Idlib', *The Century Foundation*, 14 July 2016, https://tcf.org/content/report/assads-broken-base-case-idlib/.

MacGinty, Roger and Oliver Richmond. 'The Local Turn in Peace Building: a critical agenda for peace', *Third World Quarterly* 34, no. 5 (2013): 763–83.

Magyar, Balint. 'Towards a terminology for Post-Communist Regimes', in *Stubborn Structures: Reconceptualizing post-Communist Regimes*, edited by Balint Magyar, 139–40. Budapest: Central European University, 2018.

Maier, Hans. 'Political Religion: A Concept and its Limitations', *Politics, Religion & Ideology* 8, no. 1 (2007): 5–16.

Makdisi, Samir and Marcus Marktanner. 'Trapped by Consociationalism: The Case of Lebanon', *Topics in Middle Eastern and African Economies* 11 (2009): available online https://meea.sites.luc.edu/volume11/PDFS/Paper-by-MakdisiMarktanner.pdf.

Makdisi, Ussama. *The Culture of Sectarianism: Community, History, and Violence in Nineteenth-Century Ottoman Lebanon*. Berkeley: University of California Press, 2000.

Makdisi, Ussama. 'Moving beyond Orientalist Fantasy, Sectarian Polemic and Nationalist Denial', *International Journal of Middle Eastern Studies* 40, no. 4 (2008): 559–60, https://doi.org/10.1017/S0020743808081488.

Malkasian, Carter. *Illusions of Victory: The Anbar Awakening And The Rise of The Islamic State*. Oxford: Oxford University Press, 2017.

Manjikian, Sevan. Բեսաք Շրջանի Հայրիթեան Միսակագրութիւն: *2006–2007*. Aleppo: Hamazkayin Press, 2010.

Manjikian, Sevan. Բեսաք *2014:* Մեղահանութիւն և Մերադարձ. NA: Arevelk, 2017.

Mann, Michael. *The Sources of Social Power*. Cambridge: Cambridge University Press, 2012.

Martinez, Jose. 'Stifling Stateness: The Assad Regime's Campaign Against Rebel Governance', *Security Dialogue* 49, no. 4 (2018): 235–53.

Marx, Karl. 'The German Ideology', in *The Marx-Engels Reader*, edited by Robert C. Tucker, 146–202. New York: W. W. Norton & Co., 1972.

Mazur, Kevin. 'State Networks and Intra-Ethnic Group Variation in the 2011 Syrian Uprising', *Comparative Political Studies* 52, no. 7 (2019): 995–1027.

Mazur, Kevin. *Revolution in Syria: Identity, Networks and Repression*. Cambridge: Cambridge University Press, 2021.

McGarry, John. 'Demographic engineering: The state directed movement of ethnic groups as a technique in conflict regulation', *Ethnic and Racial Studies* 21, no. 4 (1998): 613–38.

Menkhaus, Ken. 'Making Sense of Resilience in Peacebuilding Contexts: Approaches, Applications, Implications', *The Geneva Peacebuilding Platform*, 2013, 1–10.

Migdal, Joel. *State in Society: Studying How States and Societies Transform and Constitute One Another*. Cambridge: Cambridge University Press, 2001.

Migliorino, Nicola. 'Kulna Suriyyin? The Armenian community and the State in contemporary Syria', *Revue des mondes musulmans et de la Méditerranée*, 2006, 115–16.

Mikati, Najib. 'My country cannot cope with the Syrian refugee crisis', *The Telegraph*, 21 January 2014. https://www.telegraph.co.uk/news/worldnews/middleeast/le

banon/10587174/Lebanon-PM-My-country-cannot-cope-with-the-Syrian-refugee-crisis.html.

'Minaret of Historic Syrian Mosque Destroyed in Aleppo', *The Guardian*, 24 April 2013, https://www.theguardian.com/world/2013/apr/24/minaret-historic-syrian-mosque-destroyed-aleppo.

Morland, Paul. *Demographic engineering: Population strategies in ethnic conflict*. Burlington: Ashgate, 2014.

Mourtada, Hania. 'Rebels Reassure Christians After Capturing Key Syrian Border Town', *Time*, 27 March 2014, https://time.com/40378/syria-kessab-christians/.

Mourtada, Hania and Anne Barnard. 'Dozens of Shiites Reported Killed in Raid by Syria Rebels', *The New York Times*, 12 June 2013. http://mobile.nytimes.com/2013/06/13/world/middleeast/syria.html?from=global.home.

Neumann, Peter. 'Suspects into collaborators', *London Review of Books*, 36, no. 7 (2014): 19–21.

Newman, David. 'On borders and power: A theoretical framework', *Journal of Borderlands Studies* 18, no. 1 (2003): 13–25.

Nicholson, Madeline. 'Public Ritual Sacrifice as a Controlling Mechanism for the Aztec', Honors Scholar Theses: University of Connecticut, 2017.

Nome, Martin A. and Nils B. Weidmann. 'Conflict Diffusion via Social Identities: Entrepreneurship and Adaptation', in *Transnational Dynamics of Civil War*, edited by Jeffrey Checkel, 173–201. Cambridge: Cambridge University Press, 2014.

'No One's Left: Summary Executions by Syrian Forces in al-Bayda and Baniyas', Human Rights Watch, 13 September 2013, https://www.hrw.org/report/2013/09/13/no-ones-left/summary-executions-syrian-forces-al-bayda-and-baniyas.

Ocalan, Abdullah. *The Political Thought of Abduallah Ocalan: Kurdistan, Women's Revolution and Democratic Confederalism*. London: Pluto Press, 2017.

'Our Living After Surviving', *JRS Syria*, 2018, https://jesuitmissions.org.uk/wp-content/uploads/2018/03/JRS-Al-Sakhour-2018.pdf.

Paasi, Anssi. 'Bounded spaces in a "borderless world": Border Studies, power and the anatomy of territory', *Journal of Power* 2, no. 2 (2009): 213–34.

Paffenholz, Thania. 'Perpetual Peacebuilding: A New Paradigm to Move Beyond the Linearity of Liberal Peacebuilding', *Journal of Intervention and Peacebuilding* 15, no. 3 (2021): 367–85.

People's Council of Syria. 'حسن فهمي : عضو مجلس الشعب', *Syrian Arab Republic: The People's Council*, http://www.parliament.gov.sy/arabic/index.php?node=211&nid=1162&RID=26&Last=252&First=0&CurrentPage=0&FName=&LName=&City=&Cat=&Mem=&Com=&Aso=&or=&.

Phillips, Christopher. 'Sectarianism and Conflict in Syria', *Third World Quarterly* 36, no. 2 (2015): 357–76.
Pierret, Thomas. *Religion and State in Syria: The Sunni Ulama from Coup to Revolution*. Cambridge: Cambridge University Press, 2013.
Pierret, Thomas. 'The Syrian Islamic Council (CIS)', *Diwan*, 13 May 2014, http://carnegie-mec.org/diwan/55580.
Pierret, Thomas. 'Salafis at war in Syria: Logics of fragmentation and realignment', in *Salafism After the Arab Awakening: Contending with People's Power*, edited by Francesco Cavatorta and Fabio Merone, 275–313. Oxford: Oxford University Press, 2017.
Pierret, Thomas. 'An Excommunication in Damascus', Interview with Michael Young, 19 November 2021, Carnegie Middle East Centre.
Pierret, Thomas and Laila Alrifaai. 'Religious Governance in Syria amid Territorial Fragmentation', in *Islamic Institutions in Arab States: Mapping the Dynamics of Control, Co-optation, and Contention*, edited by Frederic Wehrey, 53–72. Beirut: Carnegie Endowment for International Peace, 2021.
Podolny, Joel and James Baron. 'Resources and Relationships: Social Networks and Mobility in the Workplace', *American Sociological Review* (1997): 673–93.
Purnell, Derecka. *Becoming Abolitionists: Police, Protests, and the Pursuit of Freedom*. New York: Astra House, 2021.
Rathmell, Andrew. 'Syria's Intelligence Services: Origins and Development', *Journal of Conflict Studies* 16, no. 2 (1996): 75–96.
Reno, William. *Warlord Politics and African States*. Boulder, CO: Lynn Rienner, 1998.
Reno, William. 'Predatory Rebellions and Governance: The National Patriotic Front of Liberia, 1989–1992', in *Rebel Governance in Civil War*, edited by Ana Arjona, Nelson Kasfir and Zachariah Mamphily, 265–85. Cambridge: Cambridge University Press, 2017.
Richmond, Oliver. 'Resistance and the Post-liberal Peace', *Journal of International Studies* 38, no. 3 (2010): 665–92.
Rihawi, Abdul Qadir. *Arabic Islamic Architecture: Its Characteristics and Traces in Syria*. Damascus: The Ministry of Culture and National Leadership, 1979.
Roberts, David. *The Ba'th and the Creation of Modern Syria*. London: Routledge, 1987.
Rotberg, Robert (ed.). *When States Fail: Causes and Consequences*. Princeton: Princeton University Press, 2005.

Rotberg, Robert. 'The Failure and Collapse of Nation-States: Breakdown, Prevention and Repair', in *When States Fail: Causes and Consequences*, edited by Robert Rotberg, 1–49. Princeton: Princeton University Press, 2005.

Sabra, George. 'Ya hurriyyeh', interview by Suad Qatanani, Syria TV, 19 July 2018, https://www.youtube.com/watch?v=9N8Amxu4riQ.

Saeed, Haidar. *The Sect and the Nation: A theoretical attempt with references to Iraq*, Striking from the Margins Conference Presentation, 16 January 2019, Beirut: American University of Beirut, https://youtu.be/tP1QDza28TI?t=3097 (51:36 — 1:20:50).

Sahner, Christian. *Among the Ruins: Syria Past and Present*. Oxford: Oxford University Press, 2014.

Salamandra, Christa. *A New Old Damascus*. Indiana: Indiana University Press, 2004

Salamandra, Christa. 'Sectarianism in Syria: Anthropological Reflections', *Middle East Critique* 22, no. 3 (2013): 303–6.

Saleh, Yassin al-Haj. *The Impossible Revolution*. London: Hurst, 2017.

Sampson, Robert and Per-Olof Wikstrom. 'The Social Order of Violence in Chicago and Stockholm Neighborhoods: A Comparative Perspective', in *Order, Conflict, and Violence*, edited by Stathis Kalyvas, Ian Shapiro and Tarek Masoud, 97–119. Cambridge: Cambridge University Press, 2008.

Schlichte, Klaus (ed.). *Dynamics of States: The Formation and Crisis of State Outside the OECD*. Aldershot: Ashgate, 2005.

Schlichte, Klaus. 'A Historical-Sociological Perspective on Statehood', in *The Oxford Handbook of Governance and Limited Statehood*, edited by Thomas Risse et al., 48–67. Oxford: Oxford University Press, 2018.

Scott, James C. *Seeing Like a State: How Certain Schemes to Improve the Human Condition Have Failed*. New Haven: Yale University Press, 1999.

Seale, Patrick. *Assad: The Struggle for the Middle East*. Berkeley: University of California Press, 1989.

Sending, Ole, and Iver Neumann. 'Governance to Governmentality: Analyzing NGOs, States, and Power', *International Studies Quarterly* 50, no. 4 (2006): 889–910.

Shahab, Sofya and Benjamin Isakhan. 'The ritualization of heritage destruction under the Islamic State', *Journal of Social Archaeology* 18, no. 2 (2018): 212–33.

Shaheen, Kareem. 'Up to 15,000 Isis victims buried in mass graves in Syria and Iraq – survey', *The Guardian*, 30 August 2016, https://www.theguardian.com/world/2016/aug/30/up-to-15000-bodies-may-be-buried-in-mass-graves-in-syria-and-iraq-survey.

Shahhoud, Annsar. 'Medical genocide: Mass Violence and the Health Sector in the Syrian Conflict (2011–2019)' (MA thesis, University of Amsterdam, 2020), https://t.co/gMSYf92kOq.

Shami, Seteney and Cynthia Miller-Idriss. *Middle East Studies for the New Millennium: Infrastructures of Knowledge*. New York: New York University Press, 2017.

Solnick, Steven. *Stealing the State: Control and Collapse in Soviet-Institutions*. Cambridge, MA: Harvard University Press, 1998.

Sonnentag, Sabine. 'Recovery from fatigue: The role of psychological detachment', in *Cognitive fatigue: Multidisciplinary perspectives on current research and future applications*, edited by Philip L. Ackerman, 253–72. Washington, DC: American Psychological Association, 2011.

Spencer, Herbert. *The Principles of Sociology*. New York: Appleton and Company, 1896.

'Statement of the formation of the Shariah Committee in Aleppo and its countryside', *AMC*, 11 November 2012, https://www.youtube.com/watch?v=XvH0iRsucBE.

Stewart, Megan A. *Governing for Revolution: Social Transformation in Civil War*. Cambridge: Cambridge University Press, 2021.

Stollenwerk, Eric. 'Measuring Governance and Limited Statehood', in *The Oxford Handbook of Governance and Limited Statehood*, edited by Thomas Risse et al., 106–29. Oxford: Oxford University Press, 2018.

'Strengthening Social Cohesion: Conceptual Framing and Programming Implications', UNDP, 27 February 2020, 17, https://www.undp.org/publications/strengthening-social-cohesion-conceptual-framing-and-programming-implications.

Stubbs, Jack and Humeyra Pamuk. 'Russian raids repeatedly hit Syrian Turkmen areas, Moscow's data shows', *Reuters*, 27 November 2015, https://www.reuters.com/article/us-mideast-crisis-russia-turkey-airstrik-idUSKBN0TG1YQ20151128.

'Swelling As-Sweida Protests Highlight Discontent Across Government Areas', *COAR*, 14 February 2022, https://coar-global.org/2022/02/14/swelling-as-sweida-protests-highlight-discontent-across-government-areas/.

'Syrian Armed Opposition Coastal Offensive', *The Carter Center*, 1 April 2014, https://www.cartercenter.org/resources/pdfs/peace/conflict_resolution/syria-conflict/2014CoastalOffensive-April1.pdf.

Syrian British Consortium. *A Decade after Daraya: Documenting a Massacre*. London: Syrian British Consortium, 2022.

Szanto, Edith. 'Sayyida Zaynab in the State of Exception: Shi'i Sainthood as "Qualified Life" in Contemporary Syria', *International journal of Middle East Studies* 44, no. 2 (May 2012): 285–99.

Tainter, Joseph. *The Collapse of Complex Societies*. Cambridge: Cambridge University Press, 1988.

Tcholakian, Hagop. *The Three Days of Kessab: 21–23 March, 2014*. Yerevan: self-published, 2015.

Tilly, Charles. 'War Making and State Making as Organized Crime', in *Bringing the State Back*, edited by Peter Evans, Dietrich Rueschemeyer and Theda Skocpol, 169191. Cambridge: Cambridge University Press, 2010.

Tlass, Moustafa. مرآة حياتي, vol. III (2005).

Tokmajyan, Armenak. 'The war economy in Northern Syria', *The Aleppo Project*, December 2016, https://theblueshield.org/wp-content/uploads/2018/06/Tokmajyan_War-Economy_N-Syria.pdf.

Trencsenyu, Balazs, 'What Should I Call You? The Crisis of Hungarian Democracy in a Regional Interpretative Framework', in *Twenty-Five Sides of a Post-Communist Mafia State*, edited by Balint Magyar and Julia Vasarhelyi, 3–19. Budapest: Central European University Press, 2017.

Turner, Jonathan. *Human Institutions: A Theory of Societal Evolution*, Lanham, MD: Rowman and Littlefield, 2003.

Ugarit News – Syria, '6 9 Aleppo أعداد المشيعين في جنازة تشييع الشيخ إبراهيم, أوغاريت حلب السلقيني في الجامع الأموي ج2', *YouTube*, 6 September 2011, https://www.youtube.com/watch?v=iu162V1_PBo.

UN General Assembly's Human Rights Council's report A/HRC/21/50, https://undocs.org/pdf?symbol=en/A/HRC/21/50.

UNDP. *Capacity Assessment Methodology*. New York: United Nations Development Programme, 2008.

UNDRR. 'Resilience', *United Nations Office for Disaster Risk Reduction*, 18 March 2015, https://www.undrr.org/terminology/resilience.

Ungor, Ugur. *Paramilitarism: Mass Violence in the Shadow of the State*. Oxford: Oxford University Press, 2020.

UNHCR. *On Faith-Based Organizations, Local Faith Communities and Faith Leaders*. Geneva: UNHCR, 2014.

Van Dam, Nikolaos. *The Struggle for Power In Syria: Politics and Society under Assad and the Ba'th Party*. London: I. B. Tauris, 2012.

Vignal, Leila. 'The changing borders and borderlands of Syria in a time of conflict', *International Affairs* 93, no. 4 (2017): 809–27.

Vignal, Leila. *War-Torn: The Unmaking of Syria 2011–2021*. Oxford: Oxford University Press, 2021.
Volkov, Vadim. *Violent Entrepreneurs: The Use of Force in the Making of Russian Capitalism*. New York: Cornell University Press, 2002.
Wacquant, Loïc. 'Habitus', in *International Encyclopaedia of Economic Sociology*, edited by Jens Becket and Zafirovski Milan, 316. London: Routledge, 2005.
Wedeen, Lisa. *Ambiguities of Domination: Politics, Rhetoric, and Symbols in Contemporary Syria*. Chicago: University of Chicago Press, 1999.
Weiner, Myron and Michael Teitelbaum. *Political demography, demographic engineering*. New York: Berghahn Books, 2001.
Weinstein, Jeremy. *Inside Rebellion: The Politics of Insurgent Violence*. Cambridge: Cambridge University Press, 2006.
Wellman, Barry. 'Network Analysis: Some basic Principles', *Sociological Theory* (1983): 155–200.
White, Benjamin. *The Emergence of Minorities in the Middle East: The Politics of Community in French Mandate Syria*. Edinburgh: Edinburgh University Press, 2011.
Wieland, Carsten. 'Alawis on the Syrian Opposition', in *The Alawis of Syria: War, Faith and Politics in the Levant*, edited by Michael Kerr and Craig Larkin, 274–90. Oxford: Oxford University Press, 2015.
Williams, Raymond. *Keywords: A Vocabulary of Culture and Society*. Oxford: Oxford University Press, 2015.
Williams, Sara E. 'The invasion of Kassab: "We were evicted"', *al Jazeera*, 30 April 2014, https://www.aljazeera.com/news/2014/4/30/the-invasion-of-kassab-we-were-evicted.
Wilson, Geoff A. 'Community resilience: path dependency, lock-in effects and transitional ruptures'. *Journal of Environmental Planning and Management* 57, no. 1 (2014): 1–26.
Wood, Paul, 'Christians Targeted by Foreign Jihadis in Syrian War', *BBC*, 18 July 2013. http://www.bbc.com/news/world-23361938.
Woodruff, David. *Money Unmade: Barter and the Fate of Russian Capitalism*. New York: Cornell University Press, 1999.
Working Papers, 2015, 1–10, http://cadmus.eui.eu/bitstream/handle/1814/37015/RSCAS_2015_61.pdf.
'World Development Indicators: Databank (Syrian Arab Republic: Preview)', *The World Bank*, 21 March 2020, https://databank.worldbank.org/reports.aspx?source=2&country=SYR.

Wrong, Dennis. *The Problem of Order: What Unites and Divides Society*. Cambridge, MA: Harvard University Press, 1995.

Yassin-Kassab, Robin and Leila al-Shami. *Burning Country: Syrians in Revolution and War*. London: Pluto Press, 2016.

Ye'or, Bat. *The Decline of Eastern Christianity under Islam*. Madison: Fairleigh Dickinson University Press, 1996.

'"You can still see their blood": Executions, Indiscriminate Shootings, and Hostage Taking by Opposition Forces in Latakia Countryside', Human Rights Watch, 10 October 2013, https://www.hrw.org/report/2013/10/10/you-can-still-see-their-blood/executions-indiscriminate-shootings-and-hostage.

Yousef, Bassam. حجر الذاكرة: بعض من جحيم السجون السورية. Paris: Maysaloun Press, 2018.

Youssef, Dellair. 'In Assad's Syria School Is Prison: Mini Dictatorships and State Violence in the Classroom', *Syria Untold*, 18 November 2021, https://syriauntold.com/2021/11/18/in-assads-syria-school-is-prison/.

Zakzak, Sawsan. 'القبيسيات في السياق المجتمعي السوري', *Jadaliyya*, 5 July 2018: https://www.jadaliyya.com/Details/37730.

Zelin, A.Y. 'New Statement from Jabhat al-Nusrah: "Bombing of the Headquarters of the Military Security and Air Force Intelligence in Dayr az-Zor (Deir el-Zor)"', *Jihadology*, 20 May 2012, www.jihadology.net/2012/05/20/new-statement-from-jabhat-al-Nusrah-bombing-of-the-headquarters-of-the-militarysecurity-and-air-force-intelligence-in-dayr-az-zur-deir-al-zour/.

Ziadeh, Radwan. السلطة والاستخبارات في سوريا. Beirut: Riad El-Rayyes, 2013.

Zubaida, Sami. *Islam, The People and The State: Political Ideas and Movements in the Middle East*. London: I. B. Tauris, 2009.

Index

abolition, 1, 2, 3, 4
administrative capacity, 209
administrative functions, 65
administrative structures, 68, 98, 101–2, 188–9, 213
agricultural production, 187, 193, 203
Ahmad, Aijaz, 12
al-Abdallah, Mounir, 56
Alawi, 49, 53–4, 109, 117, 119–20, 122, 124–6, 130, 157, 159–60, 163, 196, 198–201, 204, 206, 214, 223–4, 234
    community, 195, 217
    population, 163, 196
    villages, 97
al-Azmeh, Aziz, 12, 237
al-Dardari, Abdallah, 60
al-Jundi, Abd al-Karim, 35–6
al-Khuly, Muhammad, 36
al-Qaeda, 4, 83, 97, 128
al-Za'im, Issam, 60
antagonistic perceptions, 233
Arab nationalism, 110
Arab Spring, 1, 13
Armenian organisations, 158, 167, 199, 215
Armenian religious organisations, 163, 165
    Armenian Apostolic Church, 157, 161, 205–6
    Armenian Catholic Church, 162
    Armenian Catholicosate of Antioch, 162
    Armenian Catholicosate of Cilicia, 161
    Armenian Evangelical Church, 161, 165, 198
    Armenian Orthodox Church, 161, 165

Armenians, 110, 119, 121, 124, 159, 161, 163, 196–7, 199, 216
    churches, 157, 170, 197, 219
    communities, 158, 198, 201
    population, 165, 172, 217, 219
    Catholic Armenians, 193
Asad, Talal, 12–13
Assad, Bashar, 5, 8, 23–4, 26, 31–3, 35, 40, 43, 45–6, 48–9, 51–5, 59, 60–3, 67–8, 70, 79, 146
    Hafez, 5, 8, 23–4, 31, 33, 35, 37–46, 48–9, 51–5, 60, 64, 68, 70
    Maher, 51, 55, 79, 231
    Rif'at, 35
authenticity, 10
authoritarian power, 52, 171
authoritarian state, 145
Awqaf, 139, 142, 164–6, 169

Ba'th Party, 23, 31, 33–4, 37–8, 45, 49, 52, 63, 132, 189
    Regional Command, 37, 39
bargaining processes, 20, 22, 72, 155
Barout, Jamal, 62
Borderlands, 25, 83–5, 87–90, 92, 101–2
borders, 7, 79, 83–9, 92, 101, 159, 177, 194
Bou Nassif, Hicham, 53

centre–periphery, 161, 211–12, 216
charity, 64, 142–4, 151, 153, 157, 172, 187, 219
churches, 99, 124, 144, 155, 161, 195, 199, 206, 219
civil society, 56, 59, 65, 140, 230

civilians, 26, 28, 71–2, 74–5, 81–2, 97, 112, 173–5, 177–9, 181–2, 188, 211, 213, 228
  agency, 32, 173, 175, 228, 230
  autonomy, 104, 180, 191, 212, 214
class, 10, 41, 60–1, 123, 125, 143, 190, 201, 220, 235
clientelism, 7, 43, 68, 141, 144, 231
clientelistic arrangements, 61, 65, 146, 158
collapse, 5, 22, 26, 73, 99, 169, 174
community protection, 7, 32, 173–5, 177–8, 180, 183, 188, 196, 199, 203, 209–13, 221, 223, 229
  coping strategies, 175, 177, 230
  survival strategies, 24, 177
  transformative strategies, 177, 211
constitution, 4, 33, 35, 39, 42, 46, 60–1
  constitutional change, 30, 45
  Court, 41, 43, 48
corruption, 7, 67–8, 183, 188

Dahi, Sami, 56
Dallal, Ahmad, 237
Darwish, Samer, 56
defections, 51, 71, 73
dehumanisation, 105, 114–15, 119, 121–2, 130, 133, 135
demographic engineering, 101
denomination, 54, 219
detained, 35, 55–6, 106–7, 124, 146, 181, 192
detainees, 56–9
de-territorialisation, 22
developmentalism, 23, 26, 45, 62, 68, 137, 145, 154
devolution, 19, 62, 71, 88–9, 105, 137, 232
devolution of state capacity, 5, 68, 83
devolution of state functions, 8, 31, 104, 170
devolution of state violence, 26, 28
devolution of violence, 7, 26–8, 71, 104–5, 122, 138
Dhadha, Ali, 36
displacement, 10–11, 88, 92–3, 141, 157, 161, 178–9, 183, 195, 198, 202, 206, 207–10, 211–12, 221, 226
distributive functions, 23, 136, 141–2
Durkheim, Émile, 14

early warning, 179, 201, 203, 205, 209–12
economic government, 59–61
economic modernisation, 59–60, 62
economic responsibility, 27, 59, 65
emergency laws, 43, 48, 55
Enayat, Hadi, 12
essentialism, 12, 232, 237
ethno-religious belonging, 25, 196, 222, 224
ethno-religious differentiation, 115, 117, 135
ethno-religious identity, 111, 115, 117
ethno-religious relations, 109, 117, 120–1, 123, 128
ethno-religious solidarity, 122
ethno-religious subjectivities, 113, 167
evacuation, 160, 182, 200, 202, 208–10
exclusion, 19, 221–3
  exclusionary discourses, 94, 100
  measures, 94
executive authority, 28
  branches, 24, 30, 41, 43, 45, 48, 65, 151
  functions, 95
  powers, 5, 28, 30, 40, 46, 48
exploitation, 60, 100
extraction, 7, 65, 100, 142, 187

Fadel, Nibras, 60
Free Independent Judiciary Council, 146, 149

Graeber, David, 4
Greek Orthodox Patriarchate of Antioch, 141, 152, 158

Hallaq, Wael, 12
heterarchy, 75–6, 79, 170
Hezbollah, 72, 77–8, 82, 84–5, 198, 228
hierarchy, 2, 18, 41, 43, 51, 58, 75, 104, 147, 191, 231, 241
hinterland, 228
humanitarian solidarity, 224

identity, 101, 105, 109, 111–12, 117, 224, 232–3, 235
inclusion, 19, 221
in-group solidarity, 93

institutional arrangements, 3, 7, 8, 11, 13, 19, 21, 23–4, 26, 28–30, 31, 33, 52, 58, 71, 74, 82, 114, 161, 164, 171, 214, 235, 239
   domain, 16, 18–19, 20–2, 24, 26, 28, 68, 165, 167, 234, 239
   ecology, 16, 20–1, 24, 32, 83, 228
   superstructure, 21
   theory, 18
institutions of violence, 21, 28, 52, 80, 89, 126, 144, 231
   Air Force Intelligence, 39, 49, 51
   Fourth Armoured Division, 54–5
   General Intelligence Directorate, 49, 51
   Military Intelligence Directorate, 49, 51
   Political Security Directorate, 49
   Republican Guard, 51, 54–5
   Syrian Air Force, 49
   Syrian Arab Army, 194
Islam, 112, 236, 237
Islamic groups, 98, 117, 123, 128–9
Islamic Revolutionary Guards Force, 72, 77, 112
Islamism, 10

Jabra, Iyad, 54
Jadid, Izzat, 38
Jadid, Salah, 38–9
Jamil, Naji, 39
Jihadi groups, 82, 120, 236, 239
Jihadis, 84, 97
judiciary, 33, 41, 48, 57, 75, 95–6, 149, 151, 186

Kabe, Mariame, 3
Kallas, Fuad, 36
Khatib, Ahmad, 40
Knowledge Production, 10
Kurdish, 124
   forces, 92, 121
   history, 121
   population, 121, 123
   presence, 85
   separatism, 12
Kurdish Regional Government, 85
Kurdistan, 3, 84, 123, 128
Kurds, 119, 121, 123–4
Kweiris airport, 181–2

legislation, 40, 45, 165–7
   decree, 43
   legislative branches, 24, 33, 43, 45
   powers, 33, 40, 48
   process, 43
Liberal Peace, 11–12
Lijan Sha'biyyeh, 75, 159
Liwa' al-Baqr, 112
Liwa' al-Imam Zein al-Abidin, 112
local autonomy, 32, 173, 216, 217
Local Coordination Committees, 103–4
Local Councils, 103–4
localism, 12
localities, 10–11, 28, 82, 90, 105, 143, 144, 156, 213, 217, 223

Ma'touk, Khalil, 56
Mahmoud, Saba, 12–3
Makhlouf, Hafez, 51
Makhlouf, Rami, 161
Mann, Michael, 15
material conditions, 14, 113, 237
Middle East, 2, 7, 12, 109, 232, 234
   Iraq, 11, 53, 59, 82, 85, 89, 97–8, 128, 182–3, 188, 228
   Islamic Republic of Iran, 7, 77–8, 81–2, 85, 128, 228, 231
   Israel, 35, 37
   Lebanon, 11, 29, 35, 42, 52, 59, 80, 111, 115, 160, 162, 195, 206, 224
   Saudi Arabia, 128
   Turkey, 62, 85, 86, 89, 92, 102, 128, 149, 156, 187, 188, 194, 231
Middle East Council of Churches, 155
militants, 28, 76–7, 92, 97, 156, 159, 181
militarisation, 5, 10, 26, 28, 35, 51, 53, 68, 70–1, 74, 82–3, 107, 141, 147, 156, 175, 179, 193, 196, 198, 231
ministries, 4, 104, 165
   of Defence, 50, 54, 77
   of Education, 140
   of Health, 142
   of Social Affairs and Labour, 142, 154
   of the Interior, 50, 79, 80
modalities of violence, 11
   assassination, 50, 51, 59
   indiscriminate violence, 92, 98–9, 172, 175

modalities of violence (*cont.*)
   kidnapping, 80, 89, 121, 178, 184, 188, 210, 223
   killings, 1, 57, 59, 71–2, 74, 97, 121, 191
   mass violence, 28, 72, 112, 211
   massacres, 71–2, 112, 128, 205
   punishments, 91, 95, 98, 183
   spectacular violence, 94
   state violence, 28, 43, 71, 73, 75–6, 78, 81–2, 147
   torture, 38–9, 43, 56, 58, 111, 191, 239
modes of production, 202
monopoly of violence, 28, 30, 71, 88, 91, 145
mosque, 142–4, 147, 153, 219
Muslim Brotherhood, 43, 144, 146, 152–3, 239

Najib, Atef, 51–2
neoliberalisation, 60, 68
neoliberal government, 62
   models, 65
   modes, 11, 20, 68, 137, 174, 232
   policies, 8, 64–5
   turn, 24, 141, 174
neo-patrimonialism, 23, 41, 51, 145–6, 168, 171, 191; *see also* patrimonialism
nepotism, 19, 42, 126

opposition forces, 78, 81, 83, 86, 109, 147–9, 194
   Ahrar al-Sham, 94, 96–8, 112, 151–3, 182–3, 189, 191, 195
   Ansar al-Sham, 194
   Faylaq al-Rahman, 112
   Jaysh al-Fateh, 96
   Jaysh al-Islam, 112, 152
   Katibat Abu Dujana, 180–3, 188, 191, 215
   Liwa' al-Tawhid, 112, 151–3, 182
   Nusra, 4, 82–3, 91, 94–8, 111–12, 124, 151–3, 156, 163, 194–5
   Sham al-Islam, 194
oppression, 2, 57, 97, 116, 119, 121, 124–5, 128, 130, 221
organisational capacity, 32, 178, 192, 217
   culture, 67
   structure, 49

paramilitary, 28, 71, 75, 77–8, 82, 84, 96, 156, 159, 165, 197–9, 215
parliament, 4, 31, 189
patrimonialism, 22, 32, 105
peace-building, 11–12
peaceful protests, 163, 187, 208
perceptions, 16, 105, 113, 117, 119, 126, 128, 132–3, 135, 223, 225, 235
personalisation, 45, 52, 57
personalisation of state, 41
polarisation, 71
political Islam, 232
political subjectivities, 28
   systems, 13, 43, 68
   violence, 11, 28
population strategies, 92–3, 101, 104, 141
power consolidation, 5, 26, 30, 43, 53, 68, 99, 101, 139, 232
   relations, 7, 11, 16, 18–19, 24, 26, 70, 145, 167, 187, 213
   structures, 5, 31, 32, 58, 123, 135, 147, 159, 163, 171, 216, 238
prison, 39, 56, 58
private property, 39, 45, 195
private sector, 43
privatisation, 24, 62–3, 65, 68, 168, 232
proselytisation, 151–3
protests, 1, 10, 23, 43, 60, 71, 73, 103, 146
public administration, 41, 68
public domain, 130, 139, 141, 143–5, 147, 168, 171, 174, 232, 234, 241
public sphere, 145, 147, 168

radicalisation, 121, 236
radicalised groups, 96, 98–100, 236–8
radicalised Islamic groups, 125
reconciliation, 173, 184–6
regulatory capacity, 21
   functions, 5, 24, 68, 232
religion, 16, 19, 20, 26, 30, 70, 99, 109, 117, 119, 121, 131–2, 137, 139, 141, 144–5, 151, 167, 173, 232, 235–6, 238
religious actors, 19, 32, 43, 137, 139, 141–2, 146–8, 151–2, 155–6, 158, 161, 163, 168, 170–1, 173–4, 224, 238–9
   court, 149, 151, 185–6

field, 7, 16, 19, 24, 30, 137, 139, 140–1, 143–8, 155–6, 163, 167–8, 170–5, 239
  indoctrination, 151, 153
resettlement, 65, 92
reterritorialisation, 22
rural areas, 23, 42, 189
  periphery, 143
  strata, 146
Russia, 7, 78, 81–2, 128, 147, 231
Russian forces, 7, 82, 181, 192
  military, 86

Salafi-Jihadi, 82
scales of violence, 32, 182
Seale, Patrick, 38–9, 41, 45, 53
sect, 26, 171, 173
sectarianisation, 7, 12, 27, 29, 32, 112–14, 122, 126, 135, 173, 224, 235–36
sectarian dispositions, 239
  factions, 133
  language, 131
  modes, 30, 126, 131
  motives, 125–6
  outlook, 30, 131, 133
  strategies, 113, 126
  subjectivities, 235
sectarianism, 10, 28–9, 105, 112–15, 117, 122–3, 125–6, 128, 130–3, 135, 165, 170, 173, 232–5, 239
secularism, 125, 130
separation of powers, 41
shabbiha, 76, 80–1, 107, 159, 162
Shawkat, Assef, 52
shelters, 155, 182
Shi'a, 86, 112, 125
social formation, 16, 165
Social Market Economy, 65
social networks, 15, 18
  ordering, 21–2
  perceptions, 101, 113
  responsibility, 60, 65
  services, 64, 91, 99, 104, 141, 147, 151, 154, 171, 183, 221
  subjectivities, 28, 114, 133, 235, 238
  trust, 32, 173, 211, 223–5
socialism, 45, 60

society, 8, 12–15, 21–2, 24, 26, 30, 33–4, 51, 59, 62, 105, 113–14, 117, 120–1, 123, 125, 128, 130, 132–3, 141, 153, 159, 171, 231–5, 237, 240, 241
solidarities, 100, 122, 135, 171, 235, 238
Soviet, 3, 11, 22, 33, 37, 42, 78, 231
spaces of solidarity, 103
state atrophy, 4–6, 8, 11, 14, 19, 22–3, 28, 32, 34, 39, 71, 78, 83, 103, 112, 115, 122, 137, 139, 148, 159, 170, 173, 175, 228, 231, 239
  bureaucracy, 23, 65, 68, 70, 143, 141
  capacity, 5, 22, 24, 75, 140, 234
  capture, 3–6, 8, 12–13, 31, 33, 35, 38, 40–1, 46, 48–9, 51–4, 56–61, 63, 65, 68, 70, 168, 234, 241
  functions, 7, 32, 62, 140–1, 144, 232, 234
state–society relations, 8, 13–14, 22, 24, 30, 33, 62, 128, 171, 241
structuring capacity, 139
  role, 20, 51, 113, 135, 137, 171
subjectivities, 20, 28, 114, 144, 234, 238
Suleiman, Jamal, 96
Sunni, 54–5, 109, 119, 120–2, 124–5, 129–1, 146, 152, 163
  Islam, 144
  Arab, 117, 119–21, 123–5, 128, 132
  Kurdish, 116, 121, 123–4, 128, 131
Syria, 33, 35, 156, 194, 209, 212
  al-Bab, 180, 182, 187–8, 221
  Aleppo City, 8, 30, 80–2, 103, 141, 151, 153, 156–7, 161–3, 172, 180, 183, 189, 197–8, 210, 221, 223
  Aleppo Province, 8, 180, 189
  Bab el-Nerab, 80
  countryside, 8, 72, 82, 132, 148, 180–2, 221
  Damascus, 38, 43, 51, 60, 62, 80–2, 116, 142–4, 149, 163, 174, 180, 193, 221, 228
  Dar a Deir el-Zor, 89, 96–7, 116, 124, 128, 132
  Deir Hafer, 5, 8, 32, 173, 175, 179, 180–9, 191–2, 209–15, 217, 219, 221, 223, 225–6, 221, 223–4, 227–8
  Idlib, 56, 83, 84, 86, 96, 98, 101–2, 141, 151, 153, 173, 190, 193, 197–8

Syria (*cont.*)
   Kasab, 5, 8, 28, 30, 155–7, 159–64, 168, 169–71, 177–8, 192–3, 194–9, 200–1, 204–5, 205–10, 212–5, 216, 221–8
   Latakia City, 8, 72, 79, 154–5, 158, 161–2, 178, 192, 195, 197–8, 202, 204–5, 206, 213–4, 216, 223–4, 226
   Latakia Province, 8
   Manbij, 177, 216
   Saydnaya, 55
   Tadmur, 55
   Tartus, 71, 79
Syrian Democratic Forces, 83–5, 92, 139, 171, 183, 211
Syrian state, 8, 13–14, 22–4, 30, 34, 35, 41–2, 45, 52, 57, 59, 60, 62, 77–8, 81–2, 84–6, 89, 147, 171

Tashnak, 155–6, 160, 163, 197, 199, 200, 204, 215
territorial control, 20–2, 24, 28, 52, 71, 74, 84, 90, 104, 139, 154, 183, 208, 237
territoriality, 22
territory, 4, 22–3, 147
Tlass, Moustafa, 35–7, 41–2, 50–1
tourism, 156, 193, 195, 201
tradition, 12, 29, 236
tribe, 96, 125, 141, 185, 189, 191–2
   of al-Kharraj, 185, 189
   of Bani Jamil, 185, 191
   of Bani Sa'id, 189
   of Hadidiyin,185, 189, 191
   of Sheitaat, 96
tribesmen, 184, 189

urban areas, 64, 139, 144, 182
   centres, 23, 45, 65, 144, 220, 228
   outskirts, 228
urban–rural divides, 27, 82, 83

wealth, 7, 26, 61, 65, 83, 99, 143, 161, 179, 191, 226
Weber, Max, 14
women, 71–2, 97, 130–2, 197

EU representative:
Easy Access System Europe
Mustamäe tee 50, 10621 Tallinn, Estonia
Gpsr.requests@easproject.com